JOHN PAUL II "PILGRIMAGE OF FAITH"

JOHN PAUL II "PILGRIMAGE OF FAITH"

The First Year of the New Pope
And the Story of His Visit to the United States
Edited and Illustrated by the National Catholic News Service

With a Foreword by Fulton J. Sheen

A CROSSROAD BOOK · THE SEABURY PRESS · NEW YORK

1979
The Seabury Press
815 Second Avenue, New York, N.Y. 10017

Edited by Richard W. Daw, Director and Editor-in-Chief, National Catholic News Service, in cooperation with Agostino A. Bono, Mary Esslinger, Robert A. Strawn, Thomas N. Lorsung, Jerome F. Filteau, and Richard A. Banules, Mary Bozzonetti, Bessie J. Briscoe, James Castelli, Pamela Fleming, Jaime Fonseca, Nancy Frazier, David Gibson, James Lackey, John V. R. Lebkicher, John J. Maher, Isabelle Maneechai, Thomas S. Meldrim, Ava D. Merritt, S. J. Miragliotta, Gloria Moore, Michelle Noon, Stephenie Overman, Anna Rood, Angela M. Schreiber, Mary Lynne Woychick.

COVER: Background—Gerard A. Pottlebaum; Inset—U.P.I. FOREWORD: Wide World. PART I—KNA. October 1978: 1—NC News; 2, 3—Chris Niedenthal. November 1978: 1, 3, 4—Arturo Mari; 2, 6, 7—KNA; 5—NC News. December 1978: none. January 1979: 1—NC News; 2-7—KNA; 8—UPI; 9—Frank Smoczynski. February 1979: KNA. PART II—Msgr. John P. Foley. March 1979: KNA. April 1979: 1, 2—Arturo Mari; 3—NC News; May 1979: none. June 1979: 1, 7—KNA; 2, 3, 4, 8—Chris Niedenthal; 5—Wide World; 6—U.P.I. July 1979: none. August 1979: 1—KNA; 2—U.P.I.; 3—Wide World. September 1979: 1, 5, 7—KNA; 2, 3, 6—Arturo Mari. PART III—KNA. October 1979: none. October 1: 1—Wide World; 2—Arturo Mari; 3, 5—Jack Spratt; 4—Chris Christo; 6, 7, 8, 10—Chris Sheridan; 9—U.P.I. October 2—Chris Sheridan. October 2 and 3: 1, 2, 8, 11—U.P.I.; 3, 10, 12, 13, 14—Wide World; 4, 5—Carl Balcerak; 6, 7, 9—Chris Sheridan. October 3 and 4: 1-4—Chris Sheridan; 5, 12—U.P.I.; 6—NC News; 7-11—Wide World; 13—Robert S. Halvey. October 4: 1, 6—Chris Sheridan; 2—Wide World; 3, 8—Bob Kelly; 4, 7—Jon Jacobson; 5—Jim Shaffer. October 4, 5 and 6: 1-4—Wide World; 5, 11—Chris Sheridan; 6, 7—Joseph Jacobson; 8, 9—Dennis W. Trowbridge; 10, 12—Sheila O'Donnell. October 6: 1, 2—Chris Sheridan. October 7: 1, 6—Wide World; 2, 3—Tom Kane; 4, 7—U.P.I.; 5—James Pipkin; 8—Mark Kiryluk; 9—Bob Strawn. Epilogue October 16: none. APPENDIX—KNA.

Printed in the United States of America

Library of Congress Cataloging in Publication Data
Main entry under title:
John Paul II, pilgrimage of faith.
"A Crossword book."
1. John Paul II, Pope, 1920-   2. Popes—Voyages and travels—United States. I. National Catholic News Service.
BX1378.5.J65   262'.13'0924 [B]   79-23105
ISBN 0-8164-0109-8   ISBN 0-8164-2014-9 pbk.

Contents

Urbi et Orbi

Almost every day the Pope stands at a window overlooking Saint Peter's Square, and gives his apostolic blessing—*URBI ET ORBI*—to the "City" of Rome and to the "world." But John Paul II has in the first year of his Pontificate reversed the order, and from diverse areas of the globe has blessed *urbs*, or the city of Rome, from *orbs*, or the world itself.

This climaxes a direction his predecessors dimly foreshadowed. Picture the interior of that vast Basilica. Benedict XV was crowned Pope at the altar of the Blessed Virgin—about as far from the front door and the world as he could get. His successor, Pius XI, stepped a hundred feet closer to the front door by being crowned under the great dome at the main altar. Pius XII walked down the middle aisle and onto a balcony. And when he put his foot onto that balcony, he literally stepped into the world. John XXIII accepted his apostolic succession not only on the balcony—he stretched his great arms out like the giant columns of Bernini to embrace the whole world and then summoned about 3,000 Bishops from different parts of the earth to mingle their dust with the dust of Peter. Paul VI accepted his title of Vicar of Christ in the great piazza in front of the Basilica, where he could see the *orbs* from the *urbs*. John Paul I followed the custom briefly, but only long enough to offer the world his smile and then to say "good-bye." John Paul II, once he got into the world, never stopped moving into it—flying, walking, motoring. In the language of Francis Thompson, "he swung the world, a trinket at his wrist."

No matter where he travels in the world to feed Christ's lambs, he still keeps tethered to the city which is Rome, for it is one thing to be *in* the world, and another to be not *of* it. He has a mission in the City as was foretold by the Polish poet Slowacki a hundred years ago:

> "God has made ready the Throne for a Slav Pope;
> He will sweep out the Churches and make them clean within—
> Then God will be revealed, clear as day, in the creature world."

This book is a pictorial record of another kind of world conqueror who has won hearts without arms, and made the people of the United States and the whole world feel in a new way the truth of the words of the Latin poet, Terence:

> *Homo sum, humanum nihil a me alienum puto.*
> "I am a man, and nothing human is foreign to me."

Archbishop Fulton J. Sheen

PART I

A NEW BEGINNING

Called from a Faraway Nation

His hands folded serenely before him, Karol Wojtyla stood on the central balcony of St. Peter's Basilica and looked out over the tens of thousands of persons packed into the square below. Then he threw his arms open wide and declared in a clear, ringing voice: "May Jesus Christ be praised!"

The ancient Christian greeting fell unexpectedly on the crowd and drew only a scattered response of the traditional, "Now and forever!" It was a surprising beginning for a surprising pontificate.

From that moment on the evening of Oct. 16, 1978, when Cardinal Karol Wojtyla appeared before the world as Pope John Paul II, throughout the first year of his reign, this "son of Poland," as he referred to himself, turned the unexpected into the commonplace. He immediately put his mark on the papacy and made that mark clearer as time went by.

Having caught the estimated 300,000 persons in St. Peter's Square off guard with his greeting, he went on to do another, even more unexpected thing. Tradition called for the newly elected pope to merely stand on the balcony to be seen and cheered, to give his blessing to the crowd, and then to retire. Pope John Paul II gave a talk.

"Dearest brothers and sisters," he said. "We are all still saddened over the death of our most beloved Pope John Paul I. And now the most eminent cardinals have called a new bishop to Rome. They have called him from a faraway nation."

His words were interrupted by applause. The Polish pope was speaking Italian! And very good Italian, at that!

He continued: "Faraway, but also very near in the communion of faith and Christian tradition. I was afraid to take on this appointment."

There was a slight stirring on the balcony and an aide standing near the pope whispered, "Enough, Holiness, enough!"

The pope went on: "But I did it in a spirit of obedience to our Lord and with total trust in his mother, our Most Holy Lady."

The aide tried once more to indicate to the pope that he should stop talking.

"I don't know if I can express myself well in your — our — Italian language. If I make a mistake, correct me.

"And so I present myself to all of you to confess our common faith, our hope and our trust in the mother of Christ and the church, and also to begin again on the road, the historic road of the church, with the help of God and with the help of men."

Applause exploded and rolled up to the balcony in waves. Handkerchiefs fluttered, arms swayed rhythmically, the voices of the tens of thousands of faces turned upward to the figure standing bathed in floodlights filled the square. Turning from side to side, the new pope repeatedly opened his arms wide and then brought them together across his chest, as if to enfold everyone present in a firm embrace.

Then, in Latin, he pronounced a blessing on the city and the world, and left the balcony while the crowd continued to cheer.

Thus began the pontificate of the first non-Italian to become pope since Adrian VI, a Dutchman who reigned from 1522 to 1523. At 58, the new pope was the youngest man to be elected since Pius IX was chosen at the age of 54. Pius IX's 32-year reign, from 1846 to 1878, was the longest in history.

The conclave which had chosen Cardinal Wojtyla, archbishop of Cracow, Poland, had been composed for the first time ever of a majority of non-European cardinals, though only by a margin of one. There were 55 European cardinals and 56 non-Europeans. The decisive vote had come on the second day of balloting behind the sealed doors of the Sistine Chapel.

The man who had been selected to lead the world's 720 million Catholics and to occupy the world's most prominent religious office came onto the scene at a time when intense attention had been focused on the Vatican for more than two months. Beginning with the death of Pope Paul VI on Aug. 6, 1978, and continuing through the election and 34-day reign of Pope John Paul I, millions of television viewers around the world, Christian and non-Christian alike, had witnessed centuries-old church traditions. Never had so many people simultaneously watched such a sequence of events. The Vatican was center stage. Now John Paul II was the leading player. He was a long way from home.

In the small town of Wadowice in southern Poland, Page 549 of the parish church's register for the years 1917-1927 records the birth and baptism of Karol Jozef Wojtyla, born May 18, 1920, the son of Karol and Emilia (Kaczorowska) Wojtyla.

In 1978 the pastor, Father Edward Zacher, added beside the entry, "On 16 October A.D. 1978 he was elected to the See of Peter, assuming the name John Paul II."

The path from little Wadowice to the most important and influential post of spiritual leadership in the world was a long and often challenging one for Karol Wojtyla. Through it all, he never lost contact with his beginnings. At every major stage in the journey he returned to his roots, to the town and parish church where the people knew him by his nickname, "Lolek" (the equivalent of "Chuck" or "Charlie" for "Charles" in English).

He went back to Wadowice's Church of St. Mary for his first Mass when he was ordained a priest in 1946 after taking seminary studies in secret during the Nazi occupation of Poland. He returned for a thanksgiving Mass after he was made auxiliary bishop of Cracow in 1958, when he became archbishop of Cracow in 1964, and when he was made a cardinal in 1967.

Later, in 1979, he would return to Poland as Pope John Paul II, and he would go again to Wadowice and visit with the people and Father Zacher, who had taught him his catechism as a boy and preached at his first Mass.

The return would be symbolic — not an empty symbol, but one filled with meaning. This "son of Poland" seems to draw vast reserves of strength — intellectual, emotional and spiritual — from an almost mystical attachment to his roots.

After World War II he studied for two years in Rome, doing pastoral work there on weekends, from 1946 to 1948. As bishop, archbishop and cardinal he returned there frequently. When he was elected pope he surprised Italians not only with his knowledge of their language, but also with his awareness of their religious symbols and his ability to make them his own, as if they had always been a part of his life.

While in Rome he lived at the Belgian College, where he became fluent in French. Between school sessions he visited France and Belgium and became an avid lover of the French language and culture.

But it is his Polish heritage — an unusual blend of national and cultural history intimately linked with Catholicism — that formed the man who occupies the Chair of Peter.

3

Only by understanding that Polish heritage is it possible to fully understand the new pope.

Wadowice today is a small industrial center with a population of about 15,000. But it was much smaller when Karol Wojtyla lived there as a boy. Most of its factories, which produce chemicals and metal products, were built after World War II, and its population has more than doubled since the war.

Wadowice is situated in southern Poland on the Skawa River, at the edge of the Beskid range of the Carpathian mountains dividing Poland and Czechoslovakia, 23 miles south-southwest of Cracow.

The town dates back at least to 1327, when it is first mentioned in historical archives, and its oldest and most precious historical monument is the 14th-century parish church, St. Mary's, in the town center.

The church fronts the market square, the town center, now renamed Red Army Square. Across the square is the building that in Karol Wojtyla's youth housed the elementary school and the offices of the municipal authorities.

Just off the square, on a short street alongside the church, is a two-story house, 160 years old. In that house, 7 Koscielna Street, in a two-room apartment on the first floor, Karol Wojtyla was born.

When Karol was born, Poland was enjoying its second year as a reunited nation following almost 150 years of partition and foreign domination.

His father was an administrative army officer. The Wojtyla family originated in the village of Czaniec near Andrychow, a few miles west of Wadowice. His grandfather, Maciej, was a sailor.

When the elder Karol married Emilia Kaczorowska, they settled in Wadowice. He was in his mid-20s, she was five years younger. Until the end of the partition and formation of the Republic of Poland in 1918, Wojtyla was a staff officer in the 12th Infantry Regiment of the Austrian army. After independence he became a member of the Polish army and later retired with the rank of captain.

The Wojtylas' first son, Edmund, was born March 27, 1906. A daughter born a few years later died in early infancy. Karol, born on May 18, 1920, was the third and last child.

A little more than a month after his birth, according to a Latin notation in the parish records, on June 20, 1920, the youngest Wojtyla was baptized "Karol Jozef" at the baptismal font of the 600-year-old church. He was named after St. Charles Borromeo, the 16th-century Milanese cardinal who was noted for his work in carrying out the church reforms following the Council of Trent. In years to come, Wojtyla would return on special occasions to that church. In 1966, celebrating the millennium of Poland's conversion to Christianity and birth as a nation, as archbishop of Cracow he would kiss the baptismal font where he had been welcomed into the community of the church. On his return as pope in 1979 he would again kiss the baptismal font and remark that it was there that, "I was given the grace to become a son of God, together with my Redeemer."

Karol's mother, a native of Silesia, was in poor health and died of a heart ailment on April 13, 1929, when Karol was not quite 9.

His brother Edmund became a doctor but died in 1932, at the age of 26, after contracting scarlet fever while working in Bielsko.

When he started school at the age of 6, Lolek had only to walk past the parish church and across the market square to reach the classrooms. He attended the 7 o'clock Mass there every morning before school and stopped again every afternoon after classes. On his return to Wadowice as pope he would tell the youngsters of the town that he, like his classmates, used to stop in the church every day for a visit and pray before an image of Our Mother of Perpetual Help. Thus he apparently began his lifelong special devotion to Mary even before his mother died, though it no doubt was deepened by the loss of his mother when he was so young.

Lolek's father, who raised him alone from the age of 9, was, according to various accounts, a stern disciplinarian who demanded obedience and diligence, but also a warm-hearted man with intellectual interests. He not only kept the house and cooked the meals, but also tutored his younger son and watched over his studies daily. Father and son were reportedly inseparable and often took long walks in the evening talking about life.

As a student he excelled in most subjects. One of his schoolmates, Wlodzimierz Piotrowski, recalls, "I don't ever remember him getting less than the best grades."

"He was the best pupil in school in Greek and Latin," said one of his former teachers, Elena Szczepanska. "At times he put us in a difficult spot because he seemed to know more than we did."

A page from the school records in the Wadowice lyceum (high school) shows that for the fall term ending Dec. 23, 1937, Karol Wojtyla received "*bardzo dobry*" (excellent) in conduct, religion, Polish, Greek, Latin, German, mathematics, introductory philosophy and physical education. He got "*dobry*" (good) in history and in physics and chemistry. The page also shows that he was absent from school six times that term, but never without an excuse.

As a teen-ager Lolek was active in the student Marian Society and served as its president for three years. He was an altar boy in the parish. He loved sports, especially soccer (where he usually played goalkeeper or defense), swimming, skiing and skating.

In school he also developed an interest in literature, music and drama. He was one of the first to join a drama group of students from his high school and a private girls' school. He played guitar and sang at local folk festivals. He began writing poetry and in his last year in high school won second prize in a local speech contest for his recitation of poetry.

Recollections of the young Wojtyla in Wadowice have obviously been blurred over the years by faulty memories and the embellishments that enter into stories told and retold. Who would have predicted when Lolek was a child that one day the small town would be flooded by journalists and biographers seeking out every last detail to reconstruct his early life?

But embellished or not, some of the stories are worth recounting. It is said that when he was a baby and his mother was wheeling him around town in a carriage, she used to tell her neighbors, "Just watch, my Lolek will become a famous man."

Elena Szczepanska said that she visited him just after news of his brother's death arrived in 1932. "Poor boy, you've lost your brother," she said.

The 12-year-old Karol looked at her thoughtfully, she recalled, and responded simply, "It was God's will."

The people of Wadowice who knew him as a child remember him as athletic, humorous, witty and friendly, but at the same time deeply religious and with a pensive, meditative side. It is said that he and his friends used to get scolded by the parish priest when they played soccer in the street in front of his house and kicked the ball against the church. It is also said that he often helped his classmates who had a harder time with their studies than he, and he was well liked despite his superior abilities.

A month before his high school graduation in 1938, he was chosen to give a welcoming speech to then Archbishop Adam Sapieha of Cracow, who was visiting the school. The archbishop was known as Prince Sapieha, since he was a prince by birth. The speech was dignified and delivered fluently and beautifully. The prince-archbishop (who would later be made a cardinal) turned to Father Zacher, the parish priest, and asked, "Do you think we could make a priest out of him?"

Father Zacher said, "I don't know. He's in love with the teacher and they've talked him into taking Polish philology."

"A very great pity. We need someone like him," said Archbishop Sapieha.

(Variations on this story have the archbishop addressing young Karol himself on the possibility of becoming a priest, and Wojtyla telling him that he likes theater and wants to study philosophy or Polish language and literature. The variations on the same basic story can be attributed to frequent retelling.)

A month later Karol Wojtyla graduated from high school with honors. Three years later he would be studying for the priesthood, secretly because the Nazis had closed the seminaries.

Shortly after his graduation, Karol and his father moved to Cracow's Debnicki district, across the Vistula River from the ancient town center and historic Wawel Hill. Karol, then 18, entered the Jagiellonian University.

Also called the University of Cracow, the Jagiellonian University is the second-oldest in central Europe. It was founded in 1364, only 16 years after the University of Prague and one year before the University of Vienna. In one of its most brilliant periods, covering most of the 15th century, it had 40 percent of the students in Polish universities, including the famous astronomer Nicolas Copernicus, and leading scholars who played an important role in the flourishing Polish culture. Again in the late 19th century the university was the heart of a movement that made Cracow the most important center of Polish culture from the 1870s until World War II.

The Wojtylas moved into a cramped basement apartment at 10 Tyniecka St. For six weeks during the summer the young Wojtyla joined a road-building crew, carting and hauling construction materials.

In the fall he entered the philosophy department of Jagiellonian University, aiming at a degree in Polish philology.

His first year at the university was an exciting, happy one. Even though the growing military might and expansionist policy of Nazi Germany clouded the horizon, "peace in our time" was the slogan of the day.

The philosophy department's teaching staff had some of the leading scholars of the time in Polish language and literature. In addition to carrying a full set of courses in his field, Wojtyla enrolled in optional elocution classes, continued writing poetry and joined the Cracow Theater Fraternity, which had just been formed. The following summer he played a small part in a presentation of the dramatic poem, "The Knight of the Moon" by Marian Nizynski — a legend about a man who sold his soul to the devil but escaped as he was being carried off to hell by saying a prayer.

Karol became close friends with a fellow student, Juliusz Kydrynski, who would later become a well-known writer. The two attended opening nights of practically every play staged in Cracow that year. They also got together frequently at Kydrynski's apartment for literary evenings or poetry-writing sessions.

Wojtyla also joined the Polish Language Society, a professional group which rarely accepted undergraduates. He at least occasionally visited Cracow cafes, where intellectuals and literary figures often engaged in discussion and debate into the wee hours of the morning.

Another close friendship he formed that year was with the Szkocki family, whom he often visited with Kydrynski. Mrs. Szkocki was a lover of Polish romantic literature, Mr. Szkocki was a music teacher, and their married daughter Zofia Pozniakowa frequently played classical music on the piano for them. One of their lodgers was Wojtyla's French teacher at the university.

That last untroubled year before the war also gave Wojtyla a chance to learn the city of Cracow, whose rich treasure of history, culture and architecture had, by the 16th century, earned it the title *"Totius Poloniae Urus Celeberrima"* — "the most celebrated city of all Poland."

The city that Wojtyla would someday rule as archbishop and cardinal is most noted for Wawel Hill, the castle-cathedral-fortress complex at the edge of the old city, strategically overlooking the Vistula River. In the Wawel Cathedral is buried St. Stanislaus Szczepanow, one of the first bishops of Cracow and patron saint of Poland, who was beheaded because he opposed the king. Also buried there are 14

Polish kings, religious leaders, great cultural and literary figures, and national heroes. The latter include Tadeusz Kosciuszko, who led the Polish revolt against the combined armies of Russia, Austria and Prussia and was one of the military heroes of the American War of Independence, and Marshal Jozef Pilsudski who led the newly independent Poland out of the shambles of World War I.

Wojtyla visited the cathedral often. He had been a friend of the vicar, Msgr. (then Father) Kazimierz Figlewicz, since the priest's days in Wadowice. Every first Friday he served Mass for Father Figlewicz in the cathedral.

Another favorite church of his in Cracow was St. Mary's, a magnificent twin-towered edifice built in the 13th and 14th centuries on the northeast corner of the Old Town Market Square. Wojtyla spent hours praying before the 15th-century main altar, carved in wood by Wit Stwosz, which is a masterpiece of European Gothic art. One of the most valuable wood carvings in Europe, it was taken to Nuremberg by the Germans during World War II but returned in 1945 and restored.

When Karol Wojtyla was elected pope in 1978, he was the first pope in at least a century who had not spent his teen-age years in a strict Italian seminary. Intrigued by the oddity of a pope who had gone through adolescence and into young adulthood "in the world," Italian newspapers and magazines quickly produced rumors of a young wartime bride or fiancee killed in a concentration camp, or of other steady girlfriends or secret sweethearts. In Wadowice he had been popular with girls and according to several reports had a steady girlfriend. After he moved to Cracow he was also very popular and there were a number of young women in his circles of friends and acquaintances. But serious reporters and writers have dismissed as fiction the various stories about a special girlfriend, fiancee or bride.

At the end of the academic year in the summer of 1939, Wojtyla passed all his exams. Along with the rest of the students he joined the Academic Legion — compulsory basic military training for university students which lasted until mid-August. The students then returned home for a few weeks' rest before the next school year.

On Friday, Sept. 1, at 4:45 a.m., the German invasion of Poland began. In a classic blitzkrieg offensive, 75 German divisions and 2,400 tanks smashed across the border. Two thousand planes flew in to hit the Polish forces and bomb major cities behind the lines in order to sow terror and confusion. Cracow was among the first cities bombed. But it was First Friday and Karol Wojtyla went through the bombs and rubble to Wawel Cathedral, where he served Mass for Father Figlewicz.

The German invaders quickly overran the country. The Nazi occupation ended 21 years of independence for the Polish republic in which the church had flourished.

The fortunes of church and nation in Poland have been inextricably linked in a way that could be said of few if any other nations. Poland's birth as a nation is generally counted from A.D. 966, when the Piast Prince Mieszko I was baptized after marrying the Czech Princess Dabrowka. In 990 he placed his land in a kind of vassalage under the protection of the pope to counteract expansion efforts of the German church and Ottoman emperors. It has been Poland's fate ever since to find itself victimized by its neighbors, sometimes partitioned, sometimes occupied, seldom existing as a sovereign nation. Through it all, the Polish people have clung steadfastly to two primary symbols of their identity — their Polish language and their Catholic religion.

During the brief lifespan of the Polish republic, which was born two years before Karol Wojtyla and died with the German occupation when he was 19, Polish culture and the Catholic Church prospered side by side. The number of bishops more than doubled from 23 to 51, the number of priests increased 43 percent to 13,000, new dioceses were established and religious orders grew rapidly. Parishes also multiplied quickly, and revived or revitalized Catholic societies and church social services soon touched almost every area of life. By 1939 every diocese had its own Sunday paper, and more than 250 Catholic periodicals, many of them Eastern Rite, were being published.

Seventy-five percent of the people in the reunited nation were Catholic, about 10 percent were Orthodox, another 10 percent were Jews, and 3 percent were Protestants. About one-sixth of the Catholics belonged to Eastern Rites.

Hitler's attitudes toward the Poles were clear. Poland was to be "a vast Polish labor camp," he said. "Poles will never be raised to a higher level." The German occupiers set out systematically to crush Polish intellectual, cultural and spiritual life.

One of their first attacks was directed against Jagiellonian University, the country's leading intellectual and cultural institution. Barely more than a month after Warsaw fell, on Nov. 6, the university's teachers were called to a meeting in the institution's great hall. When they were assembled, they were arrested en masse by the Gestapo — 138 professors and lecturers, which was most of the teaching faculty. They were sent to the Sachsenhausen concentration camp. Some were released after three months of interrogation, but most never came back.

Nevertheless, before the end of the year many students and the few teachers who had avoided arrest set up an underground university — a network of secret communications and classroom sites in homes and apartments. Wojtyla and Kydrynski were among the first students back at school. To avoid detection, which would have meant arrest and possibly death, the students would slip into the prearranged site one at a time, and after a hushed, tense period of lecture and discussion, slip out again in ones and twos.

Kydrynski's third-floor apartment at 10 Felicjanek St. in Old Cracow was one of the secret classrooms. Once the Gestapo arrived an hour before a meeting and found chairs already set up for 30 people. His mother talked the German agents into believing that they were simply preparing for a party.

The whole fabric of university life, including tuition, examinations and final grades, and even makeshift laboratories for science courses, was set up in secret. By 1942 the floating university had been organized into five faculties with more than 130 teachers and 800 students.

Wojtyla's first problem after the Nazi occupation was to find a job. He had to support himself and his father, whose army pension was cut off with the occupation. But more significantly, he needed a work card proving he was employed or else risk deportation to a labor camp. With the help of Kydrynski and the Szkockis' daughter Zofia, he got work in a limestone quarry at Zakrzowek, just outside Cracow, along with Kydrynski.

He and his father still lived in their basement apartment in Debnicki, and two aunts on his mother's side lived above them. His daily routine began with an early morning visit to a nearby church run by the Salesian Fathers.

After a day's work at the quarry, he attended evening classes, studied, wrote poetry or engaged in underground theater activities, which were a form of intellectual and cultural resistance to the Nazis.

At the quarry, Wojtyla was put to work digging out and wheeling away the dirt around the stone and sometimes pumping water out of the quarry with an archaic hand pump. The regular quarrymen sympathized with the plight of students forced to do unskilled labor as a cover for their illegal activities. They did what they could to make the work easier for the students and became good friends with them.

After several months at the wheelbarrow and pump, Wojtyla was advanced to the stone hammers, breaking the large stones blasted out of the quarry walls into chunks small enough to load into carts. Each quarryman was expected to fill at least a wagon a day.

For a while Wojtyla stood up to the hard routine of manual labor all day and studies into the late evening. But one evening on his way home he collapsed from exhaustion in the street. A German truck hit him as he fell, fracturing his skull. The driver did not stop. Wojtyla lay unconscious in the street until the next morning when a passerby found him and took him to a hospital.

The foreman at the quarry had meantime taken a special liking to Wojtyla. When an opportunity arose he "promoted" him to the dangerous but less exhausting work of packing explosives into bore holes in the rock and stringing the fuses for the "shot firer," who was responsible for blasting the rock from the quarry walls.

In the winter of 1940-41 Wojtyla's father, who was 61, suffered a heart attack and was forced to stay in bed. Young Wojtyla began to go home with Kydrynski every night and pick up meals from Kydrynski's mother which he would then take home and warm up for his father. On Feb. 18, 1941, he picked up some medicine for his father, stopped at the Kydrynski home and went with Kydrynski's sister to his home across the river. As she went into the kitchen to re-heat the meal cooked earlier by her mother, he went to visit his father. A moment later he reappeared and brokenly announced that his father was dead.

Juliusz Kydrysnki, who came to join Karol in his grief, stayed in the next room that night while the 20-year-old Wojtyla knelt for 12 hours in prayer and grief at his father's bedside. Some who knew him say that that long night of prayer beside the corpse of his father, who had been his closest companion and the chief influence in his life, was the point at which Karol Wojtyla decided to become a priest.

His father was buried, alongside his mother and older brother Edmund and other members of his mother's side of the family, in Cracow's Radowicki military cemetery.

Friends from that time say that Wojtyla smiled less and became more thoughtful and meditative after his father's death. But it was certainly not only the death of his father that was affecting him. Immersed in Polish history and culture, he could see the devastation being wreaked by Hitler's occupation government. The occupation governor, Hans Frank, ensconced in the former royal castle of Wawel in Cracow, boasted that "the very concept of 'Polish' will be erased for centuries" and that "all the forests of Poland" could not provide the paper needed to print execution orders.

The few rumors of atrocities in the concentration camps that leaked out were too terrible to be believed or comprehended, but acquaintances and neighbors arrested on the streets were never heard from again. In Wojtyla's underground meetings with the resisting intelligentsia and through priest friends he must have heard of the arrest or disappearance of leading cultural and religious figures, the destruction of libraries and cultural treasures, the closings of churches and restrictions on the clergy.

Like others in his closest circle of friends, Wojtyla responded with stiffened, though secret, resistance. The underground university was not the only illegal activity he was engaged in. Among others, two that began early and played a particularly important role in his life were the parish Catholic Youth Association and the Rhapsodic Theater.

Before the war the Catholic Youth Association was an open group in the Salesian parish in Debnicki. After the occupation it might have disappeared like so many banned groups, but it was started up again secretly by a quiet, ascetic tailor who had little formal education, Jan Tyranowski. Wojtyla was chairman of the clandestine group.

Tyranowski, though uneducated, was a deeply spiritual man who read carefully the writings of St. John of the Cross and Henri de Montfort. At meetings of the association there were often long discussions of scripture and St. John of the Cross' mystical writings, led by Tyranowski. He also formed "living rosaries" in prayer meetings at his apartment. Many say that Tyranowski was a major spiritual influence on Wojtyla in the war years and might have been one of the decisive influences leading to his decision to study for the priesthood. Several years later Wojtyla's doctoral dissertation in Rome would be on St. John of the Cross. One of his first articles in Tygodnik Powszechny, the Cracow Catholic weekly, was on Tyranowski's personality and spirituality. As a cardinal he once referred to him as "an apostle of God's love."

Wojtyla saw his work with the Rhapsodic Theater as an important part of the resistance to the Nazis. It was a way to keep alive that which had enabled his countrymen to endure many other oppressions — their culture. As long as Polish culture was not destroyed, Poland could not be destroyed.

During one clandestine staging of an epic poem, Wojtyla was reading one of the poem's most dramatic passages when loudspeakers in the streets began to blare an announcement of a German battle victory. Wojtyla neither faltered nor changed his voice but continued reading as if the outside noise did not exist.

In the meantime he continued to work, to write poetry and plays, to take classes and study music and French. He was transferred from the limestone quarry owned by Solway chemical works to a nearby Solway factory, where he was in charge of mixing the chemical agents to purify boiler water. He also took part in efforts to improve working conditions there and provide recreational facilities for the workers. Later as pope he would declare that his experiences as a worker were more valuable to him than his academic degrees.

At some point he decided to study for the priesthood. Even his closest friends such as Juliusz Kydrynski and Zofia Pozniakowa, the Szkocki's daughter, were unaware of the fact. "I had no idea he was studying theology. He kept it a secret," said Kydrynski later.

Msgr. Nikolaj Kuczkowski, who was then a vicar at Wawel Cathedral, recalls that one day, impressed by Wojtyla's character and religious practice, he took an old friend of Wojtyla's from Wadowice and paid a call on the young man to try to talk him into studying for the priesthood. "You're too late, I'm already studying theology privately," Wojtyla told them.

Wojtyla tried to join the Carmelites, a strict monastic order. According to Bishop Julian Groblicki, auxiliary of Cracow, the Carmelite superiors turned him away with the comment, "You are destined for greater things."

His formal studies in Cracow's underground seminary began in 1942. Records of his grades from two and a half years of secret studies are still preserved in Polish archives. They show him receiving "very good" or "excellent" in 20 courses, and a grade as low as "good" in only one, psychology.

Wojtyla was also engaged in another activity that the Nazis considered subversive, one that could be far more dangerous than his theater or school activities — protecting Jews.

As a child in Wadowice Karol Wojtyla had counted among his close friends Jerzy Kluger, whose father was chairman of the Jewish community association in Wadowice. They maintained their contact over the years, and among the first visitors Pope John Paul II received in private audience after his election was the Kluger family.

During the war Wojtyla collaborated with the Christian democratic organization UNIA in an underground group helping Jews to hide, obtain false identities and escape. It has been reported that his activities in this area got his name on a Nazi blacklist. By the end of the war only about 500 Jews remained in the once large and flourishing Jewish community in Cracow. After the war Wojtyla helped organize the care of the Jewish cemetery.

In the summer of 1944 the Red Army was pushing back the Nazis and marching on Warsaw. On July 29 Moscow Radio told the Poles that liberation was at hand and it was time to rise up against the occupiers. It was a brutal ploy to destroy the Polish resistance movement, the country's best and most courageous sons. On Aug. 1 the Warsaw Uprising began. It took the Nazis 63 days to put down the rebellion, despite the Poles' lack of food, weapons and ammunition. The powerful Red Army, on orders from Moscow, sat 40 miles from Warsaw until it was over. In revenge Hitler levelled Warsaw and destroyed historic buildings and monuments in almost every other Polish city. Cracow was the only major city in the country to escape the massive destruction that preceded the German retreat and surrender.

Although Cracow's buildings escaped the Nazi terror, its people did not. Sunday, Aug. 6, went down in Cracow history as Black Sunday. Gestapo and SS units fanned through the city, rounding up every male they could find between the ages of 15 and 55 and shooting them in the streets. They passed by 10 Tyniecka St. without entering. Behind the closed but unlocked door Karol Wojtyla was kneeling in prayer.

Archbishop Sapieha decided it was time to call his secret seminarians in. The next day he brought 20 students, including Wojtyla, into the archbishop's palace. The spacious drawing room was converted into a somewhat cramped dormitory for them. They removed their civilian clothes and put on cassocks. In the new Nazi rage they could not be sure of safety there either, but if they died, it at least would be as what they were. The time for secrecy had passed.

There was a certain safety factor at the palace though. The Germans had not yet dared search it, despite the archbishop's well-known antagonism toward the Nazis. He had repeatedly protested against the occupying government's acts of persecution toward the Poles. The story is told that Governor Frank repeatedly sought an invitation to dinner with the archbishop and was as often rebuffed — until one day an invitation came. Governor Frank and Archbishop Sapieha sat down to eat. The meal, served on the archbishop's most elegant, precious heirloom porcelain, consisted of thin slices of heavy black bread, covered with a thin coat of jam — the daily fare of the starving Polish population.

The seminarians who moved into the archbishop's palace would not be able to leave again until the war was over. Wojtyla's absence at the chemical factory was noted immediately, and warning notices began piling up at the doorway of his now vacant apartment. At Archbishop Sapieha's urging, one of the Polish managers in the factory somehow managed to get Wojtyla's name deleted from the factory's work lists. As far as the Nazis knew, he had ceased to exist, and the police stopped searching for him.

When the war ended in 1945 the church in Poland had a monumental rebuilding task. In some areas nearly every church, monastery and convent had been closed within the first few months of the war. Thirteen bishops had been arrested or exiled, four of whom died. Of 3,647 priests, 389 clerics, 341 brothers and 1,117 nuns sent to concentration camps, 1,996 priests, 113 clerics and 238 nuns had been exterminated. Among them was Franciscan Father Maximilian Kolbe, beatified in 1971, who was one of the 4 million killed at Oswiecim, a few miles from Cracow. Six million Polish citizens had perished during the Nazi occupation, including thousands of Catholic lay leaders. The Polish city of Oswiecim in the Cracow archdiocese, better known by its German name Auschwitz, became the leading symbol not only to Poland but to the world of the degrading depths to which human cruelty can plunge.

On Nov. 1, 1946, the prince-archbishop of Cracow ordained Karol Wojtyla a priest in the private chapel of the archbishop's palace. The next day he celebrated his first Mass in Wawel Cathedral's St. Leonard Crypt, where Poland's great kings and heroes are buried. Also buried there is Juliusz Slowacki, the 19th-century poet whose works were among several performed by Wojtyla in the Rhapsodic Theater. One of Slowacki's poems, which Wojtyla had almost certainly read, predicted the election someday of a Slavic pope.

A few days later Father Wojtyla went back to Wadowice to celebrate a first Mass in his home town among his childhood friends. Seeing in Father Wojtyla a man of intellect and character who would move ahead in the church, Archbishop

11

Sapieha wanted to broaden his studies and experience. He sent him to Rome to work for a degree in philosophy at the Pontifical University Angelicum — the Dominican-run school named after St. Thomas Aquinas (the "Angelic Doctor") which stands as the church's chief university in philosophical studies.

During his two years in Rome Father Wojtyla lived at the Belgian College. The Polish College, closed during the war, had not yet been reopened. This gave him a chance to further improve his French, already well advanced. In the summers he toured France and Belgium, doing pastoral work among Polish emigrants and displaced persons in those areas. During the school year he helped out on weekends in the Garbatella quarter of Rome, then a postwar shantytown sadly lacking in social and pastoral services. More than 30 years later, one of his first pastoral visits as bishop of Rome would be Garbatella. He would find conditions only slightly improved.

Father Wojtyla's trip to Rome was his first outside Poland, the beginning of a series of international contacts that would grow steadily through the next three decades.

He did his thesis under Father Reginald Garrigou-Lagrange, a French Dominican philosopher-theologian whom many considered the best thinker in Rome in those fields at the time. Father Wojtyla came to appreciate the philosophy of St. Thomas, which in one letter he called "so marvelously beautiful, so delightful, and at the same time so uncomplicated."

But unlike many Catholic philosophy students of the same era, Father Wojtyla did not simply try to immerse himself in St. Thomas and make it his own system of thought. In the same letter, written to Mrs. Szkocki in Cracow, he said, "but I still have far to travel before I hit upon my own philosophy."

Father Wojtyla received his licentiate in 1947 with a perfect score on his examinations. He did his doctoral thesis on "The Doctrine of Faith in St. John of the Cross," for which he was given nearly perfect marks by his examining professors. In defending his thesis he was again awarded a perfect score, 50 points out of a possible 50. He graduated as a doctor of divinity, magna cum laude, on April 30, 1948.

His native Poland, meanwhile, was beginning to see the wartime Nazi repression replaced by the postwar Stalinist repression. The Nazis had attacked the church because it was seen as a unique and powerful protector of Polish life and culture. The communists attacked it simply because it was the church.

For a time after the war, it appeared the church would be able to reorganize much that had been broken down by the occupation. But in September 1945, the new Soviet-backed Polish government revoked the 1925 concordat with the Holy See, and the beginnings of a new church repression could be seen. One of the first steps was the nationalization of Catholic presses and the censorship of Catholic publications.

When Father Wojtyla returned to Poland in 1948, his doctoral thesis could not be published there because of the communist government's restrictions on publications. The theology department of the Jagiellonian University, however, accepted his studies and awarded him a doctorate of divinity in December.

He was assigned as a vicar to a parish in the rural village of Niegowic. The pastor there was about to celebrate his 50th anniversary in the priesthood, and the parishioners were in the midst of discussions on a fitting way to celebrate the event. They were talking about repainting the old church, but the new priest suggested that they build a new church instead. They did.

In 1949 Father Wojtyla was transferred to St. Florian Church in Cracow. In his two years there he performed 160 marriages and more than 200 baptisms. He spent long hours with young people, teaching religion, playing ball, and joining philosophical and religious discussions in the evenings with university students.

It was still a period of relative freedom in Poland. There was freedom of movement and work. Although Polish media were censored, it was not illegal to listen to foreign broadcasts. But it was not to last.

In the period 1948-1950 Catholic youth associations were banned, the Catholic charities agency dissolved, church-run hospitals nationalized and some 500,000 acres of church property — more than half its holdings — expropriated.

Archbishop Stefan Wyszynski succeeded Cardinal Augustyn Hlond as archbishop of Warsaw and Gniezno and primate of Poland after the latter's death in 1948. The new primate was a key figure in engineering a church-state agreement in 1950 that was supposed to guarantee church rights in the areas of teaching, liturgy and religious education in return for church opposition to "misuse of religious sentiments for anti-state aims."

The agreement did not work out as church officials had expected or hoped. Church-state relations were not normalized and the pressures continued. Bishop Czeslaw Mieczyslaw Kaczmarek of Kielce was arrested in 1951. Archbishop Wyszynski was made a cardinal in 1953, but was arrested soon afterward. The following year brought the arrest of Bishop Antoni Baraniak, then auxiliary and later archbishop of Poznan.

A 1953 government decree declared that the jurisdiction of bishops was subject to approval by the state. The government office on religious affairs was given absolute authority over church affairs. Several major and minor seminaries, including those of religious orders, were closed. In 1954-55 Catholic theological faculties at universities were closed, and several measures were taken against the Catholic University of Lublin. In January 1955, religious instruction in elementary schools was prohibited. A number of priests were arrested, monasteries were expropriated by the state, and police searches of private residences of priests and religious became commonplace.

The government also exploited left-right political divisions among Catholics, promoting so-called "patriotic priests" and "progressive Catholics" of the political left, which since World War I had been a major force in Polish politics. Prominent Catholics of a leftist orientation were organized into the Pax Movement which had its own Pax Press — still alive a quarter century later when Karol Wojtyla became pope.

In the first decade under communism the number of churches and chapels declined 30 percent, religious monasteries and convents by more than 40 percent. Many parishes could be manned only on a temporary basis because of the number of priests arrested and banished or imprisoned.

In Cracow Father Wojtyla was gaining a reputation as a preacher and an ascetic. He still showed his love of drama, often attending movies or plays with young people, but when he received gifts he usually gave them to the poor, and his clothing was frayed and often secondhand. Some say he sometimes slept on the floor instead of his bed.

In the 1950s, poems and dramas he had written during and after the war began to appear in the Cracow Catholic paper Tygodnik Powszechny and the intellectual Catholic monthly Znak. He used a variety of pseudonyms for his published works, but the most common was Andrzej Jawien, the name of a hero in a Polish novel who lost his faith and later regained it. The reason he chose this pseudonym is a matter of speculation.

Father Wojtyla resumed his studies at the Jagiellonian University in 1951, while continuing to work at St. Florian's Church in Cracow. The university awarded him a junior professorship in theology.

In October 1953, he began lecturing on ethics at Cracow's theological seminary. The same year he was invited to give several lectures at the Catholic University of Lublin — the only Catholic university still functioning in countries within the Soviet orbit.

The next year he became a regular lecturer at Lublin. Two years later, at the **13** age of 36, he became a full professor and received the chair of ethics, becoming head of the university's Institute of Ethics.

The post gave Father Wojtyla a demanding schedule. He still lived in Cracow and did parish work there, but Lublin was more than 150 miles away by train. He regularly commuted by night train, using a train seat as his bed at least two nights a week. Because of his rapport with students, he was dubbed by some "the eternal teen-ager." Students packed his classes. He frequently led their retreats and organized other student activities. After classes he often sat conversing with groups of students into the late evening before catching the train back to Cracow.

Father Wojtyla also found time in his schedule for hiking, camping, canoeing and skiing in the Carpathian Mountains, sometimes with two or three close friends, but often with groups of students. On overnight trips he frequently played the guitar and led songfests around a campfire or engaged in long philosophical or religious discussions with the students. He would celebrate Mass for the group along the trail, often strapping two branches or canoe paddles together to form a cross for a makeshift altar.

It was while he was on a canoe trip in July 1958, that word reached him that the Polish primate, Cardinal Wyszynski, wanted to see him in Warsaw. When Father Wojtyla arrived, the cardinal told him that Pope Pius XII had chosen him to be auxiliary bishop of Cracow. Father Wojtyla said he would accept the nomination as bishop, then added: "But that doesn't mean I can't go back canoeing, does it?" A few hours later he was back on the water.

Cracow had been without any bishop from 1951, when Cardinal-Prince Sapieha died, until 1956, when Archbishop Eugeniusz Baziak, Latin-Rite archbishop of Lvov in the Ukraine, was named apostolic administrator. Most of the Archdiocese of Lvov had been incorporated into the Soviet Union in 1939, leaving only a few parishes in the Poland that was reconstituted at the end of the war. From 1952 to 1956 Archbishop Baziak was prevented from working even in the small Polish territory under his jurisdiction.

Then in the fall of 1956 the newly named chief of the Polish Communist Party, Wladislaw Gomulka, initiated a new era in church-state relations. He freed imprisoned priests and bishops, including Cardinal Wyszynski, and rescinded the 1953 decree subordinating all jurisdiction of bishops to the approval of the state. Religious instruction was again allowed in the schools, though only as an elective course and before or after regular school hours.

Under the thaw initiated by Gomulka the church began once again to enter into national life, though in nowhere near the same degree that it had during the days of the Polish kingdom or the country's brief period of independence between the two world wars. In 1957 the hierarchy began a nine-year novena in preparation for the 1966 celebration of the millennium of the nation and of Polish Christianity.

On Sept. 28, 1958, Archbishop Baziak ordained Father Wojtyla a bishop in the Wawel Cathedral where he had celebrated his first Mass 12 years earlier. At 38, he was the youngest bishop in Poland.

Bishop Wojtyla went on teaching at Lublin, giving away his small annual stipend for student scholarships. The major difference after he became bishop was that, with his added work load, he could not travel regularly to Lublin. So his students traveled weekly to Cracow. He held the seminars in his small apartment at 21 Kanoniczna St., near Wawel Cathedral. These were lengthy sessions, beginning in midafternoon and running until midnight, when the students had to catch the train back to Lublin. He also combined classes with mountain outings, lecturing or conducting seminars while seated on a log or rock with his students around him. This way he was able to get his needed exercise, teach and still maintain his busy office schedule in Cracow.

14

Bishop Wojtyla continued teaching at Lublin as an archbishop and cardinal and, when he was elected pope, the university announced the post would remain his for life, even though he could no longer return to deliver lectures. His stipend is still used for student scholarships.

In 1961 Bishop Wojtyla was named vicar general of the Cracow archdiocese. On June 15, 1962, Archbishop Baziak died. Bishop Wojtyla became in effect head of the diocese, though without a formal title. Pope Paul VI made him the archbishop of Cracow on Jan. 13, 1964, and a cardinal three years later, in the consistory of June 26, 1967. At the time he was 47 years old and the second-youngest cardinal in the church.

Cardinal Wojtyla was obviously a man to be watched.

By the time the College of Cardinals went into conclave to elect a pope on the afternoon of Oct. 14, 1978, all of them were well aware not only of the name of Karol Wojtyla, but of the man himself. He had assumed a number of prominent roles in the church's international affairs and was widely respected for his intellectual ability and charismatic personality.

He was known as an avid reader and a prolific writer. In addition to his constant output of poetry and drama, including a book-length radio play, he had written at least 120 articles on philosophical and theological themes and two major books on ethics. When he preached a Lenten retreat for Pope Paul VI in 1976, Pope Paul was so impressed that he insisted the sermons be published in book form.

In addition to his work in Cracow, Cardinal Wojtyla took on a variety of roles in international church affairs. He was still only a bishop when the Second Vatican Council began in 1962, but he played an important role in the development of several of its documents. Latin was the official language of the council and many of the oral interventions by bishops were clearly simple translations into Latin from their native languages. But the Cracow bishop's speeches were delivered in excellent, polished Latin that showed a true fluency in the language.

At the council the Eastern European bishops were particularly interested in a strong statement on religious freedom. Bishop Wojtyla, while sharing the same interest, insisted that a statement that was too strong would be counterproductive. He criticized an early draft on grounds that it made the church appear authoritarian. He helped fight off critics of some of the most important passages in the council's "Declaration on Religious Liberty," a landmark document that says freedom of religion is a basic human right with which civil authorities have no power to interfere.

He also insisted on avoiding an oversimplified approach to atheism, reminding the council fathers that there were differences in personal reasons for non-belief and in expressions of it. The critical point of attack, he said, must be on atheism as a socially and politically enforced system.

He also made significant contributions to the editing of the council's "Pastoral Constitution on the Church in the Modern World," the key document declaring the church's commitment to involvement in social development and world affairs because of its concern for the dignity of man.

After the council Cardinal Wojtyla participated as a representative of the Polish hierarchy in all the general assemblies of the world Synod of Bishops, a body set up by Pope Paul to provide him with periodic consultation with the world's bishops on major issues facing the church. When he was elected pope Cardinal Wojtyla was president of the 15-member permanent Council of the Synod, of which he had been a member since 1971.

He traveled abroad a number of times as a representative of the Polish hierarchy. He visited other parts of Europe frequently and journeyed to Latin America and Australia. He also made two trips to the United States — once in 1969, when he visited 12 cities in 12 days, and again in 1976, when he spent six weeks traveling to 13 cities, including six he had gone to on his previous U.S. visit.

The church had not only a new pope. It had a new kind of pope. The year ahead would reveal just what that would mean.

1 *(above) Karol Wojtyla as a seminarian in 1944.*

2 *This is the house in Wadowice where Karol Wojtyla was born in 1920. The window shown was to his room.*

3 *Father Edward Zacher, who taught young Karol his catechism in Wadowice, makes an amendment to the parish baptismal record that his pupil has become pope.*

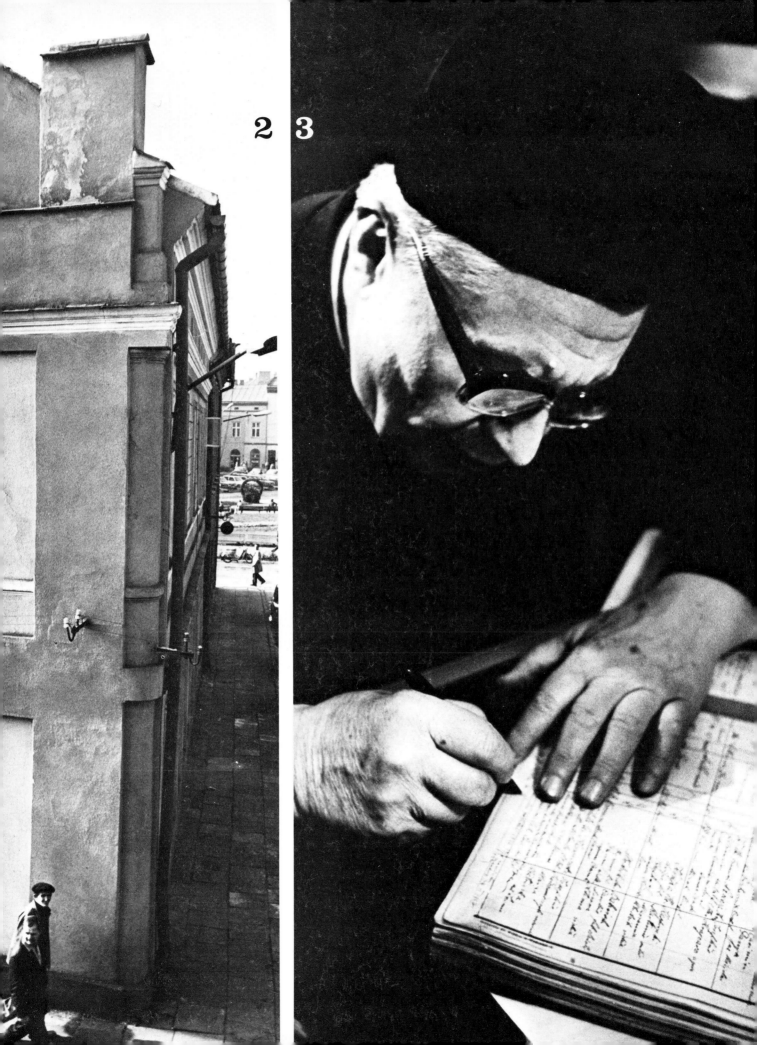

Cyclone Wojtyla

The world soon discovered the man from Poland was no ordinary pope. The signs of his strongly independent character had been immediately apparent on the day of his election, and by November it was abundantly clear: Some popes in the past may have become captives of Vatican protocol and propriety, but John Paul II had no intention of following that pattern. He was a vigorous, action-oriented man to whom spontaneity and informality seemed to come naturally, and he could move quickly and decisively when appropriate. Italian newspapers eventually dubbed him, "Cyclone Wojtyla."

From the moment of his first appearance on the balcony over St. Peter's Square, John Paul proved to be a man fully in control — aware of his own strengths and weaknesses and confident of his ability to handle the job.

The new pope's style added to the human qualities of his immediate predecessor, Pope John Paul I. In his brief reign of 34 days, the first John Paul helped humanize the papacy with a warm, shy smile and with an obvious humility that could not be submerged by the pomp and circumstance surrounding his office. To this human warmth, the athletic, younger, second John Paul added a zest for physical activity and for contact with huge masses of people.

John Paul II, humble but not inhibited, was clearly equally comfortable addressing a solemn assembly of cardinals or singing folk songs around a campfire.

The people who were first to get a detailed look at the new style were Italians. From the outset, the Polish pope wanted to forge a firm link with the Italian people, who after centuries of seeing a native in the Chair of Peter had come to consider an Italian pope as part of their natural heritage.

The pope began forging the link on Nov. 5, 1978 — scarcely three weeks after his election. He flew to Assisi to visit the tomb of St. Francis. Later that day the pope went by motorcade across Rome to the tomb of St. Catherine of Siena. The two saints are the patrons of Italy. The pope described the pilgrimage as a means "to insert myself into the history of salvation that has been impressed, so eloquently and so abundantly, in the history of Italy."

The day was filled with speaking, waving and praying. Even the new pope's prayer bore a distinctive mark. Addressing himself to St. Francis, the pope prayed: "You who brought Christ so near to your times, help us bring Christ near to our times, to our difficult and critical times. We are coming near to the year 2000 after Christ. Will they not be times that prepare us for a rebirth of Christ, for a new Advent? This is asked of you, holy son of the church, son of the Italian land, by Pope John Paul II, son of the Polish land. And he hopes that you will not refuse him, that you will help him."

Back in Rome, John Paul rode in an open-top car to the Basilica of Santa Maria Alla Minerva, a 13th-century church containing the tomb of St. Catherine of Siena, the Dominican mystic who helped end the exile of the popes in Avignon, France.

St. Catherine, he told the thousands of listeners, is "a visible sign of the mission of women in the church. The church of Jesus Christ and of the apostles is at the same time a church that is a mother and a spouse. These biblical expressions clearly reveal how deeply the mission of women is inscribed in the mystery of the church."

On that day and on earlier occasions, thousands of Italians cheered this "son of Poland" as he moved vigorously and purposefully through their midst. He was looking less and less like a foreigner.

If anyone expected the non-Italian pope to take less interest in the affairs of the Rome diocese than his Italian predecessors, they were mistaken. John Paul II made it clear within a few weeks of his election that he expected to be actively involved in diocesan affairs, and not leave them to be run almost exclusively by a cardinal designated by the pope as papal vicar for Rome, as had been the case in the past.

In early November, Cardinal Ugo Poletti, the papal vicar, announced that John Paul intended to spend a half-day a month at St. John Lateran, where the administrative offices of the Rome diocese are located, to familiarize himself with diocesan personnel and problems.

Several days later, the pope formally took possession of St. John Lateran, his cathedral as bishop of Rome. Although the taking possession is a primarily ceremonial custom dating to 324 A.D., John Paul gave it particular emphasis.

In his homily, John Paul linked himself with the previous generations of Roman bishops.

"I unite myself to these generations; I, the new bishop of Rome, Polish in origin. I stop on the threshhold of this temple and ask you to welcome me in the name of the Lord."

As he entered the basilica, the crowd inside burst into applause and cheers. They applauded and cheered again when the pope performed the symbolic act of sitting for the first time upon the chair of the bishop of Rome, to signify that he had taken over as head of the diocese and successor of St. Peter.

On his way to St. John Lateran the pope met with Giulio Argan, Rome's communist mayor, at the foot of the city's ancient Capitol Hill. He embraced Argan and seemed as much at ease hugging the mayor as embracing an old friend. The pope and Argan pledged mutual respect and support in solving the city's problems.

"It is my duty to say that Rome is not a happy city" and is "torn by social injustice, beggared by unemployment and the lack of houses, social assistance and culture," said Argan.

The pope expressed sympathy for the city administration's efforts to "improve surrounding conditions and overcome inadequate social situations." The pope said he hoped the administration would be open and attentive to the requirements of the city's religious life.

Later in November, the pope said he would begin a series of visits to Rome parishes. Concern for the spiritual and material needs of Rome's citizens was a constant theme of the pope's pastoral visits as he favored contact with parishes in low-income, working-class areas.

On Dec. 3, 1978, John Paul stepped out of the shoes of the fisherman and into the shoes of the diocesan bishop in making his first visit to a Rome parish.

The visit to San Francesco Saverino (St. Francis Xavier) Church in Rome's working-class Garbatella district was also a bit of a homecoming for the pope. In his homily he told parishioners that more than 30 years ago, when he was a student in Rome after World War II, he used to go to Garbatella on Sundays to help the priests in their pastoral duties.

The pope was accompanied by Italian security police, huge television camera lights and crowds cheering, "Long Live the Pope!" About 3,000 people unable to get inside the packed church were standing in the light rain outside when the pope arrived by motorcade at 4:30 p.m. Despite an intermittent drizzle and temperatures

19

in the 50s, the pope came in an open car. Stepping quickly out of the car, he stayed a few minutes in the square acknowledging the cheers of the crowds and touching hands outstretched across the barricades.

Then the pope headed for the courtyard, where more than 1,000 schoolchildren were waiting to greet him, waving white-and-yellow banners and cheering. There began a characteristic off-the-cuff exchange between the pope and the children

"You wish me well, and I also wish you well," the pope said to the children. "And then there is one who wishes everyone well, including you and me. And that is Jesus Christ."

Noticing a poster wishing him "Merry Christmas" in Polish, he asked the children if this was "perhaps because you think that the pope doesn't know very much Italian."

Amid the laughter, he asked the children how they were preparing for Christmas. Some responded, "By praying."

"Yes, by praying, and also by going to confession and by receiving Communion. Are you doing that?" said the pope.

"Yes, we are," the children answered.

The pope repeatedly told the children that "with children, one must be brief." But he did not take his own advice and continued laughing and joking with them. Finally, he said: "Now I must go into the church."

The children responded with a loud "No!"

The pope waved goodbye and called out: "Praised be to Christ."

During the homily inside the church, the pope recalled his earlier hope of visiting Rome parishes regularly, but said he may not be able to do this as often as he would like.

"I hope that all will understand that and be indulgent with me, in consideration with the immense weight of duties connected with my ministry," he said.

At the Offertory a dozen little children brought gifts including a basket of white carnations and two white doves in a cage. At the end of Mass the pope thanked the people for their gifts and said he had a gift for the parish — "the chalice, which comes from my former diocese, Cracow."

After the Mass, the pope visited with nuns and lay leaders in the parish. He stayed briefly at a nearby convent of cloistered Capuchin nuns. As he was leaving to return to the Vatican, a banner hanging between two windows of the neighboring nursery school caught his eye. It was a welcome to the pope. From the windows children were beckoning him to visit. The pope accepted and entered the school, where he discussed some of the problems of violence and poverty in the Garbatella area.

Even after Italians were used to the surprises of the new pope, he could still amaze them with unexpected events. When Vittoria Janni, 22-year-old daughter of a street cleaner, asked the pope if he would officiate at her wedding with Mario Maltese, 24-year-old installer of burglar alarms, John Paul quickly agreed.

He had the ornately frescoed Pauline Chapel in the Vatican's Apostolic Palace prepared, and on Feb. 25, 1979, to the accompaniment of the Sistine Choir, the marriage was performed. Popes in the past had officiated at weddings of royalty or particularly prominent people, and occasionally at group ceremonies for ordinary people. But rarely, if ever, had there been a wedding such as this.

Afterward, the pope visited briefly with the couple in his private study. He gave them a Bible and two rosaries.

"Can I give you a kiss?" the bride asked the pope.

"And why not?" he answered, giving the bride a kiss and the groom a strong embrace.

In March John Paul baptized a baby after a spur-of-the-moment request by the mother while the pope was visiting a hospital in Rome.

Italians even came up with some unexpected and strange outlets for their enthusiasm for the pope. One of these was a record called "The Wojtyla Disco Dance," with praiseworthy lyrics about "the new pope in the Vatican." The recording made a brief splash on Italy's recording charts.

Foreign visitors to Rome got a taste of the new papal style at the Wednesday general audiences. At the audiences he spent a lot of time kissing babies, shaking hands and hugging people. When the audiences were moved outdoors to St. Peter's Square in April to accommodate the huge crowds he was drawing, the pope began arriving in a white, roofless Toyota which moved at a stroller's pace through the pathways, allowing him to exchange greetings and touch outstretched hands.

At his first general audience, three days after his inaugural Mass, the pope said: "I have seen that one pope is not enough to embrace everyone. But finally there must be one. I don't know how to multiply this one."

Then quickly he added: "Thanks be to God there were not only one, but 12 apostles. Thus with collegiality we can touch everyone."

The audiences provided the initial exposure of the new Polish pope and his style to the rest of the world. The general audiences are a papal tradition and held every Wednesday, except when the pope is indisposed or traveling.

John Paul's style was quickly apparent as he bantered with the crowd, sang with them and spoke with many in their native tongues, a tribute to his linguistic ability. The papal talk is given in Italian. At the end, John Paul added summaries in various languages including English, French, German, Spanish and Portuguese.

Rather than enter the audience hall in the style of his predecessors, seated on a portable throne carried on the shoulders of aides, John Paul walked down the wide aisle. When the first John Paul had tried to initiate that practice, people had complained because those away from the aisle could not see him. The second John Paul found a solution; he had platforms set up at several points in the aisle, and he would mount these as he proceeded toward the front, standing there waving and smiling for all to see. Without the slightest thought of irreverence, some visiting churchmen commented that the pope resembled a pop star greeting his admiring fans.

The number of people attending the audiences steadily grew. Soon the pope was apologizing because the hall was too small. In order to see more people he divided the Wednesday audiences into sessions for children and adults, holding the children's gathering in St. Peter's Basilica and the audience for adults in the modern audience hall.

The audiences for children turned into wildly enthusiastic gatherings. In their anxiety to see the pope, some youngsters at the first audiences climbed atop confessionals to get an unobstructed view. At times it seemed the pope would never complete the walk down the basilica's aisle, so often did he stop to grasp the outstretched hands, to caress a cheek here, accept a kiss there, linger an extra moment to listen to a few breathless, excited words from a youngster with shining eyes experiencing a great moment in his life.

Newspapers reported in detail an exchange the pope had one day in November with Mario Arcidiacono of Pescara, Italy, one of 13,000 Italian youngsters in St. Peter's Basilica for the audience.

"My father died a few days ago," Mario told the pope. "But if it is true that you too are my father, I will feel less alone. Is it true that you too are my father?"

With his hand, the pope wiped away tears on the boy's cheeks, caressed him and kissed him. "Yes, Mario," he said. "I am your father, too."

At a February general audience for school children the pope had his aides open up the barricades to let a group of children join him on one of his movable platforms in the aisle. After chatting with them and posing for pictures, the pope motioned for them to get down from the platform. Apparently anxious to get on with greeting people, the pope did not wait for the crowded platform steps to clear. He casually dropped to one hand and jumped the two-and-a-half feet back to the floor.

The pope smiled broadly as his minor display of athletic ability brought   **21** laughter, applause and a few cheers of "Bravo!"

John Paul seemed to become particularly relaxed and informal when there were Polish pilgrims at an audience, which was often. During the Christmas season it became a routine occurrence for him to join with visiting Poles in singing Christmas carols in Polish. His firm, strong voice carried clearly through the audience hall on the loudspeaker system.

He joked publicly, often making himself the object of the joke. One day, after delivering his talk in Italian and summaries of it in several other languages, he commented in a self-deprecating tone: "You can see that the pope gives the appearance of knowing many languages."

Asking the crowd's indulgence, he said he wanted to add another language, his native Polish. The crowd cheered him as he apparently finished his brief talk in Polish. But he interrupted the cheers, saying, "Wait, I'm not done yet." He finished his remarks and then led the Polish pilgrims in singing Christmas carols.

The pope's growing popularity meant increasing crowds. At his audience on Nov. 22, a little over a month after his election, John Paul apologized because the Vatican's audience hall was not big enough to accommodate the 15,000 who came, causing many to remain outside. Many in the crowd stood on their chairs as he entered and those near the aisle climbed over each other to see him. As he walked down the aisle shaking hands, touching heads, smiling, waving, chatting, he looked like a politician on the campaign trail. He took about 20 minutes to travel the 100 yards or so between the back of the hall and the stage.

Finally, in March 1979 the pope began holding three general audiences on Wednesday and had to apologize to the last crowd for his tardiness, but added a humorous twist that this meant progress in shaking more hands extended to him.

"The pope is making continual progress because he comes a bit later each Wednesday for the audience," he said. Coming late was not his fault, he said. It was a reflection of the increased number of people who come to see him each week and his practice of exchanging greetings and handshakes with as many as possible as he works the aisles to the speaker's platform.

By the end of March total attendance at the three Wednesday audiences had passed 35,000.

Finally, in April, the pope moved the audiences outdoors to St. Peter's Square in an effort to accommodate everyone at one audience. Built and designed between 1656 and 1667 by the famous Italian sculptor Gian Lorenzo Bernini, the vast elliptical square measures 370 yards by 260 yards and can hold up to 300,000 persons. In contrast, the papal audience hall, named the Paul VI Hall after the pope who ordered it built, has a capacity of 12,000.

The need for the larger space was quickly evident. On April 25, more than 150,000 people packed St. Peter's Square for the papal audience. St. Peter's Square also provided a bigger stage for the crowd-pleasing pope.

Wearing a red cape over his white soutane, the pope entered the square in a white, roofless Toyota land cruiser. Passing through the Arch of the Bells next to St. Peter's Basilica, the jeep-like vehicle moved slowly along passages between barricades. Standing in the rear of the vehicle, the pope smiled, exchanged greetings with people in the crowd, touching their extended hands.

The Toyota went to the other end of the square, crossed over and came up the other side. The pope got out and walked along the barricades forming an aisle up to the gray-draped platform from which he spoke.

Two-and-a-half hours later, a half-hour after the audience was over, the dozens of tour buses which had brought many people to the square were causing a huge traffic jam.

Even the pope's two-month summer vacation at Castelgandolfo, about 15 miles south of Rome, was filled with innovations and whirlwind activities. One of his favorite events was gatherings with large groups of young people.

On Aug. 17 the pope held a late evening candlelight visit and songfest with youths from four apostolic groups. Under Pope Paul VI or any of his recent predecessors, such an event would have been startling. But it was only one in the series of encounters with youth that John Paul hosted during his summer vacation.

As the vacation season progressed, the meetings grew more frequent and songs and cheers wafted over the high villa walls into the village of Castelgandolfo almost every other night.

As a priest, bishop and cardinal in Poland, the pope went on frequent hikes, picnics, and camping, canoeing and skiing trips with young workers and university students. Sometimes these were the settings for spiritual retreats, sometimes for intellectual and religious discussions — and often they ended with songfests in a mountain cottage or around a blazing campfire under the open skies. As pope, he carried some of these customs to Castelgandolfo.

The gathering of Aug. 17 was typical. The pope met with youth groups from Poland and Italy. The four-hour encounter began at 6 p.m. with a concelebrated folk Mass in which the Polish and Italian youths alternated songs. Later there were talks and songs and the pope met with many of the youths individually. As darkness fell, the pope lit a large candle and passed the flame to the scores of smaller candles held by the youths.

Two nights later, the pope was entertained in the villa's Swiss Hall by the visiting Polish folk group Skalni, dressed in colorful folk costumes. The internationally known student group based in Cracow, Poland, met with the pope in the afternoon shortly after the Sunday Angelus and returned again at 8 p.m. to perform folk songs and dances for him. They closed the evening by singing a final folk song together.

A photograph in an Italian newspaper at the time showed the pope in the midst of a singing circle of Polish youths with their hands crossed in front of them and linked to the person on either side. The white-cassocked pope held hands with an archbishop on his left and a teen-age girl on his right.

Even L'Osservatore Romano, the staid Vatican daily newspaper known for its Page One formal photographs of the pope with an important visitor or presiding over a liturgical ceremony, began showing pictures of the pope lighting a bonfire amid seated youths and the pope talking to a sea of young faces shining in the candlelight.

Singing is an important part of the pope's pastoral style.

"Song is a way of being together, of communicating, of getting along across language barriers," the pope said at another informal Castelgandolfo gathering, this one with English and Italian youths.

Several days later, John Paul told French youths that joyful song is a necessary activity of Christians because the Gospel is not a gloomy pronouncement but "the happy Good News."

Songfests with youth groups around bonfires were not the only innovation John Paul brought to papal summer vacations. Traditionally, the papal vacation is a chance for popes to escape the stifling midsummer heat in Rome and they have used it as a quiet "working vacation" with few meetings and private audiences. Past popes held their customary Wednesday general audiences and led the Sunday Angelus, but rarely saw other visitors. Walking in the villa's gardens was the most strenuous exercise of the sedentary pontiffs of recent decades.

Pope John Paul held private audiences with special groups of pilgrims, had other groups join him for early morning Masses in the villa chapel and received visits from members of religious orders holding general chapter or other meetings in nearby Rome. He visited churches, convents and monasteries in the town of Castelgandolfo.

A heated swimming pool was installed to help meet the exercise needs of the first athletically inclined pope in recent memory.

A story making the rounds in Rome relates that a particular Curia official, displeased with the prospects of having a pope do such an informal thing as go swimming, hoped to head off the planned pool's construction by pointing out the expense involved. When the official tried to make his point by inquiring of John Paul how much the pool would cost, the pope is reported to have responded briskly: "It won't cost as much as another conclave."

The Sunday Angelus talks from the balcony at Castelgandolfo changed. The relatively quiet, straightforward talks of Paul VI became half-hours of bantering exchanges in various languages under John Paul II.

Before and after the Angelus talk, John Paul would greet visitors in Polish, Italian, Spanish, English, French and German. He would wave as he spotted signs from various countries, joke as people shouted greetings and often sing along when a band or choral group in the courtyard serenaded him.

John Paul sang so much that a record album starring the pope himself as singer and lyricist came out in West Germany. The album featured the pope singing six folk and religious songs alone and with students during his Polish pilgrimage in June. It also contained "The Moment of the Entire Life," a choral setting of a text by the pope performed by the symphony orchestra of Cracow, Poland.

Bernd Goeke, production chief of Crystal Records, which issued the album, said the Polish bishops had authorized the recording.

From the early days of his papacy, it was clear that John Paul would occupy the center of the world's stage. That became the case sooner than anyone expected as he set out on an intense schedule of travel outside Italy, drawing extensive coverage by newspapers, television and radio. In the weeks and months ahead, millions would line highways as he traveled to and from airports in such diverse cities as Cracow, his former archdiocese in Poland, and Mexico City. Millions more would make pilgrimages to such starkly contrasting places as the Polish Shrine of Our Lady of Czestochowa and the infamous Nazi death camps of Auschwitz I and Auschwitz II to attend outdoor Masses celebrated by the pope.

He had already shown himself adept at dealing with the news media, shattering precedent within days of his election by meeting with newsmen and answering questions rather than simply delivering a speech to them. He would do the same kind of thing again during the trips ahead, and it would leave journalists asking each other, "What kind of pope is this?" It was a question without a simple answer.

Veterans of flights with Pope Paul VI on his various trips abroad recalled that he used to visit with the press corps briefly on those trips, but only to shake hands and exchange pleasantries, rarely answering questions. Pope John Paul would not only answer questions at length; he would speak a variety of languages into the microphones thrust toward him, varying his language from questioner to questioner.

The world seemed to have an insatiable curiosity about this new pope, and he, in turn, was insatiable in his desire to know the rest of the world.

By the end of November, little doubt existed as to what type of pope the man from Poland would be. The papacy would not change him. It would merely give him a larger, more visible stage on which to perform his ministry.

A story told among Vatican insiders succinctly described the reality. According to the story, as Curia aides one day busily briefed the pope before a particular ceremony, telling him where he should stand, what he should say, John Paul brought them all to a halt with a gesture and then in a calm, even voice declared: "I am the pope. I know how to behave."

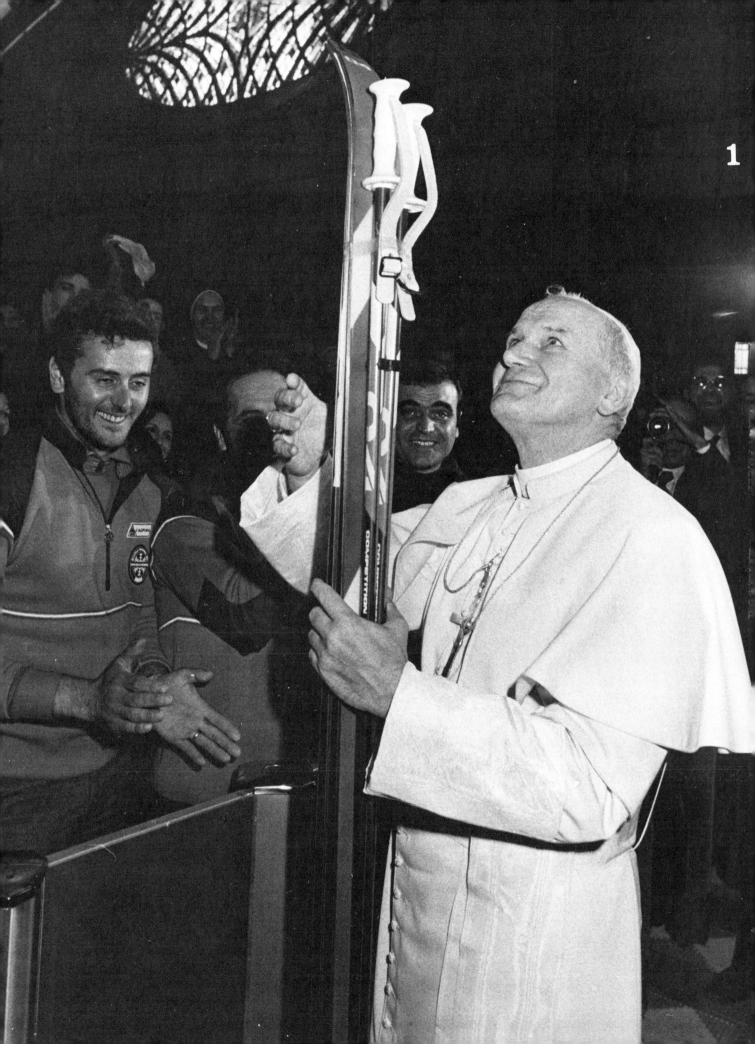

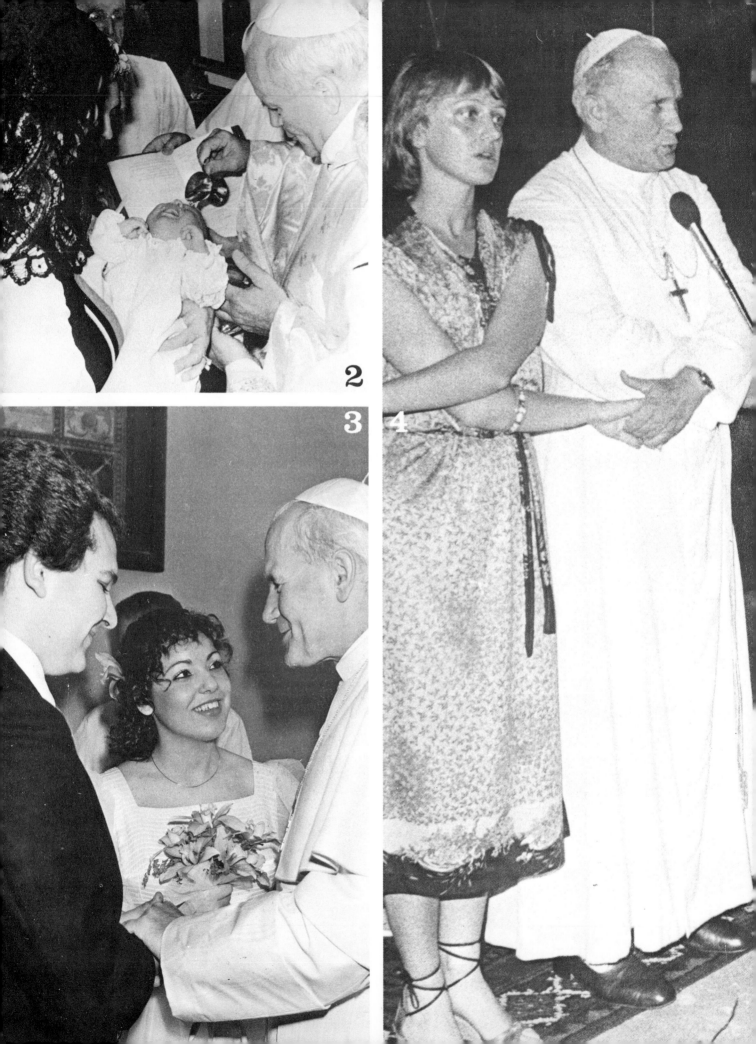

7

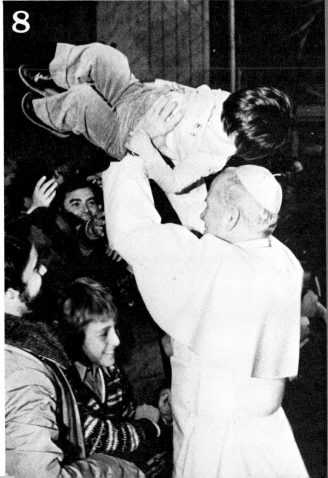

8

On the preceding pages:

1 *An avid skier for many years, the pope is presented with a gift by Italian mountaineers at an audience.*

2 *The pope baptizes seven-week old Alexis Biller at Castelgandolfo. He met the parents at an audience earlier in the year.*

3 *After officiating at their wedding at the Vatican, the pope chats with Mario and Virginia Maltese. They asked him to marry them and the pope accepted.*

4 *With a young folk group from Cracow known as Skalni, the pope joins hands and sings.*

5 *The pope received an unusual bit of praise in the form of a disco record recorded by a Milan disc jockey. It was a moderate hit in Rome.*

6 *Due to the crowds, the pope moved his weekly audience outdoors in the spring, arriving in a roofless Toyota which drove slowly through St. Peter's Square.*

7 *Pope John Paul II, being very fond of children, took the hand of a child at a November audience and strolled across St. Peter's Basilica.*

8 *In fun, Pope John Paul lifts a boy high above an audience.*

These Fundamental Values

A papacy, like a presidency, enjoys a honeymoon, a period of time when the new occupant of the office is able to bask in the glow of public admiration. The honeymoon usually lasts until the officeholder must take a stand that is less than universally popular. For John Paul II, that moment came in December.

On Dec. 17, tens of thousands of Roman school children jammed St. Peter's Square to sing Christmas carols to the pope and have him bless statuettes of Jesus they were using in their nativity scenes.

About 150,000 children and adults listened as the pope outlined the tradition of having a nativity scene. The children carefully clutched figurines of the baby Jesus, small ones and large ones, inexpensive plastic figures and exquisite hand-carved statuettes.

The tradition of setting up Christmas manger scenes was started by St. Francis of Assisi, patron saint of Italy, in 1223, said the pope, speaking from a window of his apartment high over the square.

The practice "spread through all of Italy, through Europe, through the whole world, keeping intact in diverse expressions of culture and folklore the fundamental, authentically evangelical message which Francis wanted to reach souls from the contemplation of the nativity scene — simplicity, poverty, humility," he said.

"Unfortunately, contemporary society is not always the bearer and messenger of such attitudes," the pope added. But he said the children in the square gave him great hope.

"It was for this that Jesus himself picked you as the models for those who wish to participate in his kingdom," he said. "Take home, with great care the little statue of the baby Jesus, also as a sign of the pope's love for you and your families."

The pope's remarks that day seemed to hold no particularly deep significance. But it was difficult not to recall them a few days later when John Paul found himself plunged into the midst of one of the most bitter political controversies of our times: the issue of abortion.

In Italy, as in many other countries including the United States, the church's moral position on abortion has definite political implications as governments and their constituents grapple with the issue of abortion legislation.

The new pope attacked abortion twice during the last four days of December, and Italian politicians and others promptly accused him of meddling in Italian political affairs.

In Italy, the specific political issue is the country's 1978 abortion law which allows government-funded abortion virtually on demand in the first three months of pregnancy.

The pope's first comments on abortion were directly oriented to the Italian situation. Speaking to the Association of Italian Catholic Doctors on Dec. 28, he praised the association for its defense of life and support of conscientious objection to abortion by medical personnel.

Under the law, medical personnel morally opposed to abortion cannot be required to participate in an abortion. More than half the doctors in the country signed declarations of conscientious objection, including 76 percent of the obstetricians and gynecologists from the region which includes Rome.

John Paul called the right to life "the primordial presupposition of every other human right."

"I want to express my sincere admiration for all those health care workers who, following the dictates of right conscience, are daily resisting flattery, pressures, threats and at times even physical violence for not soiling themselves with actions in every way offensive to that sacred value which is human life," the pope told the doctors.

Besides praising opponents of abortion, the pope emphasized the need for supporters of unborn life to provide the proper environment so that human life is a joyful experience at every stage of existence.

John Paul favored developing "adequate operative structures that favor the joyous welcoming of nascent life, its effective promotion during development and maturation, its attentive and delicate protection when it begins to decline and end in natural death."

The pope's second comment was made on New Year's Eve at Rome's Church of the Gesu, mother church of the world's Jesuits. These remarks were in the context of protecting the sacredness of life and the human person within the family.

"Even while maintaining respect toward all those who think differently, it is most difficult to recognize, from an objective and impartial point of view, that one conducts himself by the measure of true human dignity if he betrays matrimonial fidelity or if he allows life conceived in the mother's womb to be exterminated and destroyed," said the pope during a homily.

"As a consequence, it cannot be admitted that 'the principle of divorce' and 'the principle of abortion' serve the good of men and contribute to making human life truly most human, truly most worthy of man; that they serve the construction of a better society," he added.

"The consequence of this affirmation of the value of the person, which is expressed in the reciprocal relation between husband and wife, must be the respect of the personal value of new life, namely that of the child from the first moment of his conception," said the pope.

The church "cannot dispense itself from the obligation of protecting these fundamental values" and defending them means a fostering "of the authentic dignity of man; of the good of the person, of the family, of nations."

Papal attacks on abortion are nothing new. But abortion advocates said they had hoped that the non-Italian pope would refrain from involvement in domestic Italian political issues. The pope's remarks, coupled with earlier condemnations of the abortion law by the Italian bishops, were interpreted by abortion advocates as a sign that the Vatican was leading the campaign against the Italian law.

The church is engaged in "a new campaign to criminalize women," said the Union of Italian Women, a socialist-oriented feminist group. The attacks on the pope were joined by politicians supporting the law and were reflected in many of Italy's newspapers.

Il Tempo, a conservative independent daily in Rome, published an editorial cartoon which showed an angry couple reading a headline announcing the pope's opposition to abortion. In the caption the man was saying to the woman: "Just like the Italian popes."

The pope was also criticized, although not as strongly, by a traditional ally of the church, the Christian Democrat Party, which often receives at least tacit support from the Vatican and the Italian bishops during election campaigns. The Christian

Democrats base their political platform on Christian social teachings. The party is Italy's largest and most important political force, but it does not hold a governmental majority.

Christian Democrat leaders said they supported the right of the pope to discuss moral issues, but as one of many political parties in a pluralistic society they would abide by the expression of the majority as reflected in the laws passed by Parliament.

Flaminio Piccoli, president of the Christian Democrat Party Council, however, did not see the pope's remarks as a direct challenge to Italian politics. The pope spoke on an "exclusively religious" teaching and there are no grounds for a "war of religion" in what the pope said, added Piccoli.

Christian Democrats "insofar as we are Christians, are in complete agreement with this highest teaching," said Piccoli, but Christian Democrats "will also abide by the rules of a parliamentary democracy."

At his first general audience of 1979, John Paul defended the public stance he had taken. Responding to criticisms that he was meddling in Italian politics, the pope said abortion is a matter "of moral law, and therefore of conscience."

"It is necessary to do everything possible so that this human being, right from the beginning, from the moment of his conception, is wanted, awaited, lived as a particular value, unique and unrepeatable," he said. This belief is not unique to Christianity, but is "the logic as well of every authentic humanism."

The pope also addressed the issue of difficult pregnancies, a reason often cited by pro-abortion groups for liberal abortion laws, and linked it to the birth of Jesus.

"On Christmas night, the mother who had to give birth (a virgin birth) did not find a roof for herself. She did not find the conditions in which to accomplish in a normal way that great divine and, at the same time, human mystery of bringing a man into the world," he said.

"This fact of which I speak is a great outcry, it is a permanent challenge to each and to all, perhaps particularly in our age when a great test of moral coherence is frequently required of the expectant mother," he added. "That which has become defined euphemistically as 'an interruption of pregnancy' (abortion) cannot be valued with other authentically human categories that are not those of the moral law, and therefore of conscience."

The pope reiterated his belief that persons opposing abortion as immoral have an obligation to provide a positive environment conducive to welcoming new life into the world.

"As a result, the mother who must give birth cannot be left alone, one cannot leave her with doubts, difficulties, temptations. We must stand beside her so that she will have enough courage and trust, so that she will not overburden her conscience, so that the most fundamental bond of man's respect for man will not be destroyed."

In taking his public stance, John Paul was picking up a theme set by the Italian bishops in a statement issued on the same day he had greeted the children in St. Peter's Square and blessed their statuettes of the baby Jesus. In a 6,000-word pastoral document issued by the permanent council of the Italian Bishops Conference, the Italian churchmen had reaffirmed the church's penalty of excommunication for people having abortions or aiding in the performance of an abortion.

Excommunication for abortion is imposed because the church wishes to denounce "the gravity of the crime," said the statement, with the excommunication presupposing grave moral guilt on the part of the person obtaining or performing the abortion and awareness of the existence of the penalty.

The document was a frontal attack on the abortion law. It asked Christians not to be resigned to this "most sad reality."

The bishops said Parliament was mistaken in invoking the principle of civil tolerance in a pluralistic society when it passed the law. The application "is illegitimate and unacceptable because the state is not the source of the native and inalienable rights of the person, nor the creator and absolute arbiter of these rights, but must place itself at the service of the person and of the community through the recognition, protection and promotion of human rights," argued the bishops.

By authorizing abortions, "the state radically contradicts the very meaning of its presence and most gravely compromises the whole legal order," said the document.

The bishops also rejected the argument that abortion can be justified on grounds that the unborn child is not yet a human being.

"This concept is completely unacceptable, because only a concrete human being can originate from conception," said the statement. Modern science confirms this because the process from the fertilized cell to the birth of a child is "a unique and continuous individual development of maturation of the person."

The bishops asked Catholics to replace the abortion law with "norms totally respectful of human life."

Besides opposing the law, Catholics were asked to struggle against the causes favoring abortion, especially the sexual culture that says that procreation is not inextricably linked with sexual intercourse. The fundamental goal of the church's sex education programs should be the prevention of unwanted pregnancies by helping couples to be aware of and to choose morally permissible methods of birth regulation, said the bishops.

The document called for the establishment of family counseling centers and for the strengthening of those in existence. Such centers should teach natural family planning methods and be prepared to deal with the psychological problems of those seeking abortions, it said.

The bishops called these "centers for welcoming life" to help women with difficult pregnancies by providing moral, medical, psychological, legal, social and financial assistance.

The concerns of the Italian hierarchy were reiterated on New Year's Day by Cardinal Giovanni Benelli of Florence. If the legal abortion rate since passage of the new law continues at its present pace, "in less than five years we will have killed legally in Italy as many lives as were exterminated in World War I," he said.

Cardinal Benelli cited published figures saying 57,000 legal abortions were performed in the first six-and-a-half months of the new law thus instituting "the right to kill in Italy and placing on the state the obligation to kill."

Pro-abortion groups considered the statements of the hierarchy so strong that several legal actions were taken against Cardinal Benelli and the bishops conference for contempt of Parliament. None of the legal actions, however, resulted in a court case.

One pro-abortion group demonstrating outside the house of Cardinal Benelli handed out a release saying the bishops' statement on excommunication "is obviously an intimidating maneuver on the consciences of women to make them feel guilty about abortion and is intended to give further justification to conscientious objectors among medical personnel."

If the bishops want to excommunicate people participating in abortions because they are exterminating human life, they should also excommunicate arms traffickers and legislators who vote for military expenditures, said Marco Pannella, leader of Italy's Radical Party and initiator of efforts to get rid of Italy's previous strict abortion law.

The criticisms did not keep the pope from returning to the abortion issue. On Jan. 13 he supported the decision by the United Nations to call 1979 the International Year of the Child.

"The Holy See thinks that one can speak of the rights of the child from the moment of conception, and particularly of the right to life, for experience shows

33

more and more that the child would need special protection, in fact and in law, from before birth," said the pope in an address to the Committee of European Journalists for the Rights of the Child and the Italian Commission for the International Year of the Child.

A month later, the pope told the European Convention of the Pro-Life Movement not to be discouraged by the opposition they face.

"Do not let the difficulties, oppositions, failures that you may meet on your way discourage you. Man is in question, and when there is so much at stake, no one can enclose himself in an attitude of resigned passivity without, thereby, repudiating himself," said the pope.

John Paul placed Catholic opposition to abortion within the context of the church's support of human life and dignity at every stage of development. He referred to the Second Vatican Council's condemnation of abortion, homicide, torture, slavery, prostitution and exploitative working conditions.

"Your task is situated in this context. It consists in the first place of an intelligent and diligent activity to sensitize consciences concerning the inviolability of human life in all its stages, in such a way that the right to it may be effectively recognized in custom and in laws as the fundamental value of every society that wants to be called civil," he said.

The pope's statements brought no immediate change in the Italian abortion law. But they gave great encouragement to opponents of abortion in other countries, especially in the developed world, where abortion legislation has become increasingly liberalized.

One of the major struggles is in the United States where many religious leaders, including the Catholic bishops, have strongly supported attempts by pro-life groups to change legislation. The groups' primary concern is enactment of a constitutional amendment to prohibit abortion. Intermediate efforts are aimed at changing current legislation providing federal and state financed abortions Tactics include demonstrations, conventions, educational programs and campaigning for pro-life candidates.

These efforts are countered by abortion supporters who include some legislators and members of feminist and civil rights groups as well as other religious spokesmen. Whereas abortion opponents call themselves "pro-life" to emphasize their concern with protecting human life from the moment of conception, abortion supporters refer to themselves as "pro-choice" to underscore that they see the issue as one providing women with the freedom to choose whether to bear children.

The split between and among religious groups on the issue of abortion has grown so wide that in early 1979 the Faith and Order Commission of the National Council of Churches of Christ in the United States published guidelines calling for responsible ecumenical debate on controverted social issues. The commission said that division over such issues as abortion has polarized families, friends, congregations, communities and even the commission itself to the degree that it "has already undone some of the ecumenical advances of recent decades and is disrupting life within denominations and congregations." It said Christians have a responsibility to try to resolve these conflicts but to do so will require an understanding of the different ways Christians approach the scriptures, tradition, philosophy, science and human experience.

As the controversy in Italy over the public stand by Pope John Paul and the Italian bishops reached its height, polarization around the abortion issue in the United States increased and there was a growing militancy by some, especially pro-lifers.

On Dec. 28, the Feast of the Holy Innocents, 13 pro-lifers were arrested and charged with unlawful entry after a sit-in at a Washington abortion clinic as such sit-ins became a regular pattern across the country.

On Feb. 15, militant pro-lifers stunned feminists at a press conference sponsored by the pro-choice National Organization for Women. The pro-lifers suddenly exhibited two dead female abortion victims, bringing gasps and angry cries from others present. The pro-lifers said the well-formed fetuses had been aborted three days earlier.

But sit-ins and dramatic exhibitions of fetuses are not the main approach of pro-lifers and many pro-lifers criticized these tactics as counterproductive. The main actions to influence legislation are massive non-violent demonstrations and campaigning for pro-life candidates.

As 1978 drew to a close, pro-lifers were satisfied that they had made gains during the 95th Congress and looked forward to increased political influence in 1979.

"We gained more than we lost," said Father Edward Bryce, director of the U.S. bishops' Committee for Pro-Life Activities. "The abortion issue was very much on the minds of politicians."

Pro-life groups did not get everything they wanted in the 95th Congress, he said, but "we have to be realistic in accepting that this is a long-distance run."

There was no significant action on proposals to amend the Constitution to restrict abortion, but Congress passed laws restricting abortion funding, providing coverage for pregnant women in companies with disability programs and providing funds to help pregnant teen-agers.

Pro-lifers also had been active in the November 1978 congressional elections and scored some gains, taking credit for helping defeat several pro-abortion legislators and aiding in the re-election of pro-life congressmen. Anti-abortion votes were generally conceded to be the main reason Roger Jepsen defeated incumbent Sen. Dick Clark of Iowa, a liberal Democrat. In New Hampshire, anti-abortion Republican Gordon Humphrey beat Democratic Sen. Thomas J. McIntyre for the seat McIntyre had held since 1962.

As 1979 approached, pro-lifers turned their attention to a massive demonstration planned in Washington for Jan. 22, the sixth anniversary of the Supreme Court decisions eliminating many state restrictions on abortion.

The Supreme Court ruled on Jan. 22, 1973 that states may not regulate abortions during the first trimester (three months) of pregnancy; no state law may regulate abortion during the second trimester unless it is connected to maternal health; and during the third trimester the states may forbid abortions except where the physical or psychological health of the mother is involved. Pro-lifers say the rulings have the practical effect of allowing abortion until almost the time of birth.

On the anniversary of that decision, a crowd variously estimated at from 60,000 to 100,000 demonstrated in Washington in a huge March for Life.

The crowds shouted "Life, life" and "No compromise" as they marched. One of the speakers at the Capitol, Rep. Robert Dornan (R-Calif.), said abortion was comparable to the Nazi extermination campaign. He said official figures show that abortions claim 1.3 million lives a year but that "the unofficial cost is closer to 3 million."

Rep. Ron Paul (R-Texas), an obstetrician-gynecologist, spoke out against doctors who make "hundreds of thousands of dollars" by performing abortions. He called such activity "criminal and immoral." He said he was once "soft on abortion" but changed when he saw an abortion performed.

"All you have to do is stand in an operating room and see a two-pound infant taken from the womb and left to die," Paul told the gathering.

Prior to the Washington march, demonstrations against the Supreme Court rulings were held in other cities, including Boston, Pittsburgh and San Diego, often accompanied by statements from Catholic bishops.

Bishop Kenneth Povish of Lansing, Mich., said more political liberals should be in the pro-life camp.

"It's the liberals who claim to give priority to people over property," he said. "It's the liberals who claim to favor rights over privileges. It's the liberals who claim to be for the underdog over the top dog. Liberals are anti-privilege, anti-war, antipollution, anti-capital punishment, and usually pro-abortion. It's the most glaring inconsistency in American political life.''

Pro-choice groups were also active that day. Gloria Steinem, editor of Ms magazine, told a news conference that ''abortion was always, for women, a kind of intimate Vietnam.'' She said the issue was ''the right of reproductive freedom — the right of each individual.'' Neither the government nor any church has the right to interfere with a woman's decision to have an abortion, she said.

The Religious Coalition for Abortion Rights held a news conference to present its views. Some Protestant and Jewish leaders pledged to ''escalate the visibility and activity of the pro-choice religious community in the abortion rights controversy.'' They also said they were aware of the ''growing tensions between religious groups who are on opposing sides of the abortion controversy,'' referring to the strong Catholic pro-life position.

The pro-life people continued their political activities and at a national convention of the right-to-life movement held June 21-24 in Fort Mitchell, Ky., leaders pledged to get a constitutional amendment before the American voters by late 1982. The amendment proposed by the convention would protect all persons, including the unborn, regardless of their age, health or dependency. But it would permit abortion to prevent the death of the mother.

Pro-lifers emerged from the convention convinced and confident that they have the savvy and maturity to ''go political'' by increasing their volunteer support, educating candidates on pro-life issues, searching out and endorsing pro-life candidates and developing trained and certified lobbyists.

Yet as the year progressed, pro-lifers knew they still had a lot of work to accomplish. A Roper Poll conducted in July showed that 48 percent of the general public opposed an amendment outlawing abortion in all but cases to save the mother's life. Such an amendment was supported by 46 percent. Taxpayers surveyed opposed the amendment 50 percent to 44 percent.

In June the U.S. Catholic bishops filed a lawsuit against the federal government. It challenged government authority to force private employers to pay for abortions. The action was prompted by abortion provisions of the 1978 Pregnancy Discrimination Act.

The act requires employers to pay for abortions in cases where the life of the mother is endangered. The suit charges that the provision is tantamount to abortion on demand because of the way doctors can abuse the life-of-the-mother category. The suit also notes that the law requires employers to provide paid time off for all employees seeking abortions whether the abortion is elective or medically necessary. This could put the U.S. bishops, as employers, in the position of financing abortions, said the suit.

Such a situation puts the church's hierarchy in a position of having ''to affirm abortion as an illness and a matter of such trivial character as to be considered a fringe benefit,'' the suit noted.

''Such compulsion is not only an outrageous affront to the conscience of (the hierarchy), but is also an action on the part of Congress forbidden by the First Amendment,'' the suit said.

The U.S. bishops favor adding a clause to the law so that employers would not be forced to pay for a practice against which they have strong moral convictions.

Several weeks after the suit was filed, a new abortion-related Supreme Court decision drew renewed hierarchical criticism. In the new decision, the Supreme Court ruled that parents do not have to be consulted before an abortion is performed on an unmarried minor.

''Parental rights and family relations have become victims of the Supreme Court's obsession with abortion,'' said Archbishop John R. Quinn of San Francisco, president of the National Conference of Catholic Bishops. The court's decision "goes a long way toward tearing apart the fabric of the family."

The decision struck down a Massachusetts law requiring an unmarried minor female to obtain the consent of her parents before undergoing an abortion. The law also provided that if a minor failed to obtain her parents' consent, she could obtain consent from a judge. The Supreme Court said "every minor must have the opportunity — if she so desires — to go directly to a court without first consulting or notifying her parents."

The abortion issue was also a hotly debated controversy at a worldwide level.

In January, Msgr. James T. McHugh, former director of the U.S. bishops' Secretariat for Pro-Life Activities, asked the United Nations to exclude promotion of abortion and sterilization from its population policies.

"Families should not be forced to conform to some demographic idea in reaching responsible decisions concerning parenthood, nor should they be abandoned by society or denied basic assistance for not doing so," said Msgr. McHugh in a speech before the U.N. Population Commission at U.N. headquarters in New York.

"Neither should nations be forced to conform to population targets in order to obtain development assistance from other nations or from international agencies. There is no need or justification for invoking 'lifeboat ethics' in trying to develop programs of international assistance or partnership," added Msgr. McHugh.

In Australia, Stephen Lusher, a member of Parliament, complained that one-fourth of the country's pregnancies end in induced abortion. He said 60,000 abortions were performed in Australia in 1978 at a cost to the government of $6.8 million. Lusher asked for a tightening of legislation providing government-funded abortions.

In England, about 20,000 people marched in silence for two-and-a-half hours through central London on April 28 to protest abortion. By coincidence, the march took place the day after an aborted baby girl died after struggling for life for 38 hours at a London hospital. The march was specifically protesting Britain's liberal abortion law which allows abortion up to the 28th week of pregnancy.

A rally preceded the march and messages of support were read from Catholic leaders, including Pope John Paul. The pope said he wholeheartedly blessed the efforts to defend human life.

The Cradle of Catholicism

A little more than 100 days after his election, John Paul set out on a trip to Latin America which he described as a "pilgrimage of faith." It was an apt term not only for that trip, but for the others he would make throughout his first year.

Speaking moments before his departure on Jan. 25 for the Dominican Republic and Mexico, the pope said he was making the trip "as a messenger of the Gospel for the millions of brothers and sisters who believe in Christ."

"I want to know them, to embrace them, to say to everyone, babies, the young, the old, men, women, workers, peasants, professionals, that God loves them, the church loves them, the pope loves them," he said. He was going also, he added, "to confirm (my) brother bishops."

The pope's first destination was Santo Domingo, where he would remain overnight before continuing on to Mexico City.

During the non-stop flight of about 10 hours, the pope surprised some 60 journalists on the papal plane by spending more than an hour with them in an informal press conference during which he answered questions in several languages.

A U.S. journalist asked him whether he would visit the United States. "I suppose it will be necessary," the pope answered. "I don't know. It is not set yet."

The pope expressed a certain distrust about any form of socialism and said peace was one of the main topics during his nearly two-hour meeting with Soviet Foreign Minister Andrei Gromyko the previous evening.

Asked if he was tired from his audiences of the previous day, the pope jokingly replied: "Not from the ones in the morning, but from the one in the evening, yes."

Asked whether socialism might be the solution for Latin America's problems, he said one must first do a "historical study of what socialism is." If by socialism is meant atheistic socialism or a kind that "is incompatible with a Christian view of the world and of man and thus of Christian morality, then I think this is not acceptable," he said.

It is different, he said, if by socialism is meant a system that accepts the dimension of religion and offers guarantees of religious freedom. He quickly added that talking about freedom is easy before such a system is established. "We must see what happens afterward in practice," he said.

Introducing himself to the pope, an Italian newsman said he represented TG 2, one of two channels operated by the Italian state television network. "I am a layman," the man said. Putting his hand on the newsman's shoulder, the pope joked: "I am a priest. What have we got to talk about?"

The TV newsman then asked the pope about religion in Mexico. Religion there, the pope said, has very deep roots. With a penetrating glance at the newsman, he added, "perhaps most of all, effective ones."

On descending from the plane at the airport near Santo Domingo, the pope knelt to kiss the soil of the country known as the cradle of Catholicism in the New World. It was to the Dominican Republic that the first Christian missionaries came and there that the first Mass was celebrated in the New World.

Dominican President Antonio Guzman and his wife, members of the cabinet, Cardinal Octavio Beras Rojas of Santo Domingo, the first diocese of the Americas, other Dominican bishops, and Archbishop Giovanni Gravelli, papal nuncio to the Dominican Republic, greeted the pope, as a full honor guard in white and blue uniforms stood at attention and a 21-gun salute boomed out.

From the airport, the pope rode in an open, canopied, white vehicle along the seaside highway, lined with palm trees, into Santo Domingo. Crowds were sparse through the countryside at the beginning of the 18-mile ride, but as he neared the city limits, they swelled to tens of thousands. By 2 p.m. a huge crowd had already gathered in Independence Plaza, although the pope was not scheduled to celebrate Mass there until three hours later.

Thousands cheered as the pope entered the 16th-century Santo Domingo cathedral nearly half an hour behind schedule to greet the country's bishops and people and to ask them to pray for him. The cathedral bells pealed and the choir sang the Alleluia Chorus from Handel's "Messiah" after the pope gave his blessing and closed with his familiar prayer, "Praised be Jesus Christ."

About 30 bishops from other countries in the Americas were also present, including U.S. Cardinals Terence Cooke of New York, Humberto Medeiros of Boston, William Baum of Washington, D.C., and John Cody of Chicago.

An evening outdoor Mass before an estimated 250,000 people in the city's huge Independence Plaza capped a triumphant day.

"Evangelization constitutes the way and the vocation of the church, her most profound identity," the pope said in his homily. "She exists to evangelize."

He was quoting Pope Paul VI and, in his first major address in Latin America, he was clearly setting forth the theme of his week-long pilgrimage.

Reciting a litany of evils which must be combatted, the pope spoke of hunger, malnutrition, illiteracy, poverty, mistreatment of workers, corruption, exploitation, broken families and the gap between rich and poor.

He stressed that efforts to solve such problems should be made within the context of man's relationship to God. "But don't be content with a more human world," he said. "Make a more explicitly divine world, more according to God, governed by faith. Don't lose sight of the vertical orientation of evangelization. It can liberate man, because it is the revelation of love."

At the beginning of Mass, Cardinal Beras Rojas carried the 16th-century painting of Our Lady of Altagracia, patroness of the Dominican Republic, in solemn procession to the high arch dominating the plaza. Over the papal chair, he enshrined it on an easel under a 12-foot-high flowered arch.

In the Offertory procession, a dozen people of different ages and walks of life brought the pope gifts. At the end of the procession was President Guzman, who gave the pope a painting of the Madonna and Child.

The pope still looked fresh when Mass ended shortly after 7 p.m., although he had left Rome 16 hours earlier and had had only a brief nap on the plane. After arriving at the apostolic nunciature, where he was to spend the night, the pope gave a brief address to members of the diplomatic corps in the Dominican Republic. He received a visit from President Guzman and immediately returned the call by visiting the head of state at the presidential residence.

The next day, Friday, Jan. 26, the pope celebrated a Mass at 7 a.m. for priests, Religious and seminarians. He asked those present to have a deep faith in Christ and to live the Gospel with integrity.

Afterward, he visited a low-income neighborhood and the parish of St. Vincent de Paul, where he met with students and some of the sick from the area.

For Dominicans, the overnight papal visit was practically a national holiday with schools, government offices and most private businesses closed. Under blue, lightly clouded skies with temperatures in the 80s, about 400,000 people cheered the pope as he traveled in police-escorted motorcades or stopped at various sites for visits and ceremonies. Dozens of young motorcyclists, some of them waving Vatican flags, followed the papal motorcade around the city. They were kept a quarter of a mile behind the motorcade by soldiers stationed along the papal route.

In the morning, the pope left the Dominican Republic on an Aeromexico DC-10. After a four-hour flight, the specially equipped jet touched down shortly before 1 p.m. local time at Mexico City's Benito Juarez airport.

The country to which the pope had come was one whose people have retained a strong faith despite the strongest anti-church legislation to exist in any Catholic country. Under Mexican law, priests cannot vote, cannot be elected to public office, cannot inherit or will possessions. They cannot wear distinctive clerical garb outside churches or religious houses. The church has no juridical recognition and cannot own any property. Even church buildings legally belong to the government.

The roots of such laws go back to Mexico's revolt against Spanish rule in the last century, when the church was considered to be an ally of foreign domination. Though those conditions have long ceased to exist, the strong political organization which grew out of that revolution and subsequent ones has continued to foster an atmosphere in which government officials feel they must avoid any semblance of religious affiliation or religious sympathy.

Thus, when the pope's visit to Mexico was announced, Mexican President Jose Lopez Portillo said the pope would be welcomed as a distinguished visitor, but quickly added: "That does not mean, however, that there could be relations with the Vatican." The country buzzed with speculation over whether Lopez Portillo would meet with John Paul.

As the pope's plane landed, uncounted throngs awaited the pope along Mexico City's streets and millions of others watched the arrival on a broadcast network that covered most of Latin America and much of Europe.

Waving to the crowd and smiling, the pope descended the stairs from the plane and knelt to kiss the ground. President Lopez Portillo was in the welcoming party. His greeting, however, was brief and strained, with the president, a Catholic, addressing the pope as "Sir."

Musicians struck up typical Mexican music and the crowd chanted *"Viva el Papa!"* as he walked through the welcoming throng, shaking hands and speaking to people in the crowd. At one point a welcomer placed a broad-brimmed sombrero on the pope's head. The pope smiled, took it off after a moment and later handed it to an aide. Officials pleaded with the crowd over a public address system to let the pope move on through the crowd, but the pleas went unheeded. The pope inched his way along, at times unable to move at all. It took him 45 minutes to pass through the crowd and into a vehicle waiting to take him to Mexico City's cathedral.

For the ride into the city, the pope stood in the front of a specially adapted minibus, with members of his entourage seated behind him.

Standing eight and 10 deep in the bright, warm sun, throngs lined the route of the motorcade. They waved handkerchiefs, banners bearing the colors of Mexico and of the Vatican, or simply their upraised hands. Many chanted rhythmically, *"El Papa, El Papa."* Confetti rained from tall buildings.

The bells of the cathedral had joined those of all the city's other churches in ringing a welcome at the moment of the pope's arrival at the airport. As the papal motorcade drew near the city, the cathedral bells began to ring again. Soon the bells of other churches joined in and their peals filled the city.

The motorcade, reaching the city in an hour, drove around the Zocalo, the city's central square, and in front of the National Palace, which houses the presidential office. Waving, smiling at the cheering thousands, looking up at the bell tower of the century-old cathedral, Pope John Paul walked from his vehicle to the

40

cathedral door between two chain-link fences put up to keep the crowd from him. At the door, he stopped, knelt and kissed the stone floor. Inside, in full view of television cameras, he vested for Mass.

Complying with constitutional restrictions on public worship, Mexican television cameras scrupulously avoided focusing on the altar during the main part of that first papal Mass — and the many other Masses celebrated during the papal visit — although the sounds of the Mass were clearly audible to television viewers.

As the cathedral Mass began, Cardinal Jose Salazar Lopez of Guadalajara and Archbishop Ernesto Corripio Ahumada of Mexico City gave welcoming speeches.

Speakers carried the sound of the events inside the cathedral to the thousands gathered outside in the square, some of whom had arrived before dawn.

In his half hour homily, delivered in clear, firm Spanish with a slight Italian accent, the pope called for fidelity to the church. He recalled that his homeland is commonly described as "Poland, always faithful." When he said that the description could be applied to Mexico as well, his listeners broke into applause.

The pope held up the Blessed Virgin Mary as an example. Recalling that she sought to know the will of God, he urged the crowd to make an effort to know the mind of the church better, to study the documents of the Second Vatican Council.

"The pope expects from you," he said, "a loyal acceptance of the church. You cannot be faithful and remain attached to secondary aspects, valid in the past but already outdated. You will not be faithful either if you try to build the so-called church of the future, unrelated to the present. We must be faithful to the church born once and for all from the plan of God: at the cross, the empty tomb, Pentecost.

"The pope expects from you a coherence of your own lives and the life of the church...The church needs today a laity who will give witness to their faith and share her mission in the world, being the ferment of faith, justice and human dignity, in order to build a more human and fraternal world."

The pope used Spanish throughout the Mass, except for the final prayers and the blessing, which were in Latin.

After Mass, he walked slowly from the cathedral, shaking outstretched hands as he moved down the aisle. Outside, he spoke briefly to the crowd after Archbishop Corripio managed to quiet their cheers. "I am very happy with your enthusiasm," the pope told them.

Leaving the cathedral area, the motorcade again moved slowly through the streets with the pope standing in his special open vehicle and waving to the crowds.

Within six hours of his arrival in Mexico, the pope and President Lopez Portillo met privately for an hour and 10 minutes at Los Pinos, the presidential residence, a mansion set amid gardens and trees in Chapultepec Forest not far from the city center. The length of the visit led to speculation that the pope and president discussed matters of substance, possibly the question of diplomatic relations. A government spokesman said only that the talks "logically must have touched on themes of common interest, such as world peace, disarmament and justice."

Mexicans were intrigued by press reports that one of the things John Paul had been shown while at the presidential residence was a private chapel, set up after Lopez Portillo and his family took possession of the residence. There was even speculation that the pope had celebrated Mass there for the first family — a normal enough event in other countries, perhaps, but a subject for gossip in hushed tones in Mexico. Whatever the truth, Lopez Portillo felt it was necessary several days later in a rare public comment on religion to state that he had been raised Catholic but that he now considered himself a humanist, not aligned with any religious organization.

On Jan. 27 the pope met with several groups at the Basilica of Our Lady of Guadalupe, a shrine built on the site revered as the scene of apparitions of Mary to an Indian peasant, Juan Diego, in 1531. Juan Diego's *tilma* — a type of cloak — bearing a miraculously imprinted image of Mary hangs over the basilica's central altar. Millions of pilgrims visit the shrine each year.

Speaking to Mexican priests and men Religious, John Paul said priests should stay out of factional politics. "You are priests and members of religious orders," he said. "You are not social directors, political leaders or functionaries of a temporal power."

He reminded the priests that their vocation is based on deep-rooted convictions concerning Christian salvation. "Confronted by these truths of the faith," he said, "why do you doubt your own identity? Why do you vacillate in regard to the value of your calling? Why do you hesitate before the road you have taken?"

He told the priests and men Religious that prayer is essential to their ministry. "Today, as yesterday, this is of absolute necessity. And also be faithful to the frequent practice of the sacrament of reconciliation, daily meditation, devotion to the Blessed Virgin by means of the rosary. In a word, cultivate union with God by means of a profound interior life. Let this be your first task.

"Do not be afraid," the pope added, "that the time consecrated to Our Lord will take something from your apostolic work. On the contrary, it will be a source of fruitfulness in your ministry."

He urged the priests to be united with their bishop and obedient to him, and he reminded the members of religious orders, who are not under the local bishop's jurisdiction in the same way as diocesan priests are, that the center of unity in the local church is the bishop, with whom they should collaborate.

The pope said priests have an "irreplaceable" role to fulfill among students, the sick and needy, intellectuals, the poor, and those seeking comfort and support from them.

At a meeting with nuns in the basilica the pope praised the commitment and religious renewal of most sisters, but warned that some are confused about the nature of their vocation.

"Sometimes," he said, "prayer is left aside and action substituted for it; vows are interpreted according to a secularizing mentality that dims the religious motivations of the chosen state; community life is abandoned; socio-political stands are considered as the real goal, even with clearly defined ideological radicalizations."

Telling the sisters that with their consecrated life they have a "charism of prophecy," a spiritual gift to witness the presence of God to the world, the pope warned against losing sight of the kingdom of God in the mire of "socio-political motivations which...in the long run will be proved inopportune and self-defeating."

The next day, Jan. 28, the pope made the 70-mile drive from Mexico City to Puebla along a highway lined with enthusiastic crowds. Millions waved and cheered as the pope passed. Many had waited for as much as eight hours to catch a glimpse of him. The pope ordered his automobile to stop frequently so he could speak with people and bless religious objects they held out to him. As he neared Puebla, he moved into an open vehicle for the last 28 miles. He visited two small towns and in one of them greeted some 15,000 factory workers.

In Puebla it appeared that the entire population of 500,000 had turned out to see the pope. They sang and cheered and waved posters and banners. Homes were bedecked with flowers, with Mexican and Vatican flags and with portraits of the pope.

In the courtyard of the Palafox Seminary, a modern complex located outside the city, the pope celebrated Mass to open the Third General Assembly of Latin American bishops. In his homily, urging the bishops to promote family life, he called for efforts to make every family an *ecclesia domestica,* a church in miniature, "so that many families can be prepared for the mission of evangelizing other families, of stressing the values of family life, of helping incomplete families."

The pope lamented some of the "serious problems facing family life in Latin America," including laws permitting divorce. Consequent instability in home life affects "an alarming number of children," he said.

"There are depressing conditions of poverty and even misery, as seen in the levels of ill health, ignorance and illiteracy, as seen in inhuman housing, malnutrition and many other sad realities," he said.

The pope said he felt very close to all the families of Latin America, as if he could enter each of their homes. "Homes where there is bread and well-being, but where, perhaps, joy and peace are lacking. Homes where the family lives with modest means, uncertain of the future, yet whose members help each other to live their lives with dignity. Poor homes on the outskirts of your cities, where there is hidden much suffering, yet where the simple happiness of the poor prevails."

He appealed to families enjoying a comfortable life not to become enclosed within their own happiness. "Open up to give others what they need and you have in abundance," he said. He cautioned the poor "not to pursue luxury as an ideal."

Inviting government leaders to develop "an intelligent family policy," he warned that such a policy should not include an indiscriminate effort to reduce the birth rate "at any price."

Later that day, at the opening of deliberations of the Latin American bishops' assembly, John Paul delivered the first major address of his papacy on church and society. He lashed out against injustice, materialism and violence, and said the church's mission of preaching the Gospel demands that it do all in its power to end injustice and "make systems and structures more human."

At the same time, he sharply warned against ignoring God in the struggle for human rights and against tying the gospel message to specific political or economic systems or theories.

The pope began the following day, Jan. 29, by visiting children in a charity hospital in Mexico City. Accompanied by Mario Moreno, better known as "Cantinflas," Mexico's most popular comic and movie actor, the pope went from bed to bed, taking children's hands in his, talking with them and blessing them.

"Illness does not allow you to play with your friends," the pope told the children. "For this reason, another friend, the pope, who so many times thinks of you and prays for you, wanted to come to see you...The pope will continue to remember you. He takes with him your smiling greeting and open arms and leaves with you a hug and his blessing."

John Paul then flew to Oaxaca, about 350 miles south, where he boarded a helicopter to meet thousands of Indians in the mountain town of Cuilapan. Many of the Indians had slept overnight at the site to be sure of seeing the pope.

The area is a notably Indian part of Mexico. More than a fifth of Mexico's population is Indian and most of it is concentrated in the southeast. As a symbol of the more than 50 dialects spoken in the country, a Zapotec Indian greeted the pope in the Zapotec language.

Indians wearing huge feathered headdresses and brightly colored traditional garb danced for the pope and cheering, waving crowds were everywhere. Among the gifts presented to the pope was a wide red stole, a priestly vestment, almost the size of the traditional Mexican serape, with large white crosses on each end.

The Indians called him "little white father" and "pope of the feather headdress" after he donned part of the costume worn by the Zapotec dancers.

The pope told tens of thousands of listeners, most of them peasant farmers, all of them poor: "In light of a situation that continues to be alarming, the pope wants to be your voice, the voice of those who cannot talk or who are silenced, in order to be the conscience of consciences, the invitation to action, in order to make up for lost time, which frequently is a time of prolonged suffering and unsatisfied hopes."

John Paul told the cheering throng that he spoke not only of the rural situation in Mexico, but of that in much of the world. All peasants "have a right to be respected, a right not to be deprived of the little that they have, through maneuvers which sometimes are the same as actual thefts," he said.

The peasant "has a right to effective assistance — which is neither charity nor the crumbs of justice — so that he may have access to the development to which his human dignity and his status as a son of God give him a right,'' the pope said.

Without spelling out details, he said "urgent reforms" are needed to solve the world's rural problems, and that these actions must be "profoundly innovative."

"The church certainly defends the legitimate right to private property," he said. "But it teaches with no less clarity that, above all, private property always carries with it a social mortgage, that the lands may serve the end which God intended. And if the common good requires it, there should be no doubts even about expropriation, carried out in the proper manner."

From Cuilapan, the pope went on to Oaxaca, where hundreds of thousands tossed confetti and cheered thunderously as he rode through the streets in an open vehicle. Exposed to the region's semitropical sun, the pope showed signs of sunburn on his face and neck, but seemed to draw energy from his contact with the people.

Traveling through the Oaxaca region, he saw poverty firsthand in the shantytowns of adobe and makeshift wooden homes.

During a concelebrated Mass before a crowd of 100,000 in front of the Oaxaca cathedral, the pope instituted 25 Indians as lay ministers — 21 lectors and four acolytes. Asking the laity to become "the helpers of God," he pointed to the newly instituted men in their working clothes and said: "Precisely because these lay persons have committed themselves, of their own will, to the salvific design of God to the point that this is the reason for their existence on this earth, they must be considered as the archetype of the participation of all the faithful in the salvific mission of the church."

Catholics, through baptism and confirmation, become witnesses of Christ, the pope said, and are "called to undertake evangelization as a fundamental duty" even if they do not "participate in specific pastoral duties."

The pope returned to Mexico City in the evening. The next day, Jan. 30, began with a visit to a Catholic school, where about 60,000 children from 120 elementary schools packed the courtyard. Smiling and waving his hands, the pope listened to thousands of tiny voices combining into thunderous shouts of "Papa, Papa." Finally silencing the children by standing with his finger to his lips in a hush sign, the pope told them:

"This is a school, and we are all supposed to learn in school. Today the pope has learned something new. The pope has learned, 'Papa, Papa, rah, rah, rah.'" That set off another round of cheers.

In a speech delivered from the balcony of the school, the pope said illiteracy was a major problem and called "in the name of Christ" for action to extend education to all.

During the formal ceremony, the pope listened to a welcoming speech by one of the students and, when she had finished, kissed her. He leaned forward so that another student could place around his neck a chain with a medal of Our Lady of Guadalupe. Then he kissed her too.

Officials had trouble keeping the carefully arranged program moving according to plans, as the children kept breaking into cheers and the pope kept encouraging them. When his aides finally pulled the reluctant pope away for his next appointment, he was running far behind schedule.

He arrived at the airport of Guadalajara, Mexico's second-largest city, after 11:30 a.m., an hour and a half late. He was greeted there by Cardinal Jose Salazar Lopez of Guadalajara, other bishops of the region and the governor of Jalisco state, of which Guadalajara is the capital.

The signs at the city limits proclaim a population of 2 million, and at least that many turned out to see John Paul on his one-day visit. Despite their long wait, the crowds at the places to be visited and along the motorcade routes stayed in place, singing songs and chanting cheers to pass the time.

With temperatures in the 90s under an almost cloudless sky, a number of people — mostly elderly women and teen-age girls — fainted from the heat. At one vantage point, seven women were carried to first-aid stations in just an hour.

At the airport, about 30 young men and women in bright Mexican costumes danced native dances as the pope walked quickly along the crowd, shaking hands, smiling and waving.

Flown by helicopter to Santa Cecilia, a poor neighborhood on the outskirts of the city, the pope told the people there: "The pope loves you because you are the chosen of the Lord." He exhorted "all those who have the means and are Christians to be renewed in mind and heart...so that no one lacks food, clothing, shelter, culture, work — all that dignifies a human being."

From Santa Cecilia, he flew to Jalisco Stadium nearby, where he told a crowd of 100,000 that it is not enough to criticize injustice, but that justice must be actively sought. "Injustices hurt me," he said, "conflicts hurt me, ideologies of hate and violence that cause so many wounds to humanity hurt me."

The pope's next stop was General Lazaro Cardenas Plaza, where he switched from the helicopter to a large open bus for a motorcade to the cathedral. Obviously trying to make up for lost time, the pope said only a few words of greeting to 50,000 or more people gathered around the plaza. Through the loudspeakers he quickly greeted the inmates of Jalisco State Prison, stumbling slightly over the Spanish word for "prisoner." He then began the motorcade to the cathedral.

Everywhere children climbed trees, people lined the rooftops and groups of four or five people bulged out of every window in sight. Thousands lined the streets. When he reached the cathedral, the huge, tightly packed crowd almost turned into a mob as thousands pushed to enter areas already solidly filled.

Inside the cathedral, the pope told a group of cloistered nuns that the contemplative life is not out of date or irrelevant, but a special call to spread the kingdom of God in "a specific way" which the church greatly esteems. He then appeared at two balconies facing different directions to bless the more than 100,000 people who overflowed the plazas around the cathedral and stretched two blocks or more down every street.

During an evening Mass at the 16th-century shrine of Our Lady of the Immaculate Conception at Zapopan, just outside Guadalajara, John Paul delivered a hymn of praise to Mary as "refuge of sinners."

"If consciousness of sin oppresses us," he said, "by instinct we look for the one who has the power to forgive sins, and we look for him through Mary, whose sanctuaries are sites of conversion, repentance and reconciliation with God.

"She helps us overcome the 'structures of sin' that surround our personal, family and social life. She helps us to obtain the grace of true liberation, that with which Christ has liberated every man."

After the Mass the pope ate dinner with the Franciscan Friars Minor at their nearby monastery. He returned to Guadalajara to meet seminarians at the archdiocesan seminary before a late-night flight back to Mexico City.

The next day, Jan. 31, like a guest who is enjoying himself too much to want to go home, John Paul put a prolonged end to his visit. Although he knew he was running well behind schedule throughout the morning of his last day in Mexico, the pope continued to linger any time there was a crowd, smiling and waving as they cheered.

He began the day by meeting with Catholic university students at the Basilica of Our Lady of Guadalupe. Tens of thousands of students packed the plaza in front of the basilica, waving handkerchiefs and shouting *"Viva el Papa"* in unison.

Standing on the basilica's central balcony, the pope delivered a prepared speech. He said it is "an unrenounceable vocation of the Catholic university to give testimony to being a community which is formal and truly devoted to the scientific search, but also visibly characterized by an authentic Christian life."

Then he turned as if to leave. But when the cheering continued, he returned to the microphone and began to speak spontaneously, his Spanish coming slowly but clearly. Once again he turned to leave, and once again he halted suddenly and retraced his steps to the microphone. There was nothing more to be said; he joined the students in song and, finally and reluctantly, left.

From there, the pope flew by helicopter to a meeting with some 1,100 representatives of the news media. Quoting from a document of the Second Vatican Council, he spoke of the need people today have to "learn about events in a complete, true and accurate manner...so they can become informed participants in the affairs of humankind as a whole." In such a task, he added, the church shares the concerns of the news media because "the church loves freedom, the freedom to know the truth, to communicate the truth, to preach the truth."

The pope then went to see a *charreada*, an exhibition of the skills of Mexican horsemen, which was his last scheduled event in Mexico City.

His flight to Monterrey, the final stop in Mexico, left a few minutes before 4 p.m., two hours behind schedule, after he insisted in riding to the airport in a slow-moving open vehicle instead of taking the helicopter which was awaiting him. As word spread that he was once again moving through the city's streets, thousands hurried to the route for a final farewell.

Once at the airport, the pope spent 20 minutes walking slowly along rows of well-wishers, touching hands, bending down to kiss children, smiling, waving. He picked up one small child and held the hand of another as she walked beside him. After blessing the crowd, he walked slowly up the stairs to the waiting plane as the traditional Mexican song of farewell, *"Las Golondrinas,"* (The Starlings) was played. Dozens of starlings were released and flew skyward as the pope entered the plane.

At Monterrey, a large industrial city in northern Mexico, about 1.5 million people gathered at the dry bed of the Santa Catarina River just outside the city. The bridge over the river served as a platform for the greetings and offerings by the local people and for the pope's speech. In the crowds were about 50,000 pilgrims from the southern United States, many of them migrant workers.

Wearing his red cape in the cooler northern climate, the pope arrived by helicopter from the Monterrey airport to be greeted by a choir of 10,000 children, the cheers of the huge crowd, and the pealing of the church bells of the entire city. "Blessed be he who comes in the name of the Lord," the people chanted as the pope made his way to the throne on the bridge.

In his speech, the pope called for solutions to the problems of migrant workers. "We cannot close our eyes," he said, "to the plight of millions of men who abandon their homelands, and often their families, in search of work and bread for themselves. They go through the hardships of a new environment, not always nice or hospitable; of a language strange to them; of general conditions which corner them in loneliness and discrimination."

Even though workers migrating to various countries are foreigners, they deserve a living wage, decent housing, social security and basic human rights, he said. He criticized employers who take advantage of migrants "to offer them lower wages, cut down benefits provided by social security and other social aid, and place them in housing unworthy of a human being."

During the ceremonies, industrialists and workers gave the pope gifts symbolizing the mining and steel industries of the Monterrey area and its fine crafts. The crowd roared in approval when the pope donned a steel worker's hard hat. Scheduled to spend 90 minutes in Monterrey, the pope stayed for more than three hours before setting out for Rome. As in Mexico City, the strains of the song *"Las Golondrinas"* followed the white trail of the jet into the sky.

On the way to Rome, the papal plane stopped for refueling at Nassau in the Bahamas. After the enthusiastic fervor of the Mexicans, the religious reserve of the Bahamians was anticlimactic.

The pope landed just after midnight. After a brief ceremony at the airport he was driven along an almost deserted highway to the Queen Elizabeth Sports Centre, which was only half-filled by 5,000 people for an interfaith service. The pope drew only slight, scattered handclaps from the crowd instead of the cheers and shouts that had greeted him everywhere in Mexico.

After a procession accompanied by Catholic and Anglican hymns, the Rev. Philip Rahming, president of the Bahamas Christian Council, welcomed the pope in the name of the Bahamian churches. There was a scripture lesson and an introduction by Catholic Bishop Leonard Hagarty of Nassau, and then the pope addressed the people. Speaking in English, he greeted non-Catholic Christians and said: "Be assured of our desire to collaborate loyally and perseveringly in order to attain by God's grace the unity willed by Christ the Lord."

Going on to Rome, the pope arrived at Fiumicino airport at 5 p.m. on Feb.1 after his 15,500-mile journey. He was tanned from the Mexican sun, and he was so tired that he had difficulty reading his response to the welcomes given him by Prime Minister Andreotti and Rome Mayor Giulio Carlo Argan.

Immediately upon returning to the Vatican at about 6 p.m., the pope met with the cardinals resident in Rome in the Consistory Hall. He told them the trip was an "unforgettable experience."

On the following pages:

1 *On arrival in Santo Domingo airport, Pope John Paul II knelt down and kissed the earth.*

2 *Welcome signs were everywhere when the pope arrived in Mexico.*

3 *Confetti greets Pope John Paul II as his motorcade moves through Oaxaca.*

4 *At the Indian village of Cuilapan, the pope tries on a giant Indian headress presented to him by villagers.*

5 *At a Oaxaca hospital, the pope stops to talk with a young patient.*

6 *The pope sits with Mexican hosts during a charreada—a display of horsemanship. Broad-brimmed hats are traditional headwear of charros—Mexican cowboys.*

7 *One Mexican man awaits the arrival of the pope in his own way.*

8 *Wearing a typical straw sombrero, the pope hugs an Indian child at the village of Cuilapan.*

9 *From the balcony of the Basilica of Our Lady of Guadalupe, Pope John Paul II greets the thousands who came to see him.*

1 2

3

4

5

6

7

8

9

Go Simply to the People

"**T**he church and politics is a big question," John Paul told a reporter as he was returning on the first day of February from his eight-day trip to Latin America. "I think it is necessary to go simply to the people as they are. It is always man who is most important."

The statement was hardly needed. The pope's deep belief that man lies at the center had become abundantly clear in a multitude of ways.

Nowhere could John Paul's personal perspective be more clearly seen, however, than in the key address of his Latin American pilgrimage — his talk opening the Third General Assembly of the Latin American bishops in Puebla, Mexico, on Jan. 28. Although evangelization was the general theme of the meeting, social issues were at the forefront of the bishops' minds. Not only Latin America, but the rest of the world waited for what the first pope from a communist-governed country would say.

What he did was to carefully sidestep rightist or leftist socio-political alignments and emphasize that any such liaisons are a watering down of "the originality of Christian liberation and the energies that it is capable of releasing." He stressed that political liberation stems from liberation from sin. Christians should become involved in political and social issues because they believe in Christ's love for all mankind and not because of partisan political ideologies, he declared.

Calling the church's defense of human rights and criticism of violence a Gospel-based "commitment to the most needy," he said: "In fidelity to this commitment, the church wishes to stay free with regard to the competing systems, in order to opt only for man."

In his 8,000-word address to the 300 Latin American cardinals, bishops, priests and Religious participating in the assembly, John Paul praised the work of the bishops' Second General Assembly in Medellin, Colombia in 1968. The Medellin assembly is generally considered to have been a major turning point for the church in Latin America because of its support for social action.

The pope said the Puebla meeting would have to take as its starting point "the conclusions of Medellin, with all the positive elements that they contained, but without ignoring the incorrect interpretations at times made and which call for calm discernment, opportune criticism and clear choices of position."

Taking the Puebla theme of evangelization as a point of departure, the pope then launched into an analysis of how the church, in fulfilling its mission of preaching the Gospel, must interact with society.

He repeatedly challenged various approaches to that mission which dilute the Gospel or ignore its dimensions of God and of love.

55

Without ever explicitly mentioning Marxism, the pope clearly rejected any theories of liberation based on violence or class struggle, and said they were opposed to the Gospel. He rejected any theological effort to portray Christ "as politically committed, as one who fought against Roman oppression and the authorities, and also as one involved in the class struggle."

"This idea of Christ as a political figure, a revolutionary, as the subversive man from Nazareth, does not tally with the church's catechesis," he said.

"By confusing the insidious pretexts of Jesus' accusers with the — very different — attitude of Jesus himself, some people adduce as the cause of his death the outcome of a political conflict, and nothing is said of the Lord's will to deliver himself and of his consciousness of his redemptive mission," the pope said.

"The Gospels clearly show that for Jesus, anything that would alter his mission as the servant of Yahweh was a temptation. He does not accept the position of those who mixed the things of God with merely political attitudes. He unequivocally rejects recourse to violence. He opens his message of conversion to everybody, without excluding the very publicans."

The pope referred to trends toward Marxist social analysis in some Latin American theology of recent years, in which Jesus is depicted chiefly as a revolutionary liberator of the oppressed.

"**A**gainst such 're-readings' (of the Gospel), therefore, and against the perhaps brilliant but fragile and inconsistent hypotheses flowing from them: Jesus Christ, the Word and Son of God, becomes man in order to come close to man and to offer him, through the power of his mystery, salvation, the great gift of God."

From this faith and from the church, "we are able to serve men and women, our peoples, and to penetrate their culture with the Gospel, to transform hearts, and to make systems and structures more human."

"Any form of silence, disregard, mutilation or inadequate emphasis of the whole of the mystery of Jesus Christ that diverges from the church's faith cannot be the valid content of evangelization," the pope said.

The pope stressed the idea of "a well-founded ecclesiology" — an understanding of what the church is — as the basis of vigorous evangelical activity. The "distinctive vocation and the deepest identity of the church" is its mission to evangelize, he said.

In this context he emphasized obedience to the church's teaching authority, or magisterium. "How could there be authentic evangelizing if there were no ready and sincere reverence for the sacred magisterium, in clear awareness that by submitting to it, the people of God are not accepting the word of men but the true word of God?" he said.

In the preparatory documents for the Puebla meeting, "a certain uneasiness is at times noticed with regard to the very interpretation of the nature and mission of the church," he added.

The pope rejected any interpretation of the church that would separate it from the kingdom of God or suggest that the kingdom of God can be reached "not by faith and membership in the church, but by the mere changing of structures and social and political involvement."

He also attacked "an attitude of mistrust" toward the "institutional" or "official" church, the notion that the institutional church alienates people and is opposed to the "church of the people." This attitude, he said, tears at the unity of the church and prevents it from evangelizing effectively.

The "first and foremost" truth that the church owes to man is "a truth about man," the pope said.

"Without doubt," he continued, "our age is the one in which man has been most written and spoken of, the age of the forms of humanism and the age of anthropocentrism. Nevertheless it is paradoxically also the age of man's deepest anxiety about his identity and his destiny, the age of man's abasement to previously unsuspected levels, the age of human values trampled on as never before."

This trend is the "inexorable paradox of atheistic humanism," he said, and the church's response is its central teaching "that man is God's image."

Human dignity "is infringed on the individual level when due regard is not had for such values as freedom, the right to profess one's religion, physical and mental integrity, the right to essential goods, to life. It is infringed on the social and political level when man cannot exercise his right of participation, or when he is subjected to unjust and unlawful coercion, or submitted to physical or mental torture."

He said he was keenly aware of the questions "posed in this sphere today in Latin America" and that the bishops at Puebla would be studying the relationship between evangelization and "human advancement and liberation."

The church, by her Christian vision of man, the pope said, finds inspiration "for acting in favor of brotherhood, justice and peace, against all forms of domination, slavery, discrimination, violence, attacks on religious liberty and aggression against man, and whatever attacks life." It is because of its evangelical commitment that the church defends human rights and has a commitment to the most needy, he declared.

Taking up the delicate question of property, he stressed the church's teaching that all private property involves a social obligation, which becomes more urgent as the gap between rich and poor grows. The church's role in this area is to preach, educate, form public opinion and offer orientations for the more equitable distribution of goods, he said.

Stressing the church's role in building an international awareness of economic justice as an indispensable condition for peace, John Paul reiterated the message of Paul VI that development is the new name for peace. But he declared that economic development must not be understood simply in the materialistic sense of having more, but in the deeper sense of being more. Economic mechanisms by themselves can do nothing to bridge the rich-poor gap until ethical principles, the demands of justice, and the primary commandment to love are brought into play, he said.

Liberation, the pope said, is fundamentally the religious liberation of freedom from sin.

The speech was a strong one — almost blunt. In retrospect, it is clear and unambiguous. But at the time of its delivery, it was widely misunderstood and, particularly in the United States, was met with cries of dismay. Prestigious journals of public opinion told Americans that the new pope had taken a backward step and had thrown cold water on social activism.

At least part of the reason for the confusion were the working conditions imposed on the hundreds of newspaper and broadcast reporters who converged on Mexico to cover the pope. As a prism through which John Paul would be reflected to readers and viewers throughout the world, the reporters' access to full and accurate information, one would have thought, should have been a primary concern. That was not the case. On the day of the pope's Puebla speech, press arrangements which had been minimal, at best, hit their low point. While reporters in Puebla clamored and pleaded in vain for advance copies of the speech so they could have time to study it before having to file stories, copies sat readily available — but useless — back in Mexico City. The result was hastily filed stories that either missed the point or — in some cases — sadly misinterpreted the pope's mind.

John Paul himself, intent on maintaining a whirlwind pace and covering an amazingly broad range of subject matter in his public discourses, did little to make the reporters' job easier. At times it appeared to them — and therefore to the world — that there were three popes visiting Latin America.

— There was the pilgrim pope praying at Marian shrines, greeting people from all walks of life, waving to huge crowds wherever he traveled.

— There was the stern pastor of bishops, priests and nuns warning them to stay out of partisan politics, sharply rejecting Marxist social analysis and emphasizing the primarily spiritual nature of the priesthood and Religious life.

— There was the pastor of the poor and disenfranchised endorsing labor unions, land expropriation and redistribution of wealth and supporting the rights of emigrants, the poor, the unemployed and cultural minorities.

The first and third pope and the first and second could easily coexist. But for many, there was a tension between the second and third.

Whenever he met specifically with groups of bishops, priests or nuns, the pope warned against reducing their vocation to a social ministry. He emphasized that first and foremost they are witnesses of the gospel message of divine love and salvation.

His words to priests in Mexico City seemed to echo: "You are not social directors or political leaders or functionaries of a temporal power. You are the spiritual guides who must endeavor to orient and better the hearts of the faithful so that converted, they live the love of God and neighbor and commit themselves to the welfare and dignity of men."

The pope coupled this with the traditional church position that partisan political activity is the role of the laity. Bishops and priests are responsible for forming a social conscience at all levels, but the concrete implementation of the church's social doctrine belongs to the laity, the pope told the bishops at Puebla.

The language used in these papal encounters with bishops, priests and Religious could certainly be interpreted by opponents of social activism in the church to support views that such activity is not in accord with church teachings, that priests and Religious so engaged are disobeying papal directives and mixing politics with religion.

But there was the other John Paul. This one told Indians and poor farm workers that land expropriation was justified "if the common good requires it." He urged farm workers to organize to improve their lives. He not only endorsed the labor movement, a frequent target of political repression in many Latin American countries, but also "its rightful role of responsibility for the construction of a new world order" — a controversial aspect of the international political and economic justice advocated by Pope Paul VI.

The pope who warned priests and nuns against political involvement was the same pope who, just before he began his Latin American trip, agreed to mediate the territorial dispute between Argentina and Chile which had both nations close to war.

If Christian advocates of armed struggle against the rich found encouragement in the pope's call for special concern for the poor and the advancement of all people, they found little comfort in his rejection of revolution or class struggle as a solution to human ills.

If Christian advocates of the status quo were encouraged by the rejection of revolution, they were not comforted by the pope's repeated criticisms of poverty and injustice and the widening gap between rich and poor.

At the heart of the papal trip to Latin America was John Paul's message that the Gospel is a challenge to all. It inspires social involvement but can never be a tool of partisan politics or ideologies.

Although John Paul spotlighted the issue of the church and political activity, the Latin American bishops have been grappling with it for years. In a region marked by stark contrasts in living conditions between the minority rich and the majority poor, the Catholic Church in many countries often finds itself as the only effective spokesman for the poor and disenfranchised. Other institutions and organizations capable of social criticism — such as labor unions, political parties and universities — can be, and often are, suppressed. Repressive governments can harass church people, but they cannot apply the full strength of their iron fist against the church itself because of its moral, social and cultural influence.

As the bishops met, Amnesty International, an independent body monitoring human rights, estimated that in Latin America at least 17,000 people were political prisoners, and that close to 30,000 persons had been reported missing after being arrested or abducted by government agents.

Thus, faced with the social tensions of their home countries and the lingering controversy over the papal position on political involvement, the Latin American bishops began their deliberations Jan. 28. When the scheduled final day of their meeting was reached Feb. 12, the bishops extended the assembly one more day because they still had not finished their work.

Finally, they emerged with a document running more than 250 pages. It included a clear commitment to social action, stinging criticism of the human rights situation, strong support for the theology of liberation and encouragement of the growing trend to form "basic Christian communities," which unite small groups of Christians for common liturgical and social action activities.

Following the lead of John Paul, the bishops tied their social, political and economic stands to the divine mission of Christ and said that social action is a part of the evangelization needed in Latin America to provide spiritual and material liberation from sin.

"We must proclaim the mystery of the Incarnation, both the divinity of Christ, and all the force and reality of this human dimension in history," said the document.

"We must not fragmentize, ideologize nor disfigure the person of Christ by reducing him to a politician, leader or revolutionary agent, or even mere prophet; nor can we reduce him to the private domain, because he is the Lord of history.

"We proclaim once more the doctrine of faith about Jesus Christ....The Father sent to the world his son Jesus Christ, son of the Virgin Mary. Through Christ, God unites himself to mankind...and man acquires indescribable dignity.

"Evangelization is the call to participation in the communion of the Trinity. Family life and other human bonds of solidarity, man's temporal actions and political activities must be elevated to the level of that communion in faith, hope and love."

Regarding human rights, the bishops said widespread violations are "abuses of power typical of regimes of force...even if those at the helm call themselves Christian." This is causing "anguish among the people because of systematic, selective repression...breach of privacy, coercion, torture and exile."

The document also criticized political violence by guerrillas. "There is also anguish because of guerrilla violence, terrorism and abductions by extremist groups of opposing ideologies."

The human rights section resulted from information gathered by the conferences of bishops in each country and documentation brought before the Puebla meeting by relatives of the victims and by human rights organizations. Groups presenting data included Amnesty International and human rights agencies of the United Nations and the Organization of American States.

The document blamed a distorted view of national security for many of the violations committed by governments. This view, it said, places innocent citizens in the midst of a total war against subversion and communism encompassing "the cultural, social, political and economic fields."

"Confronted with such real or imagined danger, a situation of emergency is declared to curtail individual freedoms. The will of the state engulfs the will of the nation. Defense needs and economic growth are considered more important than the needs of the underprivileged masses....In the name of national security, individual insecurity becomes permanent," said the document.

When the document was issued, close to 230 million people of Latin America's 330 million population lived under military rule.

"We must speak with clarity in the face of deplorable violence throughout Latin America. Physical and psychological torture, kidnappings, persecution of political dissidents or suspects, or public discrimination against citizens because of their ideas are always to be condemned. If such crimes are committed by authorities **59** otherwise in charge of the common good, they are shameful, regardless of the reasons alleged," said the document.

"With the same vigor the church rejects terrorist and guerrilla violence, which is cruel and gets out of hand once launched," it added. "There is no way to justify crime as a means for liberation. Violence produces new forms of oppression and servitude, usually more serious than those it claims to eliminate. But above all, violence is an attempt against life, over which only the Creator rules. We must say too that an ideology that has recourse to violence is showing its own weakness and limitation."

The document tied the theory of national security to economic motives. "The ideology of national security is bound to a given economic and political model run by an elite with vertical power, which suppresses the people's participation in political decisions. In some countries of Latin America it pretends to justify itself as the defender of Christian civilization. It then develops a repressive system according to its idea of permanent war against subversion."

The bishops criticized liberal capitalism as an economic system, saying it leads to an "idolatry of wealth" and gives priority to profits instead of people. "The cruel contrast between luxury and extreme poverty, so widespread in our continent, further aggravated by corruption in public and professional life, shows to what degree our peoples are under the domination of the idol Mammon."

The idolatry of wealth, the bishops said, "is manifested in two opposing forms that share a common root: liberal capitalism and Marxist collectivism." That common root, they said, is materialism.

The document was strongly critical of Marxism. "Because of its materialistic premises," the bishops said, "Marxist collectivism also leads to idolatry of wealth, even if in a collective form. Its driving force is class struggle, its goal a classless society through the dictatorship of the proletariat, which is really the dictatorship of the party, closed to criticism and correction."

Human rights include the rights to life from the moment of conception, health, education, housing, jobs and social and political participation through unions and other associations, said the document.

The bishops encouraged study of liberation theology and defined Catholic teaching about liberation.

"Total liberation...is of the essence for evangelization which aims at the true fulfillment of the human person....There are two inseparable elements in it: liberation from all forms of servitude, from personal and social sin, and from all which divides man and society. Liberation is also growth of the person through communion with God and with people.

"Liberation as implemented in history — our own personal history and the history of peoples — embraces the various dimensions of existence: social, political, economic, cultural, as well as their interaction.

"The foundation of liberation is to be found in the three pillars which Pope John Paul II pointed out to us as definitive: the truth about Christ, the truth about the church and the truth about man.

"The bishops of Latin America have very grave reason to urgently foster liberating evangelization as redress for social and individual sin, because since Medellin the condition of the majority has worsened considerably. We note with joy the many attempts to give witness to liberating evangelization. Evangelization has gained from constructive aspects of theological reflection on liberation since Medellin...(but) we need a creative search to remove ambiguities and limitations."

The Puebla document noted the role basic Christian communities have played in renewing the church at the grass roots. Called *comunidades de base* in Spanish, the communities have been growing throughout Latin America since the late 1960s, principally among the poor in both urban and rural settings.

The bishops pointed with joy to the stress placed in the communities on greater personal relationships, reflection on life and the Gospel, and commitment to family, work and neighborhood.

The bishops offered this definition of the basic Christian community: "The basic community as such consists of families, both adults and youths, bound by an intimate personal relationship in the faith. Inasmuch as it is 'ecclesial,' this community celebrates the word of God, the Eucharist and other sacraments, and implements that word of God through its solidarity and commitment with the Lord's commandment. The community becomes witness to the mission of the church and to visible union with legitimate pastors through the service of approved pastoral agents. It belongs to the base or grass roots, because the small number of members are a permanent cell of the community at large."

The bishops clearly stated that the communities are not a substitute for the traditional parish structure, but draw their inspiration and union with the hierarchy through the parish. Many opponents of basic Christian communities argue that approving them would be tantamount to creating a parallel structure to the parish.

"Christians in the basic ecclesial community seek a more evangelical life at the heart of the community by deepening their loyalty to Christ. They work to challenge the selfish roots of a consumer society, to implement the vocation of communion with God and with brothers and sisters, and to offer the foundations of a new society, a civilization of love," said the bishops.

"The basic Christian community is an expression of the preferential love of the church for the poor. Popular religiosity is expressed, valued and perfected in these communities, which also give the church concrete options in its task and commitment of transforming the world."

The bishops' formal support for basic Christian communities raised hopes that the movement will grow in size and influence in coming years, especially in Latin America.

Despite the gloomy social picture presented in the document, the bishops expressed optimism about overcoming these problems and stressed the need for hard work in pastoral activities.

Picking up a phrase used by John Paul, the bishops challenged Catholics and people of good will to create a "civilization of love" from the seemingly insurmountable problems of poverty, abuse of power and moral and physical violence in Latin America.

"God is present and alive in Jesus Christ, our liberator, in the heart of Latin America. We believe in the power of the Gospel, in the efficacy of the gospel values of communion and participation to generate creativity and to promote new pastoral programs," said the final document.

Besides the final document, the bishops issued a shorter statement titled "Message to the Peoples of Latin America." The message was a shorter version of and paralleled the final document. It also expressed optimism in the resources of the Latin American people to overcome their problems, and in one portion declared:

"It is high time we tell the developed nations that they must cease to block our progress, to exploit us. On the contrary, they should help us to overcome our underdevelopment, while respecting our culture, principles, sovereignty, identity and natural resources."

John Paul's first expression of approval of the results of the Puebla meeting came on Feb. 14, the day after the bishops' conference ended. Speaking at his regular Wednesday general audience, he said he hoped the assembly would lead to a greater sense of social responsibility in the church.

"May the church in the Latin American continent, strong in the tradition of the first evangelization, become strong again with the awareness of the whole people of God, with the strength of its own priestly and religious vocations, with a profound sense of responsibility for social order founded on justice, on peace, on respect for the rights of man, on the adequate distribution of goods, and on the progress of public instruction and culture," he said.

The pope said the splendid churches he saw in Mexico were evidence that past evangelization efforts in Latin America had taken root.

"But especially, I met living men who have accepted as their own the Gospel preached to them in the New World by missionaries from the Old World, and have made it the substance of their own lives. Certainly, that meeting of the new arrivals from Europe with the natives was not an easy one. One has the impression that the natives did not completely accept what is European; that, in a certain way, they tried to hide themselves in their own tradition and native culture.

"But at the same time, one has the impression that they accepted Jesus Christ and his Gospel; that in that community of faith a meeting of the 'old' with the 'new' took place, and that this is the basis not only of the life of the church but of Mexican society itself."

He continued: "The fact of finding oneself again in Christ, which is precisely the fruit of evangelization, becomes the man's substantial liberation. Service of the Gospel is service of freedom in the Spirit. The man who has found himself in Christ, has found again the way to the consequent liberation of his own humanity through the overcoming of all his limitations and weaknesses; through liberation from his own situation of sin and from the multiple structures of sin, which weigh upon the life of society and of individuals."

J ohn Paul was stronger in his praise at his next general audience, Feb. 21. He informally endorsed the conclusions of the Latin American bishops and gave his qualified support to the theology of liberation. It was the first time a pope had publicly praised the theology of liberation as positive for the church. The pope endorsed the double stress on evangelization and liberation made by the Latin American bishops.

In a strongly worded talk, the pope said liberation theology should not be exclusively connected with Latin America. "It must be admitted that one of the great contemporary theologians, Hans Urs von Balthasar, is right when he demands a theology of liberation on a universal scale."

Liberation "is certainly a reality of faith, one of the fundamental themes of the Bible, which are a deep part of Christ's saving mission, of the work of redemption, of his teaching. This theme has never ceased to constitute the content of the spiritual life of Christians," said the pope. "The conference of Latin American bishops bears witness that this theme returns in a new historical context. Therefore, it must be taken up again in the teaching of the church, in theology and in pastoral work. It must be taken up again in its own depth and in its evangelical authenticity."

In mentioning von Balthasar, the pope, by allusion, was criticizing offshoots of liberation theology which reduce liberation to strictly political terms and seek revolution as the only answer to social ills.

A month later, the pope formally approved the conclusions of the meeting in a letter to the president of the Latin American Bishops Council, the executive agency of the hierarchy. The letter was also addressed to the bishops of the continent.

"The church in Latin America has been strengthened in its vigorous unity, in its specific identity, in the will to respond to the needs and challenges attentively studied during your meeting," the pope wrote. He invited the bishops to propose "specific plans and concrete goals" at local, regional and national levels to implement the Puebla document.

"May God grant that in a short time the whole church community may be filled and penetrated by the spirit of Puebla and by the directives of this historic meeting," said the pope.

On opposite page:

Pope John Paul II delivers his address to the Latin American bishops meeting at Puebla.

PART II

TAKING A STAND

Redeemer of Man

Pope John Paul's concept of his ministry was made clear with the publication March 15 of his first encyclical, *Redemptor Hominis* — "The Redeemer of Man."

A "Christian anthropology" might be the best way to summarize the encyclical — a papal declaration intended to have universal application as a teaching tool. The title suggests the two points of reference around which the encyclical is built: Christ, the Redeemer; and man, the redeemed. The central theme of the 24,000-word document is the supreme dignity of man proclaimed by the church through its message of redemption.

It is the first papal encyclical, at least in modern times, to have the Christian doctrine of man as its main theme. It touches on world issues such as the arms race, the gap between the rich and the poor, human rights violations, consumerism, materialism, environmental pollution, technology and international relations; but it is not a social encyclical.

At heart the encyclical is a general statement of Christian philosophy, putting into focus the church's teachings about man, about his religious striving, about the Christian answer to that striving, about the church's mission in the light of the gospel message concerning man, and what all this tells each individual concerning his duties and vocation as a Christian.

The encyclical also sets the stage for John Paul's pontificate. It opens with a kind of "state-of-the-church" message, noting that the Christian era "is already very close to the year 2000." After a short introduction — a global view of the meaning of the Incarnation and the Redemption in human history — the pope discusses the beginning of his own pontificate and the developments of the church during the papacy of Paul VI. He explicitly links his first encyclical to the first encyclical written by Pope Paul, *Ecclesiam Suam*, in which Paul outlined what he saw as the state of the church at the time and its needs.

Using the same method, John Paul lists the numerous controversies and divisions that Paul faced and concludes that the church is in a better situation now than it was when Paul took the helm. The church "is admittedly not free of internal difficulties and tensions," he said, but at the same time it is "internally more strengthened against the excesses of self-criticism...more mature in her spirit...more serviceable for her mission of salvation for all."

Among developments since Vatican II, John Paul specifically praises the progress in collegiality — shared responsibility and decision making — and in relations with other Christian churches and other religions.

The central points of John Paul's message lie in Chapters 2 and 3 of the encyclical: "The Mystery of Redemption," and "Redeemed Man and His Situation in the Modern World."

In Chapter 2, the pope declares that redemption by Jesus Christ is the central fact about man. "Only in the mystery of the Incarnate Word does the mystery of man take on light....Human nature, by the very fact that it was assumed, not absorbed, in him (Christ), has been raised in us also to a dignity beyond compare."

"Christ the Redeemer 'fully reveals man to himself,'" the pope adds. "In this dimension man finds again the greatness, dignity and value that belong to his humanity."

The pope links the religious striving of man toward God in other religions, and especially in Judaism and Islam, to the central mystery of the redemption. He says that the "amazement at man's worth and dignity" that is contained in the gospel message "is certainly of faith, but in a hidden and mysterious way it vivifies every aspect of authentic humanism."

The importance of the gospel message about God and man is also a basic demand for Christian unity, he says. "We can and must immediately reach and display to the world our unity in proclaiming the mystery of Christ, in displaying the divine dimension and also the human dimension of our redemption."

Unity is also needed in the struggle for the full dignity of every human being, says the encyclical. The pope says the church's awareness of what redemption teaches about the dignity of man "enables us to approach all cultures, all ideological concepts, all people of good will...with esteem, respect and discernment." Thus, the church's understanding of the dignity of man is linked with its insistence on freedom of conscience and religion.

Chapter 3 discusses the situation of man in the modern world. The pope says the church has a single purpose: "that every person may be able to find Christ." Because of "man's surpassing dignity, the church cannot remain insensible to whatever serves man's true welfare, any more than she can remain indifferent to what threatens it."

One of the basic questions the pope raises is the relation of technology to human values. "The man of today seems ever to be under threat from what he produces," he observes. "He is afraid that it can become the means and instrument for an unimaginable self-destruction, compared with which all the cataclysms and catastrophes of history known to us seem to fade away."

"At the same time," he says, "exploitation of the earth not only for industrial, but also for military purposes and the uncontrolled development of technology outside the framework of a long-range authentically humanistic plan often bring with them a threat to man's natural environment, alienate him in his relations with nature and remove him from nature."

The encyclical asks whether man through scientific and technological progress "is becoming truly better, that is to say more mature spiritually, more aware of the dignity of his humanity, more responsible, more open to others, especially to the neediest and the weakest, and readier to give and to aid all."

Discussing the biblical theme of man's "kingship" as being responsible dominion over the world, the encyclical comments that this consists in "the priority of ethics over technology, in the primacy of persons over things, and in the superiority of spirit over matter."

"It was the Creator's will that man should communicate with nature as an intelligent and noble 'master' and 'guardian,' and not as a heedless 'exploiter' and 'destroyer,'" it says.

Scientific and technological advances "demand a proportional development of morals and ethics," the pope declares. The question that must be asked is whether these advances "accord with man's moral and spiritual progress," he says. Much of the problem has been caused by "progress" divorced from a religious perspective. -

The encyclical rejects human slavery to material things, to production, to economic systems, saying: "A civilization purely materialistic in outline condemns man to such slavery." It also criticizes the consumer society for fostering materialism and causing much of the dichotomy between the rich and the poor of the world.

"Indeed everyone is familiar with the picture of a consumer civilization, which consists in a surplus of goods necessary for man and for entire societies — and we are dealing precisely with the rich, highly developed societies — while the remaining societies — at least broad sectors of them — are suffering from hunger, with many people dying each day of starvation and malnutrition,'' it says.

"Hand in hand go a certain abuse of freedom by one group — an abuse linked precisely with a consumer attitude uncontrolled by ethics — and a limitation by it of the freedom of the others, that is to say of those suffering marked shortages and being driven to conditions of even worse misery and destitution,'' the encyclical continues.

"So widespread is the phenomenon that it brings into question the financial, monetary, production and commercial mechanisms that, resting on various political pressures, support the world economy. These are proving incapable either of remedying the unjust social situations inherited from the past or of dealing with urgent challenges and ethical demands of the present...

"The drama is made still worse by the presence close at hand of the privileged social classes and of the rich countries, which accumulate goods to an excessive degree and the misuse of whose riches very often becomes the cause of various ills. Add to this the fever of inflation and the plague of unemployment — these are further symptoms of the moral disorder that is being noticed in the world situation and therefore requires daring creative resolves in keeping with man's authentic human dignity.''

The encyclical asks "resolute commitment by individuals and people that are free and linked in solidarity'' to end the "moral disorder'' in the distribution of the world's goods. It particularly condemns "gigantic investments for armaments'' at the expense of "investments for food at the service of life.''

"Man cannot relinquish himself or the place in the visible world that belongs to him; he cannot become the slave of things, the slave of economic systems, the slave of production, the slave of his own products,'' it says.

The U.N. Universal Declaration of Human Rights is singled out as a major symbol of modern man's concern for the welfare of humanity. But the pope questions whether the spirit of the declaration is accepted everywhere. He calls not only for each individual's rights, but also for citizens "to have the right to share in the political life of the community.''

John Paul notes in particular threats to the rights to religious freedom and freedom of conscience. The curtailment of religious freedom is not only "painful,'' but an attack on man's dignity, he says. The first pontiff from a communist-ruled country, he alludes to communist governments although he does not mention them by name.

The phenomenon of unbelief, lack of religious concern and atheism can only be understood in relation to the phenomenon of religion and faith, he observes. "It is therefore difficult, even from a 'purely human' point of view, to accept a position that gives only atheism the right of citizenship in public and social life, while believers are, as though by principle, barely tolerated or are treated as second-class citizens or are even — and this has already happened — entirely deprived of the rights of citizenship.''

The encyclical reaffirms the strong stands taken by John Paul's predecessors on social issues. It condemns the arms race and asks for sweeping changes in the world's social, political and economic life.

"Do not kill! Do not prepare destruction and extermination for men!'' the pope pleads. Money used to develop and purchase arms should be diverted to increase food production and provide other services needed by people. It criticizes developing countries for providing arms "in abundance'' to newly independent states "instead of bread and cultural aid.''

While raising world political, economic and social issues, the encyclical deals

with them in general terms as threats to human dignity. It does not offer the detailed analysis of the problems or the detailed program of principles involved in their solution presented in Pope Paul's 1967 encyclical *Populorum Progressio* ("The Progress of Peoples") or in Pope John XXIII's 1963 and 1961 encyclicals *Pacem in Terris* ("Peace on Earth") and *Mater et Magistra* ("Mother and Teacher").

Instead of specific solutions, John Paul's encyclical gives general guidelines for use in formulating answers. The pope advocates solutions based on greater solidarity among people, redistribution of wealth and an end to physical and economic domination over others by people and states.

The encyclical's final chapter, "The Church's Mission and Man's Destiny," summarizes the meaning of redemption for mankind and turns to the question of what this says about the church itself. John Paul calls the church "the social subject of responsibility for divine truth" which carries out Christ's mission of preaching God's word.

In this context, he notes that "theology has always had and continues to have great importance for the church." Theologians, says John Paul, are "servants of divine truth" and he stresses the need for them to remain united with the bishops and the pope in presenting the teaching of the church.

"If it is permissible and even desirable that the enormous work to be done in this direction should take into consideration a certain pluralism of methodology, the work cannot, however, depart from the fundamental unity in teaching of faith and morals which is at the work's end," he says.

"Nobody, therefore, can make theology, as it were, a simple collection of his personal ideas, but everybody must be aware of being in close union with the mission of teaching truth for which the church is responsible."

He also cites the role of pastors and of men and women Religious, lay catechists and parents in transmitting the church's teachings.

The pope says that the Eucharist is "the center and summit of the whole sacramental life, through which each Christian receives the saving power of redemption." While speaking of the Eucharist as "the most profound revelation of the human brotherhood of Christ's disciples and confessors," he warns against treating it "merely as an 'occasion' for manifesting this brotherhood." The "full magnitude of the divine mystery" must also be respected.

The statement was clear disapproval of shared communion services between Catholics and non-Catholic Christians, a practice being promoted by some as a way to foster unity. In his encyclical and in other ways, John Paul let it be known that his position is that unity must precede eucharistic sharing, not vice versa.

Concerning penance, the encyclical praises recent developments in the church which highlight "the community aspect of penance." But here, too, John Paul warns against reducing the sacrament to a celebration of community. He emphasizes that conversion from sin is "a particularly profound inward act" of the individual before God.

The church's defense of individual confession is a defense of "the human soul's individual right: man's right to a more personal encounter with the crucified, forgiving Christ," says the encyclical.

Discussing the church as "the people of God," the encyclical emphasizes that being part of the church "is not just a specific 'social membership'" but is rather a matter of "vocation." It stresses that each Christian has a particular vocation, a particular commitment to construct the whole body of Christ. Among specific vocations, the encyclical stresses the lifelong commitment involved in marriage, the priesthood and consecrated religious life.

The pope asks for a period of consolidation within the church with emphasis on "the centuries-old tradition of the church" and the teachings of Vatican II. As he would continue to do throughout the first year of his pontificate, he uses Vatican II as the yardstick for assessing internal church activity. He makes clear there will be

With Archbishop Giuseppe Caprio, Vatican deputy secretary of state, at his side, Pope John Paul II signs his first encyclical, "Redemptor Hominis."

no backsliding from the council, but at the same time warns Catholics not to rush ahead of it.

The encyclical closes with a plea for prayer to Mary. Mary is called "Mother of the Church" because "she gave human life to the Son of God, 'for whom and by whom all things exist' and from whom the whole of the people of God receives the grace and dignity of election."

Reaction to the encyclical was quick and varied.

The major significance of the encyclical is its clarification of the direction the pope hopes the church will take in years to come, said Bishop Thomas C. Kelly, general secretary of the National Conference of Catholic Bishops-U.S. Catholic Conference.

"We need to know where he is coming from, how he's got his act together," said Bishop Kelly at a press conference March 15 to release the document in the United States.

Some Catholics may be disappointed because the encyclical does not specifically address controversial issues facing the church, but this is "inevitable, because people like instant solutions," he said.

Bishop Kelly praised the encyclical's emphasis on human rights and social action, key areas of concern to the U.S. bishops.

The encyclical "really is an essay on redemption," said Jesuit Father Avery Dulles, professor of systematic theology at The Catholic University of America and a well-known author.

"The theology of redemption that brings together the mystery of creation and redemption overcomes the dichotomy between the sacred and the secular," Father Dulles said. "The church, the sacraments and Christ are very close to the pope's heart. Also close is his understanding of priesthood, Eucharist, penance, private confession, absolution. He is very conscious of their value. It all fits in with his Christian personalism."

The president of Catholic University, Dr. Edmund D. Pellegrino, called the new document, "a rich and broad tapestry depicting the nature and dignity of man as it is illuminated by Christ's redemption of all mankind."

Eugene Fisher, executive secretary of the U.S. bishops' Secretariat for Catholic-Jewish Relations, found the encyclical "very good on ecumenism." Dominican Sister Carol Coston, executive secretary of Network, a social justice organization, praised it as "an affirmation for those in the social justice ministry" although much of it was "rather traditional." Kevin D. Whitehead, executive vice president of Catholics United for the Faith, said John Paul is "following very faithfully and with great imagination and vigor the line laid down by John XXIII, Paul VI and John Paul I." Father James E. Ratigan, president of the National Federation of Priests Councils, said the pope's encyclical "gives us an insight into who he is at this stage. As he grows in the papacy, we'll see what future documents will say to us." Father Ratigan said the document was not written with a broad understanding of the church and does not have the point of view of someone who has the international view John Paul will have in a few years.

U.N. Secretary General Kurt Waldheim praised "the pontiff's warm affirmation of the principles of peace and justice contained in the U.N. Charter and his helpful statements concerning the many global problems on which the United Nations is making earnest efforts to find solutions."

A U.N. spokesman said John Paul's encyclical was the first one to praise specific works of the United Nations. U.N. officials saw that as a sign that the new pope wanted to increase church cooperation with the United Nations.

Before the encyclical was made public, the pope had described his intentions. Speaking to a crowd in St. Peter's Square for the Sunday Angelus March 11, John

Paul said the relationship between redemption and human dignity is "the central commitment of my new ecclesial service." He said the encyclical contains thoughts which "were pressing with particular force on my mind" at the beginning of his pontificate and which "had been maturing in me during the years of my priestly and then episcopal service."

"If Christ has called me with such thoughts, with such sentiments, it is because he wanted these expressions of intellect and heart, these expressions of faith, hope and love, to find resonance in my new and universal ministry," the pope said.

Unlike most encyclicals, which are the result of the collaboration of a team of theologians, it appeared that John Paul had written this encyclical almost singlehandedly. He at least did the first draft alone, writing it in Polish within weeks of becoming pope.

One high church official said it was as if John Paul "reached into the bottom drawer of his desk and pulled out notes on all these thoughts that had been accumulating over the years and finally put them together."

The time between the writing of the encyclical and its publication was spent in refining it, in translating it into Latin — the official language — and into other languages, and in sending it to the bishops of the world.

For the Sake of the Kingdom

One of the immediate challenges John Paul faced involved issues which, to him, struck at the very heart of the church: What to do about increasing pressures for doing away with the requirement for priestly celibacy in the Western church, what to do about the growing number of priests asking permission to leave the active ministry?

His response was characteristic. He spoke out firmly on both matters, issuing a clear "no" to those who favor married priests, and letting it be known that he would not lightly dispense anyone from his ministerial vows. Then he broke with tradition and did something no modern pope had done. On April 12, Holy Thursday, he concelebrated the Mass of the Chrism — a highly significant occasion — with about 2,500 priests of the Rome diocese. It was the first time in modern times that the pope, as bishop of Rome, had gathered with his priests for the occasion. The ceremonies for many years had been delegated to the pope's vicar for the Roman diocese.

About 8,000 persons crowded into St. Peter's Basilica for the Mass, at which oils for liturgical use during the year are blessed. The oils are used for baptism, confirmation, ordination and the anointing of the sick.

The pope stood with 22 cardinals, 40 bishops and archbishops, and his 2,500 priests. The symbolism of his gesture was clear. It is at the Mass of the Chrism each year that priests renew their vows.

During his homily, the pope asked priests for "faithfulness and perseverance" in maintaining their vows. After the homily the priests, bishops, archbishops and cardinals responded with a resounding "I will" as the pope asked them to renew their promises. Similar ceremonies took place in cathedrals throughout the world as priests renewed their vows before their bishops.

In Rome, the ceremony underscored the pope's position regarding the possibility of allowing a married clergy for the Latin-Rite church, a controversial issue in the post-Vatican II era.

The event came several days after the pope had released a document which strongly reconfirmed celibacy for Latin-Rite Catholic priests and in which the pope indicated he would not easily grant laicizations — dispensations from priestly life.

The document was a papal letter addressed "to all the priests of the church on the occasion of Holy Thursday 1979." The pope said objections raised against priestly celibacy are based on criteria "whose 'anthropological' correctness and basis in fact are seen to be very dubious and of relative value." The Latin church continues to wish "that all those who receive the sacrament of orders should embrace this renunciation (of marriage) 'for the sake of the kingdom of heaven.'"

In a shorter companion letter addressed to the world's bishops, the pope stressed "the brotherly communion of the whole of the church's episcopal college or 'body.'" He asked bishops to intensify their unity with the priests of their dioceses and urged "every possible effort" to encourage new vocations to the priesthood.

Both letters were linked in their titles to Holy Thursday and bore April 8 (Palm Sunday) as the date of issuance. The Vatican made the letters public April 9.

In the 35-page letter to priests, the pope also placed strong emphasis on lifelong fidelity to the priestly vocation. "It is a matter here of keeping one's word to Christ and the church," he said.

The pope rejected laicization as an easy answer to a crisis in one's vocation. The words of the letter did not rule out all possibilities of granting laicization, and the text did not say what the pope would do with laicization requests. But his words indicated he would not grant such requests readily.

Priests were urged to call on their resources of faith and prayer in moments of crisis "and not have recourse to a dispensation, understood as an 'administrative intervention,'" when the issue is "a profound question of conscience and a test of humanity."

John Paul opened the letter by calling priests "my brothers by virtue of the sacrament of orders." He said: "For you I am a bishop, with you I am a priest."

Priests should re-read sections of Vatican II documents which highlight the common priesthood of all Christians and the essential difference between that priesthood and the ordained priesthood, added the pope. He emphasized church teachings that the priesthood is sacramental, hierarchical and ministerial. The priesthood is a gift for the Christian community which "comes from Christ himself."

Because of their "likeness to Christ, the good shepherd," he said, "you priests are expected to have a care and commitment which are far greater and different from those of any lay person." While noting that priests are engaged in a wide variety of activities, he added that "within all these differences, you are always and everywhere the bearers of our particular vocation."

"And this you can never forget; this you can never renounce; this you must put into practice at every moment, in every place and in every way," he said. "The priestly personality must be for others a clear and plain sign and indication. This is the first condition for our pastoral service."

Repeating his call in Mexico, the pope told priests not to reduce their vocation to a simply secular ministry.

"Those who call for the secularization of priestly life and applaud its various manifestations will undoubtedly abandon us when we succumb to temptation. We shall then cease to be necessary and popular," he said.

Priests must be "close to people and all their problems" but this must be done "in a priestly way," said the pope. Priests must be men of prayer and witnesses to "the perspective of eternal salvation" in their service.

The pope called celibacy "a heritage of the Latin Catholic Church, a tradition to which she owes much and in which she is resolved to persevere, in spite of all the difficulties to which such fidelity could be exposed, and also in spite of the various symptoms of weakness and crisis in individual priests."

In treasuring the discipline of celibacy, the church is not downgrading the value of marriage or "succumbing to a Manichean concept for the human body and its functions," he said. "Celibacy is precisely a 'gift of the Spirit.' A similar though different gift is contained in the vocation to true and faithful married love."

The pope closed by entrusting all priests "to the mother of Christ, who in a special way is our mother: the mother of priests." He referred to "the wonderful and penetrating dimension of nearness to the mother of Christ" in the priesthood. And he added: "I am referring especially to my own personal experience."

In the much shorter letter to bishops, eight pages long, the pope said, "the gift of sacramental fullness of the priesthood is greater than all the toils and also all the sufferings involved in our pastoral ministry in the episcopate." Bishops should renew their love for the priests "entrusted to you as the closest collaborators in the pastoral office."

"Take care of them like beloved sons, brothers and friends," said the pope. "Be mindful of all their needs. Have particular solicitude for their spiritual advancement, for the perseverance in the grace of the sacrament of the priesthood."

Bishops were especially asked to foster vocations. "The full reconstitution of the life of the seminaries throughout the church will be the best proof of the advancement of the renewal to which the council directed the church," said the pope.

The backdrop of the pope's letters was the severe vocations crisis affecting the Catholic Church since Vatican II. In the years immediately following the council, there had been a sharp drop in priestly ordinations as well as a sharp rise in priests leaving the active ministry. Although the sharp decline in the total number of priests began leveling off before the Polish pope took office, the church was still faced with the problem of too few priests for an ever growing population.

On April 27, L'Osservatore Romano, the Vatican daily newspaper, reported that the total number of priests in the world at the end of 1977, the latest year for which figures were available, was 406,717. Five years earlier, the total had been 435,848, almost 30,000 more.

In 1977, the number of priests who left the active ministry was 2,506, nearly 300 below the 2,802 departures of the previous year, and only about two-thirds of the number that left in 1971 (3,872). The figures published by L'Osservatore Romano were taken from the 1977 statistical yearbook prepared by the Vatican.

Ordinations and deaths in 1977 were down, according to the statistics. There were 6,034 ordinations, down 144 from the previous year. There were 6,820 deaths, 120 fewer than in 1976.

Taken together, the figures showed a net decline of 3,292 priests around the world from the end of 1976 to the end of 1977; but this was lower than the net decline in 1976, which was 3,566.

Initial statistics for 1978 and the data on seminarians indicated that the final 1978 figures will show an increase in ordinations, said the Vatican newspaper.

The newspaper said that the statistics on departures include all priests who left the ministry, not just those who applied for and received laicization. The figures included diocesan priests and those in religious orders.

The statistical table produced by L'Osservatore Romano also showed the ratio of deaths, departures and ordinations per 100 priests. Over the seven years covered by the table (1971-77), the ratio of deaths to living priests remained stable at about 1.6 per 100. The ratio of ordinations dropped from 1.65 per 100 priests in 1971 to 1.44 in 1977.

The biggest relative drop was in the incidence of departures from the ministry. In 1971, there were .88 departures per 100 priests. That ratio remained relatively steady over the next three years. But in 1975, 1976 and 1977, the ratio dropped. In 1977, it was down to .59 departures per 100 priests.

Even before John Paul's letter dealing with the subject was published, he already had begun rejecting requests by priests for laicization.

The procurator general of a religious order said he got his first answer on a pending laicization request by a member of his order on April 9, the same day the pope's letter was published. The answer was "no." He said that the previous week, at a meeting in Rome of procurators general, several told him they also had received negative answers to pending cases. None reported positive answers.

During the 15 years of the reign of Pope Paul VI, an estimated 2,000 laicizations were granted per year. In the 34-day pontificate of Pope John Paul I, a number of dispensations were given. In one religious order alone, seven dispensations were granted by the pope.

After the election of Pope John Paul II, the processing of cases came to an abrupt halt and Vatican sources said the new pope wanted to reconsider the question. The pope was said to be disturbed at the effect of the large number of laicizations on the morale of priests remaining in the ministry. He was worried also about the effect on the attitude of seminarians.

The vast majority of laicization requests submitted in recent years cited difficulty with celibacy and a desire for marriage as prompting the request, according to church sources.

Pope Paul speeded up the laicization process and began granting requests more readily. The requests usually also involved complex factors such as serious psychological problems.

But the process can change easily from one pope to another and a pope can stop the laicization process without changing church law. The reason is that under church law, dispensation from priestly duty is considered a "gift" or "grace" granted by the pope. It is not something to which a priest has a right to receive under determined circumstances.

The prohibition regarding married clergy affects only the Western church, properly known as the Latin Rite, the rite most common in the United States, Canada, Europe and most of the world. Eastern-Rite Catholic churches hold to legislation enacted in 692 by the Synod of Trujillo which allows men who are already married to become deacons and priests, but bars men from marrying once they are ordained. Only men who are unmarried may become Eastern-Rite bishops, however.

In the Western church, celibacy developed in the early centuries at a time when the clergy included both celibates and married men. The first local legislation on the subject was enacted by a local council held in Elvira, Spain in 306, forbidding bishops, priests and deacons from having wives. Subsequently, similar enactments were passed by other local councils. By the 12th century, particular laws regarded marriage by clerics in major orders to be unlawful and null and void. The latter view was translated by the Second Lateran Council in 1139 into what is believed to be the first written universal law making ordination to holy orders exclude marriage. In 1563 the Council of Trent ruled definitively on the matter and established the discipline still in force — with only a minor variation — in the Western church. Under Pope Paul VI, legislation was established which allows married men to become deacons. But deacons who are not married at the time of their ordination must take a vow of celibacy, and deacons who become widowers may not remarry.

John Paul's stand was not a popular one. He obviously did not expect it to be. But just as obviously, he considered it necessary to speak out. Even in Italy, where tradition and custom in matters ecclesiastical are slower to change than in many other countries, a wave of opposition to celibacy was building. About a month before the pope issued his letter, a survey by an Italian priest-sociologist indicated that a third of Italian men and women Religious preferred a temporary vow of chastity and 20 percent considered chastity impractical. Father Silvano Burgalassi, professor of sociology at the University of Pisa and the Catholic University of Milan, said men Religious experience the greatest difficulties with chastity, according to the survey, due to the greater contact they have with people outside their religious order. Chastity for them requires a particular equilibrium not possessed by everyone, he said. The survey did not include diocesan priests, but Father Burgalassi said he felt sure the preference among them for temporary celibacy would be even stronger.

In the United States, proponents of a married priesthood were predictably disappointed. It was obvious that the debate would continue.

The pope seemed to be answering some of his critics when he issued a message specifically encouraging Catholics around the world to pray for vocations and asking young men to answer the call to the priesthood.

"You will meet difficulties," the pope said. "Do you think perhaps that I do not know about them? I am telling you that love overcomes all difficulties. The true response to every vocation is the work of love. The response to the priestly, religious or missionary vocation can only spring from a deep love of Christ."

The message was issued April 21 by the Vatican and was written for the World Day of Prayer for Vocations on May 6.

John Paul urged priests and bishops to "go among your young people" and call them to priestly and religious life. Christ's calls for disciples and followers "are entrusted to our apostolic ministry and we must make them heard," he said.

"So, do not be afraid to call. Go among your young people. Go and meet them personally and call them. The hearts of many young people, and not so young people, are ready to listen to you," he added. He said the call to vocations goes beyond the ordained ministry and includes calls to special ministries for women and the laity in general.

The pope said his message was also addressed to heads of religious orders, secular institutes and leaders of missionary organizations. Young people were asked to recall the immediate and total acceptance of Christ's call by his disciples and apostles.

"From the time when the Gospel was first proclaimed right up to our time, a very large number of men and women have given their personal response, their free and deliberate response, to the call of Christ," the pope said. "They have chosen the priesthood, the religious life, life in the missions, as the reason for the ideal of existence. They have served the people of God and humanity, with faith, intelligence, courage and love. Now it is time for you. It is up to you to respond."

Life is a gift from God and a religious vocation is a call from God to an "extraordinary adventure" of "total dedication to God," said the papal message.

In several talks on the same day, the pope continued his encouragement of priests to overcome the difficulties of their ministry by faith in God and adherence to the church.

"We have been called. This is the fundamental truth that must instill in us courage and gladness," the pope said to a group of priests from Milan, Italy, who were celebrating the 25th anniversary of their ordination. "The call has been first of all interior, mysterious, caused by various motives. But then, after the long and necessary preparation in the seminary, under the direction of sagacious and responsible superiors, it has become official, guaranteed, when the church called us and consecrated us through the bishop."

Without the strength given by the call "no one in fact would dare to become a minister of Christ, in continuous contact with the most high," he said. "No one would have the courage to burden himself with the weight of consciences and to thus accept a sacred and mysterious solitude."

Christ is always ready to help in strengthening priests through the Eucharist, he said. "We can 'consecrate' and personally meet Christ with the divine power of 'transubstantiation.' We can communicate with Jesus, living, true, real. We can distribute to souls the word, incarnate, dead and risen for the salvation of the world. Every day we are in private audience with Jesus."

On April 21, the pope also spoke to 18 deacons preparing for the priesthood at the pontifical Irish, Scots and Rosminian colleges in Rome.

"Like the apostles you too must feel impelled to proclaim by word and deed the resurrection of the Lord Jesus. You too must experience the need to do good, to render service in the name of the crucified and risen Jesus — to bring God's word into the lives of his holy people," John Paul said. "Your ability to communicate the Gospel will depend on your adherence to the faith of the apostles."

John Paul had spoken previously of women in committed religious life. In a speech to 12,000 nuns from the Diocese of Rome, he urged them to "be spiritual mothers and sisters for all the men of this church." He asked them to provide aid "especially for the sick, the suffering, the abandoned, children, the young, families in difficulty."

"Go meet them. Don't wait for them to come to you. Seek them yourselves," he said.

A religious vocation "derives from a living faith, consistent to the point of extreme consequences, which opens man to the final perspective, that is to the perspective of meeting with God himself, who alone is worthy of a love 'above everything,' a love that is exclusive and matrimonial," he said.

"This vocation, once accepted, once confirmed solemnly by means of vows, must be continuously nourished by the richness of faith, not only when it brings with it interior joy, but also when it is united with difficulties, to aridity, to interior suffering, called the 'night' of the soul," he added.

Religious vocations are "a living sign of the 'future world,' a sign that, at the same time, is rooted (even through your religious habit) in the daily life of the church and society and permeates its most difficult tissues," he said.

The pope encouraged activities to stimulate religious vocations through prayer and by the witness of the nuns' lives. This witness, he said, consists of:

— "Sincere consistency with gospel values and the charisma proper to your institute. Any yielding to compromise is a disappointment for those who draw near to you. Do not forget it."

— "A humanly successful and mature personality, which knows how to enter into relation with others without unjustified suspicions or ingenuous imprudence, but with cordial openness and serene balance."

— "Your joy, a joy which may be read in your eyes and in your attitude and also in your words."

On another occasion, speaking to about 600 nuns belonging to the international Union of Superiors General, the pope outlined what the criteria for renewal of religious orders should be. He quickly eliminated renewal guided solely by the trends of public opinion.

Superiors of congregations have to deal with rapid changes, reduced numbers, experimentation and the demands of the young, said the pope. "Welcome these realities. Take them seriously, never tragically," he said.

"Calmly seek progressive, clear, courageous solutions," he said. "In ever-renewed fidelity to the charism of the founders, congregations must strive to correspond to the expectation of the church, to the commitments that the church, with its pastors, considers most urgent today."

The pope recommended that nuns wear "a simple and adapted religious habit" as an external sign of consecration to God. "It is the means of reminding you constantly of your commitment which breaks with the spirit of the world. It is silent, but eloquent testimony."

The church and the world need "men and women who sacrifice all to follow Christ in the manner of the apostles," the pope said. "The sacrifice of conjugal love, of material possessions, of the totally autonomous exercise of freedom become incomprehensible without the love of Christ. This radicalism is necessary to announce in a prophetic, but always a very humble way, this new humanity according to Christ."

At no time did John Paul touch directly on the issue of the ordination of women. Less than two years before his election, a declaration approved by Pope Paul VI had said the church "does not consider herself authorized to admit women to priestly ordination." The new pope seemed to consider the matter closed. An active and vocal segment of the church in the United States thought differently. Whether they would get the pope's attention during his trip later in the year to the United States remained to be seen. Whether getting his attention would bring about the kind of change they seek appeared remote, indeed.

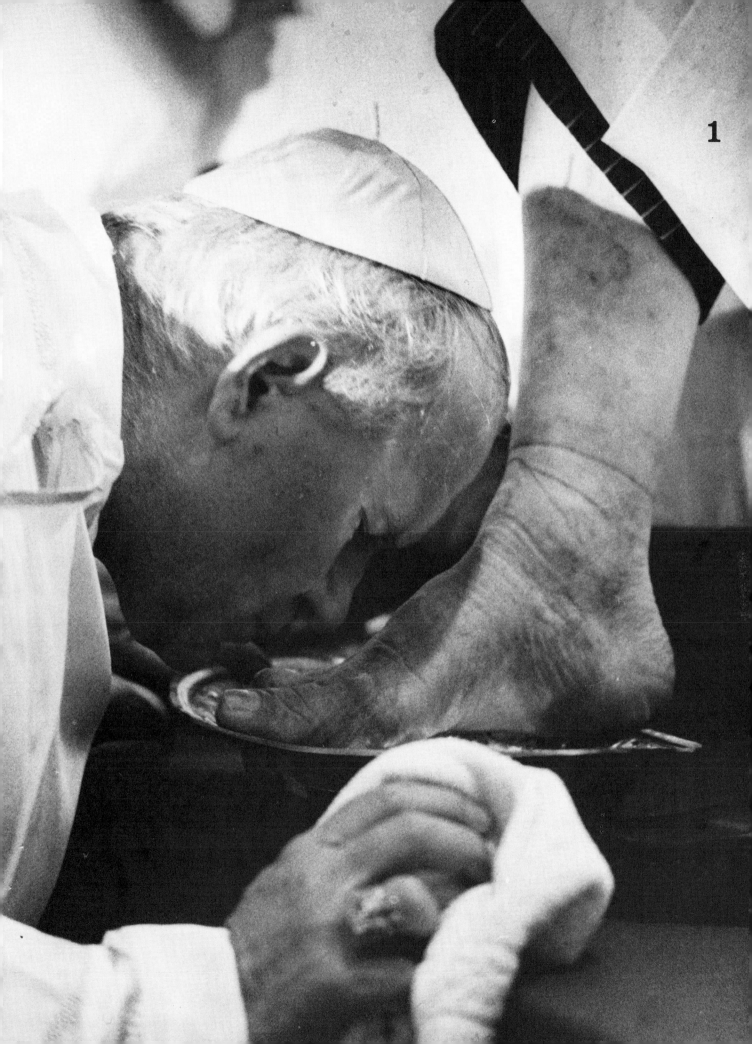

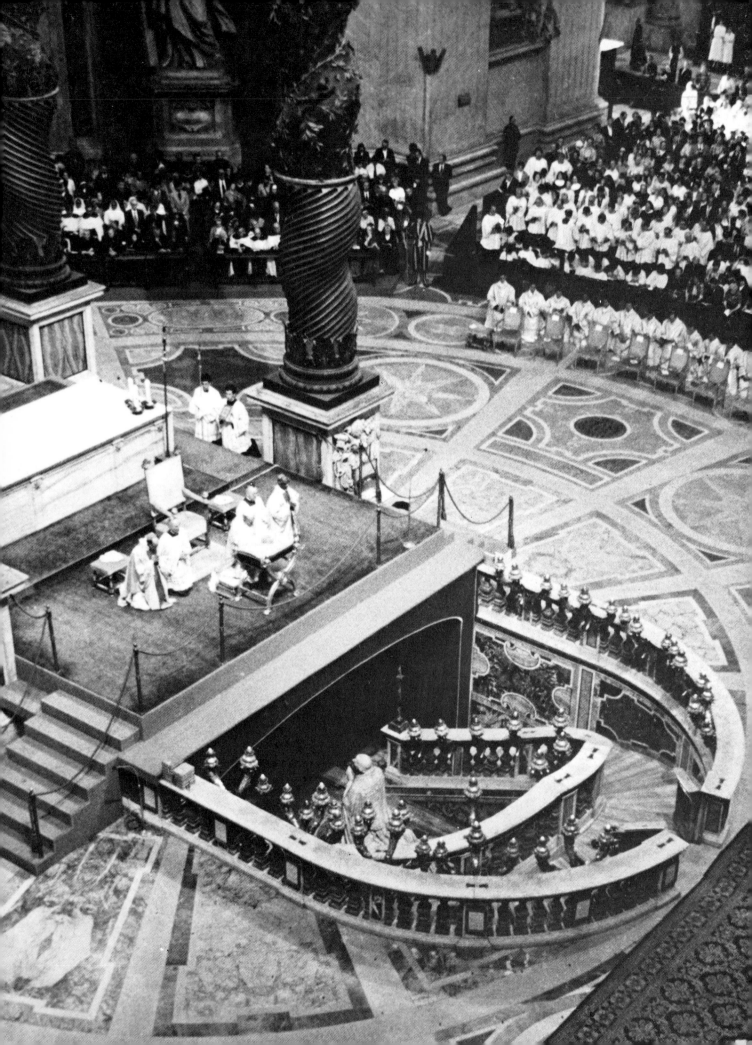

On the preceding pages:

1 *As Jesus did with his apostles, the pope washes and kisses the feet of a seminarian during a traditional Holy Thursday ceremony.*

2 *St. Peter's Basilica is the setting as Pope John Paul II ordains 26 new bishops from 12 nations.*

3 *Mother Teresa of Calcutta kisses the hand of the pope during an audience. To many, Mother Teresa symbolizes a life of service the pope asks of all women religious.*

We Yearn for This Hour

The papal transition period had been marked by singular demonstrations of Christian unity. Non-Catholic religious leaders gathered at the Vatican in unprecedented numbers for the various ceremonies; the presence of Anglican Archbishop Donald Coggan of Canterbury marked the first time since the Reformation that a primate of the Church of England had attended the solemn beginning of a pontificate. Hopes for a new impetus toward reconciliation soared. The new pope obviously shared those hopes, but by May it was clear that anyone who expected some new and sudden breakthrough was going to be disappointed. John Paul's approach to ecumenism was to temper his deep desire for unity with a frank recognition of reality.

Two events of May symbolized John Paul's approach:

— In a formal speech, he cautioned against sharing the Eucharist with non-Catholics, saying the Eucharist can be shared only after full Christian unity is achieved.

— In a highly unusual action, he made a leading Protestant theologian and ecumenist a Knight of St. Gregory the Great, a distinction usually reserved for Catholics.

Receiving the papal honor was the Rev. George Huntson Williams of the Unitarian Christian Fellowship, an old friend of the pope. Mr. Williams, 65, was an observer at Vatican II. In 1972 he lectured at the University of Lublin in Poland and renewed his friendship with the university's chancellor, the then Cardinal Karol Wojtyla. In 1976, Mr. Williams, Hollis Professor of Divinity at Harvard University, arranged for Cardinal Wojtyla to speak at Harvard. Mr. Williams has been active in civil rights, peace, ecology and anti-abortion activities. In 1951, Mr. Williams wrote a book, *Public Aid to Parochial Education*, which saw Catholic support for public aid to parochial schools as a social justice issue, not a sign of sectarian selfishness.

The pope's cautioning on the Eucharist came in an address to the 15 bishops of the Antilles gathered in Rome to meet with him. "Fidelity to Jesus Christ requires that we should pursue with vigor the cause of Christian unity," said the pope.

"We must continue to work humbly and resolutely to remove the real divisions, to restore that full unity in faith which is the condition for sharing the Eucharist," he said. The Eucharist manifests and realizes the communion of the church in all its dimensions, he added.

"Sharing in the Eucharist, therefore, presupposes unity in faith," he said, explaining his call for caution. "Intercommunion between divided Christians is not the answer to Christ's appeal for perfect unity. God has set an hour for the realization of this salvific design for Christian unity."

"As we yearn for this hour, in common prayer and dialogue, and endeavor to offer an ever more purified heart to the Lord, we must also wait for the Lord's action. It must be said and said again that the restoration of Christian unity is above all a gift of God's love," said the pope. "Meanwhile, on the basis of our common baptism and the patrimony of faith that we already share, we must intensify our common witness to the Gospel and our common service to humanity."

Ecumenism was on the mind of other churches as well. On May 8, the Anglican Consultative Council held its annual meeting in Canada, bringing together Anglican leaders from around the world. One of the topics on the agenda was ways of achieving visible unity with the Roman Catholic Church.

Bishop John Howe, secretary general of the Anglican body, said there were "generally encouraging" responses by Anglican churches throughout the world to the three agreed statements drawn up by the Anglican-Roman Catholic International Commission. The statements were on the Eucharist, on ministry and ordination, and on authority. The statements were seen as an important step toward unity and were to be studied carefully by officials of both churches.

Bishop Howe favored a next stage including another commission to deal with "subjects on which there may be important differences but which can now be discussed with a reality that was not apparent before."

Hopes such as those had been expressed by a variety of interfaith leaders from the moment of the new pope's election. Particular note was taken of John Paul's Polish background.

"I think that because of the politically oppressive situation out of which he came, he would have a very wonderful respect for religious traditions that would be different than his own," said Father Kevin McMorrow, superior general of the Atonement Friars, who sponsor the Week of Prayer for Christian Unity each year.

"He would want to ensure that all churches and all religions have the freedom to express themselves and their teachings relative to the meaning of God and the meaning of man," said Father McMorrow.

The World Council of Churches issued a statement from Geneva, Switzerland, praising John Paul II for bringing to the papacy "the rich tradition and spirituality of the Polish people as well as his pastoral and ecumenical experience as archbishop of Cracow." It expressed hopes that he would continue in the traditions of his predecessors.

"Remembering the life and witness of his two predecessors, the World Council looks toward the new pope with open and sincere expectation," the statement said. "The WCC hopes for a continuation of the tradition of the Second Vatican Council, particularly the growing ecumenical cooperation and fellowship between the Roman Catholic Church and the member churches of the World Council."

Richard Maass, president of the American Jewish Committee, said: "In view of the magnitude of Jewish suffering in Poland during World War II, we look forward to the opportunity for creating a new chapter in relationships between the Catholic Church and the Jewish people, not only in Poland but throughout the entire world."

David Hyatt, president of the National Conference of Christians and Jews, called the pope "a most worthy successor" to John Paul I. "The fact that he is predominantly a pastor as well as a scholar will help him to heal some of the divisions within the church," he said.

"I applaud the fact that in today's world, it now appears that this tremendously powerful position can be held by persons of other nationalities and ethnic origins," Hyatt added.

Claire Randall, general secretary of the U.S. National Council of Churches, praised the pope's initial remarks on the universality of the church and said his selection "is a powerful symbol of that truth."

"His reputation as a 'worker's cardinal' and his choice of the name John Paul II have demonstrated that his primary intention is to be a pastor to all the people of God," she said. "It is our prayer that he will be significant for us all in helping to heal the painful divisions that separate Christians."

Prayers for the new pontiff came from Archbishop Iakovos, primate of the Greek Orthodox Archdiocese of North and South America. "We pray to Almighty God to protect, guide and inspire him in responding to his global responsibilities, which include the rebirth of the faith and the reassurance of all believers that Christianity, the religion of love, justice and peace, is ready to compassionately lean over the weak, the defenseless, the suffering, the poor and the victims of bigotry and social injustice," he said.

Rabbi Saul Teplitz, president of the Synagogue Council of America and the Rabbinical Assembly, said:

"As Jews, ours is the hope that he will continue the path set by his namesake with the determined desire that peace will be established in the Middle East as well as throughout the world.

"We are looking forward to ongoing cooperative efforts toward the enhancement of the human condition," he added.

The Rev. George Tuttle, moderator of the United Church of Canada, pledged his church's cooperation and support. "We rejoice that God has called you to serve the church at a time when the world needs strong and dynamic leadership," he said in a message to the pope. "We pray for the unity of the church so that the Gospel of Jesus Christ may be declared to all humanity in word and deed."

American Lutherans also sent their greetings and good wishes. A message on behalf of the Lutheran World Ministries, the Lutheran Church in America, the American Lutheran Church and the Association of Evangelical Lutheran Churches rejoiced that "a man of your gifts has become the chief pastor and shepherd of the church."

"We are especially pleased that you look forward to a day when we shall celebrate full communion," said the message signed by the Rev. James Crumley, president of Lutheran World Ministries, and Paul A. Wee, general secretary. "We join you in this hope and this task, asking the Lord of the church to bless you richly in his spirit."

Howard M. Squadron, president of the American Jewish Congress, praised the election of John Paul II as "a bold and historic step." He said that because of his background, the new pontiff "must understand and appreciate the struggle of the 3 million Jews of the Soviet Union who have faced even greater oppression because of their efforts to live as Jews and to become reunited with their families outside the Soviet Union."

"And we believe he will understand and support the efforts of Jews from around the world to make a new life for themselves in the ancient homeland of the Jewish people, the state of Israel," Squadron added. "We congratulate Pope John Paul II on his election and wish him well."

Archbishop Coggan sent the pope a telegram assuring him of the prayers of Anglicans throughout the world "for your ministry as supreme pastor of the Roman Catholics at this time of new beginnings."

Ecumenism was very much on the new pope's mind. On the day after his election, he told the College of Cardinals:

"The ecumenical cause is actually so great and delicate that we cannot now let it go unmentioned. How many times have we meditated together on the last will of Christ that asks the Father to give his disciples unity.

"And who does not recall the insistence of St. Paul on the 'communion of the spirit,' which leads one to be united in love with common purpose and a common mind in the imitation of Christ the Lord? It does not seem possible that there would still remain the drama of division among Christians — a cause of confusion and perhaps even scandal. We intend, therefore, to proceed along the way already begun, by favoring those steps which serve to remove obstacles. Hopefully, then, thanks to a common effort, we might arrive finally at full communion.''

The speech also contained the foundations for his caution against moving too quickly, a caution which he expressed about all aspects of church teachings.

"Venerable brothers, dear sons and daughters, it is obvious that fidelity also demands adherence to the teaching of Peter especially in the field of doctrine. The objective importance of the 'magisterium' should always be kept in mind and safeguarded,'' he said.

In their ecumenical activities, Catholics should be guided by the teachings of Vatican II, said the pope when he addressed the members of the Vatican Secretariat for Christian Unity Nov. 18, 1978.

The Catholic Church, "faithful to the orientation taken at the council, not only wants to continue to advance on the road that leads toward restoration of unity, but desires, as far as it can and in full docility to the suggestions of the Holy Spirit, to intensify at all levels its contribution to this great movement of all Christians,'' he said.

Ecumenism "does not stop, must not stop before reaching its goal,'' said the pope. Catholics "must strain forward to pursue our course with faith that knows no fear.''

In reaching the goal, Catholics should follow the caution of Vatican II to avoid "any superficiality, any imprudent zeal which might harm the progress toward unity,'' he said.

"An illness is not cured by administering pain-killers but by attacking its causes,'' he declared.

Vatican II teaches that the church is manifested principally in the assembly of its members for the celebration of the Eucharist presided over by the bishop assisted by the body of priests, he said.

"Even if such a solemn eucharistic celebration is rarely realized in our modern world, it remains nonetheless true that in each eucharistic celebration the entire faith of the church is put into operation,'' he said. "It is the ecclesial communion in all its dimensions that is manifested and realized. Its components cannot arbitrarily be disassociated. To act that way would be to give proof of that superficiality that the council asks us to avoid. It would mean not perceiving all the riches, requirements and close relations of the Eucharist and the unity of the church.''

"I know that the more we meet as brothers in the charity of Christ, the more it is painful to us not to be able to participate together in this great mystery,'' the pope said. "Have I not said that the divisions among Christians are becoming intolerable?''

"This suffering must stimulate us to overcome the obstacles that still separate us from the unanimous profession of the same faith, from reunification, through a same sacramental ministry, of our divided communities. We cannot dispense ourselves from resolving together these questions which have divided Christians. It would be a badly enlightened charity that would express itself at the expense of truth,'' he said.

On the eve of the Week of Prayer for Christian Unity in January, John Paul again addressed himself to ecumenism. Speaking at his regular Wednesday general audience, he said Christian unity involves every baptized person, not just church authorities.

He called ecumenism "this important theme which involves all baptized persons, pastors and faithful, each according to his own capacity, his own function and the place he occupies in the church.''

He called prayer a "privileged instrument for participation in the search for the unity of all Christians.'' He recalled that Jesus at the Last Supper prayed to the Father "that all might be one.''

"Prayer places us first of all before the Lord, purifies our intentions, our feelings, our heart, and produces that 'interior conversion,' without which there is no true ecumenism. Prayer then reminds us that unity, in the final analysis, is a gift of God, a gift for which we must ask and for which we must prepare ourselves so that it be given," he said.

The pope noted that the theme of this Christian unity week — "Serve One Another for the Glory of God" — was taken from the First Letter of St. Peter.

"The time in which we live is the eschatological time, that is, the time between the redemption carried out by Christ and his glorious return. Therefore we must live in active expectation," he added.

The theme "proposes to us to live together as much as possible the heritage common to Christians," he said. "Contacts, cooperation, mutual love, reciprocal service make us know one another better, make us rediscover what we have in common and make us see, too, how much there is still different between us. These contacts push us, too, to find the ways to overcome such differences."

John Paul briefly reviewed Catholic relations with other churches.

"With the Orthodox Church of the East the dialogue of charity has made us rediscover an almost full communion, even if yet imperfect. It is a reason for comfort to see that this new attitude of understanding is not limited only to the higher authorities of the churches but gradually penetrates into the local churches, because the change of relations on the local level is indispensable for any further progress," he said.

Noting that theological dialogue between the Roman Catholic Church and the Greek Orthodox Church was about to begin with the goal of eliminating obstacles to eucharistic concelebration and full unity, the pope asked for prayers for success.

He said dialogues also are in progress with Anglican, Lutheran, Methodist and Reformed churches. He said that "on subjects that in the past constituted profound divergences, consoling convergences have been found."

He referred to relations with the World Council of Churches and other Christian confessional and interconfessional organizations.

"The journey however is not finished and we must continue it to reach the goal. Let us, therefore, renew our prayer to the Lord, so that he may give to all Christians light and strength to do everything possible to attain as soon as possible full unity in truth," he said.

The pope led those in the audience hall in a brief prayer service for Christian unity.

John Paul summarized his position on ecumenism in his encyclical *Redemptor Hominis* which said:

"True ecumenical activity means openness, drawing closer, availability for dialogue, and a shared investigation of the truth in the full evangelical and Christian sense; but in no way does it or can it mean giving up or in any way diminishing the treasures of divine truth that the church has constantly confessed."

The encyclical also noted the criticisms of ecumenism within the Catholic Church:

"There are people who in the face of the difficulties or because they consider that the first ecumenical endeavors have brought negative results would have liked to turn back. Some even express the opinion that these efforts are harmful to the cause of the Gospel, are leading to a further rupture in the church, are causing confusion of ideas in questions of faith and morals and are ending up with a specific indifferentism."

To the criticism, the pope answered:

"To all who, for whatever motive, would wish to dissuade the church from seeking the universal unity of Christians the question must once again be put: Have we the right not to do it? Can we fail to have trust — in spite of human weakness and all the faults of past centuries — in our Lord's grace as revealed recently through what the Holy Spirit said and we heard during the council?"

The general principles guiding Catholic relations with other Christian churches also apply to relations with non-Christians "although in another way and with due differences," said the encyclical. This means "activity for coming closer together with the representatives of the non-Christian religions, an activity expressed through dialogue, contacts, prayer in common, investigations of the treasures of human spirituality, in which, as we know well, the members of these religions are not lacking."

In various religions "though the routes taken may be different, there is but a single goal to which is directed the deepest aspiration of the human spirit as expressed in its quest for God and also in its quest, through its tending toward God, for the full dimension of humanity, or in other words for the full meaning of human life."

Among non-Christian religions, the encyclical singles out Judaism and Islam as having special significance for Catholics:

"The council gave particular attention to the Jewish religion, recalling the great spiritual heritage common to Christians and Jews. It also expresses its esteem for the believers of Islam, whose faith also looks to Abraham."

During John Paul's first year in office, several reports were issued by consultative commissions of Catholics and other Christian religions. Although the commissions were set up under Pope Paul VI, the uninterrupted continuance of their work under the Polish pope was another sign of his commitment to carry forward the work of his predecessor.

The Anglican-Roman Catholic International Commission (ARCIC) reported "real convergence" on the highly divisive issues of papal primacy and infallibility at their meeting held in Venice, Italy, from Aug. 28 to Sept. 6, 1979.

This convergence, though it fell short of complete agreement, encouraged the commission to hope that it might be able to offer its final report to the authorities of the Anglican and Roman Catholic churches within two years, an ARCIC communique said.

The meeting, under the co-chairmanship of Anglican Archbishop Henry McAdoo of Dublin, Ireland, and Catholic Bishop Alan Clark of East Anglia, England, continued working on the problems connected with papal primacy that had been left unresolved at the conclusion of its 1976 agreed statement on authority.

The previous June, the commission published "elucidations" of its first two agreed statements, on the Eucharist and on ministry and ordination.

On Feb. 22, 1979, the General Synod of the Church of England, the mother church of world Anglicanism, endorsed a recommendation by ARCIC that the Vatican reappraise its decision that Anglican orders are null and void. The synod also approved ARCIC statements on the Eucharist, authority, ministry and ordination saying the statements were "significantly congruent with Anglican teaching to provide a basis for further dialogue."

The synod also asked for the establishment of a permanent Anglican-Roman Catholic commission as recommended in the 1968 Malta Report after formal dialogue between the two churches was established. The permanent commission should be representative of the entire membership of the churches and not just theologians as is ARCIC, said the synod.

The Vatican declaration that Anglican orders are null and void is contained in *Apostolicae Curae* ("Apostolic Priesthood"), a bull issued by Pope Leo XIII in 1896. The decision means that, according to the Vatican, the Anglican priesthood does not follow the apostolic succession established by Christ and the apostles.

The ARCIC statement asking for the reappraisal was published June 7, 1979. It said, regarding Anglican orders and mutual recognition of ministries, that a consensus had been formed placing these questions in a new context because of the agreements reached between Anglicans and Catholics on the essential eucharistic faith and the understanding of ministry and ordination.

John Paul took advantage of two trips outside Rome in September to speak out   **87** anew on ecumenism.

At the end of a day-long visit to the Marian Shrine at Loreto and the nearby Adriatic port of Ancona, the pope sent a greeting across the Adriatic "to the peoples of the nearby East." He said:

"**B**oth to the sons of the church and to separated brothers who live there, I want to point out 'in the body of Jesus Christ' the permanent ideal of ecclesial communion, hoping — as did so many of my predecessors, especially John XXIII and Paul VI in recent times — for the recomposition of the perfect unity among all who believe in Christ, and hastening in charity and prayer that truly happy day when this prayer will be fulfilled."

The next day, he visited the abbey at Grottaferrata, the only Byzantine-Rite monastery in Italy, and told the Basilian monks there:

"It is precisely because you represent this Greek monastic tradition that you ought to be distinguished by another quality, that of a special ecumenical sensitivity. By your position, by your formation, you can do much in this regard, committing yourself in dialogue and above all in prayer to the goal of promoting the hoped-for unity between Catholics and Orthodox."

The previous June, the pope told a delegation from the Pan-Orthodox Patriarchate of Constantinople that "it is God who provokes the desire for unity." The delegation, headed by Metropolitan Meliton of Chalcedon, was in Rome to join with the pope in marking the Feast of Sts. Peter and Paul. The visit returns the visit of a Catholic delegation to Ecumenical Orthodox Patriarch Dimitrios I of Constantinople each Nov. 30, the Feast of St. Andrew, chief patron of the Orthodox churches.

"The exchange of delegations between Rome and Constantinople on the occasion of these patron saints of our church is not merely a meeting which can become a habit," the pope said. The exchange "has a very rich significance that is full of hope. The apostolic faith, the deposit of which has been given to us, is the unshakable basis of all our contacts."

Reciprocal contacts at various levels, he said, "contribute to teaching us to live together in prayer, in consultation with a view toward common solutions to be given to problems facing the churches today, in mutual aid, in fraternal life." The pope praised the "depth of communion" already existing between the Catholic and Orthodox churches and hoped this would be furthered by the top-level theological dialogues occurring "to resolve the doctrinal and canonical difficulties which constitute, up to the present moment, an obstacle to full unity."

The previous December in the United States, the Eastern Orthodox-Roman Catholic Consultation, established to investigate matters of mutual concern, released a statement saying the two churches have a common understanding of the sacramental nature of marriage.

Christian tradition defines marriage as "the fundamental relationship in which a man and woman, by total sharing with each other, seek their own growth in holiness and that of their children, and thus show forth the presence on earth of God's kingdom," said the statement.

"Given this vision of reality, Christian tradition recognizes that the total devotion of the married partners implies as its goal a relationship with God. It teaches, moreover, that the love which liberates them to seek union with God and which is the source of sanctification for them, is made possible through the presence of the Spirit of God within them," it said.

Differences exist, notably on divorce, said the statement. "The Orthodox Church, out of consideration of the human realities, permits divorces, after it exhausts all possible efforts to save the marriage, and tolerates remarriages in order to avoid further human tragedies" while Catholicism "recognizes the dissolution of sacramental non-consummated marriages either through solemn religious profession or by papal dispensation."

Both churches teach that "sacramental marriage requires both the mutual consent of the believing Christian partners and God's blessing imparted through the ministry of the church," it added, but different understandings exist of the way the ministry is exercised.

The Orthodox recognize only those marriages blessed by an Orthodox priest, it said. "The Catholic Church accepts as sacramental the marriages which are celebrated before a Catholic priest or even a deacon, but it also envisions some exceptional cases in which, by reason of a dispensation or the unavailability of a priest or deacon, Catholics may enter into a sacramental marriage in the absence of an ordained minister of the Church."

During the first 12 months of John Paul's pontificate other joint statements were issued on ecumenical relations. They included statements with Lutherans, Methodists, Baptists and Disciples of Christ.

Only a few days after John Paul's election — on Oct. 24 — Catholic and Lutheran theologians from the United States issued a document on papal infallibility which concluded that ultimately, Christians trust in Christ, not in scriptural, ecclesiastical or papal infallibility. Differences remain between the Catholic and Lutheran understanding of papal infallibility, the theologians said, but "need not, of themselves, preclude a closer union than now exists between the two churches."

"Catholics look upon the papacy, in view of its high responsibilities and the promises given to Peter, as especially assisted by the Holy Spirit. Lutherans think Catholics have overconfidently identified the focus of the work of the Spirit with a particular person or office," added the 9,000-word document.

In December 1978 nine Catholic and nine Disciples of Christ theologians met in Rome to form the International Commission for Dialogue between the Disciples of Christ and Roman Catholic Church. After the meeting the group issued a press release saying the sharp divergence in practice between the two churches "was considerably mitigated during this meeting in Rome by the amount of common understanding on the necessity and significance of baptism."

On Feb. 12, 1979, the joint International Catholic-Methodist Commission issued a statement saying the two churches are more united than divided in their understanding of the Holy Spirit. The commission met in Rome and said it hoped to formulate a more complete document on faith in the Holy Spirit by 1981.

"The doctrine of the Holy Spirit has never been a point of division between us and our discussions have shown that traditional stresses and differentiated forms of expression are complementary and mutually enriching, rather than a cause of division and dissent," said the statement.

The statements by these joint commissions do not automatically bind authorities of the churches involved to accept them. However, the high level of scholarship and the expertise of the theologians involved make it difficult to ignore the findings in future relationships among the churches. In the case of the Catholic Church, the statements must eventually be approved by the pope.

John Paul also spoke out strongly against anti-Semitism, declaring at a meeting March 12 with representatives of world Judaism:

"I believe that both sides must continue their strong efforts to overcome the difficulties of the past, so as to fulfill God's commandment of love and to sustain a truly fruitful and fraternal dialogue that contributes to the good of each of the partners involved and to our better service of humanity."

The Homecoming

When John Paul went home to Poland, the visit became a movable feast. Wherever he went, he was followed by crowds so large it was impossible to reliably estimate their numbers. People stood for hours with no sign of complaint. They prayed. They sang. They burst into vigorous applause at the slightest opportunity. One of their own had come home. The "son of Poland" had returned.

The return had not come without difficulty. The pope had wanted to make the visit in May, to coincide with the 900th anniversary of the death of St. Stanislaus, who was executed by King Boleslaw the Bold for opposing royal policies, and who has stood in Polish history ever since as a symbol of church resistance to oppression. The communist government saw too many political implications in that. John Paul could be cast in the role of the modern defender of the people against currently unpopular policies. The word was passed to the Vatican: May is out, but June would be acceptable.

John Paul agreed to June, expressed regret that he could not get home in May, and then — to the great chagrin of the Polish government — announced that by papal decree he was extending the celebration of the St. Stanislaus anniversary long enough to cover the dates of his June visit. Moving to Rome had not lessened the political ingenuity he had shown so many times in his years of dealing with his country's government.

The world watched with curiosity and interest. The intense media coverage John Paul had received had made him a familiar figure. His unique, freewheeling style had made him a popular figure. Now he was going home, back to the communist-ruled country from which he had come, the first pope to make such a visit. What would he say? What would he do?

John Paul's trip began June 2 and ended June 10. It was a religious pilgrimage marked by Masses, a lengthy visit to the Shrine of Our Lady of Czestochowa and a speech to the Polish bishops. It was also a political mission. The pope defended religious liberty in a state which officially advocates atheism. He criticized farm policies. He challenged the state to strengthen family life. Yet he couched it all in careful and diplomatic terms, and he pledged to work for church-state cooperation rather than antagonism.

The political implications of his trip were clear to John Paul, and as he did during his Latin American voyage, he quickly stressed that his purpose was to communicate with concrete people and not get involved in ideological battles. On the plane taking him to Poland he discussed his feelings at an impromptu press conference.

"There is but one Poland," he said. "I think all these differences — capitalism, communism — are differences from above. Below, however, are the people, and this is the human reality, a primordial reality."

The visit started simply enough. The pope descended the plane at Okecie Airport near Warsaw, the capital, and kissed the ground as he set foot once again on his native soil.

As he descended the steps from the plane, a 50-member military band broke into the national anthem.

The pope inspected representatives of the Polish military forces, standing stiffly erect in the 90 degree heat, then shook hands with government officials and diplomats. Finally he greeted more than three dozen waiting bishops, warmly embracing many of them.

John Paul stressed that "my visit has been dictated by strictly religious motives" and said he hoped that it would "serve the great cause of rapprochement and of collaboration among nations."

At the same time he expressed hope that his visit would aid the "development of the relations between the state and the church."

Hundreds of thousands cheered the pope as he rode triumphantly into Warsaw. All along the motorcade route into the city white-and-yellow papal flags hung side-by-side with the Polish red and white from almost every apartment that was within sight of the papal vehicle.

The motorcade came to a halt at St. John's Cathedral. The pope made a brief stop at the Shrine of the Merciful Mother of God, patroness of Warsaw, and went to the residence of Cardinal Stefan Wyszynski, primate of Poland, for lunch.

At 2 p.m. John Paul visited Poland's top government officials.

The first secretary of the Polish Communist Party, Edward Gierek, greeted the pope warmly. "We are glad to play host to Your Holiness in the land of our fathers," he said. "At the same time I, personally, am truly glad to meet Your Holiness."

A few minutes after 4 p.m., the pope and Cardinal Wyszynski stopped to pray silently for several minutes at the Polish Tomb of the Unknown Soldier lit by an eternal flame in Warsaw's Victory Square. Then they walked across the square and the pope began Mass at a large white altar beneath a monumental 50-foot cross erected for the occasion.

The pope's homily turned out to be the keynote address of his visit. It is "impossible without Christ to understand the history of the Polish nation," he said.

Standing before a crowd of at least 170,000 Poles in Warsaw's Victory Square, the pope hurled the basic challenge of the Catholic Church to efforts by the communist government to make the country atheistic. His voice and image were also carried live on national television.

In trying to view Poland without Christ and Christianity, John Paul said, "we lay ourselves open to a substantial misunderstanding. We no longer understand ourselves." He interpreted his own election as pope as a call to Poland to become "the land of a particularly responsible witness" to Christ and the church.

The homily was perhaps the most impassioned public talk delivered by John Paul since his election. At times his rich, trained voice gradually swelled to a crescendo to emphasize a point. At other times it dropped to an almost inaudible whisper and the crowd strained to hear as he softly caressed the words.

Behind the altar was the colossal cross, a steel-pipe frame structure completely encased in wood, which Warsaw residents had erected two days earlier. Draped across the arms of the cross and hanging to about 10 feet from the ground was a 70-foot to 80-foot stole of crimson cloth simply marked with gold crosses at each end.

The pope's first Mass during his homecoming ended with more than 100,000 voices singing "God Bless Poland."

On the following day, speaking at a Mass in Gniezno, Poland's primatial See, he declared himself an apostle of and to the Slavs. He expressed a conviction that God has called him, as pope, to play a particularly important role in the unity of Christians in Eastern and Western Europe.

"Is it not Christ's will, is it not what the Holy Spirit disposes, that this pope...should in a special way manifest and confirm in our age the presence of these (Slavic) peoples in the church and their specific contribution to the history of Christianity?" John Paul asked.

"Is it not Christ's will, is it not what the Holy Spirit disposes, that this Polish pope, this Slav pope, should at this precise moment manifest the spiritual unity of Christian Europe?" he added.

"Although there are two great traditions — that of the West and that of the East — to which it is indebted, through both of them Christian Europe professes 'one faith, one baptism, one God and Father of all,'" he said.

John Paul's remarks had to be considered carefully to be fully understood. He was referring to the fact that while Western European countries are all non-Slavic, the Eastern European communist-run countries of the Warsaw Pact are predominantly Slavic. And throughout Eastern Europe, the Catholic Church faces severe restrictions at best, and harsh persecution is not uncommon. The "son of Poland" was truly at home. His public utterances took on the indirectness in which criticism and challenge must be voiced.

On June 4, John Paul made a pilgrimage to Poland's most famous Marian shrine and consecrated himself and the Catholic Church around the world to Mary.

The occasion was his visit to the Monastery of Jasna Gora (Hill of Light), which houses the world-famous Shrine to Our Lady of Czestochowa. Located outside the city of Czestochowa, the centuries-old "black Madonna" icon draws hundreds of thousands of Polish pilgrims every year. Our Lady of Czestochowa is the queen and patroness of Poland.

The midday papal Mass drew hundreds of thousands of visitors. Estimates ran from 500,000 to 1 million. It also caused the first public outburst in the always fragile and tense relations between Poland's Catholic Church and the communist government.

At one point in the Mass, one of the Pauline Fathers, who run the monastery, called over the loudspeakers for silence in the crowds further down the hill who were trying to get closer.

"You represent thousands of people who were stopped around Czestochowa under the faked reason of needing invitations, despite the promise of free access to Czestochowa, given to the bishop of Czestochowa, for all believers," the announcer said. "Thousands of them are kept outside the city. So you represent them and pray for them."

As they did elsewhere before and after that day's incident, police had blockaded certain traffic routes well before the pope's arrival and kept them blocked until the pope had passed. But police denied they did anything else to prevent visitors from reaching the monastery and no clear evidence of obstructive activity was immediately available.

A spokesman for Interpress, the government news agency, said the agency made an independent check of the charges and considered them unfounded.

Despite the incident, the Mass was a joyful time for the pope.

In his homily, he sang the praises of the Madonna of Czestochowa, to whom he has long had a special devotion.

"The Poles are accustomed to link with this place, this shrine, the many happenings of their lives: the various joyful or sad moments, especially the solemn, decisive moments, the occasions of responsibility, such as the choice of the direction for one's life, the choice of one's vocation, the birth of one's children, the final school examinations, and so many other occasions," he said.

He called the power of the shrine a mystery, "an inward bond in Polish life, a force that touches the depths of our hearts and holds the entire nation in the humble, yet strong attitude of fidelity to God, to the church and to her hierarchy."

John Paul departed from his prepared text many times. In one departure, as he used the word "brother," he began to look along the lines of the Polish bishops concelebrating the Mass with him. His voice trailed off and he moved away from the microphone, struggling to regain his composure. He moved as if to resume speaking several times, but each time he stopped and looked away from the microphone again. Finally, the stillness was broken by a few voices — then many — singing "God Bless Poland." The difficult moment was over. He smiled and continued his talk.

"Brothers, brothers," he said, and spoke of the many faces he recognized. He started citing other countries also represented among the assembled prelates, with the crowd applauding for each one.

At one point the crowd began singing *"Sto-Lat,"* a Polish song wishing a person 100 years of life. He turned to 78-year-old Cardinal Wyszynski, primate of Poland for three decades, and praised him as the driving force behind the Polish church. As he wished the cardinal a "long, long life," the worshippers broke into another *"Sto-Lat"* for their primate.

The pope continued ad-libbing for a full 20 minutes. He ended jokingly, "Again the pope speaks too long. Again they will cry at me, 'What can you do with this Slavic pope? What can you do with him?'"

If the political sensitivity of the pope's words and actions had not yet become clear to anyone, the events of the following day would make it apparent.

John Paul addressed the 169th general assembly of the Polish Bishops Conference, speaking at a closed session in Jasna Gora which began at 10 a.m. Although it had been expected that Vatican press officials would routinely distribute copies of the papal text — which had been prepared for the press in five languages — they refused, without explanation, to do so. It was six hours later before the text was finally made available. Obviously, sensitivity to the political situation caused the delay. But who ordered it? It never became clear. The Vatican said the Polish bishops asked that the text be held until they had a chance to study it. The press secretary for the Polish bishops said it was the Vatican which wanted it held.

The speech was subtle but challenging.

John Paul told the Polish bishops that they must work for "fundamental human rights, including the right to religious liberty" as a means of attaining normalization of church-state relations. He also warned them that "obviously, the episcopal ministry has sometimes exposed bishops to the peril of losing their lives and thus of paying the price of proclaiming the truth and the divine law."

He cited the life of St. Stanislaus as an example of "how deeply the moral order penetrates...in the structures and levels of the life of the nation as a state, in the structures and levels of political life."

That reference and others to St. Stanislaus were the sort that Polish censors regularly delete from Catholic newspapers. Such references immediately conjur up particular images in Polish minds. Because the saint opposed the king's political policies, the king had the saint murdered. But after murdering the saint, the king was toppled from the throne and lived the remainder of his life as a penitent in exile.

"St. Stanislaus is the expression, symbol and patron of (the moral) order. Given that the moral order is the basis of all culture, the national tradition rightly sees St. Stanislaus' place at the basis of Polish culture" John Paul said.

"The Polish episcopate must add to its present mission and ministry a particular solicitude for the whole Polish cultural heritage, of which we know to what degree it is permeated by the light of Christianity," he added. "It is well known that it is precisely culture that is the fundamental proof of the nation's identity."

The effort to normalize church-state relations, the pope said, "constitutes a practical proof" of state recognition of religious liberty and other rights. "Thought of in this way, normalization is also a practical manifestation of the fact that the state understands its mission to society according to the principle of subsidiarity, namely that it wishes to express the full sovereignty of the nation."

St. Stanislaus' life showed how "both subjects and rulers" are bound by the moral law, John Paul said. "Only when we begin from this law, namely the moral law, can the dignity of the human person be respected and universally recognized," he added. "Therefore, morality and law are the fundamental conditions for social order. Upon the law are built states and nations, and without it they perish."

In the most specific part of his speech, the pope said the Polish bishops always point out "threats of a moral nature" faced by the people today. Among these he cited the "grave sin against nascent life" — a clear reference to Polish laws allowing abortion — and "the sins of immorality and abuse," as Poland suffers a high rate of alcoholism.

Regarding normalization of church-state relations, the pope gave clear backing to the Vatican policies of detente with Eastern European governments started by Pope Paul VI. Moving beyond strictly Polish issues, the pope spoke of Christianity as the cement for future European unity.

"Europe, which during its history has been several times divided, Europe, which toward the end of the first half of the present century was tragically divided by the horrible world war. Europe, which despite its present and long-lasting divisions of regimes, ideologies and economical and political systems, cannot cease to seek its fundamental unity, must turn to Christianity," the pope said. "Christianity must commit itself anew to the formation of the spiritual unity of Europe," he added. "Economic and political reasons alone cannot do it. We must go deeper: to ethical reasons."

But the entire day was not given to solemn pronouncements. John Paul was also a country pastor, visibly at ease and enjoying himself as he continued to thrill large crowds and special groups with his relaxed manner and his straying from prepared texts.

At an early morning Mass for nuns at the Shrine of Our Lady of Czestochowa, he called the theme of religious vocations "one of the most beautiful of which the Gospel has spoken."

Toward the end of a busy day during which he spoke frequently of the importance of the family, John Paul told a huge crowd that the family is "the first and basic human community" and declared that "everything possible has to be done" to sustain and protect it.

"How ardently I desire, I who owe my life, my faith, my language to a Polish family, that the family should never cease to be strong with the strength of God," he said.

He expanded on the family theme the next day and related it to economic policy when he greeted more than 300,000 workers from Upper Silesia and Dabrowskie Zaglebie, Poland's chief mining region.

The workers repeatedly cheered the pope as he spoke of the rights of workers and the value of work understood as a service to man rather than a dominating force. His words were an obvious challenge to the state-controlled economy and at one point he commented: "I am going to get into trouble for saying these things." That drew more cheers and prolonged applause.

Later that day, Stefan Staniszewski, spokesman for the Polish foreign ministry, said he was "surprised" at the extent of the pope's political remarks. "I did not expect so much," he said. He also complained that the foreign press was exaggerating the size of the crowds who gathered to see and hear the pope.

John Paul's speech to the workers marked the end of his three-day stay in Czestochowa. In the evening he returned to his native Archdiocese of Cracow and the homecoming was tumultuous. More than a million people turned out to welcome him.

Although late afternoon rains threatened to dampen the festivities, the rain stopped well before his 8 p.m. arrival and served to end the oppressive heat that baked the city earlier in the day.

Throughout the city, but especially along the papal motorcade routes, buildings and streets were decorated with flags, streamers, banners and saints' pictures. In a clear sign of the almost universal enthusiasm of Cracow residents, tenants of whole apartment buildings banded together to turn the faces of their buildings into integrated designs — six to 10 stories high and as many as eight windows wide — welcoming the pope.

The favorite designs were huge crosses in yellow or yellow and white — the papal colors — stretching from roof to ground and made of long bolts of cloth sewn together. Some buildings had individual balconies draped with large blue or yellow squares forming a cross.

Others turned their building facade into a huge blue "M" for Mary, similar to the design on the papal coat of arms. Hundreds of thousands cheered the pope as his helicopter landed in a large square near the center of Cracow.

That day, June 7, was a day of smiles and sorrow for John Paul. First he visited his birthplace of Wadowice and engaged in joyous reminiscing. Then he traveled to the sites of two Nazi concentration camps during World War II and with this as a backdrop, issued a somber denunciation of war and hatred.

In Wadowice, near Cracow, a huge crowd packed the large marketplace in front of the church where the pope was baptized 59 years earlier.

The crowd clapped, cheered and sang as John Paul stood on a platform in front of the church and recalled his childhood years. He had a prepared text, but he scarcely referred to it, speaking most of the time extemporaneously.

"When I look about this marketplace," he said, glancing at the house which had been his home "almost every detail is linked with the early details of my life."

"In my heart and mind I go back, not only to the house over there and the church here, but also to the primary school here in the marketplace — in that building over there — in that building that also housed the municipal authorities at the time."

He also recalled "the Wadowice secondary school, dedicated to Marcin Wadowita, that I went to." In those days, he said, it was the only secondary school in the region, and his classmates included many friends from neigboring towns.

"Now there are many more schools," he said.

He recalled many of those who lived in the town when he was a youth and have since died, mentioning especially his father, mother, brother and his sister. His sister died before he was born.

"On the human level," he said, "I want to express my feelings of deep gratitude to Msgr. Edward Zacher, who was my religion teacher in the Wadowice secondary school, who later gave the talk at my first Mass and at my first celebrations as bishop, archbishop and cardinal here in Wadowice — and that was not enough for him!"

The crowd had roared and cheered a few minutes earlier when the elderly Msgr. Zacher introduced the pope. John Paul thanked all those who had known him and helped him during the 18 years in which he was growing up in the town. He had special thanks for his schoolmates, saying that the influence of one's peers is one of the greatest influences on growing up.

He also thanked those in the town who "gave me better testimony than I really deserved" during the "onslaught of journalists" who rushed to the town for interviews after he was elected pope.

John Paul said he would like to talk about other memories "but we would have to go into details, and there are so many journalists out there."

In what seemed a reference to the many rumors, especially in Italian journals, about girlfriends in the life of Karol Wojtyla before he entered the seminary, the pope commented jokingly that what he had just said "will have many conjectures."

A moment later, as if apologizing for his comments on journalism, he said he was glad for the residents of Wadowice that so many reporters were present. "I am very grateful for that, because they will write about you all over the world. It is my fault that they will write about you — and I am glad they will write about you!"

Several times the pope asked the townspeople to pray daily for him before Our Lady of Perpetual Help in the church. He recalled that as a youth he and other students customarily stopped to pray to the Madonna every day before and after school.

"I don't know if that custom still goes on," he said.

During the visit John Paul solemnly kissed and prayed at the baptismal font at which he was baptized on June 20, 1920. He had lunch in the parish rectory before leaving one of the most pleasant and most joyful of his Polish stops to go on to one of the most solemn. His next stop was Auschwitz and Birkenau, where 4 million persons, mostly Jews and Poles, were killed by the Nazis during World War II.

John Paul used the death camp visit to bitterly denounce war, violations of national sovereignty and violations of individual rights in a solemn homily before a million people.

The pope first prayed privately at the death cell at Auschwitz of Blessed Maximilian Kolbe, a Polish Franciscan priest who offered his own life in place of another man marked for extermination.

Then the pope went by helicopter the short distance from Auschwitz to Birkenau, also known as Auschwitz II, where he concelebrated Mass with a large number of Polish priests who survived the concentration camps. One of those receiving Communion from the pope was Franciszek Gajowniczek, the man whose life was saved by Father Kolbe.

A throng estimated by some at more than a million stretched out over the flat fields that were once the prison camp. Rows of brick chimneys, the only remains of demolished detention buildings, stuck up starkly above the crowd. The high double rows of barbed-wire fences around the compound, a few of the original buildings, and the tall wooden guard towers around the perimeter also remained as reminders of the slavery, torture and death that occurred there.

John Paul began his homily by recalling the "victory through faith and love" over death and cruelty symbolized by Father Kolbe's sacrifice.

In an hour-long talk, John Paul spoke slowly, softly, stopping for long pauses to let his words sink in.

Blessed Maximilian's victory of faith was won in a place "which was built for the negation of faith — faith in God and faith in man — and to trample radically not only on love but on all signs of human dignity, of humanity," he said.

It is "a place built on hatred and on contempt for man in the name of a crazed ideology, a place built on cruelty," he added.

In view of the horrors and victories of the death camps, he asked if it can "still be a surprise to anyone" that a Polish-born pope should have dedicated his first encyclical "to the cause of man, to the dignity of man, to the threats to him, and finally to his inalienable rights that can so easily be trampled on and annihilated by his fellowmen."

"Is it enough to put man in a different uniform, arm him with the apparatus of violence? Is it enough to impose on him an ideology in which human rights are subjected to the demands of the system, completely subjected to them, so as in practice not to exist at all?"

His words, which drew sustained applause, were interpreted by many as directed chiefly at communist ideology and the communist system.

The pope mentioned the nationalities of those who died in Auschwitz and Birkenau by reading the languages of memorial inscriptions: Polish, English, Bulgarian, Romany, Czech, Danish, French, Greek, Hebrew, Yiddish, Spanish, Flemish, Serbo-Croat, German, Norwegian, Russian, Romanian, Hungarian and Italian.

96

John Paul particularly noted the inscription in Hebrew.

"The very people that received from God the commandment 'Thou shalt not kill' itself experienced in a special measure what is meant by killing. It is not permissible for anyone to pass by this inscription with indifference," he said.

Departing from his prepared text, the pope added mention of the Russian inscription.

"We know about what people it speaks. We know what the share of that people was in that war — a war for the freedom of peoples," the pope said in what observers took to be a note of strong irony. "We cannot pass by it with indifference."

Of the Polish inscription he said: "Six million Poles lost their lives during the Second World War: a fifth of the nation. Yet another stage in the centuries-old fight of this nation, my nation, for its fundamental rights among the peoples of Europe. Yet another loud cry for the right to a place of its own on the map of Europe. Yet another painful reckoning with the conscience of mankind, of modern times."

John Paul called Auschwitz a witness to "how far hatred can go, how far man's destruction of man can go, how far cruelty can go." Auschwitz is "a testimony of war."

"War brings with it a disproportionate growth of hatred, destruction and cruelty. It cannot be denied that it also manifests new capabilities of human courage, heroism and patriotism, but the fact remains that it is the reckoning of losses that prevail," he said.

The pope also spent part of June 7 at the Marian Shrine of Kalwaria Zebrzydowska in Cracow. He recalled how he used to visit the shrine often to pray when he was bishop of Cracow.

On June 8, the pope renewed the criticism of Poland's economic policies he had begun two days earlier in his talk to miners. This time he issued a thundering denunciation of agricultural collectivization and forced industrialization.

"This is the great and fundamental right of man: the right to work and the right to land," he said in a homily before 500,000 persons at Nowy Targ.

"Although economic development may take us in another direction, although one may value progress based upon industrialization, although the generation of today may leave en masse the land and agricultural work, still the right to the land does not cease to form the foundation of a sound economy and sociology," he added.

In Cracow that evening, John Paul met with 60,000 university students and members of youth groups, among them many he had come to know well in his years of active involvement in student life while he was archbishop of Cracow. He laughed and joked with the students and urged them to develop strong spiritual lives.

On June 9, the day before his departure from Poland, John Paul visited the Shrine to the Cross in Mogila, just outside the new city of Nowa Huta. Two years before, he had dedicated a massive new church after years of struggle with communist authorities to get a building permit. He had wanted to visit the Nowa Huta church, but permission was refused by the government. Creative once again, John Paul made his point by forging a verbal link between the relic of the cross at Mogila with the cross raised over the Nowa Huta church, and called the new cross a sign of a new evangelization in Poland's second millenium.

John Paul also expressed the hope that many more new churches would be built, especially in new population centers. This was a direct challenge to state authorities who have planned entire new cities without churches and who have refused church-building permits or delayed them for years.

John Paul told the crowd of more than 100,000 people that since the Nowa Huta church permit, the Polish government has granted permits for the building of several other new churches. "The efforts of many years are slowly bearing fruit," he said.

The climax of the papal trip came on June 10 at a huge, outdoor farewell Mass held on the city common of Cracow. A record-breaking crowd of about 2 million people packed the huge field. Thousands of Poles from other parts of the country slept outside the night before in order to be there. Tens of thousands from towns and villages near Cracow began hiking toward the city at dawn to get to the 10 a.m. Mass.

As John Paul traveled by open truck to the Mass site, crowds lined the three-quarter-mile route and were 15 to 20 people deep at some points. After he passed, they thronged en masse to the field, though by that time it was almost impossible to get closer than about a quarter of a mile from the altar.

"Be strong with the strength of faith," and never lose "your spiritual freedom" John Paul said in his homily, the final major talk of his visit.

Poland's Christian tradition "is not a limiting factor but a treasure of spiritual enrichment," he said.

"Can one cast this off? Can one say no? Can one refuse Christ and all that he has brought into human history?"

"Certainly not.

"It is true that man is free. But the basic question remains: Is it licit to do this? In whose name is it licit? By virtue of what rational argument, what value close to one's will and heart would it be possible to stand before yourself, your neighbor, your fellow citizens, your country, in order to cast off, to say no to all that we have seen for 1,000 years? To all that has created and always constituted the basis of our identity?"

The words were clearly aimed at the Polish government, which John Paul had repeatedly challenged for its efforts to make religion irrelevant and its practice difficult.

With a strong faith and love based on faith, Poles can engage in a "great dialogue with man and the world" for the work of peace and reconciliation. "There is therefore no need for fear," he said. "We must open the frontiers. There is no imperialism in the church, only service."

At 3:30 that afternoon, John Paul stood at the window of his former residence as archbishop of Cracow and said farewell to his countrymen.

"The time has come for me to go," he said. "You must now come to visit me in Rome."

As the cheers swelled, he left the second-story window and descended the stairs to a special van waiting to take him to the airport.

The movable feast set off by the homecoming of this "son of Poland" had followed in the wake of John Paul for nine days from Warsaw, to Gniezno, to Czestochowa, to Cracow. Now it moved along the 20 miles from Cracow to the Balice Airport.

The white line in the middle of the road was covered with flowers for the entire route. Crowds were five and six rows deep on both sides of the street throughout the city. Windows overlooking the motorcade route were jammed. The hillsides of parks were jammed with people. Bridges under which the pope passed were thronged to the point of apparent danger.

The people sang. They cheered. They waved papal banners. They threw flowers. But most of all they wept. Their pope was going back to Rome. Some were sure they would never see him again.

At the airport John Paul repeated his arrival gesture and knelt and kissed his native soil. He mounted the steps to the airplane and waved goodbye. As he prepared to enter the plane for his 5:45 p.m. flight to Rome, the small crowd invited to witness the departure began to sing *"Goralu Czy Ci Me Zai,"* a Polish mountaineers' lament for emigrants. Its words ask: "Mountain man, why are you leaving home? Why are you leaving the mountains of Tatra? Aren't you sorry to go?"

A sign strung over the road near the airport read: "You remain in our hearts."

16670

On the preceding pages:

1 At the Auschwitz prison camp, the pope places flowers and prays for the people who were killed there during World War II.

2 The faithful hold wooden crosses aloft to be blessed by the pope during a Mass for young people at St. Ann's Church in Warsaw's Old Town.

3 The pope's motorcade through the industrial town of Nowa Huta near Cracow.

4 The flag of St. Mary flies over the crowd of pilgrims at Jasna Gora Monastery near Czestochowa on the first day of the pope's visit.

5 A thoughtful Pope John Paul sits beneath a huge painting of Our Lady of Czestochowa during a ceremony at the Skalka church in Cracow.

6 At Warsaw's Victory Square, the pope waves good-bye to the people who had been moved back to clear the way for the helicopter that would carry him to Gniezno.

7 Barbed wire on a bare cross provides the backdrop as the pope blesses the crowd who had come to see him at Auschwitz.

8 As a greeting to the pope, flowers line the railway tracks at Birkenau (Auschwitz II), the former Nazi concentration camp in Southern Poland.

The Church
and the State

With the first rays of sunlight streaming through the trees, John Paul gathered in the Vatican gardens early on the morning of July 2 for Mass with Cardinal Agostino Casaroli and a small group of the cardinal's relatives and friends. During the homily, the pope referred to Cardinal Casaroli as "my primary collaborator," and declared:

"For me this is a moment of particular joy which gives me the opportunity to show my feelings of affection and lively appreciation to a man who, after long years of generous dedication in total service to the Holy See and the pope, now dons the important and grave responsibility of secretary of state."

Thus did the 65-year-old Casaroli assume the key position in the Vatican Curia, the church's central administration. For more than a decade, the cardinal, as secretary of the Council for the Public Affairs of the Church, had been a key troubleshooter for the Vatican on delicate church-state matters and the chief instrument of the Vatican's policy of delicate relations with communist governments.

The appointment indicated the stress the new pope places on the papacy's role in world affairs.

He already had shown himself ready to speak out on controversial issues, having stepped into the debate over Italy's liberal abortion law, criticized the economic policies of the Polish government and agreed to mediate a border dispute between Argentina and Chile. His trips abroad had given him platforms for discussing specific issues such as lack of religious freedom in Poland and migrant labor problems along the Mexico-United States border.

Before his pontificate was a year old, John Paul had met with top world leaders such as U.N. Secretary General Kurt Waldheim, U.S. Secretary of State Cyrus Vance, Soviet Foreign Minister Andrei Gromyko and West German Chancellor Helmut Schmidt.

Repeatedly he spelled out his stance: The church will defend moral issues and speak out, giving guidelines for human action; it has no desire to interfere in merely temporal affairs.

"Just as the church cannot be contained within the categories of earthly order, so our responsibility in approaching these burning questions of men and of nations shall be determined only by religious and moral motivation," he told the College of Cardinals on the day after his election.

In his encyclical, *Redemptor Hominis*, he outlined church opposition to totalitarianism and, in the process, gave his definition of what constitutes the role of a state.

"The essential sense of the state, as a political community, consists in that society and people composing it are master and sovereign of their own destiny. This sense remains unrealized if, instead of the exercise of power with the moral participation of society or people, what we see is the imposition of power by a certain group upon all the other members of society," he said.

The boundaries between the church's authority and the authority of the state have been a gray area throughout history. While John Paul did not clearly delineate the powers and responsibilities of each, he did give some rules of thumb. He told the Italian bishops in January 1979 that the church's "sacred right" to teach the Gospel must be respected by the state. Later that month, in Mexico, he warned priests against letting their preaching of the social implications of the Gospel spill over into involvement in partisan politics and the advocacy of political ideologies.

With these as guidelines, the pope had the task of overseeing a universal church, but one which exists in a number of countries under a number of different political systems and political ideologies. His trips during the first 12 months showed this diversity. He visited the heavily Catholic Dominican Republic where Catholicism is the state religion; Mexico, where the population is heavily Catholic, but where the laws are heavily anti-clerical; Poland, where the state officially espouses atheism; the United States, where religious freedom is enshrined in the Constitution and religious pluralism is an ingrained feature of daily life.

Initially, there was much interest in what the first pope from a communist country would do regarding the policy of detente with Eastern Europe started by Pope Paul VI. The Polish pope quickly established his position and clear intention to continue the detente policy with communist governments. The Catholic Church "does not seek to obtain privileges" but needs "vital space" for its mission, he told Bulgarian Foreign Minister Petar Mladenov at the Vatican on Dec. 13, 1978.

The church and communist governments need to work together on common causes, especially involving cultural development, John Paul said. He praised Bulgarian Catholics for remaining faithful to their church and for being exemplary citizens by making "their effective contribution to the development of the nation to which they are proud to belong." However, he asked Bulgaria to be more tolerant of religion and to respect the role of Christianity in shaping national culture.

On Jan. 24, 1979, the day before he left for Latin America, the pope met with Soviet Foreign Minister Andrei Gromyko. The one-hour-and-45-minute meeting was the longest the pope had granted to a government official until that time.

John Paul and Gromyko discussed "peace, peaceful coexistence and international cooperation," according to a brief report by the Vatican Press Office. "They also touched on problems related to the life of the Catholic Church in the Soviet Union."

About 8.5 million Catholics live in the Soviet Union where religious worship is officially discouraged. About 5 million of the total Catholics are Latin-Rite Catholics living in the once-independent Baltic republics of Lithuania, Latvia and Estonia. Another 1.5 million are Ukranians.

Catholics, especially Lithuanians, have repeatedly complained of persecution by government officials. Clandestine Lithuanian mimeographed publications smuggled out of the Soviet Union constantly accuse government officials of violating religious freedom. The publications say violations include discrimination against Catholics in jobs, limits on the number of students who can apply for seminary studies, infiltration of paid informers among the seminarians, refusal of church-building permits and spying on clergy and laity. Active Christians also face arbitrary arrest and trial.

Most likely, the papal meeting with Gromyko also involved the situation in the Eastern European countries, where the Soviet Union is the dominant political force. After the private meeting with Gromyko, the two men were joined by other high-level Soviet officials including Anatoli Kovaliev, vice minister of foreign affairs; Vassili Makarov, cabinet chief of the foreign affairs ministry; and Anatoli Adamiscin, director general of the East European section of the Soviet foreign affairs ministry.

The roots of current church efforts to establish and maintain contacts with communist governments go back to the time of Pope John XXIII. Contacts between Vatican and communist government officials have continually increased over the years. Gromyko's meeting in January was his sixth with a pope. However, important problems still remained to be resolved as the Polish pope settled into the Chair of Peter. A main issue is government permission in several countries to name bishops to fill vacant dioceses.

John Paul faced a different church-state situation in Italy, where the winds of religious freedom have blown in the direction of religious pluralism in the legal system. Both the Vatican and Italian officials have seen the need to redefine the situation under which Catholicism, as the state religion, has enjoyed a privileged position.

When John Paul took office, work on revising the Concordat, the international treaty between Italy and the Vatican, had been under way for 11 years. In February 1979 he urged prayers "so that the hoped for revision of the Concordat may soon be brought to a happy completion, as I hope, and as Paul VI and John Paul I ardently desired."

The Concordat was signed in 1929 when Italy was under Fascist rule, and was incorporated into the 1947 Italian Constitution. A draft of the revision, agreed to by the Vatican, would no longer establish Catholicism as the state religion and reduce some of the legal privileges of the church and church people. Priests and Religious would no longer be automatically exempt from military service, but would have to request such exemption. The weekly hour of religious instruction in state schools would be retained, but parents could request that children not attend. Decisions of church marriage courts would no longer be automatically binding under Italian law.

Despite support by the Vatican and key Italian political leaders for the revised version of the Concordat no action was taken by the Italian Parliament as John Paul neared his first anniversary.

John Paul also made a major initiative to normalize relations with China and with Chinese Catholics, thus healing a split fomented 30 years before.

On Aug. 19, 1979, the pope expressed optimism that relations could be re-established between the Vatican and Chinese Catholics and praised "a new respect for religion" accompanying China's opening to the West. He recalled that in 1949, the Catholic Church in China had been "a living church which maintained perfect union with the Holy See." At the time, there were more than 3 million Catholics, about 100 bishops and some 5,800 priests, 2,700 of them native Chinese.

"After 30 years, the news about these our brothers is little and uncertain, but we do not cease to nurture the hope that we can renew the links of that direct contact which was never spiritually interrupted," John Paul said.

Normal relations between the Vatican and Chinese Catholics were disrupted after the 1949 Communist revolution. Most foreign missionaries were expelled. Other priests and bishops were jailed.

The new government also fomented the creation of the National Association of Patriotic Catholics, an attempt to establish a national church divorced from the Vatican. In 1958, Pope Pius XII condemned the patriotic association. From 1957 to 1960, the Chinese government told the patriotic association to elect bishops. In that time, at least 51 priests were elected bishops, of whom 36 accepted ordination as bishops. In subsequent years additional bishops were chosen. The ordinations are illicit in that they violate church laws by not having papal approval. But they are not necessarily invalid. The status of these bishops would be a major point to be resolved in any re-establishment of normal relations between the Vatican and the church in China.

While the pope was expressing optimism, two priests headquartered in Rome were on an extended visit to China. Although they were not officially representing the Vatican, they had contacts with Chinese Catholic leaders in an effort to open dialogue. The outcome of that effort remained uncertain.

The road to normalization was certainly not going to be an easy one. After the Vatican issued a statement pointing out the illicit nature of the patriotic association's election of bishops, a spokesman for the association — presumably speaking with government support — called the Vatican statement "preposterous." The Vatican "has no right to interfere in the affairs of churches of other countries," the spokesman said.

In the Philippines, the very announcement that John Paul would visit the Asian country before the end of 1979 heightened an already tense church-state situation. Church leaders have criticized the human rights record of the martial law government of President Ferdinand Marcos. Several Catholic newspapers and radio stations have been closed because of their criticisms, and some missionaries have been expelled. Before the pope's visit was announced, Cardinal Jaime Sin of Manila said the government is "moving toward a totalitarian form" because President Marcos "disregards the Constitution." He added: "In the Philippines it is treason to aspire, to think of becoming president. The church speaks, not to try to take over leadership, but to express the feelings of the people."

But John Paul was also a peacemaker and helped ease military tensions between Argentina and Chile. On Jan. 24, 1979, the Vatican announced that John Paul had agreed to mediate a territorial dispute between Argentina and Chile which was bringing the two countries to the brink of war. At issue was sovereignty over three islands in the Beagle Channel off the southern tip of South America. As the countries began massing their armies along their 2,500-mile-long border and their navies in the disputed territorial waters, the pope decided to step in, following a call by Catholic leaders in both countries for a peaceful solution.

The territorial dispute has existed since the 19th century. It flared anew in 1978 when Argentina refused to accept a decision by an international commission which gave Chile possession of the islands.

By May, talks between those involved were under way at the Vatican, with Cardinal Antonio Samore, a man with a long record of Vatican diplomatic service in Latin America, serving as the papal mediator.

In August 1979, after prolonged Vatican efforts, Archbishop Raymond Marie Tchidimbo of Conarky, Guinea, was released from prison. The 57-year-old archbishop had been jailed in 1971 for allegedly supporting an unsuccessful invasion of the West African country. The Vatican negotiated the release through President William Tolbert of Liberia who interceded with Guinean President-for-Life Sekou Toure.

After visiting with John Paul at the Vatican, Archbishop Tchidimbo resigned as head of the Conarky archdiocese, leaving the Vatican free to give him a new assignment outside Guinea and to assign a new archbishop to Conarky.

Memories of "The Pope Who Smiled"

As the first anniversary of his election drew near, John Paul II paused to join with many others in remembering the first John Paul — the shy, smiling man who in 34 days as pope had in so many ways paved the way for this new papacy.

The day was Aug. 26, the date on which a year earlier Cardinal Albino Luciani had been elected to succeed Pope Paul VI. The place was Canale D'Agordo, the small town where Luciani had been born.

There were two popes in Canale D'Agordo that day: one very much alive and visiting the town for the first time and the other nearly a year dead but present in the hearts of many who remembered him.

Despite a driving rain, an estimated 20,000 people came to the tiny village in the Dolomite Alps to pay homage to John Paul I and to welcome his successor. Even those without umbrellas attended the outdoor papal Mass.

"He is still amidst us here today," said John Paul II of his predecessor. "Yes, dearest brothers and sisters of Canale D'Agordo. He is here: with his teaching, with his example, with his smile."

John Paul celebrated Mass on a platform in front of the Church of San Giovanni Battista, where Luciani had been baptized and confirmed, where he had celebrated his first Mass and served as assistant pastor.

"He learned to love the church here, among his mountains," John Paul said in his homily. "To love the church, to serve the church was the constant program of his life."

"My presence here today does not speak only of my sincere love for you," the pope told the thousands jammed into the tiny square, "but it is also a solemn and public sign of my pledge."

"I want to testify before the world that the mission and the apostolate of my predecessor continue to shine as the clearest light in the church, with a presence that death has not been able to extinguish."

John Paul was in an area where, according to Communist Mayor Toni Cagnati of Canale D'Agordo, there exists "a culture that has kept alive civil and religious traditions which, in the progress of society, have safeguarded the values and dignity of man."

After celebrating Mass outside the parish church, the pope visited the house where Albino Luciani was born. The family of the late pope's brother, Edoardo, still lives in the house. John Paul II entered the Luciani home smiling and departed visibly moved.

The second major stop on the pope's visit to the region was the top of Mount Marmolada, the highest peak in the Dolomites at 10,560 feet. There he blessed the statue of Our Lady Queen of the Dolomites and recited the Angelus in the midst of a snowstorm.

"Coming today to this magnificent peak of the Dolomites as part of my pilgrimage to the place of the birth and the youth of John Paul I, I wish to lift up my eyes, with the whole church, to her whose image stands from today as a resplendent crown from the heights of the Dolomites," he said.

Atop Mount Marmolada, John Paul wore the cardinal's skullcap of Albino Luciani, the stole of Gregory XVI, who also was from the Belluno region, and a white ski jacket. Because of the extreme cold, aides eventually convinced the pope to replace the skullcap with a heavy fur cap, complete with ear flaps.

The only rest for John Paul during the day came when he spent half an hour on the chair lift to the top of the mountain.

John Paul also visited the city of Belluno and delivered the homily during a Mass at the Sports Field in Belluno. About 50,000 people attended.

"Today there is a real need for a mature, resolute and courageous faith in light of uncertainties occurring among some brothers, like those who think Italy is a land already drawing away from Christian traditions, to enter the so-called post-Christian era," John Paul said.

"No, brothers. I know this is not so, and you yourselves tell me now — you have already told me with your moving welcome since this morning — that this is not so," he added.

"From the many years of knowledge that I have of Italy and Italians, from the more direct experience I have acquired daily in these months of my pontifical service, I know that this is not so," he said.

"Despite increasing snares and major dangers, the authentic face of the nation is Christian, illuminated as it is by the light of Christ and of his Gospel," he added.

Referring to Pope John Paul I, the pope said his predecessor's "greatness, you could say, was inversely proportional to the duration of his service in the See of Peter."

While in Belluno, the pope circled the city twice by motorcade, visited the Gregorian Seminary where Albino Luciani was first a student and later vice rector, and met with 14 bishops from nearby dioceses.

The final event of his day-long trip was a helicopter flight over the region where 2,000 people died on Oct. 9, 1963, from flooding of the Vajont Dam. The pope threw flowers over a local cemetery and said a prayer for the victims.

"As I prepare to leave this patch of Veneto soil, blessed and dear, dotted with steeples and alpine peaks, eloquent for its suggestive calls to contemplation and prayer, I can't hide the profound emotion that invades my spirit," John Paul said in Treviso shortly before boarding a military airplane for Rome.

"May the joy of this day of faith and of communion, never decrease but rather accompany you like a serene echo which sweetens your souls and inspires courageous certitude in moments of trial, in the conviction that the Lord is always near, as we have been able to feel him today with particularly joyful intensity," he said.

Two days later, some 700 residents of the Diocese of Vittorio Veneto, where John Paul I once served as bishop, made a pilgrimage to see the pope. They joined John Paul II at a morning Mass in the gardens of the papal summer residence in Castelgandolfo. The pilgrimage was organized to mark the first anniversary of the election of John Paul I.

"He is no longer visible among us, because thus desired the Lord," said John Paul of his predecessor during the homily.

"But he remains now and will remain forever luminous and blessed in the church and in humanity for his example and for his teaching," he added.

The pope especially praised the humility of John Paul I, his commitment to truth and his goodness.

"From his profound and convinced sense of humility was born his extreme confidence in God, who is Father, love, mercy. And from it also came his joy, his constant smile, his humor which bursts forth lively and persuasive in all his writings," John Paul said.

"How fortunate you are that for so many years you could enjoy the presence of such a good pastor," the pope told the Vittorio Veneto pilgrims.

The pilgrimage, led by Bishop Antonio Cunial of Vittorio Veneto, included 40 priests who concelebrated Mass with the pope.

John Paul's pause to recall his predecessor was a poignant time.

The bright but brief reign of Pope John Paul I might best be summed up by the 16th century mystic, St. John of the Cross: "One instant of pure love is worth all the works of the church put together."

Cardinal Albino Luciani of Venice, Italy, was elected to the papacy Aug. 26, 1978 and served for 34 days. The smiling pope, as he was called, issued no encyclicals, approved no major statements by Vatican congregations, made no major changes in the Roman Curia and never celebrated Mass as pope on the main altar of St. Peter's Basilica. His legacy was his papal style.

The smiling pope was chosen because the cardinals wanted a pastorally oriented man who could relate to people on a personal level. His dismissal of pomp, his sometimes chatty way of speaking to crowds, his constant claims of feeling a bit overwhelmed by his formidable new role paved the way for the election of Cardinal Karol Wojtyla as Pope John Paul II. The style of John Paul I also gave many people new insights into the human nature of the papacy.

"He was the first one to seem like a man," said one Vatican official. "He admitted that he was a little afraid of taking on his new job. And people said: 'Yes, that's the way he should feel. That's the way I would feel.'"

Because of his warmth and his bright and constantly photographed smile, John Paul I quickly entered the hearts of many people around the world and was deeply mourned when he died unexpectedly of a heart attack on Sept. 28, 1979.

"He passed as a meteor which unexpectedly lights up the heavens and then disappears leaving us amazed and astonished," eulogized Cardinal Carlo Confalonieri, dean of the College of Cardinals, at the funeral Mass.

The reminders of the smiling pope's papacy exist not in the symbols which remain, but those which are missing. He rejected use of the traditional triple crown (tiara) that goes to a new pope and preferred to call the Mass initiating his pontificate the "inauguration" of his papal ministry rather than a coronation.

"Pope John Paul I, whose memory is so vivid in our hearts, did not wish to have the tiara — nor does his successor wish it today," said John Paul II at his inaugural Mass.

John Paul I rarely used the majestic papal plural "we." He referred to himself as "I" or "me." John Paul II also cut down on use of the papal "we" and continued his predecessor's practice of stopping to greet people in the crowd as he arrives and leaves at functions such as papal audiences.

John Paul I spent great deal of his papacy visiting offices of the Roman Curia, admitting that he did not fully understand the workings of the church's central administration. "The first thing I did after the election was to read the *Annuario Pontificio* (Vatican Yearbook) to learn the organization of the Holy See," he laughingly told the College of Cardinals.

The humility, the smile, the friendly chats at his papal audiences, however, were not all that John Paul I brought to the papacy. He outlined the general program he wanted to follow in a speech to the cardinals the day after his election. The program emphasized continued implementation of the Second Vatican Council; revision of the Code of Canon Law; promotion of ecumenism "without hesitation"; involvement of all believers in evangelism efforts; greater use of shared decision making by the world's bishops; efforts for peace and social progress; and support for projects against hunger and illiteracy.

"We want to continue to bring to life the inheritance of Vatican II," he said. The speech, like the double name he chose, indicated the direction he desired during his papacy. He chose the name John Paul to signify his intentions to continue the policies of his predecessors, John XXIII and Paul VI.

Inevitably, John Paul I had hardly been buried before conjecture began about what might have happened had he not died. He was certainly a pope like no other before him. In time, would he not have changed much more than simply style?

While doing research on the smiling pope, Kay Withers, a Rome-based journalist, turned up what she considered to be firm evidence that Luciani seriously questioned the church's teaching against artificial contraception. Ms. Withers spoke of her research in an interview with the National Catholic News Service.

That news story reported that Luciani's former secretary, Father Mario Senigaglia, was convinced that John Paul I would have re-examined *Humanae Vitae*, the 1968 encyclical of Pope Paul VI reconfirming the church's teaching against artificial contraception.

Father Senigaglia said John Paul I would have re-studied the encyclical "not to condemn it, because that wasn't his style, but to find a possible way out. He always looked for the encyclical's mitigating clauses, and he was very aware of the pastoral difficulties."

The news story also cited an interview with Luciani in 1974 with the Venice newspaper, Il Gazzettino, and a letter to priests in 1968 when he was bishop of Vittorio Veneto, a small diocese near Venice.

In the newspaper interview, the then Cardinal Luciani said Catholics are obliged to accept the teaching on artificial contraception out of "humility, prudence and the religious obedience owed to the head of the church." But he added: "If I were 'the divine master of the law' I would abolish the law."

After Pope Paul's encyclical was published in 1968, the then Bishop Luciani issued a letter to priests printed in the official bulletin of the Vittorio Veneto diocese. The letter expressed his disappointment that the encyclical frustrated the hopes of those who expected the church's position to change.

"I confess — even if I did not let it leak out in writing — I had hoped in my heart that the very grave existing difficulties could have been overcome and that the answer of the teacher, who speaks with special charism and in the name of the Lord, could have coincided, at least in part, with the hopes engendered among many couples after a special pontifical commission was formed to study the question," said the letter. It also asked priests to be faithful to the encyclical's teaching.

Prior to the issuance of Pope Paul's encyclical, Bishop Luciani sent a letter on behalf of the bishops of the Venice area to the pope urging modification, said Father Senigaglia.

At the time, Bishop Luciani was studying the possibility that the birth control pill might be considered a "medicine" to regulate "excessive" ovulation — the way an antihistamine would be used to curb excess discharges in the respiratory tract, according to retired Bishop Gioacchino Muccin. Bishop Muccin was a friend of the smiling pope and once was his bishop when John Paul I was a priest in the Diocese of Belluno.

It is one thing to speak as a bishop, or even a cardinal, and another to bear the burden of speaking as pope. What would John Paul I have done about birth control? It remained a question that was intriguing, but unanswerable, mute. What John Paul I did do and did exemplify is summarized in his motto as bishop and pope: "Humility."

The significance of the humility, warmth and informal style of John Paul I was not lost on his successor. By choosing the same name, John Paul II indicated his desire to continue in the pastoral mold. The shoes into which he stepped were probably much larger than anyone other than he realized.

1 *Cardinal Karol Wojtyla talks with Pope John Paul I, the man he would succeed little more than a month later.*

2 *Pope John Paul II kneels in prayer before the tomb of Pope John Paul I on the first anniversary of his predecesor's death.*

3 *Pope John Paul II walks with Edoardo Luciani, younger brother of the late John Paul I, on the way to the house where the late pope was born in Canale D'Agordo.*

The
Emerald Isle

Cardinal Tomas O'Fiaich's words of greeting to John Paul on his arrival in Ireland struck directly at the heart of his mission: "He comes, a messenger of peace to a troubled land."

Indeed it was a troubled land in which John Paul arrived Sept. 29, beginning the first visit ever by a pope to one of the most Catholic of all countries. Violence between Catholics and Protestants has wracked the Emerald Isle for a decade in a dispute over the future of Northern Ireland and its people — an outgrowth of the centuries-old conflict involving British control of Ireland. That violence had spilled dramatically into the south only days before the pope's arrival with the assassination of Lord Louis Mountbatten and members of his family.

But not even the threat of violence could dim the enthusiasm of the tiers of Irish welcomers on hand to greet the pope at Dublin airport. Many of the crowd had waited patiently for up to four hours for the papal plane to arrive, including some Dubliners who had walked to the airport in pre-dawn darkness. Banners in Polish, Italian, English and Gaelic bid the pope welcome.

Arriving with a jet-fighter escort to a runway decorated with flower pots and flag-waving children, the pope descended the steps of the Aer Lingus plane, christened the "St. Patrick," which had brought him to Dublin from Rome and knelt to kiss the ground as he had done in other countries he had visited on previous trips.

First to greet the pope were Cardinal O'Fiaich of Armagh, primate of all Ireland, and the apostolic nuncio to Ireland, Archbishop Gaetano Alibrandi. Cardinal O'Fiaich said the pope's visit "serves to confirm our faith, and to remind us to examine our lives."

Buffeted by a breeze which once took away his skullcap and caused his red cape and hood to blow across his face, John Paul acknowledged the formal greeting of Irish President Dr. Patrick Hillery, reviewed the Irish Army troops and greeted members of the Irish government. Ever the linguist, he drew cheers of delight by offering the Gaelic phrase, "Praised be Jesus Christ!" after President Hillery switched to Gaelic to wish him "a hundred thousand welcomes."

John Paul told the thousands in the terminal, on its roof and down on the runway that he was "happy to walk among you — in the footsteps of St. Patrick and in the path of the Gospel that he left you as a great heritage." Symbolizing the religious nature of his visit, he placed his pastoral visit under the patronage of the Blessed Virgin Mary.

The visit to Ireland began the third "pilgrimage of faith" taken by John Paul since becoming pope. He soon explained that on this particular portion of this trip, he saw himself as a "pilgrim of peace," hoping that his moral influence could help end the violence.

John Paul's hope had been that he could visit both parts of Ireland — the Republic of Ireland, politically independent and overwhelmingly Catholic, and Northern Ireland, a part of Great Britain with a population made up of a majority of Protestants and a minority of Catholics. One of the key points of contention in the complex situation on which the violence in Northern Ireland feeds is the issue of whether Northern Ireland should remain tied to Britain or unite with the southern republic.

But before the pope left Rome, his plans to visit Northern Ireland were cancelled because of the security risk involved.

Commenting on that risk, John Paul told journalists on the plane taking him to Dublin: "I am traveling in the hands of God."

Throughout his three-day stay, John Paul pleaded, implored and encouraged people to end the fighting in Northern Ireland.

For his major denunciation of the violence, John Paul chose Drogheda — a hillside field near the border of Northern Ireland, two miles south of Killeeny in the Archdiocese of Armagh, primatial See of all Ireland. Archdiocesan boundaries cross the borders of Ireland and Northern Ireland with the See city of Armagh in Northern Ireland.

A caravan of some 600 buses brought at least 30,000 persons to Drogheda from Northern Ireland. Many private cars also crossed the border to bring crowds of northerners to hear the papal appeal. Overall, 250,000 people attended the pope's talk. People began arriving in the 35-acre hillside field in the early morning hours of Sept. 29, long before the pope arrived, and by 10 a.m., tens of thousands had gathered. John Paul arrived by helicopter at 4:45 p.m. At 5 p.m. he mounted the altar platform for a Liturgy of the Word, during which he preached an hour-long homily on justice and reconciliation. He was repeatedly interrupted by applause.

John Paul said the fighting in Northern Ireland is not the result of a religious war between Catholics and Protestants. "Christianity is decisively opposed to fomenting hatred and to promoting or provoking violence or struggle for the sake of 'struggle,'" he declared.

"I proclaim with the conviction of my faith in Christ and with an awareness of my mission, that violence is evil, that violence is unacceptable as a solution to problems, that violence is unworthy of man."

John Paul said the "tragic" decade-long civil war and terrorism in Northern Ireland "do not have their source in the fact of belonging to different churches and different confessions...this is not — despite what is so often repeated before world opinion — a religious war, a struggle between Catholics and Protestants."

Christianity forbids seeking solutions to injustices "by the ways of hatred, by the murdering of defenseless people, by the methods of terrorism," he said. The message of the Gospel is one of peace.

In denouncing violence, the pope laid equal stress on the need for justice and human dignity. "Every human being has inalienable rights that must be respected," he said.

His voice resounding with feeling, he declared: "On my knees I beg you to turn away from the paths of violence and to return to the ways of peace."

"You may claim to seek justice. I too believe in justice and seek justice," he said.

"But violence only delays the day of justice. Violence destroys the work of justice. Further violence in Ireland will only drag down to ruin the land you claim to love and the values you claim to cherish."

He appealed to young people:

"Do not listen to voices which speak the language of hatred, revenge, retaliation. Do not follow any leaders who train you in the ways of inflicting death.

"Love life, respect life; in yourselves and in others.

"Give yourselves to the service of life, not the work of death."

The pope also appealed to political leaders:

"Do not cause or condone or tolerate conditions which give excuse or pretext to men of violence.

"Those who resort to violence always claim that only violence brings about change...You politicians must prove them wrong. You must show that there is a peaceful, political way to justice."

Declaring himself "a pilgrim of peace," the pope said that his message to Protestants and Catholics "is peace and love." He called for an end to religious hatred.

"May no Irish Protestant think that the pope is an enemy, a danger or a threat. My desire is that instead Protestants would see in me a friend and a brother in Christ."

John Paul continued his peace pleas in a succession of meetings. After the Drogheda event, he returned to Dublin for an evening meeting with leaders of other Christian churches in Ireland.

He called on all Christian leaders to work together to foster justice and reconciliation. He also made a plea for united Christian action to fight materialism and moral permissiveness.

"All Christians in Ireland must join together in opposing all violence and all assaults against the human person — from whatever quarter they come — and in finding Christian answers to the grave problems of Northern Ireland," he said.

The Christian leaders meeting the pope included the bishops and general synod representatives of the (Anglican) Church of Ireland, leaders of the Presbyterian Church and one representative each from other denominations that are members of the Irish Council of Churches.

In addresses to President Hillery, government officials and the diplomatic corps, the pope challenged the Irish to be an example of reconciliation to the rest of Europe. President Hillery heard the pope utter a wish that the Irish heritage of faith, preserved through the centuries, would enable the Irish to achieve a well-being that brings "true human advancement" for all people. John Paul told government officials that Ireland will contribute "to the peaceful and just future of Europe," particularly if its people have the courage to solve the problems of Northern Ireland.

The following morning, Sept. 30, the pope went to Galway where he specifically directed his peace appeal to young people. The occasion was a gathering with 250,000 youths from parishes throughout Ireland. The meeting place was Ballybrit Racecourse.

In a homily which brought enthusiastic response, the pope warned the young people that the religious and moral principles they were raised to uphold "will be tested in many ways," not the least of which will be the stand they will have to take on violence in Northern Ireland.

"Love your enemies, do good to those who hate you," the pope said.

"You have guessed already that even by my reference to these words of the Savior I have before my mind the painful events that for more than 10 years have been taking place in Northern Ireland.

"I am sure that all young people are living these events very deeply and very painfully, for they are tracing deep furrows in your young hearts. These events, painful as they are, must also be an incitement to reflection.

"They demand that you form an interior judgment of conscience to determine where you, as young Catholics, stand on the matter."

The pope offered not his advice, but that of Jesus: "Love your enemies."

"I beg you to reflect deeply," John Paul told the cheering crowd. "What would human life be if Jesus had never spoken such words? What would the world be if in our mutual relations we were to give primacy to hatred among people, between classes, between nations?"

The young people saw for themselves at the Offertory procession a striking example of the violence between Catholics and Protestants in Northern Ireland. Thirteen-year-old Damien Irwin — walking with the aid of an artificial leg after losing his own in a 1977 Belfast bomb blast — presented the chalice to John Paul.

The pope also cautioned the young people against the lures of consumerism and sexual promiscuity. "The moral standards that the church and society have held up to you for so long a time will be presented as obsolete and a hindrance to the full development of your own personality," he warned.

Before the pope could finish his homily, the enthusiastic youths almost took the Mass away from him, interrupting him for a solid 10 minutes with clapping, cheering and singing after he told them, "Young people of Ireland, I love you."

From Ballybrit Racetrack, the pope traveled to Knock and delivered his major address of the day at the country's chief Marian shrine, which marks the spot venerated as one where Mary appeared to 15 people in 1879.

At the shrine, John Paul dedicated the Irish nation to Mary during a Mass before more than 400,000 people. He asked Mary to "cure and heal" the civil strife in Northern Ireland.

"In a very special way we entrust to you this great wound now afflicting our people, hoping that your hands will be able to cure and heal it," he said. "Great is our concern for those young souls who are caught up in bloody acts of vengeance and hatred. Mother, do not abandon these youthful hearts."

John Paul called the shrine 'the goal of my journey to Ireland." In the years that Knock's fame as a pilgrimage site has grown, there have been a number of cures reported by pilgrims. Before the Mass the pope visited with about 12,000 sick and handicapped persons in the basilica and blessed them.

The shrine basilica, a circular church surrounded by an ambulatory resting on 32 pillars representing the 32 counties of Ireland, is 100 meters (about 330 feet) in diameter and seats 20,000 people. The modern white basilica was completed in 1976. For the Mass, a large, circular, two-tiered altar platform was set against the south side of the original parish church, where the visions of Mary occurred.

On the lower level of the blue-carpeted platform were 12 elderly persons confined to beds or wheelchairs, whom the pope anointed before the Offertory. Two hundred priests concelebrated with the pope at the huge altar, which was dominated by a 58-foot Celtic cross.

In his homily, John Paul stressed his personal devotion to Mary, the strong Marian devotion of the Irish and the role of that devotion for the lives of all Catholics. He also emphasized that obeying Christian truths is more important than the seeking of earthly riches.

"So many false voices are heard...They are the voices that tell you that truth is less important than personal gain; that comfort, wealth and pleasure are the true aims of life; that the refusal of new life is better than generosity of spirit and the taking up of responsibility; that justice must be achieved but without any personal involvement by the Christian; that violence can be a means to a good end; that unity can be built without giving up hate," he said.

At the end of the Mass, John Paul lit and enshrined a family prayer candle to mark the long Irish tradition of family prayer.

As he was heading back toward the helicopter pad to return to Dublin, the crowd began singing, "He's Got the Whole World in His Hands." The helicopter lifted off a few minutes after 7 p.m., to the strains of another song: "Now Is the Hour, When We Must Say Goodbye."

On the same day, at a meeting with the bishops of Ireland and Northern Ireland, John Paul referred again to the violence in Northern Ireland, saying he had been advised to cancel his Irish trip because of it.

"These very difficulties, however, made it all the more important to be here, to share closely with all of you these uncommon trials," the pope said. He urged bishops and priests to be close to their people, sharing their sufferings and leading the struggle for human rights and dignity.

"It is difficult, but it is your duty," he declared.

John Paul linked this to the need of pastors to have "a deep personal relationship of faith and love with Jesus Christ."

"Because we are united with Jesus and sustained by him, there is no challenge we cannot meet, no difficulty we cannot sustain, no obstacle we cannot overcome for the Gospel," he added.

Commenting on strife-torn Northern Ireland, John Paul drew a parallel with the history of trials in his native Poland. Bishops can fulfill their duty "in no other way than by suffering with those who suffer, and by weeping with those who weep," he said.

"**D**uring the last two centuries, the church in Poland has struck root in a special way in the soul of the nation," he said. "Part of the reason for this is that its pastors — its bishops and priests — did not hesitate to share in the trials and sufferings of their fellow countrymen."

John Paul cited priests and bishops deported to Siberia in the Soviet Union and locked in concentration camps during World War II. Bishops especially "must reflect beforehand on how to strengthen peace, and on how to spare the people from these terrible sufferings," he said.

The pope particularly called on bishops to take a firm stand with government officials on human rights and social justice issues because bishops have "a special right and duty to influence those who wield the sword of authority." He declared that "there are deeper reasons and stronger laws to which men, nations and peoples are subject" than those of civil authority.

"It is for us to discern these reasons and in their light to become, before those in authority, spokesmen for the moral order: This order is superior to force and violence. In this superiority of the moral order is expressed all the dignity of men and nations," he said.

John Paul's visit to Ireland was more than a plea for peace in the Emerald Isle's troubled North. It was also a joyous and moving reaffirmtion of the strong faith of Irish Catholics. About 2.5 million of Ireland's 3.5 million Catholics saw the pope in person during his pilgrimage as he crisscrossed the country.

Living, breathing proof of the strong faith of the Irish was given to John Paul shortly after his arrival when about 1.2 million people gathered at Dublin's Phoenix Park for the first papal Mass of the trip.

The people clapped and cheered and sang the parts of the Mass in Gaelic, English and Latin as the pope praised their faith and faithfulness. It was the largest crowd ever to gather for any event in Ireland.

"As I stand here in the company of so many hundreds of thousands of Irish men and women, I am thinking of how many times, across how many centuries, the Eucharist has been celebrated in this land," John Paul said during his 45-minute homily.

"Small matter where the Mass was offered; for the Irish, it was always the Mass that mattered," he added. He warned the Irish to remain faithful to Christian values as they face the temptations offered by a "pervading materialism" and "false pretenses concerning freedom, the sacredness of life, the indissolubility of marriage, the true sense of human sexuality, the right attitude toward the material goods that progress has to offer."

"On Sunday mornings in Ireland, no one seeing the great crowds making their way to and from Mass could have any doubt about Ireland's devotion to the Mass. For them a whole Catholic people is seen to be faithful to the Lord's command, 'Do this in memory of me,'" the pope said.

A cross section of the Irish participated in the Offertory procession of the Mass in the 1,760-acre park. Children from Slane and Kildare, Glendalough and Clonmacnoise carried sheaves of wheat. A man from Kells had a basket of corn. A

Waterford baker and a housewife brought a loaf of homemade bread. And a man from Graiguenamanagh came with a jug of wine.

An Irish folk song rang out as the gifts were presented. Later some 2,000 priests distributed Communion to the multitude.

After Mass, cheers sounded in staccato fashion as John Paul rode in an open vehicle through the various roped-off sections of the crowd, the cries of well-wishers arising as he approached each new group, waving and offering his blessing.

John Paul's last day in Ireland, Oct. 1, began with a trip to St. Patrick's Seminary in Maynooth. There he called on Ireland's priests and Religious to be "signs of God" in the modern secular cities and also to be faithful to their religious commitment.

"Do not hesitate to be recognizable, identifiable, in the streets as men and women who have consecrated their lives to God," he said. He told priests specifically, "If you keep striving to be the kind of priest your people expect and wish you to be, then you will be holy priests."

"This is what causes such sadness to the church, such great but often silent anguish among the people of God, when priests fail in their fidelity to their priestly commitment," he said.

The pope then went to Limerick for his final open-air Mass. About 400,000 people gathered at the Limerick racecourse and heard the pope urge Catholics to resist growing pressure for the church to liberalize its stands on abortion, divorce and contraception.

The pope also rejected feminist views that place job or career advancement above the values of motherhood.

Focusing most of his remarks on the values of family life, John Paul said: "The family is the primary field of Christian action for Irish laity, the place where your 'royal priesthood' is chiefly exercised. The Christian family has been in the past Ireland's greatest spiritual resource."

Highlights of the pope's comments included:

— On divorce: "Divorce, for whatever reason it is introduced, inevitably becomes easier and easier to obtain and it gradually comes to be accepted as a normal part of life. The very possibility of divorce in the sphere of civil law makes stable and permanent marriages more difficult for everyone....May the Irish always support marriage through personal commitment and through positive social and legal action."

— On artificial birth control and abortion: "Generous openness to accept children from God as the gift to their love is the mark of the Christian couple. Respect the God-given cycle of life, for this respect is part of our respect for God himself, who created male and female, who created them in his own image, reflecting his own life-giving love in the patterns of their sexual being. Have an absolute and holy respect for the sacredness of human life from the first moment of its conception. Abortion, as the Vatican Council stated, is one of the 'abominable crimes.'"

— On parenthood: "Do not think that anything you will do in life is more important than to be a good Christian father and mother."

— On prayer: "May I express a wish: that every home in Ireland may remain, or may begin again to be a home of daily family prayer."

The Mass provided an affectionate farewell for John Paul who ended his sermon by breaking into Gaelic, saying: "God bless you and keep you forever." This brought thunderous applause.

After the Mass, he crossed the Shannon River and went to Shannon Airport where he boarded a plane for his flight to the United States. About 10,000 people cheered him as a tearful pope bid farewell.

"Ireland *semper fidelis*, always faithful," he said, in a final tribute to Ireland's strong Catholicism. He then took note of the weather, and in a humorous aside, added: "It is very nice that the rain comes on the last day of my visit."

On the following pages:

1 Dublin children excitedly wave pictures of the pope as he arrives at the Dublin airport.

2 As the pope's helicopter lowers for a landing at Gallway, eager crowds wave in anticipation of a papal Mass which will be celebrated on the altar to the right.

3 In an unscheduled stop, Pope John Paul prays at Clonmacnois, an early center of Christianity in Ireland.

4 The sun filters through light clouds as Pope John Paul II celebrates Mass beneath a 40-ton cross.

5 The "popemobile," as the vehicle carrying the pope became known, moves slowly through the crowds gathered at Phoenix Park in Dublin.

6 Pope John Paul II examines ruins in central Ireland.

7 At the Shrine of Our Lady of Knock, the pope blesses the handicapped aged and infirm who had come to see him.

3　4

PART III

THE HISTORIC VISIT TO THE UNITED STATES

The Pope
Goes West

As the "St. Patrick" roared skyward from Ireland's Shannon Airport on the afternoon of Oct. 1, John Paul's thoughts turned westward, toward the United States, the next segment of his pilgrimage. He was keenly aware of the challenge which awaited him.

The land toward which he was racing at jet-age speed would be vastly different from the one he had just left and from any of those he had previously visited in the first year of his pontificate. Each of the previous countries — Mexico, Poland, the Dominican Republic, even the Bahamas — had presented its own particular challenge. But the United States would be a new situation — an extended tour of a country which not only is non-Catholic but which still remembers an anti-Catholic past. American Catholics would embrace John Paul warmly, lovingly. But how would his words, his actions be perceived by the non-Catholic majority? Would his message be understood?

Karol Wojtyla was no stranger to the United States. As a cardinal, he visited the country twice, once in September 1969 for 12 days, and again in August and September 1976 for almost six weeks. He had been in 19 different cities during the two trips and many faces and sights were familiar to him. Now, however, he came not as Karol Wojtyla but as Pope John Paul II. The difference was not inconsequential.

The visit was billed as "pastoral and apolitical." But because of the tenor of the times, the American system and the issues that John Paul would address, there was no way to avoid political implications. The sheer length and breadth of the visit demanded attention.

When Pope Paul VI came to the United States in 1965, he stayed only 13 hours. Technically, he came to visit the United Nations, not the United States. Almost as an afterthought, he made a whirlwind tour of New York, and when he met with President Lyndon Johnson, it was privately and in a New York hotel room.

Ahead of John Paul lay a dramatically different program. He would spend seven days on tour, starting at Boston, moving on to the United Nations, then visiting New York, Philadelphia, Des Moines, Chicago and Washington. In Washington he would not only become the first pope to be received at the White House; he also would meet privately with President Carter in the Oval Office, visit with the Carter family, and address a White House gathering of top administration officials, members of the Supreme Court and Congress.

John Paul also knew that he would be surrounded by politics because of the substantive issues he would discuss — disarmament, human rights, justice and equality. He would speak from a Christian perspective; he would be heard in the reality of everyday life. It would be impossible to defend the basis of human dignity — the right to life — without that stand being translated into the terms of the political struggle surrounding the issue. He could hardly address disarmament without his listeners conjuring up the debate over the second Strategic Arms Limitation Treaty. Yet the message he brought transcended mere political concerns. Would his words be heard in the way he hoped they would be?

There might be reason for John Paul to be concerned over whether his message would be understood. But there was no doubt that the message would be heard. The news media had marshalled its forces as rarely before to catch his every word, depict his every move. It looked as if the visit would turn out to be the greatest media event the United States — or any other country — had ever seen.

The Secret Service had taken over the responsibility for John Paul's security during the visit, and thus all requests by journalists for credentials had to pass through the Secret Service's hands. They counted 14,000 applicants and declared that number an all-time record.

When planning for John Paul's visit began, the aim was to take him from coast to coast, to have him literally blanket the country. The press of time forced compromises and the plans were changed so that Des Moines — less than half-way across the country — was to be as far west as he would get. The pope himself reportedly was involved in coming to that conclusion, telling trip planners at one point that he wanted to spend as little time as possible inside airplanes and as much time as possible being with people. That approach brought the dropping of the idea of John Paul's going to California — where both Los Angeles and San Francisco had been under consideration for papal visits — and resulted in a selection of cities which would fit into a tight flight schedule.

As the "St. Patrick" headed out over the Atlantic Ocean, leaving the Emerald Isle behind, John Paul settled into the section of the airliner which had been specially equipped for him. In another section of the plane, the 270 journalists who had been fortunate enough to be chosen to travel with the pope caught their breath and prepared for the ordeal ahead. Before they returned to Rome from this pilgrimage to Ireland and the United States, they would have covered 12 cities in 10 days, traveling 11,200 air miles and documenting John Paul's activities as he delivered more than 70 speeches, rode in countless motorcades and celebrated Mass more than a dozen times, often in open-air settings which would draw tens of thousands of worshipers. The Italian newspapers do not call the pope "Cyclone Wojtyla" for nothing.

October 1 A Pilgrim in Boston

A light rain fell as the jetliner carrying John Paul from Ireland touched down at Boston's Logan International Airport. The rain would soon turn into a downpour, but no matter: The pope's spirits could not be dampened.

At 3:02 p.m., about 15 minutes after the "St. Patrick" landed, John Paul appeared at the door of the aircraft. He walked slowly down the stairway leading from the plane, waved to the crowds and knelt to kiss the ground — by now a familiar part of a papal arrival in a new country.

Among those gathered to welcome the pope were Rosalynn Carter, Sen. Edward Kennedy (D-Mass.), Speaker of the House Thomas "Tip" O'Neill (D-Mass.) and about 50 red and purple-robed U.S. cardinals and bishops. After an exchange of greetings, John Paul mounted a platform with Mrs. Carter and Cardinal Humberto Medeiros, archbishop of Boston.

"This may be your first visit to our shores as pope," Mrs. Carter said, "but you do not arrive as a stranger. You have stirred the world as few have ever done before."

She added, "At a time when materialism and selfishness threaten to overwhelm the values of the spirit, your visit reminds us that life's true meaning springs from the heart and the soul — from purposes and beliefs larger than our individual lives."

John Paul stepped forward to make an arrival statement, his first public speech in the United States.

"Praised be Jesus Christ!" he declared.

"It is a great joy for me to be in the United States of America, to begin my pastoral visit to the Catholic Church in this land, and at the same time to greet all the American people, of every race, color and creed.

"I am grateful for the cordial welcome given me on behalf of President Carter, whom I thank most sincerely for his invitation to the United States. I am looking forward to meeting the president after my visit to the United Nations.

"My thanks go also to the cardinal archbishop of Boston, who in this historic city offers me the first hospitality of this country. I am grateful to the episcopal conference and to all the individual bishops who have so kindly asked me to come. My only regret is that I cannot accept all the invitations extended to me by religious and civil officials, by individuals, families and groups.

"From so many quarters — Catholics, Protestants and Jews — America has opened her heart to me. And on my part I come to you —America — with sentiments of friendship, reverence and esteem. I come as one who already knows you and loves you, as one who wishes you to fulfill completely your noble destiny of service to the world. Once again I can now admire firsthand the beauty of this vast land stretching between two oceans; once again I am experiencing the warm hospitality of the American people.

"Although it is not possible for me to enter into every home, to greet personally every man and woman, to caress every child in whose eyes is reflected the innocence of love — still, I feel close to all of you, and you are all in my prayers.

"Permit me to express my sentiments in the lyrics of your own song: 'America! America! God shed his grace on thee; and crown thy good with brotherhood, from sea to shining sea.'

"And may the peace of the Lord be with you always — America!"

After the airport ceremonies, a motorcade took John Paul to Holy Cross Cathedral. The rain continued, but thousands lined the city's narrow streets as the motorcade drove through neighborhoods representing the ethnic diversity of the city and the United States.

At the cathedral, more than 2,000 priests and a token representation of nuns awaited the pope. He walked unhurriedly up the main aisle, shaking hands with hundreds of priests, as a thunderous ovation resounded through the vaulted space.

Cardinal Medeiros spoke to the pope on the office of the papacy and its teaching function. He noted:

"Among us (in the Boston area) we are privileged to have nearly a quarter of a million students in a large number of outstanding colleges and universities, all searching for the truth in a variety of ways, all ultimately seeking God with varying degrees of success.

"Along with the many more thousands of beloved youth in the other schools, they constitute an invigorating challenge and an inspiring hope to the church and to our society at large."

The cardinal concluded with an appeal to the pope to pray for the young people.

John Paul began his talk by greeting the audience as, "Dear brothers and several sisters," and glancing smilingly at the only nun who was highly visible, the photographer of the Boston Pilot, archdiocesan newspaper, Franciscan Sister Rita Murray.

After greeting the priests, John Paul gave a special blessing to the Religious. He said: "I pray for each of you, asking you to remain always united in Jesus Christ and his church, so that together we may display to the world our unity in proclaiming the mystery of Christ in revealing the divine dimension and also the human dimension of the redemption."

He also sent greetings "to all people of this city of Boston: to those in particular who are, in one way or another, burdened by suffering, to the sick and the bedridden, to those whom society seems to have left on the wayside, and those who have lost their faith in God and in their fellow human beings."

"To all I have come with a message of hope and peace — the hope and peace of Jesus Christ," he said.

John Paul led the assembly in singing *"Salve Regina."*

From Holy Cross Cathedral, the papal motorcade continued to the Boston Common for John Paul's first Mass in the United States. Despite leaden skies and heavy mists, 100,000 persons, many of them youngsters, had gathered for the service. Only minutes before John Paul's motorcade rolled into sight, an even heavier downpour began.

Standing in an open limousine, protected only by his red cape and red, broad-brimmed hat, John Paul waved to the cheering crowd. He mounted the white, gold and red altar platform set up on the edge of the Common.

By now jet lag should have been taking its toll. His day had begun 16 hours earlier across the Atlantic in Ireland. But he spoke with vigor and fervor in his half-hour homily and was repeatedly interrupted by applause and sustained cheers, especially when he said "The pope is your friend" and referred to "America the Beautiful."

John Paul also drew laughter after the latter comment when he ad-libbed: "Beautiful even if it rains."

"I want to meet you," the pope declared, his words and image carried by television throughout the country, "and tell you all — men and women of all creeds and ethnic origins, children and youth, fathers and mothers, the sick and the elderly — that God loves you, that he has given you a dignity as human beings that is beyond compare."

The pope praised America's "dedication to a more just and human future" and the "generosity with which this country has offered shelter, freedom and a chance for betterment to all who have come to its shores."

Most of the address was devoted to youths — teen-agers and young adults — whom he called "the future of the world." He issued the challenge of Christ to youth, recalling the gospel story in which a young man asked Jesus: "What must I do...?" The young man "received a concise and penetrating answer," the pope said, quoting the gospel narrative: "Then, Jesus looked at him with love and told him...Come and follow me."

John Paul recalled the remainder of the story: "The young man, who had shown such interest in the fundamental question, 'went away sad, for he had many possessions.' Yes, he went away and — as can be deduced from the context — he refused to accept the call of Christ."

From the gospel story the pope drew the lesson that the young are open to questions about the fundamental meaning of their lives. The fact of asking the questions "tells the world that you, young people, carry within yourselves a special openness with regard to what is good and true. This openness is, in a sense, a 'revelation' of the human spirit," he said.

"And in this openness to truth, to goodness and to beauty, each one of you can find yourself," John Paul added. He issued a call to young people: "Heed the call of Christ when you hear him say to you: 'Follow me!' Walk in my path! Stand by my side! Remain in my love!"

The pope further challenged young people:

"Do I make a mistake when I tell you, Catholic youth, that it is part of your task in the world and the church to reveal the true meaning of life where hatred, neglect or selfishness threaten to take over the world?"

John Paul went on:

"Many people will try to escape from their responsibility: escape in selfishness, escape in sexual pleasure, escape in drugs, escape in violence, in indifference and cynical attitudes."

Instead, he proposed "the option of love, which is the opposite of escape." He urged young people to find meaning in loving service to God and to other people, especially the needy, the poor, the lonely, the oppressed and the abandoned.

"Real love is demanding," he said. "It means discipline and sacrifice, but it also means joy and human fulfillment. Do not be afraid of honest effort and honest work; do not be afraid of the truth."

The rain came down even more heavily after John Paul's homily, and by Communion time people were leaving in droves as the ground of the Common turned into a sticky marsh.

From the Common, the papal motorcade traveled to the residence of Cardinal Medeiros where John Paul spent the night.

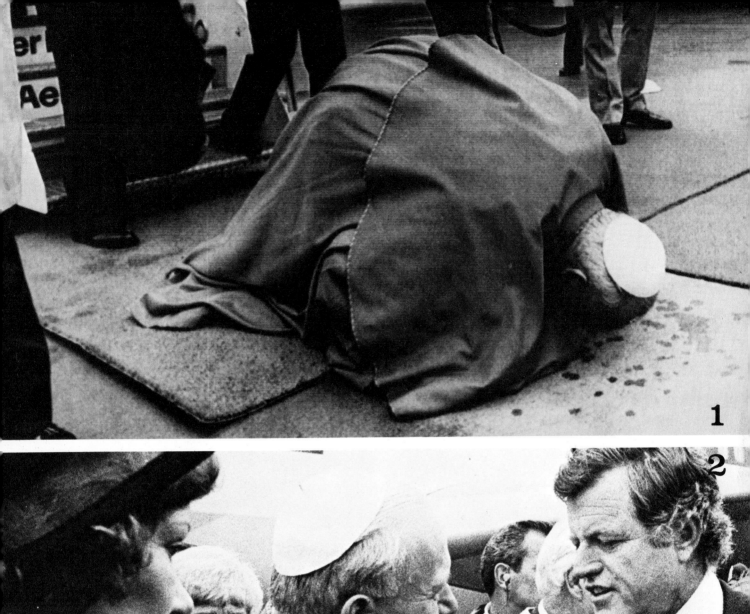

1

2

3

4

ST. ANN'S

5

WE LOVE YOU ✝ ✝ PAPA ✝

Apostolic Formation For CHRISTIAN RENEWAL

6

PROTESTANTS FOR THE POPE

7 8

9 10

On the preceding pages:

1 As he had done on his previous travels, Pope John Paul II kisses the ground on arrival in Boston.

2 At Boston's Logan airport, the pope is welcomed by Mrs. Rosalynn Carter and Sen. Edward Kennedy.

3 Boston patrolman Nick Pag uses a newspaper as improvised rainwear before heading out into the downpour which continued throughout the first day of the pope's visit.

4 A school bus, one of many which carried visitors to Boston, bears its own special window dressing.

5 Spectators, including a weary, wet photographer, crowd a Civil War monument for a better look at the pope.

6 Signs large and small carry messages for the pope.

7 A sea of umbrellas jam the Boston Common as people await the pope's arrival.

8 A lofty viewpoint offers a better chance for a snapshot.

9 Rain falls as the pope distributes Communion at the Mass on the Boston Common.

10 Pope John Paul II waves to the huge crowd gathered at the Boston Common.

The United Nations

"**T**o the task that my presence before the United Nations poses, I attribute great importance."

Pope John Paul II spoke those words from a balcony overlooking St. Peter's Square the Sunday before he began his trip to Ireland and the United States. The words indicated that his speech at the United Nations would be the major text of his trip and that he regarded the talk as the focal point of his messages. He saw the invitation as a chance to bring his moral influence and standing to a world political forum. It would be an opportunity for him to come into direct contact with diplomats responsible for protecting human rights and dignity and securing peace throughout the world, themes that John Paul had stressed repeatedly since the beginning of his pontificate.

John Paul's entire trip had come about as a result of an initial invitation which U.N. Secretary General Kurt Waldheim extended to him shortly after his election. The invitation was formalized in May when the pope and Waldheim met at the Vatican. The fall date was chosen so that the pope could speak at one of the opening sessions of the General Assembly. Traditionally, world leaders addressing the assembly are scheduled during the first few weeks of the session.

The invitations to visit Ireland and the United States fit in well with the plans and were incorporated around the U.N. visit. In terms of diplomatic protocol, the visit to the United Nations was separate from the one to the United States and separate greeting and welcoming ceremonies were held on the morning of Oct. 2 when the pope arrived at New York's LaGuardia Airport from Boston.

For the trip to New York, the pope switched from the Aer Lingus "St. Patrick" to a Trans World Airlines craft which would take him to all the cities on his U.S. tour. The TWA plane was named "Shepherd I." The two press planes which followed "Shepherd I" were dubbed by journalists "Flock I" and "Flock II."

In his airport welcome, Secretary General Waldheim said John Paul's visit to the international organization "will remind us how much we need to mobilize the moral resources of the human community and draw upon the inner strengths of your appeal to reach peace by teaching peace."

The United Nations "reflects the complete diversity of mankind," he added. "We come from many cultural traditions and religious backgrounds, but we are united in our common determination to seek peace and human betterment."

Waldheim told John Paul that "love, tolerance and understanding are the cornerstones" of the U.N. Charter and they are also "the Gospel you are preaching to the world."

142   John Paul responded:

"I reply with deep gratitude to the greetings of the secretary general of the United Nations organization. I have looked forward to this moment since the day he extended to me, immediately after the beginning of my pontificate, the invitation to address the 34th General Assembly. Your kind initiative, that honors me greatly, was thus at the basis of the journey that has first taken me to Ireland and that I shall continue in the United States of America."

Tens of thousands of people, some of them holding signs with a big red apple symbolic of New York and the words "We Love You Pope John Paul," lined the route from LaGuardia Airport to U.N. headquarters.

As John Paul left the airport at 9:40 a.m., the car top was open and he was standing. The crowds were about 10 deep near the airport. Once away from the airport exit, the car was closed by prearrangement with the United Nations. Along the route from the airport to the Triborough Bridge, there were very few people and the motorcade sped along.

After crossing the bridge, the motorcade passed along Franklin Roosevelt Drive beside the Harlem River. There the crowds varied in size at different spots and youngsters waved the "Big Apple" signs. As the motorcade passed Spanish Harlem, the signs said *"Bienvenido Papa Juan Pablo"* (Welcome Pope John Paul).

All along the parade route, police were stationed every five to 10 feet in crowded areas and more sparsely where there were fewer people. Police helicopters circled overhead and police boats patrolled the river.

Thousands of New Yorkers had begun lining up in front of the United Nations several hours before the pope's arrival. Standing behind police barricades, some of the people sang "God Bless America" while others chanted greetings to the pope in English and Spanish.

Security was tight around the international enclave of the United Nations. Guards were posted on the roofs of adjacent buildings controlling the various entrances to the headquarters building. Television cameras were mounted on the same roofs to monitor the pope's arrival and an honor guard salute for him in front of the U.N. secretariat building.

John Paul arrived shortly after 10 a.m., slightly behind schedule. He shook hands with several reporters and U.N. officials at the entrance to the secretariat building and, after a rousing cheer from the throng, entered the building to attend a reception in the office of Secretary General Waldheim.

In Waldheim's 38th-floor office, the pope shook hands with female secretaries and remarked on the fact that they outnumbered men. Waldheim answered: "It's a good sign that we have more ladies than men."

Waldheim presented an official U.N. gift to John Paul — an eight-sided inlaid wooden box, about 12 inches in diameter containing nine U.N. peace medals in silver. Eight of the medals were arranged in a circle, surrounding a silver plaque on which the ninth peace medal was mounted above the engraved signature of Kurt Waldheim.

Waldheim also presented a private gift to the pope, an early 19th-century engraving depicting St. Stephen's Cathedral in Vienna, Austria.

As John Paul went from Waldheim's office to the General Assembly Hall, U.N. officials and dignitaries lined the route to shake the pope's hand. Just before he entered the hall, a group of children dressed in the native costumes of their countries greeted him as a reminder that the United Nations declared 1979 as the International Year of the Child in an effort to promote programs to improve the quality of life of youngsters around the world. One of the girls presented the pope a bouquet of flowers and a scroll. In a typical gesture, John Paul hugged and kissed her and caressed the other participating children.

In the hall, the white-cassocked pope was ceremoniously seated in the same high-backed beige chair that had been previously occupied by world figures with such diverse reputations as John F. Kennedy, Pope Paul VI, Jimmy Carter, Yassir Arafat, Idi Amin and Queen Elizabeth.

Waldheim introduced John Paul to the overflowing crowd in the assembly hall.

"In the name of the organization, I should like to express to you how much we appreciate your addressing the General Assembly and through it the peoples of the world," Waldheim said. "You may be sure that we will hear your address not only with the greatest respect, but with a firm conviction that your message will inspire the work of the assembly. It will also give strength and hope to the peoples represented here who, in their diversity, are united in their aspirations for a better and more peaceful world."

John Paul walked to the podium as the audience applauded. After the applause died down, the native of Poland became the second pope to address the General Assembly. It was almost 14 years earlier to the day — Oct. 4, 1965 — that Pope Paul VI had spoken to the assembly.

In a slow, deep voice, John Paul delivered his speech in English. The event was carried live throughout the United States and in many countries throughout the world by radio and television. The pope prefaced his remarks by saying he would read a condensed version of his 6,700-word prepared speech in order to save time, but wanted the longer version to be regarded as the official text. For an hour and one minute, he set forth a measured plea for world leaders to put aside political differences in an effort to aid humanity.

Peace, justice and human rights dominated the message. Especially strong was the papal defense of the principles laid down in the U.N. Declaration on Human Rights.

"If the truths and principles contained in this document were to be forgotten or ignored...then the noble purpose of the United Nations organization could be faced with the threat of a new destruction," he declared.

John Paul drew an intimate link between peace and human rights and between the rights of individuals and those of nations. He particularly defended the spiritual rights of man — "in his inner relationship with truth, in his conscience, in his most personal belief, in his view of the world, in his religious faith and in the sphere of what are known as civil liberties."

John Paul said "material goods do not have the unlimited capacity for satisfying the needs of man," and for this reason they "give rise to tension, dissension and division that will often even turn into open conflict." He contrasted material goods with spiritual goods. "Spiritual goods, on the other hand, are open to unlimited enjoyment by many at the same time, without diminution of the goods themselves."

Insisting that "all political activity, whether national or international...comes from man, is exercised by man and is for man," John Paul declared that "what justifies the existence of any political activity is service to man." Political activity that works for itself and not for men "can come to contradict humanity itself."

The prepared text contained a striking list of what the pope called "some of the most important human rights." The text enumerated:

"The right to life, liberty and security of person; the right to food, clothing, housing, sufficient heath care, rest and leisure; the right to freedom of expression, education and culture; the right to freedom of thought, conscience and religion, and the right to manifest one's religion either individually or in community, in public or in private; the right to choose a state of life, to found a family and to enjoy all conditions necessary for family life; the right to property and work, to adequate working conditions and a just wage; the right of assembly and association; the right to freedom of movement, to internal and external migration; the right to nationality and residence; the right to political participation and the right to participate in the free choice of the political system of the people to which one belongs."

While declaring the "primacy given to spiritual values" and "the progress of moral life" as the chief measures of human progress, the pope also insisted on new efforts at justice in the material field.

John Paul saw "two main threats" to material and spiritual progress:

"Both concern human rights in the field of international relations and human rights within the individual states or societies. The first of these systematic threats against human rights is linked in an overall sense with the distribution of material goods. This distribution is frequently unjust both within individual societies and on the planet as a whole.''

The second threat is ''the various forms of injustice in the field of the spirit.''

Regarding unjust distribution of material goods, John Paul particularly attacked ''the frightening disparities between excessively rich individuals and groups on the one hand, and on the other hand the majority made up of the poor or indeed of the destitute, who lack food and opportunities for work and educaton and are in great numbers condemned to hunger and disease.''

He called the ''abyss'' between the rich and poor within societies ''a very grave symptom in the life of any society,'' but added: ''This must also be said with even greater insistence with regard to the abyss separating countries and regions of the earth.''

He called for steps to correct the ''serious disparity'' in material goods between various areas and regions of the world, but commented that the effectiveness of such steps will depend on ''whether peaceful cooperation will avoid imposing conditions of exploitation and economic or political dependence, which would only be a form of neocolonialism.''

Regarding injustices to spiritual life, John Paul warned of ''recurring threats and violations'' against ''the objective rights of the spirit, of human conscience and of human creativity, including man's relationship with God.''

''It is a question of the highest importance that in internal social life, as well as in international life, all human beings in every nation and country should be able to enjoy their full rights.''

''Only the safeguarding of this real completeness of rights for every human being without discrimination can ensure peace at its very roots,'' he said.

John Paul made a special plea for ''religious freedom, which I, as pope, am bound to have particularly at heart.'' But he insisted that in this area as well he was talking ''precisely with a view to safeguarding peace.''

Quoting from the Second Vatican Council's ''Declaration on Religious Freedom,'' he told the General Assembly:

''The practice of religion of its very nature consists primarily of those voluntary and free internal acts by which a human being directly sets his course toward God. No merely human power can either command or prohibit acts of this kind. But man's social nature itself requires that he give external expression to his internal acts of religion, that he communicate with others in religious matters and that he profess his religion in community.''

John Paul also discussed specific world problems. He used the International Year of the Child as a point of reference to appeal for an end to the $400 billion-per-year world arms race.

''Are the children to receive the arms race from us as a necessary inheritance?'' he asked. ''How are we to explain this unbridled race?....Can our age still really believe that the breathtaking spiral of armaments is at the service of world peace?''

He also drew attention to the problems in the Middle East. Alluding to the Egyptian-Israeli pact signed in 1978, the pope said:

''It would have no value if it did not truly represent the first stone of a general overall peace in the area, a peace that, being necessarily based on equitable recognition of the rights of all, cannot fail to include consideration and just settlement of the Palestinian question.''

Lebanon must also be included in a Middle East peace plan, he said.

''Connected with this question is that of the tranquility, independence and territorial integrity of Lebanon within the formula that has made it an example of peaceful and mutually fruitful coexistence between distinct communities, a formula

145

that I hope will, in the common interest, be maintained, with the adjustments required by the developments of the situation.''

John Paul's comments on the Lebanon formula and adjustments in it seemed to refer to the constitutional division of power along Christian and Moslem denominational lines, which had been effective for several decades. But imbalances caused by population changes without parallel power transfers caused tensions that erupted into serious civil warfare in the 1970s. He appeared to be calling for a continuation of the same kind of constitutional framework, but with the allocations of power changed to reflect current realities.

Regarding Jerusalem, John Paul said: "I also hope for a special statute that, under international guarantee — as my predecessor Paul VI indicated — would respect the particular nature of Jerusalem, a heritage sacred to the veneration of millions of believers of the three great monotheistic religions, Judaism, Christianity and Islam.''

To the surprise of many, John Paul made no mention of the world population issue. When Pope Paul VI made his precedent-setting trip to the United Nations, he clearly rejected artificial birth control as a solution to world poverty and hunger, voicing an eloquent plea for "more bread on the banquet table of life" rather than limiting the number of people allowed to the table.

The more than 900 General Assembly delegates along with the 1,000 invited guests in the assembly hall gave John Paul a standing ovation for a minute-and-a-half at the end of his speech.

John Paul spent most of that day, Oct. 2, at the United Nations. Besides addressing the General Assembly, he spoke with U.N. staff members, talked to the non-governmental organizations involved with the United Nations, addressed the journalists covering his visit and attended a reception in his honor given by Secretary General Waldheim.

In the afternoon, the pope also presented a gift to the United Nations: a mosaic of the dove of peace made by artists of the Vatican Mosaic Studio. The enamels used, the chemical composition of which is a special secret of the Vatican Mosaic Studio, were made in 1727. The gilt bronze frame was made in 1796. The mosaic itself was composed after the election of Pope John Paul.

John Paul told journalists that they can truly be "instruments of peace by being messengers of truth.''

Addressing some 600 reporters in the Economic and Social Council chambers, he said: "You are indeed servants of truth; if your reporting does not always command the attention you would desire, or if it does not conclude with the success that you would wish, do not grow discouraged. Be faithful to the truth and to its transmission, for truth endures; truth will not go away. Truth will not pass or change.''

John Paul said the service of truth is "something worthy of your best years, your finest talents, your most dedicated efforts. As transmitters of truth, you are instruments of understanding among people and of peace among nations.''

John Paul told representatives of various non-governmental organizations at the United Nations that they are privileged to witness how representatives of member countries endeavor "to chart a common course in order that life on this planet will be lived in peace, order, justice and progress for all.''

Speaking to some 600 representatives of organizations of various countries assembled in the Trusteeship Council chamber, he said no organization can alone solve the global problems if its concerns are not shared by all the people.

He said: "It is then the privileged task of the non-governmental organizations to help bring these concerns into the communities and the homes of the people and to bring back to the established agencies the priorities and aspirations of the people, so that all the solutions and projects which are envisaged be truly geared to the needs of the human person.''

He said that the delegates who drafted the 1945 U.N. Charter had a vision of united and cooperating governments. "Behind the nations, they saw also the individual and they wanted every human being to be free and to enjoy his or her fundamental rights. This fundamental inspiration must be preserved."

He said that each of the non-governmental organizations — be it in the area of food, agriculture, trade, environment, development, science, culture, education, health, disaster relief, or the problems of children and refugees — "makes a unique contribution not only to providing for people's wants, but also to fostering respect for human dignity and the cause of world peace."

John Paul concluded his short visit with representatives of agencies whose aim is to disseminate and support U.N. ideals by voicing his greetings to the various Protestant, Jewish and Moslem associations. In a particular way, he said, he extended his greetings to the representatives of international Catholic organizations.

"May your dedication and your moral sense never become blunted by difficulties, may you never lose sight of the ultimate aim of your efforts: to create a world where every human person can live in dignity and loving harmony as a child of God," he said.

The international staff of the United Nations heard the pope tell them to look upon their contributions to the aims of the world organization in terms of "growing dignity for every human being, of increased possibility for every person to advance to the fullest measure of spiritual, cultural and human completion."

He addressed some 2,000 employees from more than 100 countries in the General Assembly hall after lunch. He told the international civil servants that "each one of you is a servant of the unity, peace and brotherhood of all men."

He then said: "Your task is no less important than that of the representatives of the nations of the world, provided you are motivated by the great ideal of world peace and fraternal cooperation between all peoples; what counts is the spirit with which you perform your tasks."

He noted that the builders of the pyramids in Egypt and Mexico, of the temples in Asia and the cathedrals in Europe were not only the architects who laid out the designs or those who provided financing, but also, in no small way, "the carvers of the stones, many of whom never had the satisfaction of contemplating in its entirety the beauty of the masterpiece that their hands helped create."

John Paul told members of the U. N. staff that "you are in so many ways the carvers of the stones."

He told the international civil servants that through their works they are able to extend their love to the entire human family, to every person who has received "the wonderous gift of life, so that all may live together in peace and harmony, in a just and peaceful world, where all their basic needs — physical, moral and spiritual —may be fulfilled."

John Paul concluded his visit with a speech at a diplomatic reception calling for "a better world in freedom, in justice and in love."

He told the assembled guests from 152 countries that "peace comes down to the respect for man's inviolable rights." He said that his presence at the United Nations attests to his public and solemn commitment to collaborate with the worthy goals of the world body.

"My constant prayer for all of you is that there may be peace in justice and love," he said.

The pope ended with: "May God bless the United Nations."

There was no doubt that John Paul had left his mark at the United Nations. He scored high with the international community through his warm personality, personal dignity and obvious devotion to humanity. He impressed them with his plain and direct message that violations of human rights, including the spiritual rights of man, constitute the main threat to stability in international relations and within individual societies.

On the day following the pope's speech, Secretary General Waldheim called John Paul's address to the General Assembly "highly encouraging and inspiring." Waldheim particularly welcomed the pope's emphasis on the need for serious disarmament measures, his "strong support" for human rights and for more attention to the needs of the poor, underprivileged and oppressed.

Waldheim said he was "highly gratified at the pope's strong support for the United Nations as the supreme forum of peace and justice."

Waldheim said he "considers that the reaction of the delegates and staff to the pope's speech is clear evidence of the enthusiasm and appreciation with which his visit was received and of the inspiration which he gave to the work of the General Assembly and the United Nations."

The papal appeal for a peaceful solution to the Middle East crisis was praised by Israeli and Palestinian spokesmen at the United Nations.

Zedhi Terzi, permanent observer at the United Nations for the Palestinian Liberation Organization, characterized the pope's remarks as "most significant."

Terzi told a press conference two days after John Paul's speech that "the pope has given a guideline to the rest of the world by signifying that he agrees with those who say that peace in the Middle East rests on a just solution of the Palestinian rights question."

Yehuda Blum, Israeli representative at the United Nations, was also quick to comment on the pope's Middle East suggestions. He welcomed the papal appeal for a peaceful solution.

"Israel, too, is committed to a just and peaceful settlement of the Palestine question, and we are now engaged in negotiations to that end with Egypt and the United States," Blum said.

"We particularly welcome the pope's appeal to solve peacefully all outstanding international problems and his clear and unequivocal condemnation of violence and terrorism," Blum added.

Blum also discussed the pope's request for international guarantees for Jerusalem as a holy city for Christians, Moslems and Jews, pointing out that Israeli law guarantees members of all faiths unrestricted access to Jerusalem's holy places.

Prince Saud al Faisal, foreign minister of Saudi Arabia, also praised the pope's talk, calling it a "historical speech." But he asked for Arab sovereignty over Jerusalem instead of the proposal advocated by the pope.

Particular reference should be made to John Paul's emphasis on "the spiritual ideals and values that should be espoused by the world in facing the various facets of materialism, in order to attain peace, justice and freedom," Faisal added in a speech before the General Assembly.

"What the pontiff has advocated in his address is in consonance with what Islam and the Moslems call for. From this perspective, the followers of the three monotheistic religions must enjoy their rights of freedom of worship in the holy city of Jerusalem. In order to fulfill this objective we believe that Jerusalem must revert to Arab sovereignty so that all the faithful will enjoy complete freedom of worship on an equal footing," he said.

Peace, security and stability will not be attained in the Middle East unless there is complete and unconditional Israeli withdrawal from occupied Arab territories "including the holy city of Jerusalem," Faisal added.

Thus, John Paul left behind him an impressive moral posture but no magic formula. Spokesmen for radically opposed points of view found much to praise in the pope's address, but each continued to cling to his own particular stance as also morally correct.

John Paul probably was far better understood and received by the international

staff of the United Nations than by the diplomats and foreign ministers from the

152 countries who had fought for weeks for invitations to be in his presence.

His scripture references to human rights and religious freedom were too close for comfort for some in the General Assembly Hall. The Albanians, who last year announced that they had successfully uprooted all traces of religion in their country, chose not to attend the speech.

The Chinese also ignored the pope. U.N. officials said that diplomats invited to meet the pope included Chinese Deputy Foreign Minister Nan Nianlong and Ambassador Chen Chu, but they did not show up. The Chinese gave no reason for their absence. Lower-level members of the Chinese mission, however, attended the pope's speech.

In contrast, delegates from other communist countries — including the Soviet Union, Vietnam, Laos, Cambodia and Eastern European nations — were introduced to the pope during a reception given by Waldheim.

John Paul displayed either diplomatic tact or spiritual judgment — or perhaps a combination of the two — by not offering a blessing to the assembled dignitaries, since among them were representatives of officially atheistic states.

But the pope's attitude changed completely when he spoke to secretaries, clerks, maintenance men, lawyers, economists, interpreters and civil servants. He noted that he had been asked to give that audience his blessing and he did it with warmth and obvious joy.

During Waldheim's reception for John Paul, the Arabs thanked the pope for mentioning the Palestinian question and the need for Jerusalem to remain a holy city for Moslems, Jews and Christians. The Palestine Liberation Organization invited the pope to come "to Palestine," using their own name for Israel.

John Paul impressed U.N. diplomats with his simple yet profound conviction that "peace is possible when it is based on the recognition of the fatherhood of God and the brotherhood of all men."

Waldheim, the official host, summed up his feelings about the pope's visit by telling reporters: "This is the happiest day of my life."

Polish Prime Minister Emil Wojtaszek asked for and received a private audience with the pope in Waldheim's 38th-floor office. Present were Cardinal Agostino Casaroli, papal secretary of state, and Henryk Jarosz, Polish ambassador to the United Nations, indicating that this was a business meeting as opposed to Wojtaszek's personal interest in seeing the pope.

Another reception was held for the pope so he could greet the many non-U.N. related dignitaries and personalities who were present for his speech. The white-cassocked pope looked tired but happy at the end of this 50-minute reception which culminated his visit to the United Nations. Standing on a blue-carpeted platform beneath a massive Chinese tapestry depicting the Great Wall of China, he greeted hundreds of guests by shaking their hands, holding the gold cross around his neck with his left hand during most of the reception.

Among those John Paul greeted were Jacqueline Onassis, the widow of President Kennedy, and her daughter Caroline, and television newswoman Barbara Walters.

In his farewell speech to diplomats, John Paul returned to one of the themes of his main address.

"By proclaiming the incomparable dignity of every human being and by manifesting my firm belief in the unity and solidarity of all nations, I have been permitted to reaffirm a basic tenet of my encyclical letter: 'After all, peace comes down to respect for man's inviolable rights.'

"The message which I wish to leave with you is a message of certitude and hope: the certitude that peace is possible when it is based on the recognition of the fatherhood of God and the brotherhood of all men; the hope that the sense of moral responsibility which every person must assume will make it possible to create a better world in freedom, in justice and in love."

149

Gateway to Freedom

The "Big Apple" signs that greeted Pope John Paul II as his motorcade sped from LaGuardia Airport to the United Nations were only a warm-up for the greeting New Yorkers would give the second pontiff to visit their city. After John Paul finished his activities at the United Nations about 5 p.m. Oct. 2, he belonged to New York — at least until his trip to Philadelphia the following day.

Streamers and confetti in midtown Manhattan, tenement window watchers in Harlem and flash after flash from Instamatic cameras in the South Bronx greeted John Paul on his travels through New York for the remainder of the day. Before the day was over, New Yorkers would give him a welcome, complete with ticker-tape parade, normally reserved for war heroes and astronauts.

The first stop was St. Patrick's Cathedral. Located in the center of the city, the cathedral was packed with dignitaries of church and state as well as non-Catholic guests and rank-and-file parishioners lucky enough to get a ticket. As the pope entered, going up the sanctuary steps with Cardinal Terence Cooke of New York, he was greeted with resounding applause and cheers.

In his introduction, Cardinal Cooke noted that John Paul had visited St. Patrick's during his 1976 U.S. tour when he was "a great cardinal of Poland."

The purpose of this papal visit is "to confirm you in your holy, Catholic and apostolic faith; to invoke upon you the joy and strength that will sustain you in Christian living," John Paul said.

"On this occasion I send my greetings to all the people of New York. In a special way my heart is with the poor, with those who suffer, with those who are alone and abandoned in the midst of this teeming metropolis."

Quoting from his encyclical *Redemptor Hominis*, John Paul said he prayed that "the spires of St. Patrick's" would always reflect the thrust of the church's fundamental function: "to direct man's gaze, to point the awareness and experience of the whole of humanity toward the mystery of God, to help all men and women to be familiar with the profundity of the redemption taking place in Jesus Christ."

The church's distinctive mission is "to direct hearts to God, to keep alive hope in the world." At the conclusion of his talk, John Paul received a standing ovation, and he led the congregation in the Lord's Prayer and gave his blessing.

Retired Archbishop Fulton Sheen, whose oratory in the pulpit of St. Patrick's has inspired generations of Catholics, had a seat of honor and received a personal greeting from the pope.

Also seated in a special section in the sanctuary were representatives of other religions, including Greek Orthodox Archbishop Iakovos of North and South America, Dr. Claire Randall, general secretary of the National Council of Churches, and Rabbi Marc Tanenbaum of the American Jewish Committee.

Seated at the front of the nave were Gov. Hugh Carey of New York, Mayor Ed Koch of New York City, former New York Mayor Abraham Beame, and Sens. Jacob Javits and Daniel Patrick Moynihan.

The cathedral, which seats 2,500, was packed, and many hundreds were standing. Tickets were assigned to parishes, where they were often distributed by lot. Others came as special guests of Cardinal Cooke — people such as Hugh Grant, donor of the townhouse where the Vatican now houses its mission to the United Nations.

At the conclusion of the service, John Paul walked the length of the center aisle and through the huge bronze doors that open onto Fifth Avenue. There he greeted thousands of people who had gathered outside. Among the throng was a Polish-American folk dance group from Brooklyn, wearing Polish costumes.

The pope then went to Cardinal Cooke's residence adjacent to the cathedral for a brief rest.

Manhattan office workers delayed their dinners to crowd around the cardinal's residence at Madison and East 51st Street for a glimpse of the pope. When he finally became visible about an hour after most offices closed at 5 p.m., cheers rose up and confetti and streamers drifted down from the office workers in windows above.

Evening plans called for John Paul to travel by motorcade to Yankee Stadium via Harlem and the South Bronx so he could address black Americans and Hispanics. At the stadium, he would celebrate Mass. His police-escorted motorcade traveled through the sparsely lined roads of Central Park before turning up Seventh Avenue, the main artery of New York's predominantly black and Hispanic Harlem section, and moving onto Adam Clayton Powell Boulevard toward St. Charles Borromeo Parish.

There, as dusk fell over Harlem, John Paul was greeted by a gospel choir and by Msgr. Emerson Moore, black pastor of St. Charles Borromeo. Msgr. Moore said the pope's taking time to stop in Harlem was seen as support and encouragement "in all the Harlems of America."

John Paul acknowledged that he was speaking not only to the crowd outside St. Charles but through them "to all black Americans." He said he came as a servant of Jesus Christ and that Christ came to bring joy. "In a true sense, joy is the keynote of the Christian message."

He also encouraged evangelization, saying many people have never known the joy of Christ. "We need not look to the ends of the earth" for those people, he said. "They live in our neighborhoods, they walk down our streets. They may even be members of our own families."

Two third-graders from the parish school, Joel Fernandez and Lynda Anderson, received a papal hug and kiss when they presented gifts of Polish bread and flowers to the pope.

St. Charles Borromeo is on a side street, West 141st. Only ticket holders were admitted onto the street for the pope's visit. But the tenement windows across the street were filled with people enjoying their ringside seats. The pope gave them a smile and a wave. Thousands more lined his approach and departure routes.

As in the rest of the city, security for the pope was massive and tight. Hundreds of uniformed police kept watch over the area, some from rooftops and a helicopter. Phalanxes of motorcycle police, police cars and a swarm of Secret Service agents accompanied the papal motorcade. Secret Service agents checked the bread and flowers which were to be given to the pope and watched closely until they were presented to make sure no substitutions were made.

All went smoothly and there were no incidents. The only difficulty was one created by the enthusiasm of the crowd — so much noise that some of the statements made by and to John Paul could not be clearly heard.

Finishing with several "alleluias," John Paul returned to his car. As it drove off he lifted his eyes and hands upward to the many people who watched him from tenement and apartment windows.

From Harlem John Paul traveled to the South Bronx to address Hispanics. The **153** vicar for the South Bronx, Father Neal Connelly, said, "We are not surprised you came," referring to the pope's concern for the poor. "It tells the whole world that we count."

The site had been cleared of slum housing a week earlier to make way for a new housing project co-sponsored by the Morris-Courtland Neighborhood Association and two nearby parishes, St. Anselm and Immaculate Conception.

John Paul spoke primarily in Spanish although he added English several times. The largely Hispanic community is composed of people whose "lives are marked by pain," he said. His visit was "meant to be a sign of gratitude and an encouragement for what the church has done and is continuing to do, through her parishes, schools, health centers, institutes for assisting youth and the aging, on behalf of so many who experience inner anxiety and material deprivation."

John Paul was wildly cheered as the magnetism of his personality overcame the technical difficulties of a malfunctioning loudspeaker system which caused his words to be missed by many. Ironically, people listening and watching the pope at home on radio and television heard every word because the broadcasting apparatus was on a different hook-up than the loudspeaker system.

The pope's motorcade then proceeded to Yankee Stadium. After comforting the afflicted in Harlem and the South Bronx, John Paul afflicted the comfortable during his homily at Yankee Stadium.

John Paul told American Catholics — one of the wealthiest Catholic populations in the world — to end their easy way of life and to give to the poor until it hurts.

The poor "are your brothers and sisters in Christ. You must never be content to leave them just the crumbs from the feast. You must take of your substance, and not just of your abundance, in order to help them," he told the 80,000 people gathered in the stadium.

"It is not right that the standard of living of the rich countries should seek to maintain itself by draining off a great part of the reserves of energy and raw materials which are meant to serve the whole of humanity," he declared.

The crowd — unlike most audiences or congregations on papal trips who repeatedly interrupt the pope with applause and cheers — was silent through most of the homily. At the beginning, John Paul spoke quietly of Christ as the giver of peace, as peace and justice itself, and the one who "perfects, restores and manifests in himself the unsurpassable dignity that God wishes to give to man from the beginning."

John Paul said to the overflow crowd at the late evening service that when Christians make Christ the center of their lives, "we are caught up in the movement of the Holy Spirit who visits the poor, calms fevered hearts, binds up wounded hearts, warms cold hearts and gives us the fullness of his gifts."

He said that the task of the Christian in the modern world is an immense but "an enthralling one," and told them he was going to bring up "urgent priorities which your service to humanity ought to concentrate upon today."

He asked American Catholics to remember the needs of the poor, the suffering, the hungry, neglected, unemployed and desperate. He softened the sting of the frank words that would follow by recalling the traditional reputation of America and American Catholics for generosity to others, and the continuing value of the existing network of Catholic charitable works.

John Paul spoke of the framework of charity, emphasizing that the recipient's dignity and freedom must be respected, and that poverty and misery must be attacked on the structural level as well as the individual level. Only when he was halfway through the homily did he began to raise serious challenges to the American lifestyle.

In order to meet the challenges he was discussing, he said, "fresh spiritual and moral energy drawn from the inexhaustible divine source is needed."

"This energy does not develop easily. The lifestyle of many of the members of our rich and permissive societies is easy, and so is the lifestyle of increasing groups inside the poorer countries," he added.

Christians should be "in the vanguard in favoring ways of life that decisively break with a frenzy of consumerism, exhausting and joyless," he said. "It is not a question of slowing down progress, for there is no human progress when everything conspires to give full reign to the instincts of self-interest, sex and power. We must find a simple way of living."

He cited the parable of Lazarus and the rich man, commenting that the rich man was not condemned because he had riches, but "because he did not pay attention to the other man."

God "pronounces very harsh words against those who use their possessions in a selfish way, without paying attention to the needs of others," John Paul said.

The parable of Lazarus "must always be present in our memory; it must form our conscience. Christ demands openness to our brothers and sisters in need — openness from the rich, the affluent, the economically advanced; openness to the poor, the underdeveloped and the disadvantaged."

He called on Americans to translate the biblical parable "into contemporary terms, in terms of economy and politics, in terms of all human rights, in terms of relations between the 'First,' 'Second' and 'Third Worlds.'"

John Paul said: "We cannot stand idly by when thousands of human beings are dying of hunger. Nor can we remain indifferent when the rights of the human spirit are trampled upon...we cannot stand idly by, enjoying our own riches and freedom if, in any place, the Lazarus of the 20th century stands at our doors."

Catholics of the most affluent country in the world should realize that "riches and freedom create a special obligation," he said.

Security for the pope continued to be tight. New York police took extraordinary security measures at the stadium. They deployed bomb-sniffing dogs and scores of security police to sweep the whole stadium before the Mass. Along the motorcade route and interspersed around the stadium were hundreds of police sharpshooters scanning the crowd for any suspicious activity.

Unlike the 1965 Mass celebrated in Yankee Stadium 14 years earlier by Pope Paul VI, the Mass of Pope John Paul featured distribution of Communion to all the people who wanted to receive. Eighty thousand hosts were consecrated for the occasion and hundreds of priests were available to distribute them.

The Mass featured a band of 50 musicians on a large platform holding the altar near the center of the playing field. A choir of 1,400 voices from dioceses in Connecticut, New York and New Jersey led the singing. Because of a threat of rain, a large plastic hood had been erected over the altar. In Boston the night before, heavy rains had soaked the pope, some 30 bishops concelebrating with him, and the altar.

At Yankee Stadium it did not rain during the Mass.

The Mass was the final public event of that day for John Paul. He spent the night at Cardinal Cooke's residence at 452 Madison Ave. The first papal event of Oct. 3 took place at the neighboring St. Patrick's Cathedral.

As John Paul entered the cathedral for a morning prayer service with priests and Religious, the thousands who had waited for hours in the intermittent rain chanted "Long live the pope!"

Smiling, John Paul spoke into the microphone: "You're right." As was usual with him, he was running slightly behind schedule, arriving at 8:25 a.m. The service had been scheduled for 8 a.m.

Umbrellas opened and closed among the waiting crowd as the rain came and went. Some people had been waiting for more than two hours. One nun who had arrived early and reached a central place near the cathedral entrance became faint, but after a first-aid crew revived her, she refused to leave her hard-won location.

Another nun from New Jersey had attended the papal Mass at Yankee Stadium the previous evening, returned to New Jersey, slept for 25 minutes and rose to return to the cathedral for the morning service.

For several blocks near the cathedral Fifth Avenue was closed off and crowded. Swarms of police patrolled the area. The cathedral bells were chiming. Papal and American flags flew from flagpoles angling out from the front of the cathedral, and a papal flag flew also at Rockefeller Center across Fifth Avenue. A choir was singing inside the cathedral and loudspeakers carried their songs to the crowd outside. Booklets with the order of service were distributed.

Immediately after the first words of the service, John Paul turned from the crowd outside and went up the main aisle of the cathedral. The choir and congregation sang "All Creatures of Our God and King," a hymn attributed to St. Francis of Assisi.

The central scriptural text of the service was from St. Paul's Letter to the Romans: "Who will separate us from the love of Christ?" The pope's answer was: "Nothing, provided we remain a community of prayer." He emphasized the importance of maintaining a strong life of prayer. "The Liturgy of the Hours should be among the highest priorities of our days and of every day," he said.

The Liturgy of the Hours, more commonly known as the breviary, is the official prayer of the church by which it consecrates the various times of the day to God in prayer. It is required of priests, deacons and some Religious, and it is recommended to lay persons as a daily prayer.

"The value of the Liturgy of the Hours is enormous," John Paul told more than 2,000 priests and Religious packing the cathedral.

"In this prayer of praise we lift up our hearts to the Father of our Lord Jesus Christ, bringing with us the anguish and hopes, the joys and sorrow of all our brothers and sisters in the world," he said.

"And our prayer becomes likewise a school of sensitivity, making us aware of how much our destinies are linked together in the human family. Our prayer becomes a school of love," he added. "Through this prayer of Christ to which we give voice, our day is sanctified, our activities transformed, our actions made holy."

After finishing his talk, he led the recitation of the Our Father.

Applause broke out as the service ended. The applause continued as John Paul walked down the central aisle to the entrance of the cathedral. Outside, standing on the cathedral steps, he greeted the waiting crowd and intoned a blessing. "Very nice," he said in conclusion, referring to the enthusiasm with which the crowd had chanted the responses. Then he went off to his next appointment with youngsters waiting at Madison Square Garden.

At Madison Square Garden, about 19,000 teen-agers awaited John Paul. When he arrived, he and his audience engaged in a rollicking singing and shouting encounter that was typical of his meetings with young people.

Blue jeans, a T-shirt, rock music and a slide show helped the roaring crowd of American teen-agers give John Paul an insight into their lives.

"By our jeans, by our T-shirts we say: 'We are different,'" said a young representative of the Archdiocese of New York. The pope quickly adopted the informal atmosphere, clapping to the beat of a song from the rock opera, "Godspell," and motioning with his hands like a band leader to the theme from the movie, "Superman."

John Paul rode around inside the arena standing in the back of a white compact pickup truck specially fitted out for him and dubbed by those who saw it "the popemobile." At one point he picked up a small girl from the crowd and stood her atop the cab of the vehicle. Then he held his ears as if to shield them from the noise as he finished a trip around what is usually the home of New York's basketball Knicks and hockey Rangers.

It was a program for youth, entirely designed by New York's Catholic teen-agers.

The young people presented John Paul mementos important to them — a pair of jeans, a T-shirt, a tape of the music they listen to, a guitar, a medal of Mary and, perhaps the most significant, a pledge of thousands of hours of service and sacrifice for the people of their communities.

The pope accepted each, playfully fingering the strings of the guitar, trying on the medal and chain and warmly hugging and holding the teens who presented the gifts.

The slide show told a story of the lives of American teen-agers engaged in helping others. It was accompanied by taped voices of several youths. They told the pope what was on their minds, urging him to "mention young people" in his talks, telling him they think the pope at times is "just for adults," discussing their worries about the impoverished conditions of some of their neighborhoods.

In a burst of youthful enthusiasm, different school groups shouted their high school names and that they loved the pope as he prepared to start his talk. The groups came from New York, New Jersey and Connecticut. The pope acknowledged the cheers by waving his arms, humming and murmuring "woooo," the Polish equivalent of wow, in appreciation into the microphone.

After a few minutes John Paul was able to begin his talk. He said Catholic education is important because its purpose is "to communicate Christ to you so that your attitude toward others will be that of Christ."

"You are approaching that stage in your life when you must take personal responsibility for your own destiny," he said. "Soon you will be making major decisions which will affect the whole course of your life. If these decisions reflect Christ's attitude, then your education will be a success."

He added: "People have placed a lot of hope in you, and they now look forward to your collaboration in giving witness to Christ and in transmitting the Gospel to others."

The church and the world need young people "because it needs Christ and you belong to Christ," he said.

As John Paul left Madison Square Garden for his next stop, Battery Park on the southern tip of Manhattan, he was caught in a downpour of rain. Planned for the trip to Battery Park was a ticker-tape parade down Broadway.

The pope was attired in a plastic raincoat and protected by his wide-brimmed red hat and a black umbrella held by Cardinal Terence Cooke of New York. As he stood in his limousine, John Paul was visible to workers in offices in the Wall Street area. He continued to wave, bless the crowd and smile as the motorcade drove down the traditional ticker-tape route between City Hall and Battery Park.

The parade was marked by 68-degree temperatures with winds blowing rain up to 23 miles an hour. Despite that, the crowd was 10 deep in many places. One woman viewing the parade exclaimed, "God bless the pope; God bless the rain!"

The limousine had some wet ticker tape and flowers stuck to it as the papal entourage arrived at Battery Park where John Paul addressed a community composed of a cross section of American ethnic groups. He used the occasion to issue an address to New York and the nation, stressing how ethnic diversity and a devotion to liberty are cornerstones of the United States.

Battery Park was chosen for this speech because visible in the distance are the Statue of Liberty and Ellis Island, historic entry point for waves of European immigrants to the United States. With the Statue of Liberty at his back and the wind whipping around him, John Paul spoke.

"Every nation has its historical symbols. They may be shrines or statues or documents, but their significance lies in the truths they represent to the citizens of a nation and in the image they convey to other nations," he said. "Such a symbol in the United States is the Statue of Liberty."

The statue, one of America's most famous landmarks, "is an impressive symbol of what the United States has stood for from the very beginning of its history," he said. "This is a symbol of freedom."

The statue "reflects the immigrant history of the United States, for it was freedom that millions of human beings were looking for on these shores.

"And it was freedom that the young republic offered in compassion. On this spot, I wish to pay homage to this noble trait of America and its people: its desire to be free, its determination to preserve freedom, and its willingness to share this freedom with others. May the ideal of liberty, of freedom, remain a moving force for your nation and for all nations in the world today!"

John Paul continued: "It greatly honors your country and its citizens that on this foundation of liberty you have built a nation where the dignity of every human person is to be respected, where a religious sense and a strong family structure are fostered, where duty and honest work are held in high esteem, where generosity and hospitality are no idle words, and where the right to religious liberty is deeply rooted in your history."

But Americans should remember that "past achievements can never be an acceptable substitute for present responsibilities," he said. Freedom and justice go hand in hand, and "no institution or organization can credibly stand for freedom today if it does not also support the quest for justice, for both are essential demands of the human spirit."

"The freedom that was gained must be ratified every day by the firm rejection of whatever wounds, weakens or dishonors human life. And so I appeal to all who love freedom and justice to give a chance to all in need, to the poor and the powerless. Break open the hopeless cycles of poverty and the ignorance that are still the lot of too many of our brothers and sisters; the hopeless cycles of prejudices that linger on despite enormous progress toward effective equality in education and employment; the cycles of despair in which are imprisoned all those that lack decent food, shelter or employment; the cycles of underdevelopment that are the consequence of international mechanisms that subordinate human existence to the domination of partially conceived economic progress; and finally the inhuman cycle of war that springs from the violation of man's fundamental rights and produces still graver violation of them.

"Freedom in justice will bring a new dawn of hope for the present generation as it has done before: for the homeless, for the unemployed, for the aging, for the sick and the handicapped, for migrants and the undocumented workers, for all who hunger for human dignity in this land and in the world."

John Paul praised the diversity and pluralism of the United States "where people of different ethnic origins and creeds can live, work and prosper together in freedom and mutual respect."

"Leaders of the Jewish community whose presence honors me greatly," received a special papal greeting. John Paul praised the "fraternal dialogue and fruitful collaboration" between Catholics and Jews at an international level and in the United States.

"Several common programs of study, mutual knowledge, a common determination to reject all forms of anti-Semitism and discrimination, and various forms of collaboration for human advancement, inspired by our common biblical heritage, have created deep and permanent links between Jews and Catholics. As one who in my homeland has shared the suffering of your brethren, I greet you with this word taken from the Hebrew language: *Shalom!* Peace be with you."

John Paul at one point interrupted his address to greet Poles in the crowd in Polish. His remarks were translated as, "Long live Poland! Long live Polish-Americans!"

From Battery Park, John Paul left for the neighboring Diocese of Brooklyn and Shea Stadium for the final event on his New York itinerary. On the way, though, he overruled the plans of his own staff and the Diocese of Brooklyn in order not to disappoint some 100 children and hundreds of Polish-Americans gathered to see him outside St. James Cathedral in downtown Brooklyn.

In pouring rain, the papal procession was rerouted after it crossed the Brooklyn Bridge to the little-known cathedral where hundreds of Polish-American Catholics from Brooklyn and from other parts of metropolitan New York had been waiting for hours under umbrellas.

Originally, the cathedral stop was scheduled by the Brooklyn Diocese, but later was cancelled because of the pope's tight itinerary. In addition, the heavy rains seemed to work against the prayers and hopes of the Polish-Americans. But the children in the costumes of his homeland had the pope on their side.

By now wearing a heavy raincoat and still standing up under an umbrella in the black limousine, John Paul smiled and waved to an overjoyed crowd at the recently renovated cathedral. A white-and-yellow bouquet of flowers was thrust into his hands as he waved to well-wishers. He then got out of the limousine and mingled with the crowd for about 10 minutes.

On all sides were banners displaying the greeting in Polish: "Welcome! May you live 100 years!"

The procession then went to Shea Stadium.

At Shea Stadium, the home of the baseball Mets and the football Jets, almost 50,000 people had been waiting for hours in rain that was very heavy at times. As they waited, choirs sang and there was a prayer service at noon before the pope's arrival.

At almost 1 p.m., as the rain diminished, the papal motorcade arrived accompanied by a motorcycle-police escort and police helicopters overhead. The Secret Service asked people in seats near the platform to fold their umbrellas for security reasons.

About 1:15 p.m., the pope entered the stadium in his white open vehicle — "the popemobile." He was an hour behind schedule. Riding with him were Bishop Francis Mugavero of Brooklyn and Cardinal Cooke. As the vehicle circled the field, a band played, flashbulbs popped, the crowd chanted "Long Live the Pope," and the electronic scoreboard flashed the same sentiment.

Welcoming the pope on behalf of the people of Long Island, on which the Brooklyn Diocese is located, Bishop Mugavero said: "Welcome to a part of these United States where the faith which was brought by immigrants from faraway places has given comfort, encouragement and guidance to the lives and destinies of so many."

Attending the ceremony were Gov. Carey and Mayor Koch.

John Paul used the occasion to issue a final appeal for love to New Yorkers. He urged them to let Christian love inspire them to build every part of the city into a true community.

"From Rome I bring you a message of faith and love," he said as he addressed the crowd from a platform in center field with a huge crucifix as backdrop. Quoting from St. Paul's Letter to the Colossians, he said: "May the peace of Christ reign in your hearts."

John Paul continued: "Make peace the desire of your heart, for if you love peace, you will love all humanity without distinction of race, color or creed."

Christ's words to love your neighbor as yourself "must be your inspiration in forming true human relationships among yourselves, so that nobody will ever feel alone or unwanted or, much less, rejected, despised or hated," John Paul said.

"Jesus himself will give you the power of fraternal love. And every neighborhood, every block, every street will become a true community because you will want it so, and Jesus will help you to bring it about. Keep Jesus Christ in your hearts and you will recognize his face in every human being. You will want to help him out in all his needs: the needs of your brothers and sisters."

In a departure from his text, John Paul greeted the people of New York, New

159

Jersey, Connecticut, Brooklyn and Long Island. Persons from each place cheered as he greeted them.

Laughter erupted as John Paul mispronounced the word "skyscrapers" as "skyscrappers." Smiling, he corrected himself and then pronounced the equivalent word in French, Italian, Spanish and Polish to show that he really knew what the word meant. The crowd applauded.

After his talk in English, he greeted ethnic groups present in Spanish, Polish and Italian.

He emphasized the importance of the Hispanic community in the United States and in the church. He exhorted them "always to maintain very clearly your Christian identity, with a constant reference to the value of your faith, values that must enlighten the legitimate quest for a worthy material position for yourselves and your families."

As he spoke in Italian, the sun finally broke through the clouds. Pointing to it, he said: "At last the sun has arrived. Italy means sun, not rain."

As the roar of jets from nearby LaGuardia Airport were heard in the background, a reminder that he would soon fly to Philadelphia, John Paul concluded his remarks with: "Goodbye and God bless you." Then he led the crowd in singing the Our Father and gave his blessing.

John Paul's impact on New Yorkers went beyond the hundreds of thousands who saw him in person. It extended to the millions who saw him live on television and read about him in the newspapers.

Often, television viewers had the best seats in the house — whether it was a wheelchair, hospital bed or bar stool in the local pub. They got a close-up view. They saw the furrows in the pope's face, the curls at the ends of the pope's smile and the sparkle in the pope's eyes as he spontaneously bantered with the crowds.

One of the high points for New York's television watchers — and for those in the rest of the country where that particular segment was shown — came as John Paul, seated on a flower-decked platform in Madison Square Garden filled with thousands of cheering high school students, literally said nothing. He hummed.

As thunderous cheers and outbursts of whistles filled the hall, John Paul expressed his appreciation and admiration with sounds of his own, all clearly picked up by the microphone in front of him. "Woooooooo...woo...mmmm...mmmm," he intoned time after time. In the background, Cardinal Cooke and other prelates shifted nervously, discussing what was going on. How would they quiet the audience? The cardinal rose, but the pope waved him off. Camera crew blood pressures went up as valuable television time passed.

"Mmmm...wooo...." Then at last the pope said, "You know what it is — we shall destroy the program. Cardinal Cooke says, 'Enough!'"

A roar of laughter rose from the audience.

A gauge of John Paul's impact on New York television came when the station which provided live coverage of the Mass at Yankee Stadium checked the audience ratings. The pope drew an estimated audience of 2.5 million viewers.

It was the same for the city's newspapers. The usually staid New York Times splashed John Paul's photograph across its front page and ran column after column of stories inside. The New York Daily News, the nation's largest daily paper with a circulation of 1.6 million, printed an additional 100,000 copies and still ran short of demand.

There was no doubt about it: "Cyclone Wojtyla" certainly had been "gangbusters" in New York.

1

WITAJ

PARK HOLLOW SOCIAL & CIVIC CLUB
WELCOMES **POPE JOHN PAUL II**
BENVENUTO

WINES
LIQUORS

588

CL

POLICE LINE   DO NOT CROSS

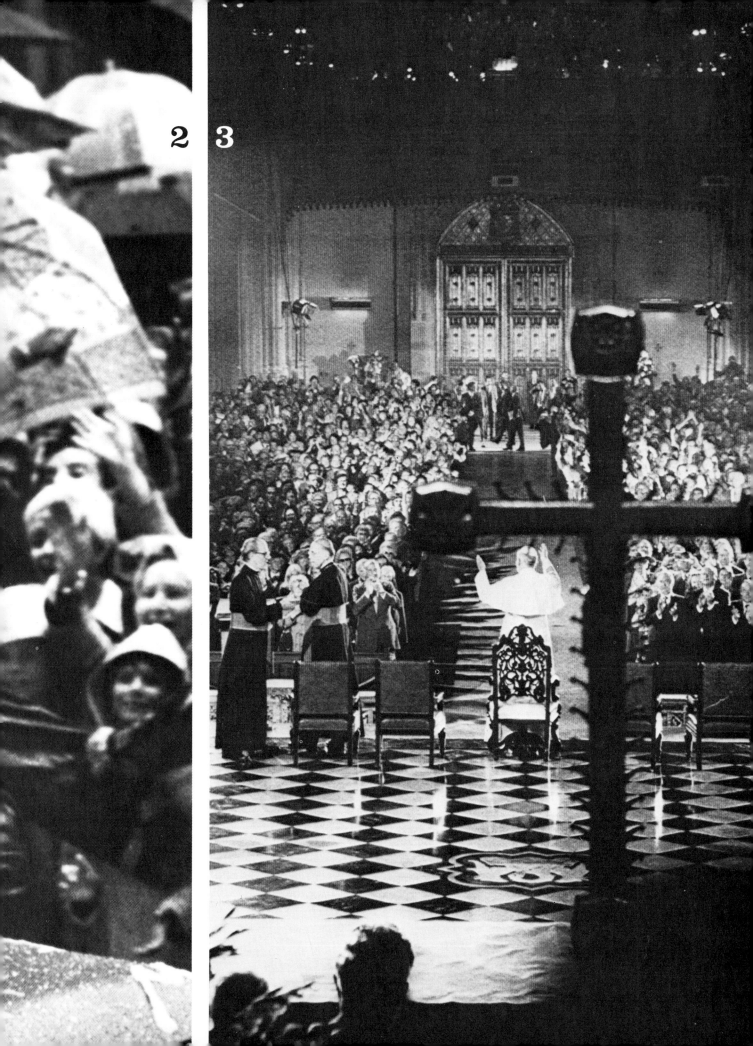

GOD BLESS YOU
POPE JOHNP

4 **5**

6

7

8 9

10 11

12 13

14

On the preceding pages:

1 People along Morris Avenue in the South Bronx wait their turn for a glimpse of the pope.

2 Even though it rained on his parade down Broadway, the pope has a warm smile and wave for those who braved the elements. Cardinal Terence Cooke holds the umbrella.

3 The pope acknowledges applause of the crowd in St. Patrick's Cathedral.

4 Students await the arrival of Pope John Paul in Harlem.

5 A girl from St. Aloysius parish in Harlem has her own special wish for the pope.

6 From a sidewalk in Harlem, Pope John Paul II addresses the crowd which had turned out to see him.

7 Cardinal Terence Cooke is embraced by Pope John Paul at St. Patrick's Cathedral.

8 Geralyn Smith is lifted atop the pope's vehicle shortly after his arrival at Madison Square Garden.

9 Pope John Paul II waves to the young people gathered at Madison Square Garden. Students from more than 200 Catholic and public high schools turned out.

10 Waving a gift from a youth at Madison Square Garden, Pope John Paul keeps time with the chanting crowd.

11 The pope smiles at the cheering crowd at Shea Stadium.

12 With the Statue of Liberty behind him, the pope takes his place on the podium at a windy Battery Park.

13 In a pouring rain, Pope John Paul II picks up a small child as he leaves Battery Park.

14 At Yankee Stadium, the pope gestures to the multitude assembled for Mass.

October 3 and 4

The City of Brotherly Love

Philadelphia scored a first when John Paul arrived on the afternoon of Oct. 3. For the first time on his U.S. journey, the pope was welcomed in sunshine. Cardinal John Krol of Philadelphia greeted him aboard the papal airplane, "Shepherd I," and they walked off the plane arm in arm. The cardinal credited the "solid foundation of prayer" in preparation for his visit as a reason for the good weather.

Also greeting John Paul were Pennsylvania Gov. Dick Thornburgh, Philadelphia Mayor Frank Rizzo and his wife Carmella, and 3,000 archdiocesan school students who cheered and sang, "Long live the pope." Gov. Thornburgh welcomed John Paul by recalling that Pennsylvania had been established by William Penn nearly 300 years ago as a place based on brotherly love where religious refugees could live in peace.

"Through the warmth of your personality, the moral force of your character and the understanding within your heart, you have breathed new life in the dream of our founder," Thornburgh told the pope.

Mayor Rizzo kneeled and kissed the pope's ring and welcomed him "with all our love and affection."

John Paul responded: "Philadelphia means brotherly love."

Already 65 minutes behind schedule, John Paul rode in a closed-car motorcade to the foot of Broad Street. Then the roof of the limousine was opened and he stood to wave at the 800,000 people lining the routes. The crowd, though, found that getting the pope's attention on the motorcade was not easy. The motorcade was supposed to travel about 3 to 6 miles per hour. Instead it traveled at speeds of up to 28 miles an hour, apparently to make up for lost time.

Nevertheless, thousands showed John Paul signs of welcome and love in an attempt to prompt him to look their way. Hand-lettered signs and banners along the route varied from *"Viva il Papa"* to a simple "Hi Pope."

A nun on Broad Street held a sign with one of the more compelling messages of the day: "My friend lies sick with cancer. Say the word and my friend will be cured."

The first stop was the Cathedral of Sts. Peter and Paul where John Paul delivered a message of love. Saying he felt "truly among friends" in the gold-leaf trimmed cathedral, he addressed 1,500 dignitaries and cathedral parishioners. He used the cathedral setting to call Philadelphia a "symbol of freedom and fraternal relations."

He added: "My greeting is also a prayer. May the common dedication and the united efforts of all your citizens — Catholics, Protestants and Jews alike — succeed in making your inner city and suburbs places where people are no strangers to each other, where every man, woman and child feels respected; where nobody feels abandoned, rejected or alone.''

Cardinal Krol welcomed the pope to the cathedral in the name of the dioceses of Pennsylvania and neighboring New Jersey. Cardinal Krol praised the loyalty and devotion of local Catholics and called the pope's visit ''an honor and a privilege. ''

After the ceremony, John Paul rested in the cathedral rectory in preparation for his first major event in Philadelphia, an outdoor Mass at Logan Circle. Crowds of people lined the route as the motorcade traveled to the site of the Mass.

At Logan Circle well over a million persons lined the Benjamin Franklin Parkway for more than one-half mile, ballooning around the altar built atop Logan Fountain. The circular location gave the huge gathering a chance to join in the celebration on all sides — a feature John Paul used to advantage by turning completely around to elevate the host and the chalice during the consecration.

In the crowd were thousands of families from the Middle Atlantic states who had made day-long journeys to see and hear the pope.

Aware that he was speaking near the birthplace of political freedom in the United States, John Paul cautioned against the abuses of freedom on such topics as human sexuality, human rights, the family, religious freedom and priestly celibacy.

With the statue of the man who gave this land its first religiously free colony — William Penn — looking down from the top of nearby City Hall, John Paul noted that the human and civil values contained in the Declaration of Independence have ''strong connections with basic religious and Christian values.'' A sense of religion itself ''is part of this heritage,'' he said.

''As citizens, you must strive to preserve these human values...As Christians, you must strengthen these human values and complement them by confronting them with the gospel message,'' he added.

John Paul said human values are strengthened when power and authority respect fundamental human rights; when freedom is seen as a gift that enables self-giving and service; and when the family is protected, when its unity is preserved and when its role as the basic cell of society is recognized and honored.

Approximately one mile from the site where the Declaration of Independence was read 203 years earlier, John Paul said man must not abuse the freedom fostered by the historic declaration, but live his life according to what is ''objectively true and morally good.''

Freedom, he said, ''can never tolerate an offense against the rights of others, and one of the fundamental rights of man is the right to worship...No freedom can exist when it goes against man in what he is, or against man in his relationship to others and to God.'' Freedom cannot be seen ''as a pretext for moral anarchy.''

John Paul noted what he called ''disturbing tendencies and so much laxity'' regarding traditional church teachings on marriage and human sexuality.

''Moral norms do not militate against the freedom of the person or the couple,'' he said. ''On the contrary, they exist precisely for that freedom, since they are given to ensure the right use of freedom. Whoever refuses to accept these norms and to act accordingly, whoever seeks to liberate himself or herself from these norms, is truly not free.''

John Paul quickly added that his thoughts also applied to the obligations of priestly celibacy.

Cardinal Krol, himself of Polish descent, joined John Paul and Bishop J. Carroll McCormick of Scranton, Pa., on the elevated altar. Some 150 selected individuals from groups such as the handicapped, students, ethnic parishes and religious superiors received Holy Communion from the pope, as did Michael Flanagan, who as a boy was cured of cancer and played a large part in the 1977 canonization of Philadelphia bishop St. John Neumann.

After the Mass, John Paul traveled by motorcade to the residence of Cardinal Krol for dinner. Students from St. Joseph's University, which borders Cardinal Krol's residence, lined the street between the two properties and welcomed the

171

motorcade by candlelight. Even though John Paul was late for dinner, for the first time in the day the motorcade slowed down and nearly stopped.

After dinner, John Paul traveled to Overbrook, Pa., where 180 seminarians awaited him at St. Charles Borromeo Seminary. John Paul received a rousing greeting when he arrived for the late evening meeting. The visit had the atmosphere of an old friend returning to renew acquaintances. He had visited the seminary twice before, in 1969 and 1976, before becoming pope.

When he arrived at the seminary's St. Martin's Chapel a few minutes before 10 p.m., John Paul was 45 minutes behind schedule.

The students greeted him with the hymn *"Christus Vincit"* (Christ Conquers) and cheers of *"Viva il papa!"* Also in the chapel were Cardinal Krol, the bishops of Pennsylvania, the seminary faculty, and 300 civic and lay leaders.

In his talk, John Paul urged the seminarians to immerse themselves in God's word and to exercise "sound discipline to prepare for a life of consecrated service in the image of Christ."

Discipline "properly exercised" will lead seminarians into a priestly life of "joyful obedience, generosity and self-sacrifice," he said. He particularly urged fidelity to the "irrevocable commitment" which at ordination they would make to the people, to Christ and to the church.

"It is important that one's commitment be made with full awareness and personal freedom," he said. "Consider whether Christ is calling you to the celibate life. You can make a responsible decision for celibacy only after you have reached the firm conviction that Christ is indeed offering you this gift, which is intended for the good of the church and for the service of others."

John Paul continued: "Perseverance in fidelity is a proof, not of human strength and courage, but of the efficacy of Christ's grace."

The chief priorities of the priesthood are "prayer and the ministry of the word," he said.

"Develop an ever greater hunger for the word of God. Meditate on this word daily and study it continually, so that your whole life may become a proclamation of Christ, the word made flesh. In this word of God are the beginning and end of all ministry."

At the end of his talk, John Paul departed from his prepared text and said he had "a good reputation" at the seminary because of his previous visits. He referred to the fact that on his first visit, the then Cardinal Wojtyla announced a school holiday from classes, and that on his second visit he announced a two-day holiday. To mark his visit as pope, he declared a three-day holiday.

The evening closed with the singing of *"Salve Regina,"* a traditional Latin hymn in honor of Mary. The pope left the seminary at 10:40 p.m. He spent the night at Cardinal Krol's residence.

The papal visit had a profound effect on all the seminarians. But one — Robert Cunningham, a first-year theology student — came away with a special recollection. Cunningham obtained a special souvenir from John Paul by exchanging his white *zucchetto* (skullcap) for the pope's. The successful exchange started in the summer when Cunningham learned of the planned papal visit. He asked a friend studying in Rome to buy him a white *zucchetto*, similar to the one worn by the pope.

"I had read that there had been an old tradition for people at papal audiences to offer the Holy Father a white *zucchetto* in exchange for the one the pope was wearing," Cunningham recalled later. "Supposedly, the custom was common during the years when Pope Pius XII was alive."

On the night of John Paul's visit, Cunningham wasn't sure he would get close enough to the pope to even attempt the exchange. As John Paul was leaving the seminary chapel, he passed Cunningham without noticing the skullcap held out to him.

Cunningham's heart sank. His opportunity had passed. Suddenly, he saw that John Paul had started back, reaching out to shake more outstretched hands.

Cunningham dashed out to the front steps. The pope had to come out that way. He would get one more chance!

As John Paul walked down the steps, Cunningham shouted "Holy Father." The pope turned and saw the *zucchetto* in the student's hand. He looked at Cunningham and asked "For me?" The student responded, "Yes, Your Holiness." John Paul took the *zucchetto* and placed it on his head, saying "great, great." He handed his own *zucchetto* to Cunningham and when the student thanked him, he responded, "No, thank you!"

For Cunningham, the words he exchanged with the pope were more memorable than his new souvenir.

"After we had exchanged *zucchettos*," Cunningham recalled, "the Holy Father looked at me briefly, and I felt that I should say something. The only thing I could think of to say was, 'We love you very much,' and he looked at me and everyone around me and replied, 'Ah, not as much as I love you.'"

The following day, Oct. 4, was the busiest and most hectic for the pope as he completed his activities in Philadelphia, traveled to rural Iowa and finally arrived in Chicago. The public day began with a visit to the tomb of St. John Neumann at St. Peter's Church.

At the church, John Paul praised the contributions of Hispanic immigrants to the United States. Speaking in Spanish to a group of Hispanics, the pope said: "St. John Neumann, too, was an immigrant, and he experienced many of the difficulties that you yourselves have encountered: the difficulties of language, of a different culture, of social adaptation."

"Everyone knows about your efforts and perseverance in preserving your own religious heritage, which is also at the same time placed at the service of the whole national community, so that it may be a witness of unity within a pluralism of religion, culture and social living," John Paul said.

St. John Neumann, a Bohemian immigrant, Redemptorist priest and fourth bishop of Philadelphia, was the first American male to be canonized.

John Paul also spoke in English and cited the Philadelphia saint as an example of holiness and the love for God that he said is the primary thing in life.

"This is the lesson we learn from the life of St. John Neumann, and the message which I leave with you today: What really matters in life is that we are loved by Christ, and that we love him in return. In comparison to the love of Jesus, everything else is secondary. And without the love of Jesus, everything else is useless."

From St. Peter's Church, the papal motorcade traveled to Immaculate Conception Ukrainian Cathedral for a religious-ethnic celebration with Ukrainian-Rite Catholics. John Paul greeted the crowd in Ukrainian. The 600 people present in the cathedral included bishops, priests, nuns and lay people. Also present were about 25 children and a few adults in Ukrainian folk dress. The pope stressed that Ukrainian tradition is an integral part of the church.

"The various traditions within the church give expression to the multitude of ways the Gospel can take root and flower in the lives of God's people," he said. "Each tradition combined particular artistic expressions and unique spiritual insights with an unparalleled lived experience of being faithful to Christ."

John Paul also provided a note of controversy by strongly indicating that he has no intention of establishing a patriarchate for Ukrainian-Rite Catholics, despite repeated support for a patriarch by many members of the rite. Immaculate Conception Cathedral is the mother church of the Ukrainian Rite in the United States.

While expressing firm support and strong appreciation for the Ukrainian Rite and other Eastern Rites, John Paul added: "The ecclesial communities that follow these traditions are called to adhere with love and respect to certain particular forms

173

of discipline which my predecessors and I, in fulfilling our pastoral responsibility to the universal church, have judged necessary for the well-being of the whole body of Christ.''

In speaking of ''certain particular forms of discipline'' for the Ukrainian church and linking his own position to that of Pope Paul VI, who resisted pressure to establish a patriarchate, John Paul indicated his own policy will follow that of Pope Paul. John Paul also asked for an end to the divisions that have developed among Ukrainian-Rite Catholics over the patriarchate issue.

''To a great extent, our Catholic unity depends on mutual charity,'' he said.

The next stop on the papal motorcade was the Philadelphia Civic Center where John Paul concelebrated Mass with representatives of priests senates from throughout the United States. The crowd in the 17,000-seat Civic Center was heavily clerical, containing priests from each of the 172 dioceses in the United States.

In contrast to the previous crowds on the pope's U.S. visit, when the congregations consisted mainly of lay people, this one featured people dressed in cassocks, surplices, Roman collars and religious habits.

The priests representing the dioceses sat on either side of the red-carpeted altar. John Paul was seated in a gold chair. During the homily, he used the occasion to specifically address priests on their role in the church.

John Paul asked the priests of the United States to remain faithful to their ministry. He reaffirmed the permanency of the priesthood, priestly celibacy and the Catholic tradition of an all-male clergy. He also praised at length the role of the priests senates and councils in helping the local bishops govern the church.

John Paul asked American priests to remain faithful to the magisterium — the teaching authority of the church — and also to strive for priestly unity. He asked Catholics everywhere to pray for priests ''so that each and every one of them will repeatedly say 'yes' to the call he has received.''

The priesthood is not ''a task which has been assigned; it is a vocation, a call to be heard again and again,'' John Paul said. In Jesus' own call to his apostles three aspects were significant: that he called his first priests individually and by name; that he called them to preach the Gospel; and that he made them his own companions, ''drawing them into that unit of life and action which he shares with his Father,'' John Paul added.

He cautioned priests about becoming ''too earthbound'' and ''too attached to our own vision of ministry, thinking that it depends too much on our own talents and abilities and at times forgetting that it is God who calls us.''

He added: ''We are called to speak the words of God and not our own, to minister the sacraments he has given to his church, and to call people to a love which he has first made possible.''

John Paul said the ''priesthood is forever — *tu es sacerdos in aeternum* — we do not return the gift once given. It cannot be that God who gave the impulse to say 'yes' now wishes to hear 'no.' ''

The world should not be surprised that the church continues to maintain a celibate priesthood, he said. ''After centuries of experience, the church knows how deeply fitting it is that priests should give this concrete response in their lives to express the totality of the 'yes' they have spoken to the Lord.''

The calling of only males to the priesthood is ''in accord with the prophetic tradition,'' he said. The fact that Jesus individually called men to be his apostles, ''the men he himself had decided on,'' should help us ''to understand that the church's traditional decision to call men to the priesthood, and not to call women, is not a statement about human rights nor an exclusion of women from holiness and mission in the church.

174

''Rather this decision expresses the conviction of the church about this particular dimension of the gift of priesthood by which God has chosen to shepherd his flock," he said.

John Paul had to switch to the alternate microphone when the first malfunctioned at the start of his homily, but he turned the nervous moment into a harmless one, saying that during his week in the United States "something had to be not OK." The audience caught the compliment and applauded.

John Paul said the concelebration of the Mass with the representatives of the priests senates was intended to affirm the past accomplishments of these bodies as well as to encourage their "enthusiasm and determination" to work for gospel values.

Noting that priests senates were called for by the Second Vatican Council, John Paul remarked: "This new structure gives a concrete expression to the unity of bishop and priests in the service of shepherding the flock of Christ, and it assists the bishop in his distinctive role of governing the diocese, by guaranteeing for him the counsel of representative advisors from among the presbyterium."

John Paul said priests senates provide an opportunity "to give visible witness to the one priesthood you share with your bishops and with one another," and to foster the unity which Jesus desired for the church.

"Unity among priests is not a unity or a fraternity that is directed toward itself. It is for the sake of the Gospel, to symbolize, in the living out of the priesthood, the essential direction to which the Gospel calls all people: to the union of love with him and one another," he said.

Calling to mind Christ's commandment to love one another, the pope added, "And how will believers receive a witness that such love is a concrete possibility unless they find it in the example of the unity of their priestly ministers?"

Just as Jesus was a "man for others" in giving himself up on the cross, "so the priest is most of all servant and 'man for others'" when he celebrates Mass, John Paul said. "All our pastoral endeavors are incomplete until our people are led to the full and active participation in the eucharistic sacrifice."

John Paul asked priests to become closer to Jesus. "No one can effectively bring the good news of Jesus to others unless he himself has first been his constant companion through personal prayer," he said.

Priests should seek a unity "lived out in fraternity and friendship," he added.

The pope told his listeners that "our zeal for the priesthood...is inseparable from our zeal for the service of the people."

As he left the Civic Center on his way to the airport, John Paul stopped to greet young people from Children's Hospital across from the arena.

At the airport, John Paul listened to a farewell in song from Little Flower High School students who strung out a long banner proclaiming, "We love you, Holy Father. Thank you for visiting Philadelphia."

John Paul was given a send-off by city officials and by Cardinal Krol and his auxiliary bishops. In one of his many spontaneous gestures, the pope also shook hands with about 20 Philadelphia policemen.

"Shepherd I" left Philadelphia about an hour and 15 minutes behind schedule, at 12:25 p.m., heading for Des Moines, Iowa.

1

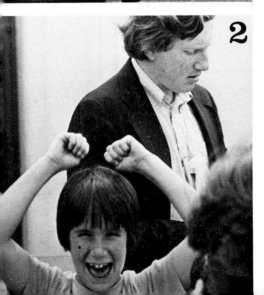

2

3

4

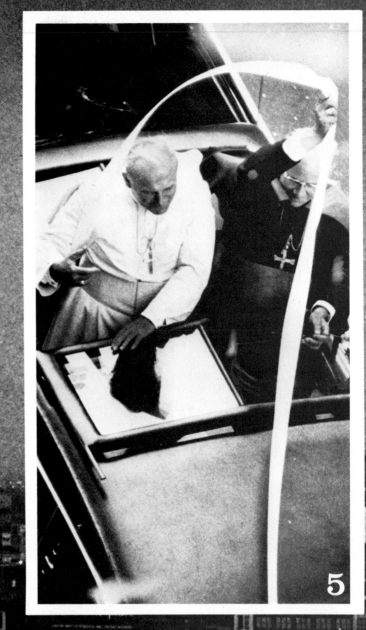

56

7

12

13

A Journey to the Heartland

I t was bright and windy — a typical Midwestern fall day — when "Shepherd I" touched down at the Des Moines airport about 1:50 p.m.

As the airport crowd cheered, John Paul was welcomed by Bishop Maurice Dingman of Des Moines, who accompanied the pope down the steps from the airplane and introduced him to state and city officials. A grade-school student, 9-year-old Thomas Anonia, who was selected at random by the Des Moines diocese, presented John Paul a bouquet of flowers.

Iowa Gov. Robert Ray gave the welcoming remarks, noting the state's "good environment" and the fact that the pope landed at the time when farmers were in the midst of the harvest.

John Paul was not expected to say anything at the airport arrival. That was fortunate, because he already was about an hour behind schedule. But after greeting dignitaries and groups of elderly and handicapped persons, he decided to take a little more time, and he gave his blessing in Latin and said, "Thank you for your coming, for your reception. God bless you."

John Paul then boarded a helicopter which took him to St. Patrick's Church, a rural parish in the small community of Irish Settlement. The helicopter landed in a farm field across from the church, and the pope and his entourage walked down a short hill next to a grain elevator and across a country gravel road to get to the church, a small building containing only 14 rows of pews.

Only the church's parishioners — slightly more than 200 persons — were allowed in the area. A security perimeter kept all others well away.

At the door of the church, John Paul was greeted by the parish's newly appointed pastor, Father John Richter.

"You are young," the pope said to the 28-year-old priest.

John Paul slowly walked up the aisle of the church, stopping to shake a hand here, to chat a moment there.

As Bishop Dingman asked the pope to "sprinkle the people with holy water," John Paul's attention was elsewhere. He was talking to the altar boy who had been chosen by lot to serve as holy water bearer. John Paul patted the boy's head and clasped his shoulder. "What is your name?" he asked. The boy, startled, couldn't immediately respond. When he finally did, the pope, who was now bending over in an effort to hear, was unable to understand him. John Paul looked up at Father Richter in a wordless plea for help.

"Bob Mulvihill," Father Richter said.

"Mulvihill," repeated John Paul. "Say the given name," he added, this time directing the request to anyone who would answer.

185

"Robert," said Bishop Dingman.

"Robert," repeated John Paul, nodding in satisfaction and approval. "Well, well."

It was like that all the way up the aisle. Spotting young Michael Kiernan in the back pew, the pope walked over, picked the boy up, hugged him and greeted his parents.

Farther up the aisle, John Paul stopped to greet 19-month-old twins Kevin and Kyle King.

When he reached the pew at the front of the church occupied by Bob Mulvihill and his family — the family of the altar boy — John Paul stood gazing admiringly at 2-year-old Sarah, who was sleeping in her father's arms.

"Look at the pretty baby," John Paul said.

Then the pope, supreme pastor of the church, knelt with the parishioners of rural St. Patrick's for several moments of silent prayer.

John Paul delivered a brief address.

"It gives me great pleasure to be here today with you, in the heartland of America, in this lovely St. Patrick Church at the Irish Settlement," he said.

"On your farms you are close to God's nature; in your work on the land you follow the rhythm of the seasons; and in your hearts you feel close to each other as children of a common Father and as brothers and sisters of Christ."

He noted that small communities such as the Irish Settlement parish are able to achieve a "more human dimension" of fellowship than is possible in big cities.

"Let your small community be a true place of Christian living and of evangelization, not isolating yourselves from the diocese or from the universal church," he said.

After delivering his address, he thanked the people of St. Patrick's for their hospitality and invited them to join him in praying the Lord's Prayer. Then, in Latin, he bestowed his apostolic blessing.

"Very nice," he concluded. And with that he was back hugging, shaking hands and asking names. On his way out, he stopped to bless an engagement ring that Joe Connor held out to him.

Once out of the church, John Paul strolled leisurely across the lawn with all of St. Patrick's parishioners crowded around him. They walked with him as far as the gravel road outside the church gate.

John Paul waved, boarded his helicopter and flew off to greet a different group — 340,000 people waiting for him at Living History Farms.

The fall weather was excellent as John Paul arrived at Living History Farms. There, he celebrated Mass atop a knoll surrounded by the crowd. In gold vestments amid the concelebrants clothed in the autumn field colors of green, gold and brown, the pope spoke of "God's gift" of the land.

"The land is God's gift entrusted to people from the very beginning. It is God's gift, given by a loving Creator as a means of sustaining the life which he created," John Paul said. "But the land is not only God's gift. It is also man's responsibility."

Christ during his life on earth often showed a "closeness to nature," expressing his teachings in terms of the land and farmers and shepherds, the pope said.

"Three attitudes in particular are appropriate for rural life," from the Christian viewpoint, he said, listing them as gratitude, conservation and generosity.

The farmer in his close dependence on sun, wind and rain is reminded daily of his dependence on God, he added.

"The farmer prepares the soil, plants the seed, and cultivates the crop. But God makes it grow. He alone is the source of life," John Paul said. "Surely it was this awareness that prompted the early Pilgrims to America to establish the feast which you call 'Thanksgiving.'"

On preservation of the land the pope said: "The land must be conserved with care since it is intended to be fruitful for generation upon generation." He called America's farming heartland "some of the earth's best land" and said farmers "are stewards of some of the most important resources God has given to the world."

John Paul pleaded for conservation: "Therefore, conserve the land well, so that your children's children and generations after them will inherit an even richer land than was entrusted to you."

He said "economic livelihood" is a legitimate goal of farming. But farming "will always be more than an enterprise of profit-making," he added. "In farming you cooperate with the Creator in the very sustenance of life on earth."

Calling for an attitude of generosity, he said: "You who are farmers today are stewards of a gift from God which was intended for the good of all humanity. You have the potential to provide food for the millions who have nothing to eat and thus help to rid the world of famine."

When Christ saw the hungry crowd on the hillside, he said, "he did not content himself with expressing his compassion," but told his disciples to feed the people.

Surrounded in the distance by the silos and barns of the Living History Farms — a complex of three working farms exhibiting farming methods of the past, present and future — John Paul said farmers "provide bread for all humanity, but it is Christ alone who is the bread of life. He alone satisfies the deepest hunger of humanity."

"Even if all the physical hunger of the world were satisfied...the deepest hunger of man would still exist," he declared.

"Therefore I say: Come all of you to Christ. He is the bread of life. Come to Christ and you will never be hungry again. Bring with you to Christ the products of your hands, the fruit of the land, that 'which earth has given and human hands have made.' At this altar these gifts will be transformed into the Eucharist of the Lord."

Each time John Paul celebrated Mass, there would be a group of persons selected beforehand to receive Communion from him. The intention was to avoid what otherwise might have turned into the world's longest single line as thousands queued up to receive the Eucharist from the hands of the pope. Communion time at Living History Farms produced a particularly poignant moment. Included in the Communion group were 10 persons particularly picked to represent rural America. One of them, however, could not receive Communion because he was not Catholic. Communion time thus became a moment when the pain of Christian division — a pain about which John Paul had spoken earlier — was acutely felt and seen.

The non-Catholic, Gustave Rhodes, a 46-year-old black plantation worker from Napoleonville, La., had been included in the group as a result of a selection process which did not include religion as a factor. It turned out that the nine others were Catholics and that Rhodes was a Baptist.

Rhodes sat in a special section with the others during the Mass, but when Communion time came, a nun from his hometown, Sister Anne Catherine Bizalion, accompanied Rhodes in the Communion line and received the Eucharist from John Paul, with Rhodes standing at her side. The procedure had been prearranged.

In a joint statement released the morning of the Mass, Rhodes and Bishop Dingman said they "experienced great pain with the decision," but recognized "that the pain is the price we must pay until that unity for which we pray becomes a reality."

"Receiving the body of Christ is a sign of unity, not the means to achieve that unity," the two said in their joint statement.

Rhodes continued to have mixed feelings. "I am sad in a way, but I am happy we were able to come to a mutual understanding," Rhodes told a newsman before the start of the Mass. But earlier he had said that "I'd love to take Communion and I do not think being Baptist should have anything to do with it."

The National Catholic Rural Life Conference, which carried out the selection process, defended its choice of Rhodes despite the stir it created. Sister of Providence Helen Vinton, research and publications director for the conference, said officials tried to choose the 10 to represent all aspects of rural life, such as migrant farm workers, cattle ranchers, wheat farmers and Indians. In doing so, she said, the conference knew a non-Catholic might be in the group since, for instance, there are few if any black Catholic plantation workers in the sugar cane fields of Louisiana.

"We thought we'd pick representative rural people and then deal with whatever problems came up," Sister Vinton said.

Another unusual situation at the Mass was visible to the people present and to the millions watching on television. As people in the special Communion line approached John Paul, some of them held out their hands to receive the Communion host — a common practice in the United States. With a clear gesture, John Paul indicated that he wanted to place the host on the tongue. Each time, after a fleeting moment of hesitation, the communicant's hands would drop and he or she would accept the host on the tongue.

The pope's action raised questions. In the United States and many other countries, Communion may be received either on the tongue or in the hand. It is optional. And church teaching is that it is the communicant who makes the choice, not the Communion minister. The minister is to follow the communicant's wishes. It would have been a minor point except that the introduction in the United States of the option of receiving Communion in the hand had been accompanied by considerable debate. Some saw Communion in the hand as a sign of what they considered a further erosion of reverence for the Eucharist and a change in the traditional understanding of the eucharistic sacrifice itself. It stood as a symbol in the continuing conservative-liberal debate in the church.

The reason for John Paul's action was explained by Father Thomas Krosnicki, director of the National Conference of Catholic Bishops' Committee on the Liturgy.

"When Pope John Paul II was informed that the practice of giving Communion in the hand was an approved practice in the United States, he decided that he would prefer to follow the practice of Rome and Poland and distribute Communion only on the tongue," Father Krosnicki said. He said that the pope's decision "should not be interpreted to mean that he does not agree" with the practice of Communion in the hand. The Vatican has permitted reception of Communion in the hand since 1969 in dioceses of any country where the bishops' conference has requested such permission and the local bishop approves the practice.

Unlike the United States, where Communion in the hand was approved by the U.S. bishops in 1977, the practice has not been approved by the bishops of either Italy or Poland.

People came from throughout the Midwest to see the pope at Living History Farms.

Alvin Teten and his wife Mary Ann, wearing matching red windbreakers, drove 200 miles from Talmadge, Neb. The Tetens grow corn, soybeans, wheat and alfalfa. Attending the Mass was something they felt they had to do.

"When I was a little girl, the pope was almost untouchable," recalled Mrs. Teten. "Now he's actually walking the earth, he's becoming more humble it seems. I hope he can do something for today's world. We need a miracle."

In another area, at the side of a shed, sat Theresa Haarhues, 26, of Van Meter, Iowa. Nestled in her arms was her 4-week-old daughter, Hannah, clad in a bulky one-piece suit and covered by a flowered quilt. They had spent the night there, braving the wind and the cold in hopes of getting a good spot from which to see John Paul.

The selection of the Des Moines area as a stop on the papal trip came at the last minute and was a surprise to many who thought John Paul would confine his visit to large urban areas. But by visiting St. Patrick's Church and the 600-acre Living History Farms, the pope emphasized themes which have become key topics of interest during his pontificate: the importance of rural life, the rights of the rural poor and the right to land. These issues were themes of papal talks in Mexico and Poland.

Four rural dioceses invited the pope to visit. Des Moines was selected because it had the best facilities to offer.

Des Moines also was a logical choice because it is the headquarters of the National Catholic Rural Life Conference. Msgr. Luigi Ligutti, former director of the conference, longtime Vatican observer at the U.N. Food and Agriculture Organization and one of the church's most articulate defenders of family farming, is a priest of the Des Moines diocese.

The invitation to the pope was formally extended by Bishop Dingman, president of the rural life conference. But the idea to bring John Paul to Iowa was conceived by Joseph A. Hays, who farms 80 acres in Truro, Iowa.

Hays said the idea came to him in mid-July as he and his pastor were watching television news reports that the pope was planning to visit the United States.

"I was serious and sincere about it right from the start," Hays recalled. He considered it a "gift of the Holy Spirit" that he had the confidence to write a letter inviting John Paul.

The farmer handed Bishop Dingman the letter of invitation on July 22, at a parish picnic. Five days later, a two-page letter by Bishop Dingman outlining 10 reasons why John Paul should visit Iowa was sent to the National Conference of Catholic Bishops.

At first, Bishop Dingman did not take Hays' idea seriously. Then, "the crucial moment came when I said to myself, 'Look, you're a bishop who says the greatest ideas always come from the people. If you've got an idea like that here, you'd better use it.'"

The first invitation drew no response. On Aug. 8, a second, more extensive invitation was sent. This one totalled nine pages and included a packet of other materials about rural issues and the proposed sites for the pope's visit.

The first the general public learned that Des Moines was under serious consideration was after the weekend of Aug. 18, when members of the papal "advance team," including Father Robert Lynch, papal visit coordinator for the U.S. bishops, and Bishop Paul Marcinkus, a Vatican official who served as advance man for the pope's trips to Latin America and Poland, visited the city.

Living History Farms is a tract of land just west of Des Moines run by a private corporation as a working model of farm history. Crops are grown and harvested using methods from previous eras of farm life. The farm also had two other advantages. Its huge site could handle the throngs expected for a papal Mass and it was situated at the intersection of two interstate highways, making it accessible to people in many big cities of the Midwest.

The farmer's idea had paid off.

On the following pages:

1 *The pope's helicopter descends for a landing at the Living History Farms museum.*

2 *Children from St. Patrick's parish in Cumming, Iowa, greet the pope outside the church which can be seen in the background. Father John Richter, pastor, is beside the pope.*

3 *The pope elevates the chalice during Mass at the Living History Farms.*

4 *A huge banner is carried through the crowd before the Mass.*

5 *One Iowa farmer might be missing the picture as the pope passes by.*

6 *With silos as a backdrop Pope John Paul II celebrates Mass in the heart of rural America.*

7 *An Amish family listens to the words of Pope John Paul at the Living History Farms.*

8 *A father manages to hold his baby and still get his picture.*

7 8

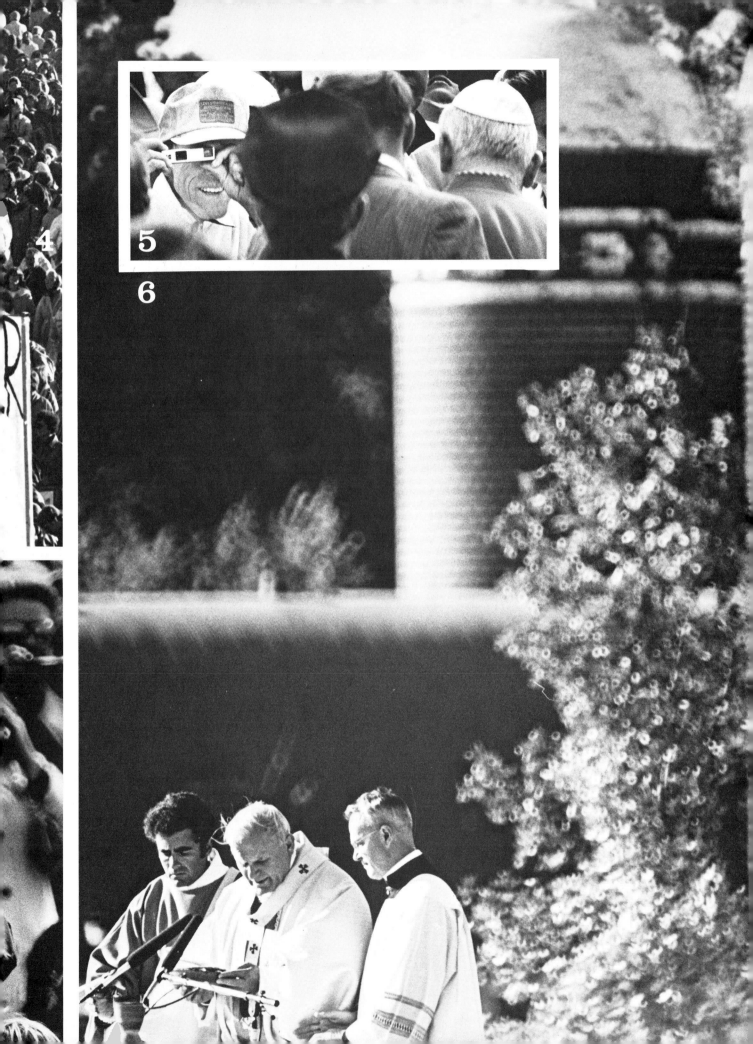

October 4, 5 and 6

The Windy City

"**F**rom Philadelphia to Des Moines, from Des Moines to Chicago! In one day I have seen a great part of your spacious land, and I have thanked God for the faith and the achievements of its people."

John Paul was standing in Holy Name Cathedral, delivering an address shortly after his arrival in Chicago Oct. 4. His words were intended to convey to his listeners a sense of the extent of his travels. But combined with the sound of his voice and the appearance of his face and posture, they also unintentionally conveyed a message of how tired the pope was. He had been pushing himself through a daily schedule of activities that would have by now worn down a man less physically fit — and less determined.

Despite the tiredness, John Paul managed to break from his prepared text and joke a little.

"Chicago is an American city," he said, ad-libbing in his careful English. "Chicago is also called the second Polish city in the world." The reference to Chicago's large Polish population — the largest of any city outside Warsaw — drew cheers.

In Latin and Polish, he added: "Praised be Jesus Christ."

Focusing in his talk on the name of the cathedral, he said there is a "great mystery expressed in the title of your cathedral: the Holy Name of Jesus, Son of God and Son of Mary."

He asked the people of Chicago to renew themselves and "do everything in the name of the Lord Jesus."

"It is in the name of Jesus that I come to you," he said. He added that "in this name — in the holy name of Jesus — there is help for the living, consolation for the dying, and joy and hope for the whole world."

John Paul had arrived at O'Hare Airport an hour earlier, again behind schedule, this time about 45 minutes. It was the third city he had visited in eight hours on the most grueling day of his U.S. tour, having started that morning in Philadelphia and stopping at Des Moines before flying to Chicago.

As he rode in a motorcade from the airport to the cathedral, John Paul was cheered by an estimated million persons lining the streets. Except along the motorcade's short expressway section, people stood 10 and 15 deep. At intersections the crowd spilled into the side streets at times for half a block. Many latecomers were unable to get closer than a block to the motorcade route. John Paul saw waving flags and signs welcoming him in English, Italian, Spanish and Polish.

Billboards along the route flashed greetings in between the time, temperature

194

and advertising messages: "Coca-Cola — welcomes — Pope John Paul II — to Chicago — 45 degrees — 8:20 p.m."

When the pope arrived at the cathedral, it was packed. The people sang "Holy God, We Praise Thy Name" as he proceeded up the aisle, and then Luciano Pavarotti, a renowned tenor now with the Chicago Lyric Opera, sang "Ave Maria."

Cardinal John Cody of Chicago extended a welcome to John Paul and then the pope delivered his brief address.

After his address, John Paul blessed those in the cathedral and moved outside where thousands were packed tightly around a small platform set up on the right side of the church. The people sang and cheered him without interruption for about 10 minutes until he stopped them by saying, "You must go sleep! Go sleep!"

John Paul gave them a quick blessing and returned to his car half a block away, pausing only a couple of times to greet people across the wooden barricades and to bless a child in a wheelchair and an elderly woman who had been brought inside the barricades on a small portable cot.

Because the pope was tired and an hour behind schedule, a scheduled brief stop at Cardinal Cody's residence was skipped. It was the first time that a stop had been eliminated in the six-day-old trip that had already covered 10 cities and more than 5,000 miles. The pope went directly to St. Peter's Church, a few blocks from the cardinal's residence to meet with a gathering of religious brothers.

The pope praised their religious consecration as "an act of love...an imitation of Christ who gave himself to his Father for the salvation of the world." He declared that commitment to the religious life requires one to be "interiorly free, spiritually free."

"The freedom of which I speak is a paradox to many," he said. "No matter what others may contend or the world may believe, your promises to observe the evangelical counsels have not shackled your freedom. You are not less free because you are obedient, and you are not less loving because of your celibacy." In fact, the opposite is true, he added.

John Paul asked the brothers to center their lives on the Eucharist and on God's word. He urged them to live their community life fully as a "concrete expression of love of neighbor" and as "the force which supports you in your mission for the church."

After the meeting with the brothers, the pope went to Cardinal Cody's residence, where he would spend the night.

By now obviously weary, John Paul waved to crowds gathered across the street as he arrived. Once inside the cardinal's residence, he moved quickly into the chapel for prayer, accompanied by his host.

It was late, almost 10:30 p.m., and John Paul had been on the go for more than 17 hours, crossing a time zone in his three-city swing. He seemed gray with exhaustion as he walked the short distance from the chapel to the reception room. He conversed quietly, in Italian, with Cardinal Cody, passing a fireplace which gave off a warm glow.

When the house was built around 1885, the reception room had been designed as a throne room — ready for a visiting pope. A small platform with a gold-colored carpet had been set up just a few days before John Paul's arrival, and on it a gilt throne had been placed.

John Paul scarcely glanced at it as he greeted relatives of Cardinal Cody and distributed small gifts.

Soon, John Paul returned from the reception room and began to climb the staircase, his feet heavy with fatigue. At the second-floor landing the pope and the cardinal stopped, and Cardinal Cody tugged at a large window, opening it and stepping out onto the roof of the original coach entrance.

There John Paul greeted the crowds gathered across the street behind the temporary snow fences. Wordlessly, he held the palms of his hands together, pressed them to his face and tilted his head to the side in a universal gesture of sleep.

A quiet dinner of prime rib was awaiting the pope. After dinner, a bedroom and study were ready on the second floor.

Across the street, the crowds still lingered. Uniformed police — there seemed to be hundreds of them — lined the pavement. Mingling with them, and standing watchfully but unobtrusively inside the residence, were solemn-faced agents of the Secret Service.

For a tired pope, a day of incredible overtime was coming to an end.

The following day, Oct. 5, John Paul's busiest in Chicago, began with a visit to the Providence of God Church, in Pilsen on Chicago's near west side. The largely Hispanic crowd of 75,000 under Chicago's Dan Ryan Expressway sensed the importance of the fact that the pope had come to their area, a poor and sometimes forgotten place.

The visit might not have taken place if the parish had not received funds from the Campaign for Human Development, the program begun a decade ago by the U.S. bishops. The money given to the parish had been used to give a shot in the arm to local businesses. John Paul's stop was designed to be a papal endorsement for continued operation of the campaign's programs.

On that particular day, however, the center of attraction was the pope himself. No effort to highlight the Campaign for Human Development — or any other program — could top the presence among these Hispanics of this smiling, waving man, so fluent in their own language, so recently a visitor to Mexico.

Much of the crowd waited all night in 30-degree temperatures and chilly winds to get a glimpse of John Paul, and for most of the time the waiting was broken only by an occasional flood of light as television crews tested equipment and illuminated for an instant some aspect of the crowd's anticipation. Then, all would be darkness and cold again.

But when the first shouts went up from the crowd about 7:40 a.m., the waiting seemed not to matter. When the police-motorcycle escort roared around the corner and pulled up in front of the church, emotions kept in check for hours suddenly overflowed.

As a tall man in the crowd shouted *"Viva el papa,"* the Spanish for "Long live the pope," the crowd surged forward, pressing against the fence, straining to catch a glimpse of John Paul. Mothers held up babies, fathers cried with joy.

The crowd shouted the pope's name in Spanish, *"Juan Pablo Segundo!"* as his white skullcap emerged through the open roof of the Cadillac limousine.

Even though it was the first stop of the day, the pope seemed tired. He read a statement in English in support of the Campaign for Human Development, calling it "a witness to the church's living presence in the world among the most needy." He commended the U.S. bishops for undertaking such a program. The crowd applauded politely.

But when he began to speak in Spanish, the crowd filled the air with shouts of *"Viva Jesus Rey"* (Long live Jesus the king). The pope acknowledged the cheers, waving a bouquet of flowers presented to him by parishioners.

During the brief encounter, John Paul was also presented a pastoral letter on the problems of the undocumented (illegal aliens) written by the priests of all the parishes in Pilsen.

Father John Harrington, pastor of the Providence of God Church, said of his parishioners: "It was a day they won't forget."

The administrator of St. Vitus Parish, Father James Colleran, was among the crowd on the steps, and he recalled the moment.

"By the time the pope arrived, most of us were pretty tired from waiting in the cold," he said. "But what we saw when he arrived was something I won't forget. He was a human being. His cassock was wrinkled. There was no golden aura, no clouds to surround him. When he looked at me, I saw a serene face filled with confidence, and I found myself practically crying."

All too soon, the visit was over. Aides pressed the pope to finish his remarks so that he might keep to his schedule as much as possible, even though he was already late when he arrived.

"Goodbye," John Paul said, in his now-familiar baritone voice. Then, he reached back into his reserve of strength for one last crowd-pleasing wave and a genuine *"Hasta la vista!"* (Until we meet again!) before his aides closed the car's roof and the motorcade sped away.

The next stop was Five Holy Martyrs Church in the predominantly Polish-American Brighton Park neighborhood.

Amid the bungalows and two-flat buildings, a different kind of Pope John Paul was seen. He was not just that charismatic figure in the white cassock. Among the Felician Sisters, who sing hymns as well in Polish as they do in English, among babushka-covered recent immigrants who speak Polish and no English at all, he was not the deliberate homilist who reads so slowly from an English text. This Pope John Paul was not reaffirming positions on church issues. He was not addressing a world problem. This Pope John Paul was talking directly — and in Polish — to everybody gathered there.

One of those there, Robert Zyskowski, managing editor of the Chicago Catholic, who was born in the neighborhood, recalled the scene like this:

"He was talking to me — a Polish-American whose grandparents had been born in the country Karol Wojtyla left to become pope. When he said that the Offertory gifts at the Mass on the parish parking lot at Five Holy Martyrs Church stood for 'all the contributions that the sons and daughters of our first homeland, Poland, have made to the history and to the life of their second homeland across the ocean,' I remembered the story dad told us about Grandma Zyskowski's boat trip.

"This different Pope John Paul reminded me that Grandma Zyskowski came over as the second oldest of three sisters, leaving their parents behind and leaving her and her big sister — all of 16 — to care for the littlest sister, age 2, on an ocean voyage and on to a new country.

"Speaking faster in his native Polish, the pope made me think about their new lives here and all they must have gone through when he recalled 'all their toil, efforts, struggles and sufferings; all the fruits of their minds, hearts and hands; all the achievements of the individuals, families and communities...but also all the failures, pains and disappointments; all the nostalgia for their homes.'"

John Paul praised the work of the men and women Religious and priests who followed their countrymen to America and helped them keep their faith, and he lauded the work of the many Polish organizations which served the immigrants.

As he looked out at the thousands crowded between Francisco and Richmond Avenues between Five Holy Martyrs School and 44th Street, the pope asked the congregation to "place on this altar an offering of everything you — the American Polonia — have represented from the very beginning, from the time of Kosciuszko and Pulaski," the Poles who helped win independence for the United States.

At the end of the homily, John Paul, now speaking in his native Polish, was ad-libbing, inserting extra lines into his prepared text to the members of some 180 Polish-American parishes from around the country.

Instead of staying with the prepared text as he had done throughout his journey through Ireland and the United States, this pope was quipping: "The number of Poles seems to have greatly increased since last year."

This was a pope telling jokes: "It's a cold day...just like in Poland. We got up early, we went to Mass early — even the pope!" And this pope was one, too, who answered the singing of *"Sto-Lat"* ("May you live 100 years") by reminding Polish-American Catholics, "No matter how many times you sing this you can't sing the whole thing because you cannot outdo the goodness of God."

John Paul went inside the parish church only briefly, walking down the aisle

197

and warmly greeting the predominantly Polish parishioners.

As he neared the fourth row of pews from the sanctuary a woman there beckoned him to stop. Debbie Spitali passed her one-week-old baby girl, Loriann, hand by hand over to the pope so he could bless her. It was feared that Loriann may have been born blind, without pupils in her eyes.

On leaving the church, John Paul traveled to Quigley Seminary for a meeting with the U.S. hierarchy and delivery of his major speech of the day and, probably after his U.N. speech, the most important of his stay in the United States.

In a one-hour-and-10-minute talk, the pope reaffirmed key aspects of church teachings which have been heavily debated by U.S. Catholics.

John Paul forcefully rejected "the ideology of contraception and contraceptive acts" supporting the position taken by his predecessor, Pope Paul VI, in his 1968 encyclical *Humanae Vitae* which reaffirms church teaching against artificial birth control.

"I myself today, with the same conviction of Paul VI, ratify the teaching of *Humanae Vitae*," John Paul said. It was the clearest, bluntest statement on contraception he had made since he began his pontificate.

In his 5,000-word speech, John Paul discussed a wide range of issues involving social and individual morality.

He put his talk within the context of collegiality — that is, shared responsibility between the pope and bishops — and often quoted from pastoral letters of individual U.S. bishops and the National Conference of Catholic Bishops. He praised these documents for their clear expression of Catholic faith and used them to emphasize key points.

John Paul proclaimed that marriage is indissoluble, condemned homosexual activity, and sexual intercourse outside marriage. He called abortion "an unspeakable crime" and rejected euthanasia, mercy killing, as "a grave moral evil...incompatible with respect for human dignity and reverence for life."

The pope praised the U.S. bishops for rejecting "racial antagonism and discrimination...the oppression of the weak, the manipulation of the vulnerable, the waste of goods and resources, the ceaseless preparations for war, unjust social structures and policies, and all crimes by and against individuals and against creation."

On religious issues facing the U.S. Catholic Church, he warned against eucharistic sharing (intercommunion) between divided Christians and called for a revival in American Catholicism of the sense of penance and conversion. He reaffirmed the need for personal confession and warned bishops against any misuse of general absolution without individual confession.

On homosexuality — an issue raised increasingly in recent years by activist groups seeking church acceptance of the practice and better pastoral care for the homosexually oriented — John Paul strongly backed the U.S. bishops' comments in a 1976 pastoral letter.

The pope said, "As authentic teachers of God's laws and as compassionate pastors you also rightly stated: 'Homosexual activity...as distinguished from homosexual orientation, is morally wrong.'"

He continued: "In the clarity of this truth, you exemplified the real charity of Christ, you did not betray those people who, because of homosexuality, are confronted with difficult problems as would happen if, in the name of understanding and compassion, or for any other reason, you had held out false hope to any brother or sister."

John Paul began the speech with praise for American Catholics and their "long tradition of fidelity to the Apostolic See" and for their sacramental life, efforts in the field of Catholic schools and religious education, and generosity to the poor and the missions.

He said he was with the bishops "because of my personal pastoral responsibility" and out of a desire "to strengthen you in your ministry of faith as local pastors, and to support you in your individual and joint pastoral activities."

Personal holiness and conversion to God are essential to the spiritual leadership of bishops, he stressed. "Holiness is the first priority in our lives and in our ministry," he said. He also emphasized the bishops' duty to preach the truth found in the "holy word of God."

Teachings on individual and social moral issues of the U.S. bishops were lauded as examples of sound doctrine and the "ministry of truth." He cited the bishops' joint pastoral letter, "To Live in Christ Jesus."

John Paul also singled out for praise two recent pastoral letters by individual bishops to their own dioceses.

"Both are examples of responsible pastoral initiatives," he said. "One of them deals with the issue of racism and vigorously denounces it. The other refers to homosexuality and deals with the issue, as should be done, with clarity and great pastoral charity, thus rendering a real service to truth and to those who are seeking liberating truth."

The pope did not identify the two bishops to whom he referred. There was speculation afterward, however, that the letter on homosexuality was either one written by Bishop Francis Mugavero of Brooklyn or one written by Cardinal Humberto Medeiros of Boston. It was suggested that the letter on racism probably was one written by Cardinal William Baum of Washington or one written by Bishop Walter Sullivan of Richmond, Va.

John Paul also emphasized the importance of the work of the Catholic press in church life. The Catholic press has a "special role" in the church's work of witnessing Christ and preaching the Gospel, he said.

"In a community of witness and evangelization, may our testimony be clear and without reproach," John Paul said. "In this regard the Catholic press and other means of social communication are called to fulfill a special role of great dignity at the service of truth and charity."

"The church's aim in employing and sponsoring these media is linked to her mission of evangelization and service to humanity," he said. Through the media, "the church hopes to promote even more effectively the uplifting message of the Gospel."

John Paul said a drop in frequency of confession among American Catholics is a serious problem. "In the face of a widespread phenomenon of our time, namely that many of our people who are among the great numbers who receive Communion make little use of confession, we must emphasize Christ's basic call to conversion," he said.

John Paul also issued what could be interpreted as a warning against a tendency to turn liturgical worship into merely a community celebration, without a divine dimension.

"Let us always recall that the validity of all liturgical development and the effectiveness of every liturgical sign presupposes the great principle that the Catholic liturgy is theocentric (God-centered)," he said.

John Paul closed his talk with pleas for special efforts for evangelization, for maintaining the unity of the church and for increased vocations to the priesthood and professed religious life.

After the meeting, Archbishop John Roach of St. Paul-Minneapolis, vice president of the National Conference of Catholic Bishops, held a news conference. He rejected suggestions that the pope's remarks might be interpreted as criticism of the American bishops for inadequate action.

The archbishop acknowledged that there seemed to be a note of warning in the pope's reminder of the strict conditions under which general absolution can be used. In recent years there have been several exchanges of views between the Vatican and U.S. bishops concerning this, and in at least two instances the Vatican is known to have disapproved of general absolution rites conducted in the United States.

Concerning the remainder of the speech, Archbishop Roach said that the tone was one of support and encouragement in areas in which the pope and the American hierarchy share essentially the same concerns and views.

The archbishop agreed with the idea that it would be unfair to infer from the emphases in the speech that John Paul probably views issues of personal morality and social consciousness as major problems in American Catholic life.

While at the seminary, John Paul also addressed special messages to the sick of Chicago and to students at Quigley South Minor Seminary.

To the sick he said:

"I would like to greet you, one by one, to bless you all individually, and to speak to you — to each of you individually — about Jesus Christ, the one who took upon himself all human suffering so that he could bring salvation to the whole world. God loves you as his privileged chidren. For two reasons you are in a special way my brothers and sisters: because of the love of Christ that binds us together, and particularly because you share so profoundly in the mystery of the cross and the redemption.

"Thank you for the suffering you bear in your bodies and your hearts. Thank you for your example of acceptance, of patience and of union with the suffering Christ. Thank you for filling up 'what is lacking in the suffering of Christ for the sake of his body, the church' (Col. 1:24)."

To the seminarians, he said: "During your years in the minor seminary, you have the privilege of studying and deepening your understanding of the faith. Since baptism you have lived the faith, aided by your parents, your brothers and sisters, and the whole Christian community. And yet today I call upon you to live by faith even more profoundly. For it is faith in God which makes the essential difference in your lives and in the life of every priest."

From the seminary, John Paul traveled by helicopter to Cardinal Cody's residence for a brief rest before going by motorcade to Grant Park to celebrate an outdoor Mass. A throng estimated at 1 million people from as far away as Santa Fe, N.M., and from throughout the Midwest covered the Grant Park site of the pope's largest public Mass in Chicago.

More than 350 bishops from around North America flanked the pope and concelebrated Mass as the crowd extended from the lip of Lake Michigan to the shadows of Chicago's Loop.

Using the setting of the United States as a nation of immigrants, John Paul preached in favor of the unity needed to follow Christ's command to bring the Gospel "to all nations." He called unity one of the conditions "necessary if we are to share in the evangelizing mission of the church." He called workers for evangelization — the theme of the Mass — "ambassadors for Christ."

John Paul continued: "In the first two centuries of your history as a nation you have traveled a long road, always in search of a better future, in search of a homestead. You have traveled 'from sea to shining sea' to find your identity, to discover each other along the way."

Each wave of immigrants brought a different culture and contributed to the distinctive richness of the United States, he said.

"Different as you are, you have come to accept each other, at times imperfectly and even to the point of subjecting each other to various forms of discrimination," he added, noting that understanding is still in the growing process.

Just as the United States has come toward unity, so must the church, he implied. "The church too is composed of many members and enriched by the diversity," he said. But "our unity in faith must be complete, lest we fail to give witness to the Gospel, lest we cease to be evangelizing."

To spread the Gospel, the pope said, Catholics must remain faithful to the magisterium, the teaching authority of the church. He suggested love as the vehicle which would best spread the word of God.

"Love is the force that opens hearts to the word of Jesus," he said. "Love is the only driving force that impels us to share with our brothers and sisters all that we are and have."

John Paul called for dialogue and prayer based on love to "build the bridges across our differences and at times our contrasting positions."

In a message alluding to Catholics in the Chicago archdiocese — where criticism of Cardinal Cody has been widely publicized — the pope said: "Let love for each other and love for truth be the answer to polarization, when factions are formed because of differing views in matters that relate to faith or to the priorities for action."

In keeping with the theme of evangelization, the Mass was preceded by a Rite of Initiation. Thirty persons studying to become Catholics were presented to the pope, and he in turn invited them "to share with us at the table of God's word."

After the Mass, John Paul returned to Cardinal Cody's residence for dinner and to rest before attending an evening concert by the Chicago Symphony.

Before going to the concert, John Paul telephoned retired Bishop Romeo Blanchette of Joliet, Ill., who lay ill in St. Francis Woods Rest Home in Mokena, Ill., dying of Lou Gehrig's disease, a disorder of the nervous system which causes progressive paralysis. As the disease advanced, Bishop Blanchette had lost most of his ability to speak, managing to utter only a few words each day at Mass. During the four-minute conversation, the bishop's voice returned. He spoke to John Paul in English, French, Italian and Latin. The pope asked for the bishop's blessing and the bishop gave it to him in Latin. The pope then offered to bless the bishop.

"Bless not only me, but my family, the people who are caring for me and pray that I may maintain my courage, joy and cheerfulness until the end," Bishop Blanchette said.

The concert by the Chicago Symphony Orchestra in Holy Name Cathedral was the final event on the pope's full schedule of the day. Conducting was Sir George Solti.

The pope entered the cathedral at intermission and was seated on a chair in the middle of the center aisle, facing the musicians who were seated in the sanctuary.

Solti came forward to be introduced to the pope, then returned to the sanctuary to conduct the last two movements of Anton Bruckner's Symphony No. 5.

John Paul appeared to be somewhat tired, after a day that had begun more than 13 hours earlier. He rubbed his eyes several times during the performance but exuded warmth and vitality in remarks to the musicians and audience afterward.

Speaking from the lectern of the cathedral, John Paul thanked the orchestra for "the artistic beauty which you have shared with me tonight." He then turned his thoughts to his predecessor, Paul VI, who "showed himself to be the friend of artists."

John Paul added: "In my own name and on behalf of the church, I reiterate my respect and admiration for your uplifting contribution to humanity, for your artistic creation that exalts what is human and reaches what is religious and divine."

After the greeting to the musicians and the audience inside the church, John Paul went out a side door to speak to the crowd assembled in the courtyard.

"Sto-Lat (May you live 100 years) is not an American expression," he said, "but it becomes American. Sto-Lat. Good evening."

Leaving the cathedral by another exit, he told the cheering crowds. "I am not the Chicago Orchestra. I am only the pope."

The symphony concert was not the last music of the day for John Paul. On his return to Cardinal Cody's residence, he joined in singing "Alleluia" with a crowd outside.

Early the following morning, Oct. 6, John Paul flew to Washington, D.C., the last stop on his trip and the site of his historic meeting with President Jimmy Carter.

On the following pages:

1 *A young boy gets a hug on the pope's arrival at Chicago's O'Hare airport.*

2 *The pope keeps time with members of the Suzuki Academy of Performing Arts as they serenade him in O'Hare airport.*

3 *At the end of a long day which included activities in three cities, the pope signals from the balcony of Cardinal John Cody's residence that it is time for bed.*

4 *The pope acknowledges applause from bishops at Holy Name Cathedral following his address to clergy and women religious.*

5 *A tired Pope John Paul fights off fatigue as he listens to the Chicago Symphony at Holy Name Cathedral.*

6 *A girl holds a single rose she hopes to give to the pope at Five Holy Martyrs Church.*

7 *Pope John Paul II celebrates Mass at Five Holy Martyrs Church.*

8 *A wall at the Copernicus Cultural and Civic Center becomes a huge greeting card.*

9 *The pope listens intently to music during Mass at Five Holy Martyrs Church.*

10 *A nun steadies her camera for a picture of the pope.*

11 *Amid Chicago skyscrapers and more than a million people, the pope arrives for a Mass in Grant Park.*

12 *Framed by bishops' miters, Pope John Paul delivers his homily at Grant Park on Chicago's lakefront.*

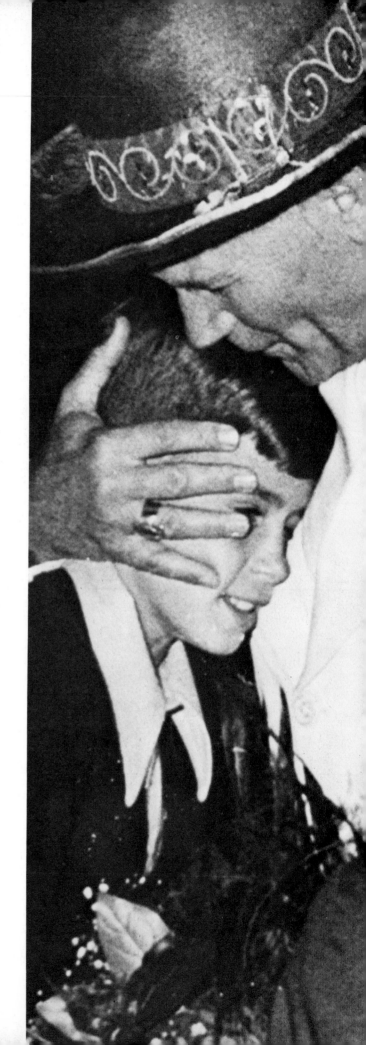

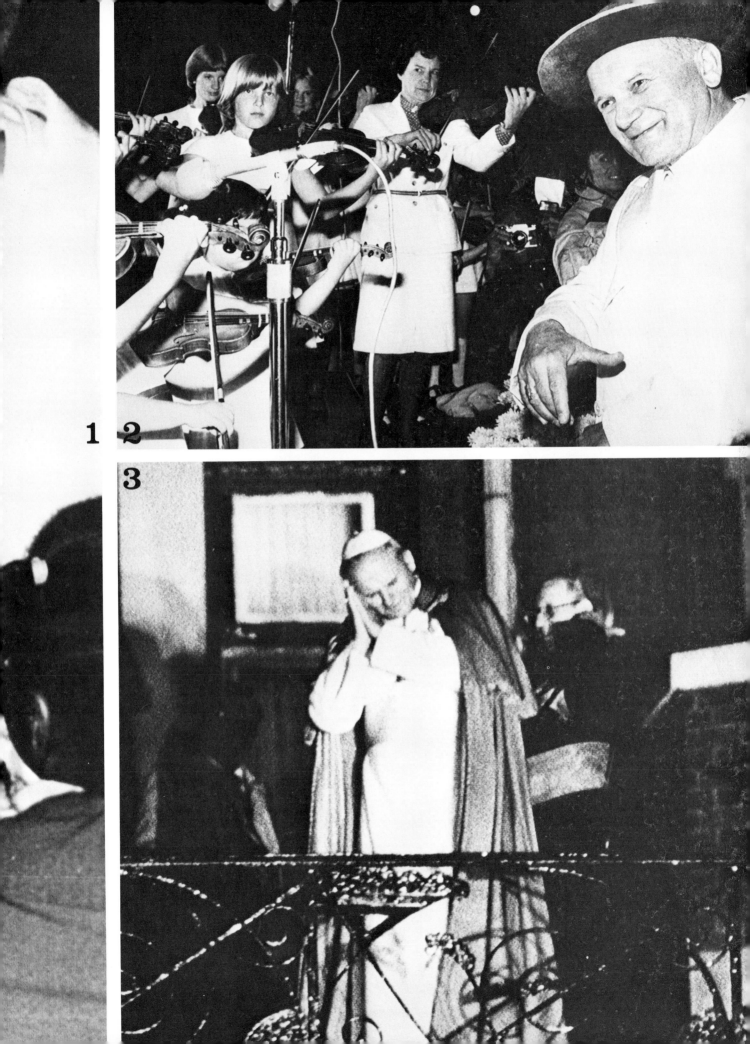

1 2

3

4 5

6

7

8

9

10

11 12

A Pope at the White House

The voice over the loudspeaker came suddenly, unexpectedly, startling the crowd waiting on the afternoon of Oct. 6 along Pennsylvania Avenue and in Lafayette Park across from the White House:

"Ladies and gentlemen, if you will please take your seats, we'll have an arrival very shortly."

The announcement obviously was for the 1,400 invited guests on the White House front lawn. The thousands waiting outside the White House had no seats to take. They had been standing for hours, hoping to catch a glimpse of Pope John Paul II as he arrived for his historic meeting with President Carter.

A large group of Poles, part of a throng lined six to eight deep all along the street, surged against the police barricades, looking to the right for the first signs of the approaching motorcade. Easily identifiable by their native dress and their Polish-language banners, they ran through one final rehearsal of the traditional Polish song *"Sto-Lat."*

Suddenly the lead car came into view, then a truck carrying photographers, then policemen on motorcycles. Finally, the open limousine carrying John Paul became visible, moving down the street at about 10 miles an hour. The pope stood, hatless on a bright fall day, waving and blessing the crowd.

Then, almost as if it had been planned all along, the pope's car stopped directly in front of the Polish-Americans, who waved and sang *"Sto-Lat"* with all the vigor they could muster. The pope waved back. Then the car pulled into the White House driveway.

The crowd across the street could hear the speeches and see the pope and the president, although the pope — more than 100 yards away — was little more than a white dot above a sea of gray business suits.

"Ooo, I see him good now," one woman exclaimed after moving a couple more feet to her left. "Ooo, I can see him great!"

One teen-age girl wasn't so lucky. Shorter than almost everyone else, she had to resort to bouncing up and down on her toes to try to catch a glimpse of John Paul.

One boy, about 8 years old, asked his father if the pope were a Democrat like President Carter.

"No, the pope doesn't have any political parties," the man explained.

"Well," the boy persisted, "what is he anyway?"

It was a good question. What — or who — was this smiling, waving man in white who for the past week had been cheered like a rock star or a sports hero at some moments, listened to like a wise, all-knowing father at others, and now was being received at the White House like...well, like what?

In a strict sense, John Paul entered the White House as a head of state — the sovereign ruler of the Vatican City State, a tiny independent dot in the midst of Rome. But no one pretended that he had any temporal power; popes gave that up many years ago, and John Paul, like his predecessors, went out of his way to emphasize that he neither had, nor wanted, any such power.

The reality was that John Paul was present as the world's conscience. At times it seemed as if he were "a voice crying in the wilderness," a spokesman for sanity in the midst of a world intent on rushing headlong into insanity.

Though many groups had threatened to demonstrate for one reason or another at the time of John Paul's arrival, few actually did.

A park police spokesman said later that the National Park Service granted no permits for demonstrations in the park that day. One man, saying he represented "Polish Freedom Fighters," held a sign urging a "holy war against the bandit state of Israel." Other Poles in the park quickly pointed out that the man's views were not representative of the Polish community.

Two more men, both with beards and wearing shirts that read, "Jesus saves; read the Bible," held large banners saying the Catholic Church misinterprets the Bible.

One group that did have a permit to demonstrate was Catholic Advocates for Equality, though its protest had to be staged on a sidewalk a block west of the White House. A member, Margaret Yanta of Beltsville, Md., a suburb of Washington, said the organization was a coalition of groups protesting the church's stand against the ordination of women as well as the lack of lay persons distributing Communion at papal Masses and the pope's refusal to give Communion in the hand while in the United States.

"While in America, the pope should 'do as the Romans do,'" she said.

There was only one major incident. A Florida man found to be carrying three guns and a number of rounds of ammunition was arrested in Lafayette Park shortly before the pope arrived at the White House. The man later told police he wanted to be arrested so that the government might straighten out a problem he had with the Veterans Administration.

As John Paul arrived at the front portico of the White House in the open limousine about 1:45 p.m., a military honor guard stood at attention, bayonets unsheathed and gleaming in the sun. A Marine Corps band played a fanfare. President Carter waved from the White House doorway. Next to Carter were his wife Rosalynn and their daughter Amy.

John Paul greeted the Carters, planting a big kiss on 11-year-old Amy. Responding to the pleadings of photographers, he kissed her again and gave her a hug.

Carter began his formal welcome speech with the words, *"Niech bedzie Bos pochwalony!"* — Polish for "May God be praised!" He called the papal visit a "milestone in the long intertwined history of our country and its faith in God."

"You have moved among us as a champion of dignity and decency for every human being, and as a pilgrim of peace among nations," Carter said. "You have offered your love. We as individuals are heartened by it. You can be sure, Pope John Paul, that the people of America return your love."

The president saw "four unique opportunities dramatized" by the pope's visit to the United States.

He said that these were the opportunities:

— "To renew our spiritual strength."

— "To recognize that our values, our beliefs, our faith are forged and made meaningful only through action."

— "To remember that the enhancement of human rights is the compelling idea and goal of our time."

— "We are dedicated to the belief that the natural and proper desire of all human beings is peace."

In his response, John Paul told Carter that he hoped their meeting would

211

"serve the cause of world peace, international understanding and the promotion of full respect for human rights everywhere." He read his speech from a prepared text but ad-libbed once at the beginning, congratulating Carter on his Polish.

John Paul told the gathered government officials: "I wish to say how profoundly I esteem your mission as stewards of the common good of all the people of America."

The meaning of history is found in the "dignity of the human person" created in the likeness of God, John Paul said.

He praised the United States as "a people that bases its concept of life on spiritual and moral values, on a deep religious sense, on respect for duty and generosity in the service of humanity."

These are "noble traits which are embodied in a particular way in the nation's capital, with its monuments dedicated to such outstanding national figures as George Washington, Abraham Lincoln and Thomas Jefferson," he said.

Before entering the White House to confer privately, the pope and the president talked briefly with some of the dignitaries in the front seats by the podium. Then they went inside. The welcoming ceremony had lasted about 20 minutes.

The talk between pope and president took place in the Oval Office. It was a private meeting which went on for about an hour.

As Carter and John Paul, accompanied by Mrs. Carter, emerged from the White House after their talk and began descending the spiral staircase to the south lawn, opera singer Leontyne Price sang the "Our Father."

Carter beckoned her to them when she finished, and she went up to the pope and kissed his ring.

In an address to the 6,000 guests assembled on the south lawn, Carter said that John Paul "comes to us as a pastor — as a scholar, a poet, a philosopher, but I think primarily as a pastor — to know us and to talk to us about gentleness, humility, forgiveness and love."

John Paul "has taught us that we are not perfect, and that we are responsible for our own behavior. He shows a particular concern for human dignity. He knows that many people are fearful, but that a person of faith need not be afraid. Our religious faith is, indeed, relevant to the modern world," Carter said.

Speaking of their private talk, Carter said, "We share a belief that 'the church must in no way be confused with the political community, nor bound to any political system.'" The quote was taken from the Second Vatican Council's "Pastoral Constitution on the Church in the Modern World."

"But we also spoke of opportunities we might pursue together," the president said. "We will work to renew the spiritual strength that can bear us beyond the blind materialism to true caring for one another."

Carter continued: "I join His Holiness in urging all individuals and nations of the world to alleviate the hunger of people and the homelessness of refugees — not as political acts but as acts of humanitarian concern."

Carter said he also joined John Paul in seeking protection of human rights, reductions of arms, and peace. He called the pope "our new friend" and urged him to visit the United States again soon.

As John Paul began to speak, a stiff breeze lifted his white cape and blew it over his head. He pushed it back down, but the wind persistently kept trying to turn the cape into a makeshift hood. Carter reached over and held the cape down so that the pope could speak without disturbance.

John Paul praised the United States for its "efforts for arms limitation, especially of nuclear weapons." He urged a "prudent and progressive reduction" of arms.

Speaking to America as a nation "blessed with a larger share of the world's goods," he praised the country for its tradition of "goodness and generosity in providing food for the hungry of the world." At the same time he challenged it to exert greater effort to achieve a more equitable distribution of the world's goods.

"The more powerful a nation is, the greater becomes its international responsibility, the greater also must be its commitment to the betterment of the lot of those whose very humanity is constantly being threatened by want and need," John Paul said.

He called for the United States to match its traditional generosity "with an equally convincing contribution to the establishing of a world order that will create the necessary economic and trade conditions for a more just relationship between all the nations of the world."

He praised the "concern for what is human and spiritual," that he said "has been a hallmark of the American people." He declared that the Catholic Church and the U.S. political community share common concerns in the areas of "safeguarding the dignity of the human person, and the search for justice and peace."

"For her part, the Catholic Church will continue her efforts to cooperate in promoting justice, peace and dignity through the commitment of her leaders and the members of her communities, and through her incessant proclamation that all human beings are created to the image and likeness of God," he said.

It was a historic moment.

There, on the south lawn of the White House, stood Pope John Paul, Catholic pilgrim from Rome, and President Jimmy Carter, Southern Baptist layman from Georgia. They chatted quietly, smilingly, as if their being together at that place were the most natural thing in the world.

Protocol demanded that no official note be taken of it, but the reality was that the visit marked a watershed for Catholicism in the United States.

Easily within memory span was the deep anti-Catholicism which would have made such a meeting impossible in past years.

"Popery" had been the cry when Al Smith, a Catholic, had run for president in 1928. The anti-Catholic feeling had become so strong and Smith's defeat so resounding that it was more than 30 years before either political party would again dare to put forward a Catholic presidential candidate.

When John F. Kennedy was tapped as the Democratic nominee in 1960 his religion immediately became an issue. He spent a great deal of time dispelling insinuations that as president he would be a tool of the Vatican.

Now Carter had not only invited John Paul to the White House, he was referring to him as "an extraordinary man."

The speeches over, the president and the pope walked side by side away from the microphone. The president spoke quietly into the pope's ear. The pope turned and retraced his steps to the microphone.

John Paul's voice once again carried out across the White House lawn: "The pope will bless you...with the permission of the president of the United States."

Then, as the Southern Baptist layman from Georgia bowed his head, the Catholic pilgrim from Rome raised his hand in sign of blessing and intoned in his clear, ringing Latin: *"Sit nomen Domini benedictum..."*

The moment was over. A page of history had been written.

Never before had a pope been in the White House. Meetings between presidents and popes had been few and far between, and all had taken place far from the White House.

Woodrow Wilson became the first president to meet with a pope when he called on Benedict XV shortly after arriving in Europe in December 1918 in preparation for conferences to draft peace treaties ending World War I.

Almost half a century passed before another such meeting. It came when Dwight D. Eisenhower met Pope John XXIII at the Vatican in December 1959 as part of an 11-nation European and Asian tour by Eisenhower.

213

John F. Kennedy met with Pope Paul VI at the Vatican on July 2, 1963, just two days after Paul's coronation.

When Pope Paul came to the United States to address the United Nations on Oct. 4, 1965, he met with President Lyndon Johnson — but Johnson went to New York and the encounter took place in a New York hotel.

Paul met two other U.S. presidents at the Vatican — Richard M. Nixon in February 1969, and Gerald Ford in June 1975.

Several days after the meeting between Carter and John Paul, Carter was asked about the meeting at a news conference. The president revealed little about their private talk.

This is a transcript of the questions and answers at the news conference about the papal visit:

Q. Mr. President, clearly the pope, on his visit to the United States and in Washington, left an extraordinary impression beyond simply the religious. Have you reflected on the meaning of the pope's visit to the United States yet?

A. Yes.

Q. Could you discuss that?

A. In addition to being with him in public and when we met with the members of my family at the White House, I had an extensive private conversation with the pope and we discussed this particular question. We were both surprised at the degree of warmth and enthusiasm among American people in welcoming the pope.

I expected the welcome to be warm and friendly, but I had no idea that it would be that enthusiastic and that large a number of people — and neither did he.

I think there's an innate hunger in our country for moral and ethical and religious principles — things that do not change during a time of rapid change brought about by a technological revolution throughout the world. I believe there's a hunger for things that are decent and honest, for principles of which we can be proud.

I think the pope, as a religious leader, accurately mirrors, for many people, those aspirations and hopes. I think it shows that this hemisphere is the most deeply religious, perhaps, in the world — certainly the most deeply religious Christian population in the world.

We had long discussions about what this meant to other nations; the threat of atheism as espoused and enforced by the state against the inherent desire of people for religious belief. But I believe that this was one of the most dramatic, and I think potentially the most beneficial, visits we've ever had from a leader in the world.

I was very thrilled to meet him and believe that his visit will have benefits for our country.

On opposite page:

1 *A comment from the pope brings a familiar grin to the face of President Jimmy Carter as the two meet for the first time on the White House lawn.*

2 *The president and the pope are nearly engulfed in a sea of secret service agents as tight security is in force at the White House.*

October 6 and 7

The Mass on the Mall

John Paul's visit to the White House was a highlight of his visit to Washington, but it was only a part of two days of frenetic activity for the pope in the nation's capital.

John Paul arrived Oct. 6, touching down aboard "Shepherd I" at Andrews Air Force Base, in Washington's outskirts, on a bright fall morning.

Among the dignitaries greeting the pope were Vice President Walter Mondale, Secretary of State Cyrus Vance and National Security Adviser Zbigniew Brzezinski, all accompanied by their wives.

The pope's plane landed at 10:36 a.m., only a few minutes behind schedule.

"It is with joy, with friendship and with honor that I welcome Your Holiness to the capital of our nation," Mondale said. Noting that the pope's U.S. tour followed earlier papal trips to Mexico, Poland and Ireland, Mondale said, "We have discovered for ourselves what it is that won the love of the world."

John Paul's trip had helped Americans discover the enduring values they sometimes forget, the vice president said. "Only a special man could do this."

John Paul said he was looking forward to "meeting the leaders of this young and flourishing country." He added that he would be "honored" to visit the headquarters of the Organization of American States (OAS) in Washington "to bring this deserving body a message of peace for all the peoples they represent."

The pope also saluted the officers and staff of the National Conference of Catholic Bishops "as well as those who in the U.S. Catholic Conference provide all the indispensable services for the whole Catholic community of this country."

After his welcoming remarks, John Paul spent several minutes shaking hands with the crowd along the fence. He kissed at least three babies and lifted them into the air. Then he boarded a helicopter for the short trip to the Reflecting Pool between the Lincoln Memorial and the Washington Monument.

Waiting at the Reflecting Pool were Washington Mayor Marion Barry, local politicians, members of the Washington Catholic hierarchy and thousands of cheering people, many of them school children.

Mayor Barry presented John Paul the key to the city of Washington, commenting that the pope already had the key to American hearts.

Many people waved papal flags and shouted their welcome, but one sign questioned "Romanists" and urged them to "read your Bible."

John Paul waved to the crowd and beckoned children forward, but police kept most of the people back. A few managed to slip through and were rewarded with a kiss, a touch or a rosary. One of the people receiving a rosary from the pope was 7-year-old John Maher. He became an instant celebrity.

Cheeks freckled and one tooth missing, the youngster stood holding the white rosary with gold cross as television cameras and reporters surrounded him. Watching over him were his parents, Gerard and Pat Maher of Gaithersburg, Md.

"How does it feel to receive a rosary from the pope?" a television reporter asked, thrusting a microphone at the boy.

"Fine," John answered and, prompted by his school principal, Madeline Ortman, he showed his gift. John and other children from St. Martin's School in Gaithersburg had waited for four hours for the pope to arrive.

The official greetings were warm and sincere.

But John Paul's visit was not without at least some discord. Before the pope arrived, Madalyn Murray O'Hair, well-known as an atheist for her various anti-religion efforts, initiated legal action to try to prevent him from celebrating Mass on Washington's Mall. The Mall Mass, set for the afternoon of Oct. 7, was scheduled as the grand finale of the pope's U.S. tour. Mrs. O'Hair contended that having the Mass on federal government property violated the separation of church and state.

Late on the afternoon of Oct. 5, the U.S. Court of Appeals rejected Mrs. O'Hair's contention.

Judge Harold Leventhal, writing for the appeals court, said that "It is an important function of government to permit large assemblies in outdoor parks by our citizens." He noted that other religious groups have been granted permission to use the Mall and that such permission is not an indication of government approval or disapproval of the activities.

Mrs. O'Hair, who 16 years earlier had successfully filed suit to ban prayer in public schools, was appealing a decision by U.S. District Court Judge Oliver Gasch, who had ruled earlier in the week that in the case of the Mall Mass freedom of speech should prevail over the principle of separation of church and state.

Mrs. O'Hair made an attempt to get the issue before the U.S. Supreme Court, but failed. The Supreme Court declined to consider the matter before the Court of Appeals ruled, and by the time that court ruled it was so late on Friday afternoon that the necessary papers could not be filed with the Supreme Court.

Thus, by the time John Paul arrived at the Reflecting Pool, whatever question had existed over the Mass on the Mall had been resolved.

From the Reflecting Pool, a motorcade took John Paul to St. Matthew's Cathedral where he would celebrate Mass.

Announcements over the loudspeaker system kept the congregation at the cathedral posted on the pope's progress from his arrival at Andrews Air Force Base to his landing by helicopter at the Reflecting Pool. He arrived at the cathedral an hour behind schedule, at noon, as the crowd outside chanted "Long Live the Pope" and screamed with delight.

Despite the enthusiastic throng in the cathedral and the thousands who jammed Rhode Island Avenue outside — some of them having waited for hours — there were signs of contradiction in evidence as well. On the building across from the cathedral, in dark-blue letters on large light-blue banners, advocates of the ordination of women had proclaimed: "'Discrimination Based on Sex Is Contrary to God's Intent' — Vatican II." The message was in English and Polish. Another banner said: "Sexism is a Sin — Repent." Another, put up by Dignity, an association of homosexual Catholics, stated in gold letters on a green background: "Dignity: Gay-Lesbian Catholics Welcome the Pope."

In an address in Philadelphia two days earlier, the pope had reaffirmed the Catholic tradition of admitting only men to the priesthood and the day before in Chicago, he restated the church's teaching that homosexual acts are sinful.

Most of the 1,400 people inside the cathedral for the Mass were priests from the Washington area, with some deacons and lay members of the archdiocesan pastoral council. They had begun filling the cathedral more than an hour before the scheduled beginning of Mass. An "Old Home Week" or class-reunion atmosphere prevailed. Commenting on the short distance from almost any spot in the building to the main altar, one priest said, "It's like being at his private Mass. You can't beat that."

The priests came from the District of Columbia, Maryland and Virginia to be with their "Supreme Pastor." When John Paul arrived, they gave him a joyous, enthusiastic welcome. The congregation applauded tumultuously as the pope entered the 80-year-old cathedral. They sang vigorously during the Mass. And they applauded and cheered at the end as the pope waved to them before leaving the sanctuary.

The pope set the tone of his relationship to the priests as he embraced the two monsignors who met him at the cathedral door.

In brief welcoming remarks before the pope's homily, Cardinal William Baum of Washington noted that the Washington archdiocese includes St. Mary's County in Maryland, site of the first foundation of the Catholic Church in the United States.

Thanking the cardinal for his words of welcome, John Paul expressed a special greeting to Cardinal Patrick O'Boyle, retired archbishop of Washington, who was present in the sanctuary with Cardinal Lawrence Shehan, retired archbishop of Baltimore.

In his homily, John Paul urged the priests "to continue to look to Mary as the model of the church, as the best example of the discipleship of Christ."

He said people should "learn from her to be always faithful, to trust that God's word to you will be fulfilled, and that nothing is impossible with God." It was Mary's "continual trust in the providence of God which most characterized her faith."

The pope added:

"All her earthly life was a 'pilgrimage of faith.' For like us she walked in shadows and hoped for things unseen. She knew the contradictions of our earthly life. She was promised that her son would be given David's throne, but at his birth, there was no room even at the inn. Mary still believed. The angel said her child would be called the Son of God; but she would see him slandered, betrayed and condemned, and left to die as a thief on the cross. Even yet, Mary 'trusted that God's words to her would be fulfilled' and that 'nothing was impossible with God.'

"This woman of faith, Mary of Nazareth, the mother of God, has been given to us as a model in our pilgrimage of faith."

John Paul listed other lessons to be learned from Mary: "From Mary we learn to surrender to God's will in all things. From Mary, we learn to trust even when all hope seems gone. From Mary, we learn to love Christ, her Son and the Son of God. For Mary is not only the mother of God, she is mother of the church as well."

After Mass, John Paul went to the cathedral rectory for lunch. The crowd in the street kept urging him to make another appearance.

Youngsters chanted in pep-rally style: "We Want You — John Paul Two." When he finally appeared on the balcony of the cathedral rectory, the pope responded: "John Paul Two — He Wants You." Then, referring to the fact that he was once again running behind schedule, this time late for his appointment at the White House, he told the crowd: "And he will say to the president of the United States that he comes late because of you." Then he gave his blessing and went inside to go down to the waiting open-top limousine that took him to the White House.

After the White House visit, John Paul traveled four blocks to the headquarters of the Organization of American States to address its General Assembly. At the time of the papal visit, the OAS had 28 member countries from the Western Hemisphere. Of these, 19 had diplomatic relations with the Vatican.

John Paul had a more than usual interest in the OAS. The United States was the fourth OAS country he had visited since becoming pope. In January, he had visited the Dominican Republic, Mexico and the Bahamas. He was mediating a territorial dispute between Argentina and Chile. The OAS Charter, signed in 1948 and updated in 1967, reflects many of the social teachings of the church. The charter's introduction states: "Solidarity and good neighborliness can only mean the affirmation on this continent, within the framework of democratic institutions, of a system of individual liberty and social justice based on respect for the essential rights of men and women." The charter establishes means to settle by peaceful negotiation all conflicts between states and for mutual economic, social and cultural aid among the member nations.

John Paul's talk to the diplomats was formal and the subjects somber, though the encounter was sometimes enlivened by shouts of *"Viva!"*

"I solemnly call on you to do everything in your power to restrain the arms race on this continent...What a relief it (disarmament) would be to your peoples, what new opportunities it would provide for their economic, social and cultural progress, and how contagious an example it would give the world," he said.

"The legitimate demand by the (member) states to participate on a basis of equality in the organization's common decisions must be matched by the will to promote within each country an ever more effective participation by the citizens in the responsibility and decisions of the nation."

John Paul criticized the theory of national security used by some governments to justify political repression. The theory allows for the suspension of human and civil rights if these are needed to preserve the government in power.

The pope said that if in the process toward political maturity "certain ideologies and ways of interpreting legitimate concern for national security were to result in subjugating man and his rights and dignity to the state, they would to that extent cease to be human."

John Paul also talked about the responsibilities of nations.

"The great cause of full development in solidarity must be given new life by those who in one degree or another enjoy these blessings," he said.

"In this field, too, you can be an example for humanity," he added. "You will discover that it is a logical requirement for you to deal with problems such as unemployment, migration and trade as common concerns" demanding unified solutions.

John Paul also mentioned one of the key topics of his pontificate, the need for religious freedom.

"The full religious freedom that the local churches ask for is in order to serve, not in order to oppose the legitimate autonomy of civil society and of its own means of action. The more all citizens are able to exercise their freedoms, the more readily will the Christian communities be able to dedicate themselves to the central task of evangelization."

In his greeting to the pope, OAS Secretary General Alejandro Orfila said that the objective of the organization is "to achieve human dignity for every individual" and to respect human rights. Noting that this is the first visit of a pope to "this house of the Americas," Orfila said John Paul's teachings encouraged OAS efforts at regional development.

The next welcome came from Jamaican Ambassador Alfred A. Rattray, president of the OAS permanent council at the time of the papal visit. Rattray began with a non-hemispheric issue:

"We have observed your concern for the plight of our brothers and sisters in Northern Ireland, and your attempt to bring the people of that strife-torn land closer together. We pray that they will respond to the challenge."

Rattray said that the pope's presence at the OAS meant that he was reaching out to the estimated 338 million Catholics in the Americas and "to all of us, whatever our religion."

"Your visit brings new hope," said Rattray, "in seeking out solutions to critical human problems." He particularly cited the work of the Inter-American Commission on Human Rights.

Both officials spoke to John Paul of the need for understanding between the rich and poor nations to spur development in the Third World.

Following the meeting with OAS representatives, John Paul appeared before a **219** group of OAS employees and invited guests waiting for him in the Aztec Garden behind the OAS building. In contrast to his meeting with the diplomats, this gathering was completely informal from the moment the pope stepped on the balcony overlooking the garden.

With a bright smile and tapping the microphone with his fingers to the rhythm of the huge crowd's chant, John Paul listened to a new salute: *"Viva el pope."*

That would be "Spanglish" for *"Viva el papa"* or "Long live the pope." Some 8,000 enthusiastic Hispanics and Anglos joined their voices under sunny skies, to greet John Paul in answer to his salute of *"Hasta la vista"* and "God bless America."

The multilingual exchange was only proper to an organization representing 28 nations having various cultures and languages.

"I pray to God that you can always look to the OAS for an echo of your legitimate aspirations of lofty ideals for human and Christian dignity," John Paul said in Spanish.

As he spoke of the Hispanic groups he met during his visit to the United States, he exhorted all the Spanish-speaking in the nation "to persevere in your values and traditions with courage" while showing solidarity with the rest of the nation.

Then turning to English, he said:

"Always when I meet with a group of people like you, I see my brothers and sisters, all children of the same Father, and I look at the beauty of human beings capable of knowing the truth, of understanding each other and of joining hands to make this world a better place to live."

After the roar of *"Viva el pope"* died down, he referred to his recent travels and added:

"It gave me joy to learn how strongly everyone believes in the real possibility of living in peace and bringing well-being to every man, woman and child in the world."

Then he gave his listeners a counsel: "Never lose sight of the things of the spirit. God gives meaning to our lives."

The crowd burst into applause. John Paul hummed into the microphone his appreciative "Woooo-woooo" and added *"Si!"* (Yes). The ovation continued and he fed the enthusiasm with *"Bien, bien,"* (Good, good). His hesitant farewell was a sonorous *"Hasta la vista"* (Until we meet again), followed by goodbye.

From the OAS, John Paul traveled to the Apostolic Delegation housed on Massachusetts Avenue amid many of the foreign embassies. He would spend the night there. But before retiring for the evening, a diplomatic reception awaited him.

As the papal motorcade came into view, a crowd outside the delegation sang American and Polish songs and shouted "John Paul II, we want you" and "You are not alone."

John Paul stepped out of his car and walked across the delegation lawn to cross a side street and greet people before going inside. He stopped at the chapel for a moment of prayer before going on to address the diplomatic corps.

The diplomats gave John Paul a polite, dignified reception in contrast to the singing, shouting welcome of the crowd outside.

John Paul spoke in French to more than 200 diplomats and their wives, then was introduced to them in a receiving line.

"Your mission as diplomats is based on the mandate you receive from those who hold responsibility for the well-being of your nations," he said. "The power you partake of cannot be separated from the objective demands of the moral order or the destiny of every human being."

He added: "Yours is a noble task. Despite unavoidable difficulties, setbacks and failures, diplomacy retains its importance as one of the roads that must be traveled in the search for peace and progress for all mankind."

Quoting his predecessor, Pope Paul VI, John Paul said, "Diplomacy is the art of making peace."

The efforts of diplomats do not always succeed in establishing or in maintaining peace, he said, but they must always be encouraged, "so that new initiatives will be born, new paths tried with the patience and tenacity that are the eminent qualities of the deserving diplomat."

John Paul made a plea for "the ever deeper insertion of the supreme values of the moral and spiritual order into the aims of peoples and into the methods used in pursuit of these aims."

First among these, he said, is truth.

"I am confident that the governments and the nations which you represent will, as they have so admirably done in the past, associate themselves once again with this lofty aim: to instill truth into all relationships, be they political or economic, bilateral or multinational," he said.

"Bringing truth into all relations is to work for peace, for it will make it possible to apply to the problems of the world the solutions that are in conformity with reason and with justice — in a word, with the truth about man.

"If it is to be true and lasting, peace must be truly human. The desire for peace is universal. It is embedded in the hearts of all human beings and it cannot be achieved unless the human person is placed at the center of every effort to bring about unity and brotherhood among nations."

As John Paul spoke, the crowd outside could be heard singing.

Oct. 7 was the final day in John Paul's U.S. tour and it was filled with activities. The morning schedule called for him to visit the area around The Catholic University of America, with the first stop the National Shrine of the Immaculate Conception, located on the campus grounds. Built by the U.S. bishops, the shrine serves as a national church for U.S. Catholics.

As John Paul's motorcade approached, three persons participating in an anti-nuclear demonstration broke through police lines and attempted to lie down in the street to block the pope's car. District of Columbia police quickly arrested them and took them away. The motorcade continued.

From the top of the stairs of the shrine, John Paul greeted Catholic University students, many of whom had kept an all-night prayer vigil.

"I thank you most cordially...for such a beautiful gift. By welcoming me with offerings of prayers, it shows you understand what is most important in your lives," he said.

Students chanted: "John Paul II. We love you." And the pope chanted in return: "I love you."

After talking to the students, praying for them and blessing them, he said, "Now with your permission — I enter," and went into the shrine where about 7,000 women Religious waited for him. Inside, John Paul was greeted by Cardinal William Baum of Washington and Sister Theresa Kane, president of the Leadership Conference of Women Religious, an organization which brings together the heads of the various orders of nuns.

The events which followed were dramatic.

In a formal speech of greeting to John Paul, Sister Kane came as close as anyone had ever come to publicly challenging the pope to his face on the church's position with regard to women. Standing at a podium a few feet away from John Paul, she said:

"As I share this privileged moment with Your Holiness, I urge you to be mindful of the intense suffering and pain which is part of the life of many women in the United States. I call on you to listen with compassion and to hear the call of women who represent half of humankind.

"As women we have heard the powerful messages of our church addressing the dignity and reverence for all persons. As women we have pondered these words. Our contemplation leads us to state that the church in its struggle to be faithful to its call for reverence and dignity for all persons must respond by providing the possibility of women as persons being included in all ministries of our church.

"I urge you, Your Holiness, to be open to and to respond to the voices coming from the women of this country who are desirous of serving in and through the church as fully participating members."

The remarks drew enthusiastic applause from some of the nuns and stony silence from others.

Her welcoming speech concluded, Sister Kane walked to where the pope was seated and as he stood, she knelt before him and he placed his hand on her head in blessing.

Sister Kane's talk came only three days after John Paul had reaffirmed in a speech in Philadelphia the church's teaching that only men may become priests.

There was some question about whether John Paul clearly heard Sister Kane's remarks. The odd acoustics of the shrine prevented some others seated near him from understanding them. As she spoke, the pope sat quietly, his expression giving no clue to his feelings.

When John Paul rose to speak, about 50 women wearing blue armbands as a sign of protest against his position on women's roles stood also. They remained standing, silently, throughout his address.

John Paul did not directly acknowledge the protest nor Sister Kane's remarks. His address, however, in a revision of what was originally prepared, emphasized the traditional role of women in the church.

Speaking of Mary and her obedience to God, John Paul pointed out that she played a major role in salvation history and yet was not present at the Last Supper, when the priesthood was established.

"This woman, this Mary of the Gospels, who is not mentioned as being at the Last Supper, comes back again at the foot of the cross, in order to consummate her contribution to salvation history," John Paul said.

By her courageous act, she prefigured and anticipated the courage of all women throughout the ages who concur in bringing forth Christ in every generation, he added.

"At Pentecost, the Virgin Mother once again comes forward to exercise her role in union with the apostles, with and in and over the church," he said.

He noted that Mary is honored as spiritual mother of all people and queen of the apostles "without herself being inserted into the hierarchical constitution of the church."

"And yet this woman made all hierarchy possible, because she gave to the world the shepherd and bishop of our souls," he said.

The talk dealt with the role of nuns and also with the clothing which the pope urged them to choose.

"It is not unimportant that your consecration to God should be manifested in the permanent exterior sign of a simple and suitable religious garb," he said. "This is not only my personal conviction, but also the desire of the church, often expressed by so many of the faithful."

As for the nuns' priorities, the pope said:

"Dear sisters in Christ: Jesus must always be first in your lives. His person must be at the center of your activities — the activities of every day. No other person and no activity can take precedence over him. For your whole life has been consecrated to him.

"Christ remains primary in your life only when he enjoys the first place in your mind and heart."

He urged nuns to unite themselves continuously with Christ in prayer and to center their lives in the Eucharist.

"Your service in the church is then an extension of Christ to whom you have dedicated your life. For it is not yourself that you put forward, but Christ Jesus as Lord," he said. "Your life must be characterized by a complete availability: a readiness to serve as the needs of the church require, a readiness to give public witness to the Christ whom you love.''

The events at the shrine added fuel to the continuing debate over the women's ordination issue and other feminist issues.

One order of nuns — the Sisters of St. Francis of the Martyr St. George — placed an advertisement in the Washington Post apologizing to the pope for Sister Kane's ''public rudeness.'' The ad stated that ''Sister Theresa was not only impertinent to the Holy Father, but she has also offended the millions of us who love him and gladly accept his teaching.''

Others took the opposite stance. Sister Clare Fitzgerald, vice president of the leadership conference, said Sister Kane showed her the statement before she spoke at the shrine.

''She asked me: 'Do you think it's all right? Do you think I should delete something?''' Sister Fitzgerald said. ''I read it quietly and prayerfully, and I thought it was fine.''

The day after her speech, as controversy swirled, Sister Kane issued a formal statement. The statement read:

''I appreciated the opportunity to greet the Holy Father and it was his openness that encouraged me to express a concern experienced by me and many other women across the country. It is my hope that such an opportunity will increase when women can dialogue further about such concerns as I expressed yesterday. I reaffirm my respect for and fidelity to the Holy Father.''

After the prayer service at the shrine, John Paul traveled the short distance to the Catholic University fieldhouse to address theologians, scholars, Catholic university presidents and educators.

Before entering the fieldhouse, John Paul paused to cheer the crowds that had been cheering him all morning. In a show of exuberance the pope shouted to the crowd: ''John Paul Two. He loves you! He loves you!''

After the cheers of the crowd died down, the pope repeated: ''John Paul Two. He loves you! John Paul Two. He loves you!''

The crowd cheered again, louder than before. The pope stood at the fieldhouse entrance smiling broadly as if drawing new energy from the crowd's adulation. As the cheering subsided, John Paul said, ''It is all my message — enough,'' and then turned to enter the fieldhouse.

John Paul, himself a former university professor in Poland, defended academic freedom for theologians, but warned against spreading theories that could trouble everyday Catholics who are unprepared to cope with them.

''It behooves the theologian to be free, but with the freedom that is openness to the truth and the light that comes from faith and from fidelity to the church,'' he said.

Academic freedom is fruitful for the church only if the theologian ''takes into account the proper functions of the bishops and the rights of the faithful,'' he added.

''It is the right of the faithful not to be troubled by theories and hypotheses that they are not expert in judging or that are easily simplified or manipulated by public opinion for ends that are alien to the truth,'' he said. It is the job of the bishop to ''safeguard the Christian authenticity and unity of faith and moral teaching.''

John Paul had warm words of praise for the work of Catholic universities. ''The church has always tried to stand by the institutions that serve, and cannot but serve the knowledge of truth,'' he said.

''As one who for long years has been a university professor — or tried to be one — I will never tire of insisting on the eminent role of the university, which is to instruct but also to be a place of scientific research. In both these fields, its activity is closely related to the deepest and noblest aspiration of the human person: the desire to come to the knowledge of truth.''

He said: ''No university can deserve the rightful esteem of the world of learning unless it applies the highest standards of scientific research and unless it excels in seriousness, and therefore, in freedom of investigation.''

When man is the object of investigation, ''no single method, or combination of methods, can fail to take into account, beyond any purely natural approach, the full nature of man,'' he said. In studying man, the Christian must ''let himself be enlightened by his faith in the creation of God and the redemption of Christ.''

Catholic universities are important to evangelization, he said.

''The cultural atmosphere in which a human being lives has a great influence upon his or her way of thinking and, thus, of acting. Therefore, a division between faith and culture is more than a small impediment to evangelization, while a culture penetrated with the Christian spirit is an instrument that favors the spreading of the Good News.''

John Paul praised the dedication and sacrifice of those involved in building and improving Catholic higher education ''despite immense financial strain, enrollment problems and other obstacles.'' He also praised people engaged in campus ministry.

John Paul was already an hour and a half behind schedule when he reached the fieldhouse. Although it was only the third event of six that were scheduled for the morning, he did not leave until a few minutes before noon. He had been scheduled to depart at 10:20 a.m.

The next stop was nearby, at Trinity College, for an ecumenical prayer service. John Paul used the occasion to urge prayer for Christian unity. But he also noted that complete unity does not yet exist in faith or in views on moral issues.

Because of that lack of unity, he said, there can be no common celebration of the Eucharist at present.

The pope strongly endorsed theological dialogue between Catholics and other Christians and discouraged ''complacency in the status quo of division in faith.''

The setting for the ecumenical service, in which about 200 Catholic, Orthodox and Protestant clergymen and clergywomen participated, was the modernized Renaissance-style Notre Dame Chapel of Washington's Trinity College, an 82-year-old Catholic women's college. A white lectern with a handsome gilded eagle, borrowed for the occasion from St. John's Episcopal Church on Lafayette Square, had been added to the chapel's usual appointments. The rector of St. John's, the Rev. John C. Harper, said he and the church's members ''feel greatly honored that a furnishing of our sanctuary is being put to the service of a great Christian leader whose visit to our city means so much to us.''

Leaders of the U.S. branches of eight other Christian churches which have been engaged in dialogue with the Catholic Church flanked John Paul in the sanctuary. Other church officials were seated behind him and the other clergy, in white albs and stoles or black academic gowns with academic hoods of green, red, gold, blue and violet filled the 13 pews on either side of the center aisle.

The service included elements of the Protestant and Orthodox liturgies, including the 100th Psalm sung in rousing style to the tune of the ''Old Hundredth'' by all present, including John Paul.

After the Rev. M. William Howard, president of the National Council of Churches of Christ, read the verses from St. Paul's Letter to the Colossians recalling God's reconciliation of everything in Christ, the pope, wearing no liturgical vestments but only his white cassock and skullcap, addressed the congregation.

John Paul praised the ecumenical dialogues between the Catholic Church and other Christian churches in the United States during the past 15 years and urged their continuation. The aim of joint theological investigation ''is always the full evangelical and Christian dimension of truth,'' he said.

"It is to be hoped that, through such investigation, persons who are well prepared by a solid grounding in their own traditions will contribute to a deepening of the full historical and doctrinal understanding of the issues," he said.

"The particular climate and traditions of the United States have been conducive to joint witness in defense of the rights of the human person, in the pursuit of goals of social justice and peace, and in questions of public morality," he added.

John Paul encouraged continued ecumenical activity in these areas and in fostering "esteem for the sacredness of marriage" and in supporting "healthy family life."

"In this context," he said, "recognition must be given to the deep division which still exists over moral and ethical matters. The moral life and the life of faith are so deeply united that it is impossible to divide them."

John Paul urged his listeners to go forward in ecumenical dialogue "with a spirit of hope."

He added: "Even the very desire for the complete unity in faith — which is lacking between us, and which must be achieved before we can lovingly celebrate the Eucharist together in truth — is itself a gift of the Holy Spirit, for which we offer humble praise to God."

John Paul recalled that the Second Vatican Council said interior conversion, holiness of life, and public and private prayer for Christian unity constitute "the soul of the ecumenical movement." To this he added:

"It is important that every individual Christian search his or her heart to see what may obstruct the attainment of full union among Christians. And let us pray that the genuine need for the patience to await God's hour will never occasion complacency in the status quo of division in faith. By divine grace may the need for patience never become a substitute for the definitive and generous response which God asks that there be given to his invitation to perfect unity in Christ."

After the pope's address, Archdeacon Methodios G. Tournas of the Greek Orthodox Archdiocese of North and South America led all present in intercessions from the Divine Liturgy of St. John Chrysostom. Bishop Papken, legate of the primate of the Armenian Apostolic Orthodox Church's Archdiocese of New York, led everyone in the Lord's Prayer.

John Paul then read the concluding prayer and gave a blessing.

As the congregation sang "Rejoice, the Lord Is King!" the pope led the procession from the chapel. As he went down the central aisle he paused along the way to shake hands and exchange greetings with many of those present.

John Paul fell further behind his schedule after the ecumenical prayer service when he took time to give personal greetings to about 300 handicapped persons who had gathered at Trinity College.

Originally, the plan had been for him to extend a greeting to the handicapped at the Mass on the Mall. Then it was decided that it would be best to hold a separate meeting so the handicapped would not have to cope with the Mall crowds. Part of that decision was that the pope would drive to the spot on the Trinity campus set aside for the handicapped and extend a blessing from his car.

But when John Paul arrived where the handicapped were gathered, he got out of the car and walked slowly down one row and up another, between the wheelchairs and stretchers, pausing often to grasp outstretched hands.

Then, speaking without a prepared text — a departure from the practice followed almost without exception during the remainder of the trip — John Paul told the handicapped persons:

"My love for you is a special love. I love in you the suffering Christ, our redeemer."

He thanked them for their prayers, which he said helped and supported him.

At the Apostolic Delegation, John Paul met with journalists covering his U.S. visit.

When he saw that only about 50 journalists had gathered in the garden in a light rain, he said: "You are a small group, so the speech will be short."

"The purpose of this journey was to permit the pope to exercise his function as a herald of peace, in the name of Christ, who was referred to as the Prince of Peace," he said. "This message of peace was announced especially in those places and before those audiences where the problem of war and peace is perceived with particular sensitivity and where there exist the conditions of understanding, of good will and of the means necessary to building peace and cooperation among all nations and among all peoples."

Journalists, he said, reported his reflections on peace, commented on them, interpreted them. Media people also "performed the service of stimulating people to think about how they might contribute to a firmer foundation for peace, for cooperation and for justice among all persons," he added.

"Now we find ourselves at the moment of parting, in this capital city of one of the most powerful nations in the world. The power of this country, I believe, comes not only from material wealth but from a richness of spirit."

Because the United States was established on a foundation "which was not only human but also profoundly religious," he said, the Catholic Church has been able to flourish in the country. "The millions of faithful who belong to the church testify to that fact, as they exercise the rights and duties which flow from their faith with full freedom," he added.

Recalling the U.S. national motto *"E pluribus unum,"* Latin for "From many, one," John Paul expressed hope that the country might never stop striving for the effective good of all its inhabitants and for the unity reflected in the motto.

He said he hoped that journalists had the opportunity to reflect anew on the Christian values which have contributed to the civilization of the United States.

"Most of all, however, we can draw hope for a peaceful world community from the example of persons of all races, of all nationalities, and of all religions living together in peace and unity," he said.

As the meeting concluded, one journalist called out to John Paul: "Come back."

The pope responded, "I hope," and added: "You Americans have supported me quite well."

John Paul had lunch and rested before traveling to the Mall for his final Mass in the United States.

Long before John Paul arrived at the Mall, people were gathering to get a good spot for the Mass. For many it was a family affair.

Entire families seated on blankets and sleeping bags made the vast area between the Capitol and the Washington Monument look like a giant outdoor picnic.

"We're calling this a 'pilgrimage-picnic,'" said Msgr. Thomas Leitch of New Cumberland, Pa., explaining how five busloads of parishioners — 200 people — came from his parish in the Harrisburg diocese. The group was gathered under a parish sign about 100 yards from the altar.

Elsewhere on the Mall were other signs of family life. Fathers hoisted their children up on their shoulders, especially when John Paul arrived, so their sons and daughters could get a glimpse of him. Babies were ferried about in strollers, and children asked their parents to explain who the pope was and how he got to his position.

Marriage Encounter groups, which see the promotion of family life as an important church ministry, were especially prominent on the Mall. One sign directly in front of the pope as he celebrated Mass said: "Worldwide Marriage Encounter Loves Pope John Paul." Other smaller Marriage Encounter signs and symbols were visible in other locations.

It was also a family affair for many non-Catholics such as the McClures.

"The pope is important for the whole world," Sally McClure of Washington said, explaining why she, her husband and daughter had come. "Plus we thought children should have this experience just like the parade at the inauguration (of the president). It's just awesome."

The mall crowd included a good percentage of teen-agers.

"The pope really appeals to youth — he's really down to earth," said Kevin Webb, vice president of a Falls Church, Va., parish Christian life community, a Catholic youth group.

"The kids at school all talk about him," Webb added. "Even the non-Catholics want to know more about him."

But a cold front — along with cloudy skies and chilly winds — that had come through Washington a few hours earlier was more than some families could take, limiting the crowd and causing some to leave early. U.S. Park Police estimated that 175,000 persons attended the Mass.

As the cold weather continued, people began wrapping themselves in the blankets which earlier covered the ground. Some had transistor radios, making it possible to hear the homily and the rest of the Mass four times — once on the radio, once from the closest speaker of the massive sound system put together for the Mass, once from another speaker farther up the Mall, and once from the speaker behind the crowd.

Also attending the Mall Mass were the ever-present vendors, many of whose prices fell as the Mass neared its end. In one place, four vendors were commiserating with each other over their difficulty in selling their poster-sized portraits of the pope superimposed on the Washington Monument and Lincoln Memorial.

The posters, originally priced at $3, were selling for $1 after the Consecration and could be had for 50 cents if one were willing to look long enough.

Some people sought shelter from the cold in the Smithsonian museums lining the Mall. In the Museum of History and Technology people wearing Pope John Paul buttons were looking at Pope John Paul books on sale in the bookstore.

Museum guards did not have a chance to see the pope. "You were AWOL if you didn't work," a museum guard said, adding that he had worked 12 hours the previous day.

"I'm glad it didn't rain, we would have had them all in here," he said.

It was a day of frustrations and joys for those trying to see the pope.

In a first-person news story, Thomas N. Lorsung, managing editor of the National Catholic News Service, captured some of those feelings in the following account:

I thought of it as "body surfing."

There was a lull in the action of editing stories on the last day of Pope John Paul II's visit to the United States, and I decided to walk to the Mall and look for myself at the papal Mass concluding the visit.

The 20-minute walk took me down deserted streets and, as the Mass site approached, past vendors selling all manner of buttons, calendars, pennants and papal flags. There was even a "special graphic," — a modern, original poster — commemorating the visit of the pope to the nation's capital.

It was not a cold day by my Milwaukee-bred resistance, but with temperatures in the low 60s and a steady breeze blowing, there was a wind-chill factor operating.

At 12th and Madison, I was at the edge of a crowd and from there could hear the pope reading the Creed in his now-familiar solid, deliberate, baritone voice.

But seeing him was another matter. From that distance, half a block away, he was just a speck on a white stage. I wanted to get closer to put some of the crowd and at least some possibly identifiable image on some Instamatic film left in my children's camera, which I stuffed in my briefcase at the last minute when I left for work.

At the crowd's edge the "body surfing" began. It did not involve surfing with the body as much as it meant surfing through bodies to edge closer to the action.

A James Taylor song says he would "ride with the tide and go with the flow." It was the way toward the front of the crowd. When someone came out, from up front, the most successful of the "body surfers" would seize the moment and slip up to fill the gap. There was a certain ebb and flow to the process, all right.

As the crowd ebbed, we surfers flowed — past the couple in their 20s praying aloud the parts of the Mass, past the two women wrapped in a quilt to keep off the wind as they sat in lawn chairs, past the short woman carrying a baby who was more intrigued by my striped tie than by the crowd towering above, past the young men who climbed 20 feet or more up into trees like Zaccheus trying to see the Lord.

But the family-history scrapbook will probably be a little light in pictures of the pope. After surfing through about two dozen rows, I lifted the lens toward the action only to see a pontifical figure in green on the white stage in front of the Smithsonian Castle. The viewfinder showed a view of the altar and castle, anyway, I thought. The only problem was that the red warning light on the camera told me that it was probably futile to shoot in the fading daytime, as dusk was accelerated by a new cloud cover. But I shot anyway. That's how surfers are. One wipeout can't stop us."

Before the Mass, John Paul got a glimpse of American history — a special exhibit of American Catholic religious figures on display in the Smithsonian Castle, a red-brick building with towers and turrets that is the headquarters of the Smithsonian.

The exhibit included a portrait by Gilbert Stuart of the first American bishop, John Carroll, and portraits of Mother Elizabeth Seton and Bishop John Neumann, the first American saints.

John Paul was met at the castle by Chief Justice Warren Burger, chancellor of the Smithsonian. The pope vested for Mass there.

A chill autumn wind was blowing as John Paul, wearing a green chasuble, concelebrated the Mass at the modernistic wooden altar on a raised platform in front of the castle. The concelebrants were about 20 bishops from around the United States and all nine U.S. cardinals.

After the entrance procession to the tune of "All Creatures of Our God and King," the thousands cheered and applauded as John Paul mounted the stairs to the 20-foot high platform, turned and waved.

Then followed the introductory rites, a reading from the Book of Genesis by a white layman, a reading from the Epistle to the Hebrews by a black laywoman and a reading from St. Mark's Gospel by a deacon.

In his homily, John Paul noted that the day's gospel reading recalled Jesus' teaching on the indissolubility of marriage and his willingness to have children surround him. He focused on the nature of marriage, on the family and on the value of life. The sermon was a summary of many of the key points he had made during his U.S. trip.

John Paul vigorously reaffirmed the sacredness of human life from conception onward and the indissolubility of the marriage bond.

To an audience which included Chief Justice Burger, the pope quoted the nation's third president, Thomas Jefferson, saying: "The care of human life and happiness and not their destruction is the just and only legitimate object of good government."

In the center of the capital of the world's richest nation, John Paul warned against the growth of selfishness among husbands and wives in a society "whose idols are pleasure, comfort and independence."

He also advised against limiting family size to provide greater material advantages and comfort.

The crowd interrupted the homily 20 times with applause as the pope:

— Proclaimed that "no one ever has the right to destroy unborn life."

— Insisted that "every child has the right to a loving and united family."

— Opposed the domination of the weak, the squandering of natural resources

and the denial of basic necessities to people.
— Called for care for the sick, aged and dying.
— Rejected discrimination based on race, origin, color, culture, sex or religion.

"I do not hesitate to proclaim before you and before the world that all human life — from the moment of conception and through all subsequent stages — is sacred, because human life is created in the image and likeness of God. Nothing surpasses the greatness or dignity of a human person. Human life is not just an idea or an abstraction. Human life is the concrete reality of a being that lives, that acts, that grows and develops. Human life is the concrete reality of a being that is capable of love and of service to humanity," he said.

"If a person's right to life is violated at the moment in which he is first conceived in his mother's womb, an indirect blow is struck also at the whole of the moral order, which serves to ensure the inviolable goods of man," John Paul said.

"**H**uman life is precious because it is the gift of a God whose love is infinite; and when God gives life, it is forever. Love is also precious because it is the expression and the fruit of love. This is why life should spring up within the setting of marriage, and why marriage and the parents' love for one another should be marked by generosity in self-giving.

"The great danger for family life, in the midst of any society whose idols are pleasure, comfort and independence, lies in the fact that people close their hearts and become selfish. The fear of making permanent commitments can change the mutual love of husband and wife into two loves of self — two loves existing side by side, until they end in separation."

The sacrament of marriage assures a baptized man and woman of the help they need to develop their love in a faithful and indissoluble union and to respond with generosity to the gift of parenthood, he said.

"In order that Christian marriage may favor the total good and development of the married couple, it must be inspired by the Gospel, and thus be open to new life — new life to be given and accepted generously. The couple is also called to create a family atmosphere in which children can be happy, and lead full and worthy human and Christian lives," John Paul said.

"Each member of the family has to become, in a special way, the servant of the others and share their burdens. Each one must show concern, not only for his or her own life, but also for the lives of the other members of the family: their needs, their hopes, their ideals.

"Decisions about the number of children and the sacrifices to be made for them must not be taken only with a view to adding to comfort and preserving a peaceful existence. Reflecting on this matter before God, with the graces drawn from the sacraments, and guided by the teaching of the church, parents will remind themselves that it is certainly less serious to deny their children certain comforts or material advantages than to deprive them of the presence of brothers and sisters, who could help them to grow in humanity and to realize the beauty of life at all its ages and in all its variety."

After the homily, the general intercessions were read in French, Polish, Italian, Korean, Vietnamese, Spanish and English by representatives of various ethnic groups.

At the beginning of the Liturgy of the Eucharist, the chalice, bread and wine were presented to John Paul by three families, one white, one Hispanic and one black.

The crowd of 175,000 on the Mall was well below the initial calculations of church planners and U.S. Park Service officials, who expected about 500,000 and had contingency plans for 1 million.

Church and government officials advanced several theories to explain why the turnout was less than anticipated.

The leading theory was that many people were frightened away by reports that there would be a huge crowd, leading to a massive post-Mass traffic and subway crunch.

Other theories mentioned were the threats of rain, the scheduling of the Mass after the pope already had visited three other metropolitan areas on the East Coast, the small number of Catholics who live in the Washington area compared to the Catholic populations of cities like Boston and Chicago, and televised football.

The figure of 1 million came up when the Archdiocese of Washington applied in early August for permission to use the Mall. The archdiocese suggested that as many as a half million might show up. The Park Service and U.S. Park Police decided to prepare for a million.

Later, when it was announced that John Paul would be visiting Boston, New York and Philadelphia in addition to Washington, officials began to scale down their estimates. But the 1 million figure stuck in the public's mind.

Transit officials made elaborate — and well-publicized — plans for fringe parking and special bus and subway service. In retrospect, a transit official said, "We may have scared people away."

U.S. Park Police used a new videotape map system to arrive at its official estimate of 175,000. After regularly photographing the crowd, police superimposed the photos on a grid map showing how many people could fit in each section.

If 1 million had shown up, the Mall would have been completely filled from the Washington Monument to the Capitol Reflecting Pool, the Park Service said.

After the Mass, John Paul returned to the Apostolic Delegation where he awaited word from Andrews Air Force Base that the chartered plane which would return him to Rome was ready.

At Andrews, Vice President Mondale, House Speaker O'Neill, dozens of other dignitaries and about 15,000 spectators gathered to see the pope off.

"You have built a bridge of friendship to all Americans," Mondale told John Paul. "Though you leave tonight, this special bridge remains, and so does this special memory."

John Paul recalled that he had met with many people and many groups, and said: "Your hospitality has been warm and filled with love, and I am grateful for all your kindnesses."

He added: "I believe strongly in the message of hope that I have held up to you, in the justice and love and truth that I have extolled, and in the peace that I have asked the Lord to give all of you."

Then, leaving in much the same way as he had arrived — quoting from American patriotic lore — John Paul declared:

"My final prayer is this: That God will bless America, so that she may increasingly become — and truly be — and long remain — 'One nation, under God, indivisible, with liberty and justice for all.'

"God bless America! God bless America!"

Late to the end, John Paul's plane took off one hour and 15 minutes behind schedule on his return flight to Rome.

4

5 6

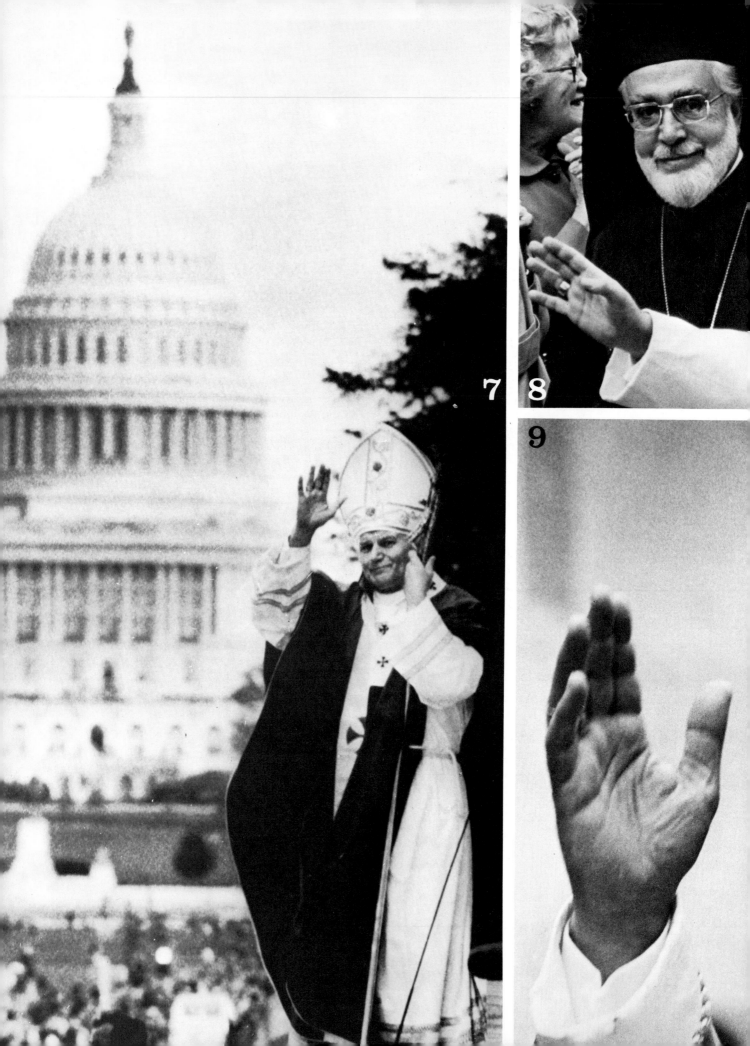

7 8

9

On the preceding pages:

1 *On arrival in Washington, Pope John Paul II looks across the reflecting pool toward the Lincoln Memorial.*

2 *Decked in flowers a little girl cranes to see the pope.*

3 *The pope waves to well-wishers as the papal motorcade rushes to St. Matthews's Cathedral.*

4 *From a balcony at the Organization of American States, Pope John Paul addresses a crowd jammed into the Aztec Garden.*

5 *In the Crypt Church at the National Shrine of the Immaculate Conception, the pope reaches out to touch the throngs who came to greet him.*

6 *At the National Shrine of the Immaculate Conception, the pope blesses Sister Theresa Kane, who only moments earlier had challenged him to expand the role of women in the church.*

7 *With the U.S. Capital behind him, Pope John Paul II blesses the people at the conclusion of the Mass on the Mall.*

8 *Following an ecumenical service at Trinity College, the pope walks with Archbishop Iakovos, primate of the Greek Orthodox Church in North and South America.*

9 *Pope John Paul II bids farewell to the press corps that had covered his trip and gives them his blessing before his departure for Rome.*

Epilogue
October 16

"Quo Vadis, Domine?"

High above St. Peter's Square, in his Vatican apartment, John Paul could hear the singing. It sounded as if it were coming from directly below his window. And — could it be? — yes, the song was in Polish!

It was 9 p.m. on the evening of Oct. 16, the first anniversary of the day when Karol Wojtyla's fellow cardinals had chosen him to become the 263rd successor of Peter as Christ's vicar. John Paul went to the window of his apartment and looked down into the vast square.

There below were hundreds of members of an Italian youth group, holding lighted candles and displaying a 20-foot banner reading, "We love you!"

"I can't see you," he said. "All I see is the light of the candles. And this is significant, because you must be a light. You must always remain visible to others."

The youths began to sing again in Polish, and John Paul joined in, his voice strong and clear and enthusiastic. But because he was so high above the square, he had trouble keeping in time.

"I would like very much to sing with you," he said. "But from here it is impossible to sing together. I am too far away."

Except for that moment of singing, John Paul took no public notice of the fact that the day marked the end of his first year as pope. It had been a busy year, a challenging year. What would the next year bring? And the years after that?

On the day he was elected, he had admitted plainly and unashamedly that he was afraid of the task to which he had been called. He said he accepted it in obedience and trust. Later, at his inaugural Mass, he recalled the ancient tradition of how during the persecution of Christians by Nero, Peter wanted to leave Rome. On the road out of the city, Peter met Christ, and asked him: *"Quo vadis, Domine?"* — "Where are you going, Lord?" — and the Lord answered, "I am going to Rome, to be crucified again." Peter turned back immediately and remained in Rome until he was crucified, head downward, near the spot where St. Peter's Basilica now stands. John Paul compared himself to Peter.

In that first, full, active year, it had become clear that John Paul would be a strong and decisive leader. He would go to the heart of issues, speak clearly and plainly the truth — the Lord's will — as he saw it. In his first year, he had addressed those controversial issues which command great — perhaps undue — public attention: priestly celibacy, women's ordination, birth control. He also had spoken out forcefully on matters which potentially are of greater import yet which get much less public attention: the dignity of each person, the proper distribution of the world's goods, the right to individual liberty, the sharing of responsibility in administering the church.

At 59 years of age, he appeared to be in excellent health, and he had shown time after time that his intellectual capacity was extraordinary. He would continue to use that extraordinary intellect in writing, in speaking.

He would continue to travel. About that there was no doubt. Wags were wont to say that the only mistake the Vatican Curia had made so far in its dealings with the new pope was to give him an air-travel card. Now they could not keep him home. He had made three major trips in his first year and plans were moving ahead for others. He clearly intended to travel as much as possible. He saw these trips as a means of carrying out his role as universal pastor.

He would continue to meet problems head-on. When he concluded that disagreement in the Dutch church had grown so serious that Vatican intervention was necessary, he dealt with it by calling the Dutch bishops to Rome for a special synod.

John Paul's first year had, indeed, been a pilgrimage of faith. The pilgrimage had left a deep impression not only on the places he had visited, but on the whole world. And the pilgrimage had left a deep impression on John Paul himself.

In his first general audience after returning to the Vatican from his trip to Ireland, the United Nations and the United States, John Paul said he was surprised by the huge welcome he got in the United States.

Referring to Catholics in the United States, he said: "Their church is still young because their great society is still young."

He continued: "I want to thank everyone for the welcome they gave me, for the response they gave to this visit, to this necessarily brief presence.

"I confess that I was surprised by such a welcome, by such a response.

"We stuck it out under the rain that fell during the Mass for young people the first evening in Boston. The rain accompanied us on the streets of that city, as it did afterward on the streets of New York, among the skyscrapers. That rain didn't stop so many men of good will from persevering in prayer, from waiting for the moment of my arrival, my words, my blessing."

The visits to Harlem and the South Bronx, with thousands of youths in Madison Square Garden, in Battery Park "under torrential rains and a raging storm," in Shea Stadium and in Yankee Stadium, all "remain unforgettable for me," he said.

"And then, renowned Philadelphia, the first capital of the independent states, with its Liberty Bell, and perhaps 2 million participants in the afternoon Mass in the center of the city.

"And the encounter with rural America in Des Moines. And next, Chicago, where the analogy on the theme 'E pluribus unum' could be developed in a most appropriate way.

"And finally, the city of Washington, capital of the United States, with a whole heavy schedule up to the final Mass on the Mall."

He said that, following "the footsteps of the Good Shepherd" in his U.S. visit, he had "sought to live together with you the reality of the church that emerges from the teaching of the Second Vatican Council, with all the depth and rigorousness that this teaching carries with it."

He added: "It seems indeed that all this was accompanied, above all, by a great joy for the fact that we are this church, that we are the people to which the Father offers redemption and salvation in his Son and in the Holy Spirit."

John Paul called his visit to the United Nations a "special fruit" of his trip. "What else could I have said before that supreme forum of a political nature, if not that which constitutes the core of the gospel message?"

That core is "the words of a great love for man," he said. "If political activity, in the dimensions of the individual states and in its international dimensions, must assure a real primacy for man on earth, if it must serve his true dignity, the witness of the Spirit and of truth rendered by Christianity and the church is necessary."

He also recalled his welcome by President Carter "in the historic meeting at the White House with him and his dear family, as well as with all the high authorities gathered there."

Behind John Paul's words seemed to lie a clear answer to the future as he saw it. Anyone who would ask "Where are you going, John Paul?" could imagine the response: "To the world."

237

at least some of the inalienable rights of man. Permit me to enumerate some of the most important human rights that are universally recognized: the right to life, liberty and security of person; the right to food, clothing, housing, sufficient health care, rest and leisure; the right to freedom of expression, education and culture; the right to manifest one's religion either individually or in community, in public or in private; the right to choose a state of life, to found a family and to enjoy all conditions necessary for family life; the right to property and work, to adequate working conditions and a just wage; the right of assembly and association; the right to freedom of movement, to internal and external migration; the right to nationality and residence; the right to political participation and the right to participate in the free choice of the political system of the people to which one belongs. All these human rights taken together are in keeping with the substance of the dignity of the human being, understood in his entirety, not as reduced to one dimension only. These rights concern the satisfaction of man's essential needs, the exercise of his freedoms and his relationships with others; but always and everywhere they concern man, they concern man's full human dimension.

14. Man lives at the same time both in the world of material values and in that of spiritual values. For the individual living and hoping man, his needs, freedoms and relationships with others never concern one sphere of values alone, but belong to both. Material and spiritual realities may be viewed separately in order to understand better that in the concrete human being they are inseparable, and to see that any threat to human rights, whether in the field of material realities or in that of spiritual realities, is equally dangerous for peace, since in every instance it concerns man in his entirety. Permit me, distinguished ladies and gentlemen, to recall a constant rule of the history of humanity, a rule that is implicitly contained in all that I have already stated with regard to integral development and human rights. The rule is based on the relationship between spiritual values and material or economic values. In this relationship, it is the spiritual values that are pre-eminent, both on account of the nature of these values and also for reasons concerning the good of man. The pre-eminence of the values of the spirit defines the proper sense of earthly material goods and the way to use them. This pre-eminence is therefore at the basis of a just peace. It is also a contributing factor to ensuring that material development, technical development and the development of civilization are at the service of what constitutes man. This means enabling man to have full access to truth, to moral development, and to the complete possibility of enjoying the goods of culture which he has inherited, and of increasing them by his own creativity. It is easy to see that material goods do not have unlimited capacity for satisfying the needs of man: They are not in themselves easily distributed and, in the relationship between those who possess and enjoy them and those who are without them, they give rise to tension, dissension and division that will often even turn into open conflict. Spiritual goods, on the other hand, are open to unlimited enjoyment by many at the same time, without diminution of the goods themselves. Indeed, the more people share in such goods, the more they are enjoyed and

drawn upon, the more then do those goods show their indestructible and immortal worth. This truth is confirmed, for example, by the works of creativity — I mean by the works of thought, poetry, music, and the figurative arts, fruits of man's spirit.

15. A critical analysis of our modern civilization shows that in the last hundred years it has contributed as never before to the development of material goods, but that it has also given rise, both in theory and still more in practice, to a series of attitudes in which sensitivity to the spiritual dimension of human existence is diminished to a greater or less extent, as a result of certain premises which reduce the meaning of human life chiefly to the many different material and economic factors — I mean to the demands of production, the market, consumption, the accumulation of riches or of the growing bureaucracy with which an attempt is made to regulate these very processes. Is this not the result of having subordinated man to one single conception and sphere of values?

16. What is the link between these reflections and the cause of peace and war? Since, as I have already stated, material goods by their very nature provoke conditionings and divisions, the struggle to obtain these goods becomes inevitable in the history of humanity. If we cultivate this one-sided subordination of man to material goods alone, we shall be incapable of overcoming this state of need. We shall be able to attenuate it and avoid it in particular cases, but we shall not succeed in eliminating it systematically and radically, unless we emphasize more and pay greater honor, before everyone's eyes, in the sight of every society, to the second dimension of the goods of man: the dimension that does not divide people but puts them into communication with each other, associates them and unites them.

I consider that the famous opening words of the Charter of the United Nations, in which the peoples of the United Nations, determined to save succeeding generations from the scourge of war, solemnly reaffirmed "faith in fundamental human rights, in the dignity and worth of the human person, in the equal rights of men and women and of nations large and small," are meant to stress this dimension.

Indeed, the fight against incipient wars cannot be carried out on a merely superficial level, by treating the symptoms. It must be done in a radical way, by attacking the causes. The reason I have called attention to the dimension constituted by spiritual realities is my concern for the cause of peace, peace which is built up by men and women uniting around what is most fully and profoundly human, around what raises them above the world about them and determines their indestructible grandeur — indestructible in spite of the death to which everyone on earth is subject. I would like to add that the Catholic Church, and I think I can say, the whole of Christianity sees in this very domain its own particular task. The Second Vatican Council helped to establish what the Christian faith has in common with the various non-Christian religions in this aspiration. The church is therefore grateful to all who show respect and good will with regard to this mission of hers and do not impede it or make it difficult. An analysis of the history of mankind, especially at its recent stage, shows how important is the duty of revealing more fully the range of the goods that are linked with the spiritual dimension of human existence. It shows how important this task is for building peace and how serious is any threat to human rights. Any violation of them, even in a peace situation, is a form of warfare against humanity.

It seems that in the modern world there are two main threats. Both concern human rights in the field of international relations and human rights within the individual states or societies.

17. The first of these systematic threats against human rights is linked in an overall sense with the distribution of material goods. This distribution is frequently unjust both within individual societies and on the planet as a whole. Everyone knows that these goods are given to man not only as nature's bounty; they are enjoyed by him chiefly as the fruit of his many activities, ranging from the simplest manual and physical labor to the most complicated forms of industrial production and highly qualified and specialized research and study. Various forms of inequality in the possession of material goods, and in the enjoyment of them, can often be explained by different historical and cultural causes and circumstances. But, while these circumstances can diminish the moral responsibility of people today, they do not prevent the situations of inequality from being marked by injustice and social injury.

People must become aware that economic tensions within countries and in the relationship between states and even between entire continents contain within themselves substantial elements that restrict or violate human rights. Such elements are the exploitation of labor and many other abuses that affect the dignity of the human person. It follows that the fundamental criterion for comparing social, economic and political systems is not, and cannot be, the criterion of hegemony and imperialism; it can be, and indeed it must be, the humanistic criterion, namely the measure in which each system is really capable of reducing, restraining and eliminating as far as possible the various forms of exploitation of man and of ensuring for him through work, not only the just distribution of the indispensable material goods, but also a participation, in keeping with his dignity, in the whole process of production and in the social life that grows up around that process. Let us not forget that, although man depends on the resources of the material world for his life, he cannot be their slave, but he must be their master. The words of the book of Genesis, ''Fill the earth and subdue it'' (Gn. 1:28), are in a sense a primary and essential directive in the field of economy and of labor policy.

18. Humanity as a whole, and the individual nations, have certainly made remarkable progress in this field during the last hundred years. But it is a field in which there is never any lack of systematic threats and violations of human rights. Disturbing factors are frequently present in the form of the frightful disparities between excessively rich individuals and groups on the one hand, and on the other hand the majority made up of the poor or indeed of the destitute, who lack food and opportunities for work and education and are in great numbers condemned to hunger and disease. And concern is also caused at times by the radical separation of work from property, by man's indifference to the production enterprise to which he is linked only by a work obligation, without feeling that he is working for a good that will be his or for himself. It is no secret that the abyss separating the minority of the excessively rich from the multitude of the destitute is a very grave symptom in the life of any society. This must also be said with even greater insistence with regard to the abyss separating countries and regions of the earth. Surely the only way to overcome this serious disparity between areas of satiety and areas of hunger and depression is through coordinated cooperation by all countries. This requires above all else a unity inspired by an authentic perspective of peace. Everything will depend on whether these differences and contrasts in the sphere of the possession of goods will be systematically reduced through truly effective means, on whether the belts of hunger, malnutrition, destitution, underdevelopment, disease and illiteracy will disappear from the economic map of the earth, and on whether peaceful cooperation will avoid imposing conditions of exploitation and economic or political dependence, which would only be a form of neocolonialism.

19. I would now like to draw attention to a second systematic threat to man in his inalienable rights in the modern world, a threat which constitutes no less a danger than the first to the cause of peace. I refer to the various forms of injustice in the field of the spirit.

Man can indeed be wounded in his inner relationship with truth, in his conscience, in his most personal belief, in his view of the world, in his religious faith, and in the sphere of what are known as civil liberties. Decisive for these last is equality of rights without discrimination on grounds of origin, race, sex, nationality, religion, political convictions and the like. Equality of rights means the exclusion of the various forms of privilege for some and discrimination against others, whether they are people born in the same country or people from different backgrounds of history, nationality, race and ideology. For centuries the thrust of civilization has been in one direction: that of giving the life of individual political societies a form in which there can be fully safeguarded the objective rights of the spirit, of human conscience and of human creativity, including man's relationship with God. Yet in spite of this we still see in this field recurring threats and violations, often with no possibility of appealing to a higher authority or of obtaining an effective remedy.

Besides the acceptance of legal formulas safeguarding the principle of the freedom of the human spirit, such as freedom of thought and expression, religious freedom and freedom of conscience, structures of social life often exist in which the practical exercise of these freedoms condemns man, in fact if not formally, to become a second-class or third-class citizen, to see compromised his chances of social advancement, his professional career or his access to certain posts of responsibility, and to lose even the possibility of educating his children freely. It is a question of the highest importance that in internal social life, as well as in international life, all human beings in every nation and country should be able to enjoy effectively their full rights under any political regime or system.

Only the safeguarding of this real completeness of rights for every human being without discrimination can ensure peace at its very roots.

20. With regard to religious freedom, which I, as pope, am bound to have particularly at heart, precisely with a view to safeguarding peace, I would like to repeat here, as a contribution to respect for man's spiritual dimension, some principles contained in the Second Vatican Council's declaration *Dignitatis Humanae:* "In accordance with their dignity, all human beings, because they are persons, that is, beings endowed with reason and free will and therefore bearing personal responsibility, are both impelled by their nature and bound by a moral obligation to seek the truth, especially religious truth. They are also bound to adhere to the truth once they come to know it and to direct their whole lives in accordance with its demands" (*Dignitatis Humanae*, 2).

"The practice of religion of its very nature consists primarily of those voluntary and free internal acts by which a human being directly sets his course toward God. No merely human power can either command or prohibit acts of this kind. But man's social nature itself requires that he give external expression to his internal acts of religion, that he communicate with others in religious matters and that he profess his religion in community" (*Dignitatis Humanae*, 3).

These words touch the very substance of the question. They also show how even the confrontation between the religious view of the world and the agnostic or even atheistic view, which is one of the signs of the times of the present age, could preserve honest and respectful human dimensions without violating the essential rights of conscience of any man or woman living on earth.

Respect for the dignity of the human person would seem to demand that, when the exact tenor of the exercise of religious freedom is being discussed or determined with a view to national laws or international conventions, the institutions that are by their nature at the service of religion should also be brought in. If this participation is omitted, there is a danger of imposing, in so intimate a field of man's life, rules or restrictions that are opposed to his true religious needs.

21. The United Nations organization has proclaimed 1979 the Year of the Child. In the presence of the representatives of so many nations of the world gathered here, I wish to express the joy that we all find in children, the springtime of life, the anticipation of the future history of each of our present earthly homelands. No country on earth, no political system can think of its own future otherwise than through the image of these new generations that will receive from their parents the manifold heritage of values, duties and aspirations of the nations to which they belong and of the whole human family. Concern for the child, even before birth, from the first moment of conception and then throughout the years of infancy and youth, is the primary and fundamental test of the relationship of one human being to another.

And so, what better wish can I express for every nation and the whole of mankind, and for all the children of the world than a better future in which respect for human rights will become a complete reality throughout the third millennium, which is drawing near.

22. But in this perspective we must ask ourselves whether there will continue to accumulate over the heads of this new generation of children the threat of common extermination for which the means are in the hands of the modern states, especially the major world powers. Are the children to receive the arms race from us as a necessary inheritance? How are we to explain this unbridled race?

The ancients said: *Si vis pacem, para bellum.* But can our age still really believe that the breathtaking spiral of armaments is at the service of world peace? In alleging the threat of a potential enemy, is it really not rather the intention to keep for oneself a means of threat, in order to get the upper hand with the aid of one's own arsenal of destruction? Here too it is the human dimension of peace that tends to vanish in favor of ever new possible forms of imperialism.

It must be our solemn wish here for our children, for the children of all the nations on earth, that this point will never be reached. And for that reason I do not cease to pray to God each day so that in his mercy he may save us from so terrible a day.

23. At the close of this address, I wish to express once more before all the high representatives of the states who are present a word of esteem and deep love for all the peoples, all the nations of the earth, for all human communities. Each one has its own history and culture. I hope that they will live and grow in the freedom and truth of their own history. For that is the measure of the common good of each one of them. I hope that each person will live and grow strong wth the moral force of the community that forms its members as citizens. I hope that the state authorities, while respecting the just rights of each citizen, will enjoy the confidence of all for the common good. I hope that all the nations, even the smallest, even those that do not yet enjoy full sovereignty, and those that have been forcibly robbed of it, will meet in full equality with the others in the United Nations organization. I hope that the United Nations will ever remain the supreme forum of peace and justice, the authentic seat of freedom of peoples and individuals in their longing for a better future.

Homily at Mass in Yankee Stadium, Oct. 2

1. "Peace be with you!"

These were the first words that Jesus spoke to his apostles after his resurrection. With these words the risen Christ restored peace to their hearts, at a time when they were still in a state of shock after the first terrible experience of Good Friday. Tonight, in the name of the Lord Jesus Christ, in the power of his spirit, in the midst of a world that is anxious about its own existence, I repeat these words to you, for they are words of life: "Peace be with you!"

Jesus does not merely give us peace. He gives us his peace accompanied by his justice. He is peace and justice. He becomes our peace and our justice.

What does this mean? It means that Jesus Christ — the Son of God made man, the perfect man — perfects, restores and manifests in himself the unsurpassable dignity that God wishes to give to man from the beginning. He is the one who realizes in himself what man has the vocation to be: the one who is fully reconciled with the Father, fully one in himself, fully devoted to others. Jesus Christ is living peace and living justice.

Jesus Christ makes us sharers in what he is. Through his incarnation, the Son of God in a certain manner united himself with every human being. In our inmost being he has recreated us; in our inmost being he has reconciled us with God, reconciled us with ourselves, reconciled us with our brothers and sisters: He is our peace.

2. What unfathomable riches we bear within us and in our Christian communities! We are bearers of the justice and peace of God! We are not primarily painstaking builders of a justice and peace that are merely human, always wearing out and always fragile. We are primarily the humble beneficiaries of the very life of God, who is justice and peace in the bond of charity. During Mass, when the priest greets us with these words: ''The peace of the Lord be with you always,'' let us think primarily of this peace which is God's gift: Jesus Christ our peace. And when, before Communion, the priest invites us to give one another a sign of peace, let us think primarily of the fact that we are invited to exchange with one another the peace of Christ, who dwells within us, who invites us to share in his body and blood, for our joy and for the service of all humanity.

For God's justice and peace cry out to bear fruit in human works of justice and peace, in all the spheres of actual life. When we Christians make Jesus Christ the center of our feelings and thoughts, we do not turn away from people and their needs. On the contrary, we are caught up in the eternal movement of God's love that comes to meet us; we are caught up in the movement of the Son, who came among us, who became one of us; we are caught in the movement of the Holy Spirit, who visits the poor, calms fevered hearts, binds up wounded hearts, warms cold hearts, and gives us the fullness of his gifts. The reason why man is the primary and fundamental way for the church is that the church walks in the footsteps of Jesus: It is Jesus who has shown her this road. This road passes in an unchangeable way through the mystery of the incarnation and redemption; it leads from Christ to man. The church looks at the world through the very eyes of Christ; Jesus is the principle of her solicitude for man (cf. *Redemptor Hominis*, 13-18).

3. The task is immense. And it is an enthralling one. I have just emphasized various aspects of it before the General Assembly of the United Nations, and I shall touch upon others during my apostolic journey across your country. Today, let me just dwell on the spirit and nature of the church's contribution to the cause of justice and peace, and let me also mention certain urgent priorities which your service to humanity ought to concentrate upon today.

Social thinking and social practice inspired by the Gospel must always be marked by a special sensitivity toward those who are most in distress, those who are extremely poor, those suffering from all the physical, mental and moral ills that afflict humanity including hunger, neglect, unemployment and despair. There are many poor people of this sort around the world. There are many in your own midst. On many occasions, your nation has gained a well-deserved reputation for generosity, both public and private.

Be faithful to that tradition, in keeping with your vast possibilities and present responsibilities. The network of charitable works of each kind that the church has succeeded in creating here is a valuable means for effectively mobilizing generous undertakings aimed at relieving the situations of distress that continually arise both at home and elsewhere in the world. Make an effort to ensure that this form of aid keeps its irreplaceable character as a fraternal and personal encounter with those who are in distress; if necessary, re-establish this very character against all the elements that work in the opposite direction. Let this sort of aid be respectful of the freedom and dignity of those being helped, and let it be a means of forming the conscience of the givers.

4. But this is not enough. Within the framework of your national institutions and in cooperation with all your compatriots, you will also want to seek out the structural reasons which foster or cause the different forms of poverty in the world and in your own country, so that you can apply the proper remedies. You will not allow yourselves to be intimidated or discouraged by oversimplified explanations, which are more ideological than scientific — explanations which try to account for a complex evil by some single cause. But neither will you recoil before the reforms — even profound ones — of attitudes and structures that may prove necessary in order to recreate over and over again the conditions needed by the disadvantaged if they are to have a fresh chance in the hard struggle of life. The poor of the United States and of the world are your brothers and sisters in Christ. You must never be content to leave them just the crumbs from the feast. You must take of your substance and not just of your abundance in order to help them. And you must treat them like guests at your family table.

5. Catholics of the United States, while developing your own legitimate institutions, you also participate in the nation's affairs within the framework of institutions and organizations springing from the nation's common history and from your common concern. This you do hand in hand with your fellow citizens of every creed and confession. Unity among you in all such endeavors is essential, under the leadership of your bishops, for deepening, proclaiming and effectively promoting the truth among man, his dignity and his inalienable rights, the truth such as the church receives it in revelation and such as she ceaselessly develops it in her social teaching in the light of the Gospel. These shared convictions, however, are not a ready-made model for society (cf. *Octogesima Adveniens*, 42). It is principally the task of lay people to put them into practice in concrete projects, to define priorities and to develop models that are suitable for promoting man's real good. The Second Vatican Council's pastoral constitution *Gaudium et Spes*, tells us that ''lay people should seek from priests light and spiritual strength. Let the people not imagine that their pastors are always such experts, that to every problem which arises, however complicated, they can readily give a concrete solution, or

even that such is their mission. Rather, enlightened by Christian wisdom and giving close attention to the teaching authority of the church, let the lay people assume their own distinctive role" (*Gaudium et Spes*, 43).

6. In order to bring this undertaking to a successful conclusion, fresh spiritual and moral energy drawn from the inexhaustible divine source is needed. This energy does not develop easily. The lifestyle of many members of our rich and permissive societies is easy, and so is the lifestyle of increasing groups inside the poorer countries. As I said last year to the plenary assembly of the Pontifical Commission Justice and Peace, "Christians will want to be in the vanguard in favoring ways of life that decisively break with the frenzy of consumerism, exhausting and joyless" (Nov. 11, 1978). It is not a question of slowing down progress, for there is no human progress when everything conspires to give full reign to the instincts of self-interest, sex and power. We must find a simple way of living. For it is not right that the standard of living of the rich countries should seek to maintain itself by draining off a great part of the reserves of energy and raw materials that are meant to serve the whole of humanity. For readiness to create a greater and more equitable solidarity between peoples is the first condition for peace.

Catholics of the United States, and all you citizens of the United States, you have such a tradition of spiritual generosity, industry, simplicity and sacrifice that you cannot fail to heed this call today for a new enthusiasm and a fresh determination.

It is in joyful simplicity of a life inspired by the Gospel and the Gospel's spirit of fraternal sharing that you will find the best remedy for sour criticism, paralyzing doubt and the temptation to make money the principal means and indeed the very measure of advancement.

7. On various occasions, I have referred to the gospel parable of the rich man and Lazarus. "Once there was a rich man who dressed in purple and linen and feasted splendidly every day. At his gate lay a beggar named Lazarus who was covered with sores. Lazarus longed to eat the scraps that fell from the rich man's table" (Lk. 16:19). Both the rich man and the beggar died and were carried before Abraham, and there judgment was rendered on their conduct. And the scripture tells us that Lazarus found consolation, but that the rich man found torment. Was the rich man condemned because he had riches, because he abounded in earthly possessions, because he "dressed in purple linen and feasted splendidly every day?" No, I would say that it was not for this reason. The rich man was condemned because he did not pay attention to the other man. Because he failed to take notice of Lazarus, the person who sat at his door and who longed to eat the scraps from his table. Nowhere does Christ condemn the mere possession of earthly goods as such. Instead, he pronounces very harsh words against those who use their possessions in a selfish way, without paying attention to the needs of others. The Sermon on the Mount begins with the words: "Blessed are the poor in spirit." And at the end of the account of the Last Judgment as found in St. Matthew's Gospel, Jesus speaks the words that we all know well: "I was hungry and you gave me no food, I was thirsty and you gave me no drink.

I was away from home and you gave me no welcome, naked and you gave me no clothing. I was ill and in prison and you did not come and comfort me" (Mt. 25:42-43).

The parable of the rich man and Lazarus must always be present in our memory; it must form our conscience. Christ demands openness from the rich, the affluent, the economically advanced; openness to the poor, the underdeveloped and the disadvantaged. Christ demands an openness that is more than benign attention, more than token actions or half-hearted efforts that leave the poor as destitute as before or even more so.

All of humanity must think of the parable of the rich man and the beggar. Humanity must translate it into contemporary terms of economy and politics, in terms of all human rights, in terms of relations between the First, Second and Third Worlds. We cannot stand idly by when thousands of human beings are dying of hunger. Nor can we remain indifferent when the rights of the human spirit are trampled upon, when violence is done to the human conscience in matters of truth, religion and cultural creativity.

We cannot stand idly by, enjoying our own riches and freedom if, in any place, the Lazarus of the 20th century stands at our doors. In the light of the parable of Christ, riches and freedom mean a special responsibility. Riches and freedom create a special obligation. And so, in the name of the solidarity that binds all together in a common humanity, I again proclaim the dignity of every human person; the rich man and Lazarus are both human beings, both of them equally created in the image and likeness of God, both of them equally redeemed by Christ, at a great price, the price of "the precious blood of Christ" (1 Pt. 1:19).

8. Brothers and sisters in Christ, with deep conviction and affection I repeat to you the words that I addressed to the world when I took up my apostolic ministry in the service of all men and women: "Do not be afraid. Open wide the doors for Christ. To his saving power open the boundaries of states, economic and political systems, the vast fields of culture, civilization and development. Do not be afraid. Christ knows what is in man; he alone knows it" (Oct. 22, 1978).

As I said to you at the beginning, Christ is our justice and our peace, and all our works of justice and peace draw from this source the irreplaceable energy and light for the great task before us. As we resolutely commit ourselves to the service of all the needs of the individuals and of the peoples — for Christ urges us to do so — we shall nevertheless remind ourselves that the church's mission is not limited to this witness to social fruitfulness of the Gospel. Along this road that leads the church to man, she does not offer, in the matter of justice and peace, only the earthly fruits of the Gospel; she brings to man — to every person — their very source: Jesus Christ himself, our justice and our peace.

Address to Youth
at Madison Square Garden, Oct. 3

Dear young people,

1. I am happy to be with you in Madison Square Garden. Today this is a garden of life, where young people are alive: alive with hope and love, alive with the life of Christ. And it is in the name of Christ that I greet each one of you today.

I have been told that most of you come from Catholic high schools. For this reason I would like to say something about Catholic education, to tell you why the church considers it so important and expends so much energy in order to provide you and millions of other young people with a Catholic education. The answer can be summarized in one word, in one person, Jesus Christ. The church wants to communicate Christ to you.

This is what education is all about, this is the meaning of life: to know Christ. To know Christ as a friend: as someone who cares about you and the person next to you, and all the people here and everywhere — no matter what language they speak, or what clothes they wear, or what color their skin is.

And so the purpose of Catholic education is to communicate Christ to you, so that your attitude toward others will be that of Christ. You are approaching that stage in your life when you must take personal responsibility for your own destiny. Soon you will be making major decisions which will affect the whole course of your life. If these decisions reflect Christ's attitude, then your education will be a success.

We have to learn to meet challenges and even crises in the light of Christ's cross and resurrection. Part of our Catholic education is to learn to see the needs of others, to have the courage to practice what we believe in. With the support of a Catholic education we try to meet every circumstance of life with the attitude of Christ. Yes, the church wants to communicate Christ to you so that you will come to full maturity in him who is the perfect human being, and at the same time, the Son of God.

2. Dear young people: You and I and all of us together make up the church, and we are convinced that only in Christ do we find real love and the fullness of life.

And so I invite you today to look to Christ.

When you wonder about the mystery of yourself, look to Christ who gives you the meaning of life.

When you wonder what it means to be a mature person, look to Christ who is the fullness of humanity.

And when you wonder about your role in the future of the world and of the United States, look to Christ. Only in Christ will you fulfill your potential as an American citizen and as a citizen of the world community.

3. With the aid of your Catholic education, you have received the greatest of gifts: "I believe nothing can happen that will outweigh the supreme advantage of knowing Christ Jesus my Lord. For him I have accepted the loss of everything and I look on everything as so much rubbish if only I can have Christ and be given a place in him" (Phil. 3:8-9).

Be always grateful to God for this gift of knowing Christ. Be grateful also to your parents and to the community of the church for making possible, through many sacrifices, your Catholic education. People have placed a lot of hope in you and they now look forward to your collaboration in giving witness to Christ, and in transmitting the Gospel to others. The church needs you. The world needs you, because it needs Christ, and you belong to Christ. And so I ask you to accept your responsibility in the church, the responsibility of your Catholic education: to help — by your words and, above all, by the example of your lives — to spread the Gospel. You do this by praying and by being just and truthful and pure.

Dear young people: By a real Christian life, by the practice of your religion you are called to give witness to your faith. And because actions speak louder than words, you are called to proclaim, by the conduct of your daily lives that you really do believe that Jesus Christ is Lord!

Address at Battery Park,
New York, Oct. 3

Dear friends of New York,

1. My visit to your city would not have been complete without coming to Battery Park, without seeing Ellis Island and the Statue of Liberty in the distance. Every nation has its historical symbols. They may be shrines or statues or documents; but their significance lies in the truths they represent to the citizens of a nation and in the image they convey to other nations. Such a symbol in the United States is the Statue of Liberty. This is an impressive symbol of what the United States has stood for from the very beginning of its history; this is a symbol of freedom. It reflects the immigrant history of the United States, for it was freedom that millions of human beings were looking for on these shores. And it was freedom that the young republic offered in compassion. On this spot, I wish to pay homage to this noble trait of America and its people: its desire to be free, its determination to preserve freedom, and its willingness to share this freedom with others. May the ideal of liberty, of freedom, remain a moving force for your nation and for all the nations in the world today!

2. It greatly honors your country and its citizens that on this foundation of liberty you have built a nation where the dignity of every human person is to be respected, where a religious sense and a strong family structure are fostered, where duty and honest work are held in high esteem, where generosity and hospitality are no idle words, and where the right to religious liberty is deeply rooted in your history.

Yesterday, before the General Assembly of the United Nations, I made a plea for peace and justice based on the full respect of all fundamental rights of the human person. I also spoke of religious freedom because it regards a person's relationship to God and because it is related in a special way to other human rights. It is closely allied with the right to freedom of conscience. If conscience is not secure in society, then the security of all other rights is threatened.

Liberty, in all its aspects, must be based on truth. I want to repeat here the words of Jesus: "The truth will make you free" (Jn. 8:32). It is then my wish that your sense of freedom may always go hand in hand with a profound sense of truth and honesty about yourselves and about the realities of your society. Past achievements can never be an acceptable substitute for present responsibilities toward the common good of the society you live in and toward your fellow citizens. Just as the desire for freedom is a universal aspiration in the world today, so is the quest for justice. No institution or organization can credibly stand for freedom today if it does not also support the quest for justice, for both are essential demands of the human spirit.

3. It will always remain one of the glorious achievements of this nation that, when people looked toward America, they received together with freedom also a chance for their own advancement. This tradition must be honored also today. The freedom that was gained, must be ratified each day by the firm rejection of whatever wounds, weakens or dishonors human life. And so I appeal to all who love freedom and justice to give a chance to all in need, to the poor and the powerless. Break open the hopeless cycles of poverty and ignorance that are still the lot of too many of our brothers and sisters; the hopeless cycles of prejudices that linger on despite enormous progress toward effective equality in education and employment; the cycles of despair in which are imprisoned all those that lack decent food, shelter or employment; the cycles of underdevelopment that are the consequence of international mechanisms that subordinate the human existence to the domination of partially conceived economic progress; and finally the inhuman cycles of war that spring from the violation of man's fundamental rights and produce still graver violation of them.

Freedom in justice will bring a new dawn of hope for the present generation as it has done before: for the homeless, for the unemployed, for the aging, for the sick and the handicapped, for the migrants and the undocumented workers, for all who hunger for human dignity in this land and in the world.

4. With sentiments of admiration and with confidence in your potential for true human greatness, I wish to greet in you the rich variety of your nation, where people of different ethnic origins and creeds can live, work and prosper together in freedom and mutual respect. I greet and I thank for the cordial welcome all those who joined me here: businessmen and laborers, scholars and managers, social workers and civil servants, old and young. I greet you with respect, esteem and love. My warm greetings go to each and every group, to my fellow Catholics, to the members of the different Christian churches with whom I am united in the faith in Jesus Christ.

And I address a special word of greeting to the leaders of the Jewish community whose presence here honors me greatly. A few months ago, I met with an international group of Jewish representatives in Rome. On that occasion, recalling the initiatives undertaken following the Second Vatican Council under my predecessor Paul VI, I stated that "our two communities are connected and closely related at the very level of their respective religious identities," and that on this basis "we recognize with

utmost clarity that the path along which we should proceed is one of fraternal dialogue and fruitful collaboration" (*L'Osservatore Romano*, March 12-13, 1979).

I am glad to ascertain that this same path has been followed here in the United States by large sections of both communities and their respective authorities and representative bodies. Several common programs of study, mutual knowledge, a common determination to reject all forms of anti-Semitism and discrimination, and various forms of collaboration for human advancement, inspired by our common biblical heritage, have created deep and permanent links between Jews and Catholics. As one who in my homeland has shared the suffering of your brethren, I greet you with the word taken from the Hebrew language: *Shalom!* Peace be with you.

And to everyone here I offer the expression of my respect, my esteem and my fraternal love. May God bless all of you! May God bless New York!

Address at Shea Stadium, New York, Oct. 3

Dear friends in New York,

It gives me great joy to have the opportunity to come and greet you on my way to La Guardia Airport, at the end of my visit to the archdiocese and to the metropolis of New York.

Thank you for your warm welcome. In you I wish to greet once again all the people of New York: all your parishes, hospitals, schools and organizations, your sick and aged. And with special affection I greet the young people and the children.

From Rome I bring you a message of faith and love. "May the peace of Christ reign in your hearts!" (Col. 3:15). Make peace the desire of your heart, for if you love peace, you will love all humanity, without distinction of race, color or creed.

My greeting is also an invitation to all of you to feel personally responsible for the well-being and the community spirit of your city. A visitor to New York is always impressed by the special character of this metropolis: skyscrapers, endless streets, large residential areas, housing blocks and, above all, the millions of people who live here or who look here for the work that will sustain them and their family.

Large concentrations of people create special problems and special needs. The personal effort and loyal collaboration of everybody are needed to find the right solutions, so that all men, women and children can live in dignity and develop their potential to the full without having to suffer for lack of education, housing, employment, and cultural opportunities. Above all, a city needs a soul if it is to become a true home for human beings. You, the people, must give it this soul. And how do you do this? By loving each other. Love for each other must be the hallmark of your lives. In the Gospel Jesus Christ tells us: "You shall love your neighbor as yourself" (Mt. 22:39). This commandment of the Lord must be your inspiration in forming true human relationships among yourselves, so that nobody will ever feel alone or unwanted, or much less, rejected, despised or hated. Jesus himself will give you the power of fraternal love. And every neighborhood, every block, every street will become a true community because you will want it so, and Jesus will help you to bring it about.

Keep Jesus Christ in your hearts, and you will recognize his face in every human being. You will want to help him out in all his needs: the needs of your brothers and sisters. This is the way we prepare ourselves to meet Jesus, when he will come again on the last day as the judge of the living and the dead and he will say to us: "Come, you have my Father's blessing! Inherit the kingdom prepared for you from the creation of the world. For I was hungry and you gave me food, I was thirsty and you gave me drink. I was a stranger and you welcomed me, naked and you clothed me. I was ill and you comforted me, in prison and you came to visit me....I assure you as often as you did it for one of my least brethren, you did it for me" (Mt. 25:34-35, 39).

I now wish to address a very cordial welcome to each and every member of the Spanish-speaking colony, coming from various countries, here in this stadium.

In you, I see and I wish to greet, with great affection, the whole of the numerous Hispanic community living in New York and many other places in the United States.

I wish to assure you that I am well aware of the place that you occupy in American society and that I follow with lively interest your accomplishments, aspirations and difficulties within the social fabric of this nation, which is your homeland of adoption or the land that welcomes you. For this reason, from the very moment that I accepted the invitation to visit this country, I thought of you, who are an integral and specific part of this society, a very considerable part of the church in this vast nation.

I wish to exhort you, as Catholics, always to maintain very clearly your Christian identity, with a constant reference to the value of your faith, values that must enlighten the legitimate quest for a worthy material position for yourselves and your families.

Since you are generally immersed in the environment of heavily populated cities and in a social climate where sometimes technology and material values take first place, make an effort to provide a spiritual contribution to your life and your neighborhood. Keep close to God in your lives, to the God who calls you to be ever more worthy of your condition as human beings with an eternal vocation, to the God who invites you to solidarity and to collaboration in building up an ever more human, just and fraternal world.

I pray for you, for your families and friends, above all for your children, for the sick and suffering, and to all of you I give my blessing. May God be with you always! Goodbye, and God bless you.

Homily at Mass on Logan Circle, Philadelphia, Oct. 3

Dear brothers and sisters of the church in Philadelphia,

1. It is a great joy for me to celebrate the eucharist with you today. All of us are gathered together as one community, one people in the grace and peace of God our Father and of the Lord Jesus Christ; we are gathered in the fellowship of the Holy Spirit. We have come together to proclaim the Gospel in all its power, for the eucharistic sacrifice is the summit and enactment of our proclamation:

Christ has died, Christ is risen, Christ will come again!

From this altar of sacrifice, there arises a hymn of praise and thanksgiving to God through Jesus Christ. We who belong to Christ are all part of this hymn, this sacrifice of praise. The sacrifice of Calvary is renewed on this altar, and it becomes our offering too — an offering for the benefit of the living and the dead, an offering for the universal church.

Assembled in the charity of Christ, we are all one in his sacrifice: the cardinal archbishop who is called to lead this church in the path of truth and love; his auxiliary bishops and the diocesan and religious clergy, who share with bishops in the preaching of the word; men and women religious, who through the consecration of their lives show the world what it means to be faithful to the message of the Beatitudes; fathers and mothers, with their great mission of building up the church in love; every category of the laity with their particular task in the church's mission of evangelization and salvation. This sacrifice offered today in Philadelphia is the expression of our praying community. In union with Jesus Christ we make intercession for the universal church, for the well-being of all our fellow men and women, and, today in particular, for the preservation of all the human and Christian values that are the heritage of this land, this country and this very city.

2. Philadelphia is the city of the Declaration of Independence, that remarkable document, containing a solemn attestation of the equality of all human beings, endowed by their Creator with certain inalienable rights: life, liberty and the pursuit of happiness, expressing a "firm reliance on the protection of divine providence." These are the sound moral principles formulated by your founding fathers and enshrined forever in your history. In the human and civil values that are contained in the spirit of this declaration there are easily recognized strong connections with basic religious and Christian values. A sense of religion itself is part of this heritage. The Liberty Bell which I visited on another occasion proudly bears the words of the Bible: "Proclaim liberty throughout the land" (Lv. 25:10). This tradition poses for all future generations of America a noble challenge: "One nation under God, indivisible, with liberty and justice for all."

3. As citizens, you must strive to preserve these human values, to understand them better and to define their consequences for the whole community and as a worthy contribution to the world. As Christians, you must strengthen these human values and compliment them by

confronting them with the gospel message, so that you may discover their deeper meaning, and thus assume more fully your duties and obligations toward your fellow human beings, with whom you are bound in a common destiny. In a way, for us, who know Jesus Christ, human and Christian values are but two aspects of the same reality: the reality of man, redeemed by Christ and called to the fullness of eternal life.

In my first encyclical letter, I stated this important truth: "Christ, the redeemer of the world, is the one who penetrated in a unique unrepeatable way into the mystery of man and entered his 'heart.' Rightly therefore does the Second Vatican Council teach: 'The truth is that only in the mystery of the incarnate word does the mystery of man take on light. For Adam, the first man, was a type of him who was to come (Rom. 5:14), Christ the Lord. Christ the new Adam, in the very revelation of the mystery of the Father and his love, fully reveals man to himself and brings to light his most high calling'" (*Redemptor Hominis*, 8). It is then in Jesus Christ that every man, woman and child is called to find the answer to the questions regarding the values that will inspire his or her personal and social relations.

4. How then can a Christian, inspired and guided by the mystery of the incarnation and redemption of Christ, strengthen his or her own values and those that are embodied in the heritage of this nation? The answer to that question, in order to be complete, would have to be long. Let me, however, just touch upon a few important points. Those values are strengthened when power and authority are exercised in full respect for all the fundamental rights of the human person, whose dignity is the dignity of one created in the image and likeness of God (Gn. 1:26); when freedom is accepted, not as an absolute end in itself, but as a gift that enables self-giving and service; when the family is protected and strengthened; when its unity is preserved, and when its role as the basic cell of society is recognized and honored. Human-Christian values are fostered when every effort is made so that no child anywhere in the world faces death because of lack of food, or faces a diminished intellectual and physical potential for want of sufficient nourishment, or has to bear all through life the scars of deprivation. Human-Christian values triumph when any system is reformed that authorizes the exploitation of any human being; when upright service and honesty in public servants is promoted; when the dispensing of justice is fair and the same for all; when responsible use is made of the material and energy resources of the world — resources that are meant for the benefit of all; when the environment is preserved intact for the future generations. Human-Christian values triumph by subjecting political and economic considerations to human dignity, by making them serve the cause of man — every person created by God, every brother and sister redeemed by Christ.

5. I have mentioned the Declaration of Independence and the Liberty Bell, two monuments that exemplify the spirit of freedom on which this country was founded. Your attachment to liberty, to freedom, is part of your heritage. When the Liberty Bell rang for the first time in 1776, it was to announce the freedom of your nation,

the beginning of the pursuit of a common destiny independent of any outside coercion. This principle of freedom is paramount in the political and social order, in relationships between the government and the people, and between individual and individual. However, man's life is also lived in another order of reality: the order of his relationship to what is objectively true and morally good. Freedom thus acquires a deeper meaning when it is referred to the human person. It concerns in the first place the relation of man to himself. Every human person, endowed with reason, is free when he is the master of his own actions, when he is capable of choosing that good which is in conformity with reason, and therefore with his own human dignity.

Freedom can never tolerate an offense against the rights of others, and one of the fundamental rights of man is the right to worship God. In the Declaration on Religious Freedom, the Second Vatican Council stated that the "demand for freedom in human society chiefly regards the quest for the values proper to the human spirit. It regards in the first place, the free exercise of religion in society....Religious freedom, which men demand as necessary to fulfill their duty to worship God, has to do with immunity from coercion in civil society. Therefore it leaves untouched traditional Catholic teaching on the moral duty of men and societies toward the true religion and toward the one church of Christ" (*Dignitatis Humanae*, 1).

Christ himself linked freedom with the knowledge of truth. "You will know the truth and the truth will make you free" (Jn. 8:32).

In my first encyclical, I wrote in this regard: "These words contain both a fundamental requirement and a warning: the requirement of an honest relationship with regard to truth as a condition for authentic freedom, and the warning to avoid every kind of illusory freedom, every superficial unilateral freedom, every freedom that fails to enter into the whole truth about man and the world" (*Redemptor Hominis*, 12).

Freedom can therefore never be construed without relation to the truth as revealed by Jesus Christ and proposed by his church, nor can it be seen as a pretext for moral anarchy, for every moral order must remain linked to truth. St. Peter, in his first letter, says: "Live as free men, but do not use your freedom for malice" (1 Pt. 2:16). No freedom can exist when it goes against man in what he is or against man in his relationship to others and to God.

This is especially relevant when one considers the domain of human sexuality. Here, as in any other field, there can be no true freedom without respect for the truth regarding the nature of human sexuality and marriage. In today's society, we see so many disturbing tendencies and so much laxity regarding the Christian view on sexuality that have all one thing in common: recourse to the concept of freedom to justify any behavior that is no longer consonant with the true moral order and the teaching of the church. Moral norms do not militate against the freedom of the person or the couple; on the contrary, they exist precisely for that freedom, since they are given to ensure the right use of freedom. Whoever refuses to accept these norms and to act accordingly, whoever seeks to liberate himself or herself from these norms, is not truly free. Free indeed is the person who models his or her behavior in a responsible way according to the exigencies of the objective good. What I have said here regards the whole of conjugal morality, but it applies as well to the priests with regard to the obligations of celibacy. The cohesion of freedom and ethics has also its consequences for the pursuit of the common good in society and for the national independence which the Liberty Bell announced two centuries ago.

Divine law is the sole standard of human liberty and is given to us in the Gospel of Christ, the Gospel of redemption. But fidelity to this Gospel of redemption will never be possible without the action of the Holy Spirit. It is the Holy Spirit who guards the life-giving message entrusted to the church. It is the Holy Spirit who ensures the faithful transmission of the Gospel into the lives of all of us. It is by the action of the Holy Spirit that the church is built up day after day into a kingdom: a kingdom of truth and life, a kingdom of holiness and grace, a universal kingdom of justice, love and peace.

Today, therefore, we come before the Father to offer him the petitions and desires of our hearts, to offer him praise and thanksgiving. We do this from the city of Philadelphia for the universal church and for the world. We do this as "members of the household of God" (Eph. 2:19) in union with the sacrifice of Christ Jesus, our cornerstone, for the glory of the most Holy Trinity. Amen.

Address at St. Charles Seminary, Philadelphia, Oct. 3

Beloved brothers and sons in Christ,

One of the things I wanted most to do during my visit to the United States has now arrived. I wanted to visit a seminary and meet the seminarians. And through you I would like to communicate to all seminarians how much you mean to me, and how much you mean for the future of the church — for the future of the mission given to us by Christ.

You hold a special place in my thoughts and prayers. In your lives there is great promise for the future of evangelization. And you give us hope that the authentic renewal of the church which was begun by the Second Vatican Council will be brought to fruition. But in order for this to happen, you must receive a solid and well-rounded preparation in the seminary. This personal conviction about the importance of seminaries prompted me to write these words in my Holy Thursday letter to the bishops of the church: "The full reconstitution of the life of the seminaries throughout the church will be the best proof of the achievement of the renewal to which the council directed the church."

1. If seminaries are to fulfill their mission in the church two activities in the overall program of the seminary are crucially important: the teaching of God's word and discipline.

The intellectual formation of the priest, which is so vital for the times in which we live, embraces a number of the human sciences as well as the various sacred sciences. These all have an important place in your preparation for the priesthood. But the first priority for seminaries today is the teaching of God's word in all its purity and integrity, with all its demands and in all its power. This was clearly affirmed by my beloved predecessor Paul VI, when he stated that sacred scripture is "a perpetual source of spiritual life, the chief instrument for handing down Christian doctrine, and the center of all theological study" (Apostolic Constitution *Missale Romanum*, April 3, 1969). Therefore if you, the seminarians of this generation, are to be adequately prepared to take on the heritage and challenge of the Second Vatican Council, you will need to be well trained in the word of God.

Second, the seminary must provide a sound discipline to prepare for a life of consecrated service in the image of Christ. Its purpose was well defined by the Second Vatican Council:

"The discipline required by seminary life should not be regarded merely as a strong support of community life and of charity. For it is a necessary part of the whole training program designed to provide self-mastery, to foster solid maturity of personality, and to develop other traits of character which are extremely serviceable for the ordered and productive activity of the church" (*Optatam Totius*, 11).

When discipline is properly exercised, it can create an atmosphere of recollection which enables the seminarian to develop interiorly those attitudes which are so desirable in a priest, such as joyful obedience, generosity and self-sacrifice. In the different forms of community life that are appropriate for the seminary, you will learn the art of dialogue: the capacity to listen to others and to discover the richness of their personality, and the ability to give of yourself. Seminary discipline will reinforce rather than diminish your freedom for it will help develop in you those traits and attitudes of mind and heart which God has given you, and which enrich your humanity and help you to serve more effectively his people. Discipline will also assist you in ratifying day after day in your hearts the obedience you owe to Christ and his church.

2. I want to remind you of the importance of fidelity. Before you can be ordained, you are called by Christ to make a free and irrevocable commitment to be faithful to him and to his church. Human dignity requires that you maintain this commitment, that you keep your promise to Christ no matter what difficulties you may encounter, and no matter what temptations you may be exposed to. The seriousness of this irrevocable commitment places a special obligation upon the rector and faculty of the seminary — and in a particular way on the spiritual director — to help you to evaluate your own suitability for ordination. It is then the responsibility of the bishop to judge whether you should be called to the priesthood.

It is important that one's commitment be made with full awareness and personal freedom. And so during these years in the seminary, take time to reflect on the serious obligations and the difficulties which are part of the priest's life. Consider whether Christ is calling you to the celibate life. You can make a responsible decision for celibacy only after you have reached the firm conviction that Christ is indeed offering you this gift, which is intended for the good of the church and for the service of others (cf. "Letter to Priests," 9).

To understand what it means to be faithful we must look to Christ, the "faithful witness" (Rv. 1:5), the Son who "learned to obey through what he suffered" (Heb. 5:8); to Jesus who said: "My aim is to do not my own will, but the will of him who sent me" (Jn. 5:30). We look to Jesus, not only to see and contemplate his fidelity to the Father despite all opposition (cf. Heb. 23:3), but also to learn from him the means he employed in order to be faithful, especially prayer and abandonment to God's will (cf. Lk. 22:39ff).

Remember that in the final analysis perseverance in fidelity is a proof, not of human strength and courage, but of the efficacy of Christ's grace. And so if we are going to persevere we shall have to be men of prayer who, through the eucharist, the Liturgy of the Hours and our personal encounters with Christ, find the courage and grace to be faithful. Let us be confident then, remembering the words of St. Paul: "There is nothing that I cannot master with the help of the one who gives me strength" (Phil. 4:13).

3. My brothers and sons in Christ, keep in mind the priorities of the priesthood to which you aspire, namely prayer and the ministry of the word (Acts 6:4).

"It is the prayer that shows the essential style of the priest; without prayer this style becomes deformed. Prayer helps us always to find the light that has led us since the beginning of our priestly vocation, and which never ceases to lead us....Prayer enables us to be converted continually, to remain in a state of continuous reaching out to God, which is essential if we wish to lead others to him. Prayer helps us to believe, to hope and to love." ("Letter to Priests," 10).

It is my hope that during your years in the seminary you will develop an ever greater hunger for the word of God (cf. Am. 8:11). Meditate on this word daily and study it continually, so that your whole life may become a proclamation of Christ, the word made flesh (cf. Jn. 1:14). In this word of God are the beginning and end of all ministry, the purpose of all pastoral activity, the rejuvenating source for faithful perseverance and the one thing which can give meaning and unity to the varied activities of a priest.

4. "Let the message of Christ, in all its richness, find a home with you" (Col. 3:16). In the knowledge of Christ you have the key to the Gospel. In the knowledge of Christ you have an understanding of the needs of the world. Since he became one with us in all things but sin, your union with Jesus of Nazareth could never, and will never, be an obstacle to understanding and responding to the needs of the world. And finally, in the knowledge of Christ, you will not only discover and come to understand the limitations of human wisdom and of human solutions to the needs of humanity, but you will also experience the power of Jesus, and the value of human reason and human endeavor when they are taken up in the strength of Jesus, when they are redeemed in Christ.

May our Blessed Mother Mary protect you today and always.

5. May I also take this opportunity to greet the lay people who are present today at St. Charles Seminary. Your presence here is a sign of your esteem for the ministerial priesthood, as well as being a reminder of that close cooperation between laity and priests which is needed if the mission of Christ is to be fulfilled in our time. I am happy that you are present and I am grateful for all that you do for the church in Philadelphia. In particular I ask you to pray for these young men, and for all seminarians, that they may persevere in their calling. Please pray for all priests and for the success of their ministry among God's people. And please pray the Lord of the harvest to send more laborers into his vineyard, the church.

Address to Priests at Philadelphia Civic Center, Oct. 4

Dear brother priests,

1. As we celebrate this Mass, which brings together the presidents or chairmen of the priests senates, or councils, of all the dioceses of the United States, the theme that suggests itself to our reflection is a vital one: the priesthood itself and its central importance to the task of the church.

In the encyclical letter *Redemptor Hominis*, I described this task in these words: "The church's fundamental function in every age and particularly in ours is to direct man's gaze, to point the awareness and experience of the whole of humanity toward the mystery of God, to help men to be familiar with the profundity of the redemption taking place in Christ Jesus" (*Redemptor Hominis*, 10).

Priests senates are a new structure in the church, called for by the Second Vatican Council and recent church legislation. This new structure gives a concrete expression to the unity of bishop and priests in the service of shepherding the flock of Christ, and it assists the bishop in his distinctive role of governing the diocese, by guaranteeing for him the counsel of representative advisers from among the presbyterium.

Our concelebration of today's eucharist is intended to be a mark of affirmation for the good that has been achieved by your priests senates during these past years, as well as an encouragement to pursue with enthusiasm and determination this important aim, which is "to bring the life and activity of the people of God into greater conformity with the Gospel" (cf. *Ecclesiae Sanctae*, 16:1).

Most of all, however, I want this to be the special occasion on which I can speak through you to all my brother priests throughout this nation about our priesthood. With great love I repeat the words that I wrote to you on Holy Thursday: "For you I am a bishop, with you I am a priest."

Our priestly vocation is given by the Lord Jesus himself. It is a call which is personal and individual: We are called by name as was Jeremiah. It is a call to service. We are sent out to preach the good news, to "give God's flock a shepherd's care." It is a call to communion of purpose and of action: to be one priesthood with Jesus and with one another, just as Jesus and his father are one — a unity so beautifully symbolized in this concelebrated Mass.

Priesthood is not merely a task which has been assigned. It is a vocation, a call to be heard again and again. To hear this call and to respond generously to what this call entails is a task for each priest, but it is also a responsibility for the senates of priests. This responsibility means deepening our understanding of the priesthood as Christ instituted it, as he wanted it to be and to remain, and as the church faithfully explains it and transmits it.

Fidelity to the call to the priesthood means building up this priesthood with God's people by a life of service according to apostolic priorities: concentration "on prayer and the ministry of the word" (Acts 6:4).

In the Gospel of St. Mark the priestly call of the twelve apostles is like a bud whose flowering displays a whole theology of priesthood. In the midst of Jesus' ministry we read that "he went up the mountain and summoned the men he himself had decided on, who came and joined him. He named twelve as his companions whom he would send to preach the good news...."

The passage then lists the names of the twelve (Mk. 3:13-14). Here we see three significant aspects of the call given by Jesus. He called his first priests individually and by name; he called them for the service of his word, to preach the Gospel; and he made them his own companions, drawing them into that unity of life and action which he shares with his Father in the very life of the Trinity.

2. Let us explore these three dimensions of our priesthood by reflecting on today's scripture readings. For it is in the tradition of the prophetic call that the Gospel places the priestly vocation of the twelve apostles of Jesus.

When the priest reflects on Jeremiah's call to be a prophet, he is both reassured and disturbed. "Have no fear...because I am with you to deliver you," says the Lord to the one whom he calls. "For look, I place my words in your mouth."

Who would not take heart at hearing such divine assurance? Yet when we consider why such reassurance is needed, do we not see in ourselves that same reluctance we find in Jeremiah's reply? Like him, at times, our concept of this ministry is too earth-bound; we lack confidence in him who calls us.

We can also become too attached to our own vision of ministry, thinking that it depends too much on our own talents and abilities, and at times forgetting that it is God who calls us, as he called Jeremiah from the womb. Nor is it our work or our ability that is primary. We are called to speak the words of God and not our own; to minister the sacraments he has given to his church; and to call people to a love which he has first made possible.

Hence the surrender to God's call can be made with utmost confidence and without reservation. Our surrender to God's will must be total — the "yes" given once for all which has as its pattern the "yes" spoken by Jesus himself. As St. Paul tells us, "As God keeps his word, I declare that my word to you is not 'yes' one minute and 'no' the next. Jesus Christ...was not alternately 'yes' and 'no'; he was never anything but 'yes'" (1 Cor. 1:18-19).

This call of God is grace. It is a gift, a treasure "possessed in earthen vessels to make it clear that its surpassing power comes from God and not from us" (2 Cor. 4:7). But this gift is not primarily for the priest himself; it is rather a gift of God for the whole church and for her mission to the world.

Priesthood is an abiding sacramental sign which shows that the love of the good shepherd for his flock will never be absent. In my letter to you priests last Holy Thursday, I developed this aspect of the priesthood as God's gift. Our priesthood, I said, "constitutes a special *ministerium*, that is to say 'service,' in relation to the community of believers. It does not, however, take its origin from that community, as though it were the community that 'called' or 'delegated.' The sacramental priesthood is truly a gift for this community and comes from Christ himself, from the fullness of his priesthood" (Letter, n. 5). In this gift-giving to his people, it is the divine giver who takes the initiative; it is he who calls the ones "he himself had decided on."

Hence when we reflect on the intimacy between the Lord and his prophet, his priest — an intimacy arising as a result of the call which he has initiated — we can better understand certain characteristics of the priesthood and realize their appropriateness for the church's mission today as well as in times past:

a) Priesthood is forever — *Tu es sacerdos in aeternum* — we do not return the gift once given. It cannot be that God who gave the impulse to say "yes" now wishes to hear "no."

b) Nor should it surprise the world that the call of God through the church continues to offer us a celibate ministry of love and service after the example of our Lord Jesus Christ. God's call has indeed stirred us to the depths of our being. And after centuries of experience, the church knows how deeply fitting it is that priests should give this concrete response in their lives to express the totality of the "yes" they have spoken to the Lord who calls them by name to his service.

c) The fact that there is a personal, individual call to the priesthood given by the Lord to "the men he himself had decided on" is in accord with the prophetic tradition. It should help us, too, to understand that the church's traditional decision to call men to the priesthood, and not to call women, is not a statement about human rights, nor an exclusion of women from holiness and mission in the church. Rather this decision expresses the conviction of the church about this particular dimension of the gift of priesthood by which God has chosen to shepherd his flock.

3. Dear brothers: "God's flock is in your midst; give it a shepherd's care." How close to the essence of our understanding of priesthood is the role of shepherd. Throughout the history of salvation it is a recurring image of God's care for his people. And only in the role of Jesus, the Good Shepherd, can our pastoral ministry as priests be understood.

Recall how, in the call of the twelve, Jesus summoned them to be his companions precisely in order to "send them out to preach the good news." Priesthood is mission and service; it is being "sent out" from Jesus to "give his flock a shepherd's care." This characteristic of the priest — to apply an excellent phrase about Jesus as the "man for others" — shows us the true sense of what it means to "give a shepherd's care." It means pointing the awareness of humanity to the mystery of God, to the profundity of redemption taking place in Christ Jesus.

Priestly ministry is missionary in its very core. It means being sent out for others, like Christ sent from his Father, for the sake of the Gospel, sent to evangelize. In the words of Paul VI, "evangelizing means bringing the good news into all the strata of humanity...and making it new." (*Evangelii Nuntiandi*, 18).

At the foundation and center of its dynamism, evangelization contains a clear proclamation that salvation is in Jesus Christ, the son of God. It is his name, his teaching, his life, his promises, his kingdom and his mystery that we proclaim to the world. And the effectiveness of our proclamation, and hence the very success of our priesthood, depends on our fidelity to the magisterium, through which the church guards "the rich deposit of faith with the help of the Holy Spirit who dwells within us" (2 Tm. 1:14).

As a pattern for every ministry and apostolate in the church, priestly ministry is never to be conceived in terms of an acquisition. Insofar as it is a gift, it is a gift to be proclaimed and shared with others.

Do we not see this clearly in Jesus' teaching when the mother of James and John asked that her sons sit on his right hand and his left in his kingdom? "You know how those who exercise authority among the Gentiles lord it over them; their great ones make their importance felt. It cannot be like that with you. Anyone who aspires to greatness must serve the rest, and whoever wants to rank first among you must serve the needs of all. Such is the case with the Son of Man who has come, not to be served by others, but to serve, to give his own life as a ransom for the many" (Mt. 20:25-28).

Just as Jesus was most perfectly a "man for others" in giving himself up totally on the cross, so the priest is most of all servant and "man for others" when he acts *in persona Christi* in the eucharist, leading the church in that celebration in which this sacrifice of the cross is renewed. For in the church's daily eucharistic worship, the good news that the apostles were sent out to proclaim is preached in its fullness; the work of our redemption is re-enacted.

How perfectly the fathers at the Second Vatican Council captured this fundamental truth in their Decree on Priestly Life and Ministry: "The other sacraments, as every ministry of the church and every work of the apostolate, are linked with the holy eucharist and are directed toward it....Hence the eucharist shows itself to be the source and the summit of all evangelization" (*Presbyterorum Ordinis*, 5).

In the celebration of the eucharist, we priests are at the very heart of our ministry of service, of "giving God's flock a shepherd's care." All our pastoral endeavors are incomplete until our people are led to the full and active participation in the eucharistic sacrifice.

4. Let us recall how Jesus named the Twelve as his companions. The call to priestly service includes an invitation to special intimacy with Christ. The lived experience of priests in every generation has led them to discover in their own lives and ministry the absolute centrality of their personal union with Jesus, of being his companions. No one can effectively bring the good news of Jesus to others unless he himself has first been his constant companion through personal prayer, unless he has learned from Jesus the mystery to be proclaimed.

This union with Jesus, modeled on his oneness with his Father, has a further intrinsic dimension, as his own prayer at the Last Supper reveals: "That they may be one, Father, even as we are one" (Jn. 17:11). His priesthood is one, and this unity must be actual and effective among his chosen companions. Hence unity among priests, lived out in fraternity and friendship, becomes a demand and an integral part of the life of a priest.

Unity among priests is not a unity or fraternity that is directed toward itself. It is for the sake of the Gospel, to symbolize in the living out of the priesthood the essential direction to which the Gospel calls all people: to the union of love with him and one another. And this union alone can guarantee peace and justice and dignity to every human being. Surely this is the underlying sense of the prayer of Jesus when he continues: "I pray also for those who believe in me through their word, that all may be one as you, Father, are in me, and I in you" (Jn. 17:20-21).

Indeed, how will the world come to believe that the Father has sent Jesus unless people can see in visible ways that those who believe in Jesus have heard his commandment to "love one another"? And how will believers receive a witness that such love is a concrete possibility unless they find it in the example of the unity of their priestly ministers, of those whom Jesus himself forms into one priesthood as his own companions?

My brother priests: Have we not here touched upon the heart of the matter — our zeal for the priesthood itself? It is inseparable from our zeal for the service of the people.

This concelebrated Mass, which so beautifully symbolizes the unity of our priesthood, gives to the whole world the witness of the unity for which Jesus prayed to his Father on our behalf. But it must not become a merely transient manifestation, which would render fruitless the prayer of Jesus. Every eucharist renews this prayer for our unity: "Lord, remember your church throughout the world; make us grow in love, together with John Paul, our pope,...our bishop, and all the clergy."

Your priests senates, as new structures in the church, provide a wonderful opportunity to give visible witness to the one priesthood you share with your bishops and with one another, and to demonstrate what must be at the heart of the renewal of every structure in the church: the unity for which Jesus himself prayed.

5. At the beginning of this homily, I charged you with the task of taking responsibility for your priesthood, a task for each one of you personally, a charge to be shared with all the priests and especially to be a concern for your priests councils. The faith of the whole church needs to have clearly in focus the proper understanding of the priesthood and of its place in the mission of the church. So the church depends on you to deepen ever more this understanding and to put it into practice in your lives and ministry: in other words, to share the gift of your priesthood with the church by renewing the response you

have already made to Christ's invitation — "Come, follow me" — by giving yourselves as totally as he did.

At times we hear the words, "Pray for priests." And today I address these words as an appeal, as a plea, to all the faithful of the church in the United States. Pray for priests, so that each and every one of them will repeatedly say yes to the call he has received, remain constant in preaching the gospel message and be faithful forever as the companion of our Lord Jesus Christ.

Dear brother priests: As we renew the paschal mystery and stand as disciples at the foot of the cross with Mary, the mother of Jesus, let us entrust ourselves to her. In her love we shall find strength for our weakness and joy for our hearts.

Homily at Mass
in Living History Farms,
Des Moines, Oct. 4

Dear brothers and sisters in Christ,

Here in the heartland of America, in the middle of the bountiful fields at harvest time, I come to celebrate the eucharist. As I stand in your presence in this period of autumn harvest, those words which are repeated whenever people gather for the eucharist seem to be so appropriate: "Blessed are you, Lord God of all creation, through your goodness we have this bread to offer which earth has given and human hands have made."

As one who has always been close to nature, let me speak to you today about the land, the earth and that "which earth has given and human hands have made.."

The land is God's gift entrusted to people from the very beginning. It is God's gift, given by a loving Creator as a means of sustaining the life which he had created.

But the land is not only God's gift. It is also man's responsibility. Man, himself created from the dust of the earth (cf. Gn. 3:7), was made its master (cf. Gn. 1:26). In order to bring forth fruit, the land would depend upon the genius and skillfulness, the sweat and the toil of the people to whom God would entrust it. Thus the food which would sustain life on earth is willed by God to be both that "which earth has given and human hands have made."

To all of you who are farmers and all who are associated with agricultural production I want to say this: The church highly esteems your work. Christ himself showed his esteem for agricultural life when he described God his Father as "the vinedresser" (Jn. 15:1). You cooperate with the Creator, the "vinedresser," in sustaining and nurturing life. You fulfill the command of God given at the very beginning: "Fill the earth and subdue it" (Gn. 1:28).

Here in the heartland of America, the valleys and hills have been blanketed with grain, the herds and the flocks have multiplied many times over. By hard work you have become masters of the earth and you have subdued it. By reason of the abundant fruitfulness which modern agricultural advances have made possible, you support the lives of millions who themselves do not work on the land, but who live because of what you produce. Mindful of this,

I make my own the words of my beloved predecessor Paul VI:

"It is the dignity of those who work on the land and of all those engaged in different levels of research and action in the field of agricultural development which must be unceasingly proclaimed and promoted" (Address to the World Food Conference, Nov. 9, 1974, n. 4).

What then are the attitudes that should pervade man's relationship to the land? As always we must look for the answer beginning with Jesus for, as St. Paul says: "In your minds you must be the same as Jesus Christ" (Phil. 2:5).

In the life of Jesus, we see a real closeness to the land. In his teaching, he referred to the "birds of the air" (Mt. 6:26), the "lilies of the field" (Mt. 7:17). He talked about the farmer who went out to sow the seed (Mt. 13:4ff). He referred to his heavenly Father as the "vinedresser" (Jn. 15:1), and to himself as the "good shepherd" (Jn. 10:14).

This closeness to nature, this spontaneous awareness of creation as a gift from God, as well as the blessing of a close-knit family — characteristics of farm life in every age including our own — these were part of the life of Jesus. Therefore I invite you to let your attitudes always be the same as those of Christ Jesus.

Three attitudes in particular are appropriate for rural life.

In the first place: gratitude. Recall the first words of Jesus in the Gospel we have just heard, words of gratitude to his heavenly Father: "Father, Lord of heaven and earth, to you I offer praise." Let this be your attitude as well. Every day the farmer is reminded of how much depends upon God. From the heavens come the rain, the wind and the sunshine. They occur without the farmer's command or control. The farmer prepares the soil, plants the seed and cultivates the crop. But God makes it grow; he alone is the source of life.

Even the natural disasters, such as hailstorms and drought, tornadoes or floods, remind the farmer of his dependence upon God. Surely it was this awareness that prompted the early pilgrims to America to establish the feast which you call Thanksgiving.

After every harvest, whatever it may have been that year, with humility and thankfulness the farmer makes his own the prayer of Jesus: "Father, Lord of heaven and earth, to you I offer praise."

Second, the land must be conserved with care since it is intended to be fruitful for generation upon generation. You who live in the heartland of America have been entrusted with some of the earth's best land: the soil so rich in minerals, the climate so favorable for producing bountiful crops, with fresh water and unpolluted air available all around you. You are stewards of some of the most important resources God has given to the world. Therefore conserve the land well, so that your children's children and generations after them will inherit an even richer land than was entrusted to you.

But also remember what the heart of your vocation is. While it is true here that farming today provides an economic livelihood for the farmer, still it will always be more than an enterprise of profit-making. In farming, you cooperate with the Creator in the very sustenance of life on earth.

In the third place, I want to speak about generosity, a generosity which arises from the fact that "God destined the earth and all it contains for all men and all peoples so that all created things would be shared fairly by all mankind under the guidance of justice tempered by charity" (*Gaudium et Spes*, 69). You who are farmers today are stewards of a gift from God which was intended for the good of all humanity. You have the potential to provide food for the millions who have nothing to eat and thus help to rid the world of famine. To you I direct the same question asked by Paul VI five years ago:

"If the potential of nature is immense, if that of the mastery of the human genius over the universe seems almost unlimited, what is it that is too often missing...except that generosity, that anxiety which is stimulated by the sight of the sufferings and the miseries of the poor, that deep conviction that the whole family suffers when one of its members is in distress?" (Address to the World Food Conference, Nov. 9, 1974, n. 9).

Recall the time when Jesus saw the hungry crowd gathered on the hillside. What was his response? He did not content himself with expressing his compassion. He gave his disciples the command: "Give them something to eat yourselves" (Mt. 14:16).

Did he not intend those same words for us today, for us who live at the closing of the 20th century, for us who have the means available to feed the hungry of the world? Let us respond generously to his command by sharing the fruit of our labor, by contributing to others the knowledge we have gained, by being the promoters of rural development everywhere and by defending the right to work of the rural population, since every person has a right to useful employment.

Farmers everywhere provide bread for all humanity, but it is Christ alone who is the bread of life. He alone satisfies the deepest hunger of humanity. As St. Augustine said: "Our hearts are restless until they rest in you" (*Confessions* I, 1).

While we are mindful of the physical hunger of millions of our brothers and sisters on all continents, at this eucharist we are reminded that the deepest hunger lies in the human soul. To all who acknowledge this hunger within them Jesus says: "Come to me, all you who are weary and find life burdensome, and I will refresh you."

My brothers and sisters in Christ: Let us listen to these words with all our heart. They are directed to every one of us. To all who till the soil, to all who benefit from the fruit of their labors, to every man and woman on earth, Jesus says: "Come to me...and I will refresh you." Even if all the physical hunger of the world were satisfied, even if everyone who is hungry were fed by his or her own labor or by the generosity of others, the deepest hunger of man would still exist.

We are reminded in the Letter of St. Paul to the Galatians: "All that matters is that one is created anew." Only Christ can create one anew; and this new creation finds its beginning only in his cross and resurrection. In Christ alone all creation is restored to its proper order. Therefore, I say: Come, all of you, to Christ. He is the bread of life. Come to Christ and you will never be hungry again.

Bring with you to Christ the products of your hands, the fruit of the land, that "which earth has given and human hands have made." At this altar these gifts will be transformed into the eucharist of the Lord.

Bring with you your efforts to make fruitful the land, your labor and your weariness. At this altar, because of the life, death and resurrection of Christ, all human activity is sanctified, lifted up and fulfilled.

Bring with you the poor, the sick, the exiled and the hungry; bring all who are weary and find life burdensome. At this altar they will be refreshed, for his yoke is easy and his burden light.

Above all, bring your families and dedicate them anew to Christ, so that they may continue to be the working, living and loving community where nature is revered, where burdens are shared and where the Lord is praised in gratitude.

Address to Religious Brothers, Chicago, Oct. 4

Brothers in Christ,

"I thank my God whenever I think of you; and every time I pray for you, I pray with joy, remembering how you have helped to spread the Good News from the day you first heard it right up to the present" (Phil. 1:3-5). These words of St. Paul express my feelings this evening. It is good to be with you. And I am grateful to God for your presence in the church and for your collaboration in proclaiming the Good News.

Brothers, Christ is the purpose and the measure of our lives. In the knowledge of Christ, your life is sustained. For he has called you to follow him more closely in a life consecrated through the gift of the evangelical counsels. You follow him in sacrifice and willing generosity. You follow him in joy "singing gratefully to God from your hearts in psalms, hymns and inspired songs" (Col. 3:16). And you follow him in fidelity, even considering it an honor to suffer humiliation for the sake of his name (cf. Acts 5:42).

Your religious consecration is essentially an act of love. It is an imitation of Christ who gave himself to his Father for the salvation of the world. In Christ, the love of his Father and his love for mankind are united. And so it is with you. Your religious consecration has not only deepened your baptismal gift of union with the Trinity, but it has also called you to greater service of the people of God. You are united more closely to the person of Christ, and you share more fully in his mission for the salvation of the world.

It is about your share in the mission of Christ that I wish to speak this evening.

Let me begin by reminding you of the personal qualities needed to share effectively with Christ in his mission. In the first place, you must be interiorly free, spiritually free. The freedom of which I speak is a paradox to many; it is even misunderstood by some who are members of the church. Nevertheless it is the fundamental human freedom, and it was won for us by Christ on the cross. As St. Paul said, "We were still helpless when at his appointed moment Christ died for sinful men" (Rom. 5:6).

This spiritual freedom which you received in baptism you have sought to increase and strengthen through your willing acceptance of the call to follow Jesus more closely in poverty, chastity and obedience. No matter what others may contend or the world may believe, your promises to observe the evangelical counsels have not shackled your freedom: You are not less free because you are obedient; and you are not less loving because of your celibacy. On the contrary. The faithful practice of the evangelical counsels accentuates your human dignity, liberates the human heart and causes your spirit to burn with undivided love for Christ and for his brothers and sisters in the world (cf. *Perfectae Caritatis*, 1, 12).

But this freedom of an undivided heart (cf. 1 Cor. 7:32-35) must be maintained by continual vigilance and fervent prayer. If you unite yourself continually to Christ in prayer, you shall always be free and ever more eager to share in his mission.

Second, you must center your life around the Eucharist. While you share in many ways in the passion, death and resurrection of Christ, it is especially in the Eucharist where this is celebrated and made effective. At the Eucharist, your spirit is renewed, your mind and heart are refreshed and you will find the strength to live day by day for him who is the Redeemer of the world.

Third, be dedicated to God's word. Remember the words of Jesus: "My mother and my brothers are those who hear the word of God and put it into practice" (Lk. 8:21). If you sincerely listen to God's word, and humbly but persistently try to put it into practice, like the seed sown in fertile soil, his word will bear fruit in your life.

The fourth and final element which makes effective your sharing in Christ's mission is fraternal life. Your life lived in religious community is the first concrete expression of love of neighbor. It is there that the first demands of self-sacrifice and generous service are exercised in order to build up the fraternal community. This love which unites you as brothers in community becomes in turn the force which supports you in your mission for the church.

Brothers in Christ, today the universal church honors St. Francis of Assisi. As I think of this great saint, I am reminded of his delight in God's creation, his childlike simplicity, his poetic marriage to "Lady Poverty," his missionary zeal and his desire to share fully in the cross of Christ. What a splendid heritage he has handed on to those among you who are Franciscans, and to all of us.

Similarly, God has raised up many other men and women outstanding in holiness. These too he destined to found religious families which, each in a distinctive way, would play an important role in the mission of the church. The key to the effectiveness of every one of these religious institutes has been their faithfulness to the original charism God had begun in their founder or foundress for the enrichment of the church.

For this reason, I repeat the words of Paul VI: "Be faithful to the spirit of your founders, to their evangelical intentions and to the example of their holiness....It is precisely here that the dynamism proper to each religious family finds its origin" (*Evangelica Testificatio*, 11-12). And this remains a secure basis for judging what specific ecclesial activities each institute, and every individual member, should undertake in order to fulfill the mission of Christ.

Never forget the specific and ultimate aim of all apostolic service: to lead the men and women of our day to communion with the most holy Trinity. In the present age, mankind is increasingly tempted to seek security in possessions, knowledge and power. By the witness of your life consecrated to Christ in poverty, chastity and obedience, you challenge this false security. You are a living reminder that Christ alone is "the way, the truth and the life" (Jn. 14:6).

Religious brothers today are involved in a wide range of activities: teaching in Catholic schools, spreading God's word in missionary activity, responding to a variety of human needs by both your witness and your actions, and serving by prayer and sacrifice. As you go forward in your particular service keep in mind the advice of St. Paul: "Whatever you do, work at it with your whole being. Do it for the Lord rather than for men" (Col. 3:23). For the measure of your effectiveness will be the degree of your love for Jesus Christ.

Finally, every form of apostolic service, of either an individual or a community, must be in accord with the Gospel as it is put forward by the magisterium. For all Christians service is aimed at spreading the Gospel; and all Christian service incorporates gospel values. Therefore be men of God's word: men whose hearts burn within them when they hear the word proclaimed (cf. Lk. 24:32); who shape every action according to its demands; and who desire to see the Good News proclaimed to the ends of the earth.

Brothers, your presence in the church and your collaboration in promoting the Gospel are an encouragement and joy to me in my role as pastor of the whole church. May God give each of you long life. May he call many others to follow Christ in the religious life. And may the Virgin Mary, mother of the church and model of consecrated life, obtain for you the joy and consolation of Christ her Son.

Address to U.S. Bishops, Chicago, Oct. 5

Dear brothers in our Lord Jesus Christ,

1. May I tell you very simply how grateful I am to you for your invitation to come to the United States. It is an immense joy for me to make this pastoral visit, and in particular, to be here with you today.

On this occasion I thank you, not only for your invitation, not only for everything you have done to prepare for my visit, but also for your partnership in the Gospel from the time of my election as pope. I thank you for your service to God's holy people, for your fidelity to Christ our Lord, and for your unity with my predecessors and with me in the church and in the college of bishops.

I wish at this time to render public homage to a long tradition of fidelity to the Apostolic See on the part of the American hierarchy. During the course of two centuries, this tradition has edified your people, authenticated your apostolate and enriched the universal church.

Moreover, in your presence today, I wish to acknowledge with deep appreciation the fidelity of your faithful and the renowned vitality that they have shown in Christian life. This vitality has been manifested not only in the sacramental practice of communities but also in abundant fruits of the Holy Spirit.

With great zeal your people have endeavored to build up the kingdom of God by means of the Catholic school and through all catechetical efforts. An evident concern for others has been a real part of American Catholicism, and today I thank the American Catholics for their generosity. Their support has benefited the dioceses of the United States and a widespread network of charitable works and self-help projects, including those sponsored by Catholic Relief Services and the Campaign for Human Development. Moreover, the help given to the missions by the church in the United States remains a lasting contribution to the cause of Christ's Gospel.

Because your faithful have been very generous to the Apostolic See, my predecessors have been assisted in meeting the burdens of their office; and thus, in the exercise of their worldwide mission of charity, they have been able to extend help to those in need, thereby showing the concern of the universal church for all humanity. For me, then, this is an hour of solemn gratitude.

2. But even more, this is an hour of ecclesial communion and fraternal love. I come to you as a brother bishop: one who, like yourselves, has known the hopes and challenges of a local church, one who has worked within the structures of a diocese, who has collaborated within the framework of an episcopal conference; one who has known the exhilarating experience of collegiality in an ecumenical council as exercised by bishops together with him who both presided over this collegial assembly and was recognized by it as *totius ecclesiae pastor* — invested with "full, supreme and universal power over the church" (cf. *Lumen Gentium*, 22).

I come to you as one who has been personally edified and enriched by participation in the Synod of Bishops; one who was supported and assisted by the fraternal interest and self-giving of American bishops who traveled to Poland in order to express solidarity with the church in my country. I come as one who found deep spiritual consolation for my pastoral activity in the encouragement of the Roman pontiff with whom, and under whom, I served God's people, and in particular in the encouragement of Paul VI, whom I looked upon not only as head of the college of bishops, but also as my own spiritual father. And today, under the sign of collegiality and because of a mysterious design of God's providence, I, your brother in Jesus, now come to you as successor of Peter in the See of Rome and therefore as pastor of the whole church.

Because of my personal pastoral responsibility, and because of our common pastoral responsibility for the people of God in the United States, I desire to strengthen you in your ministry of faith as local pastors and to support you in your individual and joint pastoral activities by encouraging you to stand fast in the holiness and truth of our Lord Jesus Christ. And in you I desire to honor Jesus Christ, the shepherd and bishop of our souls (cf. 1 Pt. 2:25).

Because we have been called to be shepherds of the flock, we realize that we must present ourselves as humble servants of the Gospel. Our leadership will be effective only to the extent that our own discipleship is genuine — to the extent that the Beatitudes have become the inspiration of our lives, to the extent that our people really find in us the kindness, simplicity of life and universal charity that they expect.

We who, by divine mandate, must proclaim the duties of the Christian law, and who must call our people to constant conversion and renewal, know that St. Paul's invitation applies above all to ourselves: "You must put on the new man created in God's image, whose justice and holiness are born of truth" (Eph. 4:24).

3. The holiness of personal conversion is indeed the condition for our fruitful ministry as bishops of the church. It is our union with Jesus Christ that determines the credibility of our witness to the Gospel and the supernatural effectiveness of our activity. We can convincingly proclaim "the unsearchable riches of Christ" (Eph. 3:8) only if we maintain fidelity to the love and friendship of Jesus, only if we continue to live in the faith of the Son of God.

God has given a great gift to the American hierarchy in recent years: the canonization of John Neumann. An American bishop is officially held up by the Catholic Church to be an exemplary servant of the Gospel and shepherd of God's people, above all because of his great love of Christ. On the occasion of the canonization, Paul VI asked: "What is the meaning of this extraordinary event, the meaning of this canonization?" And he answered, saying: "It is the celebration of holiness." And this holiness of St. John Neumann was expressed in brotherly love, in pastoral charity, and in zealous service by one who was the bishop of a diocese and an authentic disciple of Christ.

During the canonization, Paul VI went on to say: "Our ceremony today is indeed the celebration of holiness. At the same time, it is a prophetic anticipation — for the church, for the United States, for the world — of a renewal of love: love for God, love for neighbor." As bishops, we are called to exercise in the church this prophetic role of love and, therefore, of holiness.

Guided by the Holy Spirit, we must all be deeply convinced that holiness is the first priority in our lives and in our ministry. In this context, as bishops we see the immense value of prayer: the liturgical prayer of the church, our prayer together, our prayer alone. In recent times many of you have found that the practice of making spiritual retreats together with your brother bishops is indeed a help to that holiness born of truth. May God sustain you in this initiative so that each of you, and all of you together, may fulfill your role as a sign of holiness offered to God's people on their pilgrimage to the Father. May you yourselves, like St. John Neumann, also be a prophetic anticipation of holiness. The people need to have bishops who are trying to anticipate prophetically in their own lives the attainment of the goal to which they are leading the faithful.

4. St. Paul points out the relationship of justice and holiness to truth (cf. Eph. 4:24). Jesus himself, in his priestly prayer, asks his Father to consecrate his disciples by means of truth and he adds: "Your word is truth" — *Sermo tuus veritas est* (Jn. 17:17). And he goes on to say that he consecrates himself for the sake of the disciples, so that they themselves may be consecrated in truth. Jesus consecrated himself so that the disciples might be consecrated, set apart, by the communication of what he was: the truth. Jesus tells his Father: "I gave them your word" — "Your word is truth" (Jn. 17:14, 17).

The holy word of God, which is truth, is communicated by Jesus to his disciples. This word is entrusted as a sacred deposit to his church, but only after he had implanted in his church, through the power of the Holy Spirit, a special charism to guard and transmit intact the word of God.

With great wisdom, John XXIII convoked the Second Vatican Council. Reading the signs of the times, he knew that what was needed was a council of a pastoral nature, a council that would reflect the great pastoral love and care of Jesus Christ the Good Shepherd for his people. But he knew that a pastoral council — to be genuinely effective — would need a strong doctrinal basis. And precisely for this reason, precisely because the word of God is the only basis for every pastoral initiative, John XXIII on the opening day of the council — Oct. 11, 1962 — made the following statement: "The greatest concern of the ecumenical council is this: that the sacred deposit of Christian doctrine should be more effectively guarded and taught."

This explains Pope John's inspiration. This is what the new Pentecost was to be. This is why the bishops of the church — in the greatest manifestation of collegiality in the history of the world — were called together: "so that the sacred deposit of Christian doctrine should be more effectively guarded and taught."

In our time, Jesus was consecrating anew his disciples by truth, and he was doing it by means of an ecumenical council. He was transmitting by the power of the Holy Spirit his Father's word to new generations. And, what John XXIII considered to be the aim of the council, I consider as the aim of this postconciliar period.

For this reason, in my first meeting last November with American bishops on their *ad limina* visit I stated: "This then is my own deepest hope today for the pastors of the church in America, as well as for all the pastors of the universal church: that the sacred deposit of Christian doctrine should be more effectively guarded and taught." In the word of God is the salvation of the world. By means of the proclamation of the word of God, the Lord continues in his church and through his church to consecrate his disciples, communicating to them the truth that he himself is.

For this reason the Vatican Council emphasized the bishop's role of announcing the full truth of the Gospel and proclaiming "the whole mystery of Christ" (*Christus Dominus*, 12). This teaching was constantly repeated by Paul VI for the edification of the universal church. It was explicitly proclaimed by John Paul I on the very day he died and I too have frequently reaffirmed it in my own pontificate. And I am sure that my successors and your successors will hold this teaching until Christ comes again in glory.

5. Among the papers that were left to me by Paul VI there is a letter written to him by a bishop, on the occasion of the latter's appointment to the episcopacy. It is a beautiful letter; and in the form of a resolution it includes a clear affirmation of the bishop's role of guarding and teaching the deposit of Christian doctrine, of proclaiming the whole mystery of Christ. Because of the splendid insights that this letter offers, I would like to share part of it with you.

As he pledged himself to be loyal in obedience to Paul VI and to his successors, the bishop wrote: "I am resolved:

— "To be faithful and constant in proclaiming the Gospel of Christ.

— "To maintain the content of faith, entire and uncorrupted, as handed down by the apostles and professed by the church at all times and places."

And then with equal insight, this bishop went on to tell Paul VI that, with the help of almighty God, he was determined:

— "To build up the church as the body of Christ, and to remain united to it by your link, with the order of bishops, under the authority of the successor of St. Peter the apostle.

— "To show kindness and compassion in the name of the Lord to the poor and to strangers and to all who are in need.

— "To seek out the sheep who stray and to gather them into the fold of the Lord.

— "To pray without ceasing for the people of God, to carry out the highest duties of the priesthood in such a way as to afford no grounds for reproof."

This then is the edifying witness of a bishop, an American bishop, to the episcopal ministry of holiness and truth. These words are a credit to him and a credit to all of you.

A challenge for our age — and for every age in the church — is to bring the message of the Gospel to the very core of our people's lives — so that they may live the full truth of their humanity, their redemption and their adoption in Jesus Christ — that they may be enriched with "the justice and holiness of truth."

6. In the exercise of your ministry of truth, as bishops of the United States you have through statements and pastoral letters collectively offered the word of God to your people, showing its relevance to daily life, pointing to the power it has to uplift and heal, and at the same time upholding its inherent demands.

Three years ago you did this in a very special way through your pastoral letter, so beautifully titled "To Live in Christ Jesus." This letter, in which you offered your people the service of truth, contains a number of points to which I wish to allude today.

With compassion, understanding and love, you transmitted a message that is linked to revelation and to the mystery of faith. And so with great pastoral charity you spoke of God's love, of humanity and of sin — and of the meaning of redemption and of life in Christ. You spoke of the word of Christ as it affects individuals, the family, the community and nations, you spoke of justice and peace, of charity, of truth and friendship. And you spoke of some special questions affecting the moral life of Christians: the moral life in its individual and social aspects.

You spoke explicitly of the church's duty to be faithful to the mission entrusted to her. And precisely for this reason you spoke of certain issues that needed a clear reaffirmation, because Catholic teaching in their regard had been challenged, denied or in practice violated. You repeatedly proclaimed human rights and human dignity and the incomparable worth of people of every racial and ethnic origin, declaring that "racial antagonism and discrimination are among the most persistent and destructive evils of our nation." You forcefully rejected the oppression of the weak, the manipulation of the vulnerable, the waste of goods and resources, the ceaseless preparations for war, unjust social structures and policies, and all crimes by and against individuals and against creation.

With the candor of the Gospels, the compassion of pastors and the charity of Christ, you faced the question of the indissolubility of marriage, rightly stating: "The covenant between a man and a woman joined in Christian marriage is as indissoluble and irrevocable as God's love for his people and Christ's love for his church."

In exalting the beauty of marriage you rightly spoke against both the ideology of contraception and contraceptive acts, as did the encyclical *Humanae Vitae*. And I myself today, with the same conviction of Paul VI, ratify the teaching of this encyclical, which was put forth by my predecessor "by virtue of the mandate entrusted to us by Christ" (*AAS*, 60, 1968, p. 485).

In portraying the sexual union between husband and wife as a special expression of their covenanted love, you rightly stated: "Sexual intercourse is a moral and human good only within marriage, outside marriage it is wrong."

As "men with the message of truth and the power of good" (2 Cor. 6:7), as authentic teachers of God's law and as compassionate pastors you also rightly stated: "Homosexual activity...as distinguished from homosexual orientation, is morally wrong." In the clarity of this truth, you exemplified the real charity of Christ; you did not betray those people who, because of homosexuality, are confronted with difficult moral problems, as would have happened if, in the name of understanding and compassion, or for any other reason, you had held out false hope to any brother or sister. Rather, by your witness to the truth of humanity in God's plan, you effectively manifested fraternal love, upholding the true dignity, the true human dignity, of those who look to Christ's church for the guidance which comes from the light of God's word.

You also gave witness to the truth, thereby serving all humanity, when, echoing the teaching of the council — "from the moment of conception life must be guarded with the greatest care" (*Gaudium et Spes*, 51), — you reaffirmed the right to life and the inviolability of every human life, including the life of unborn children. You clearly said: "To destroy these innocent unborn children is an unspeakable crime....Their right to life must be recognized and fully protected by the law."

And just as you defended the unborn in the truth of their being, so also you clearly spoke up for the aged, asserting: "Euthanasia or mercy killing...is a grave moral evil....Such killing is incompatible with respect for human dignity and reverence for life."

And in your pastoral interest for your people in all their needs — including housing, education, health care, employment and the administration of justice — you gave further witness to the fact that all aspects of human life are sacred. You are, in effect, proclaiming that the church will never abandon man, nor his temporal needs, as she leads humanity to salvation and eternal life. And because the church's greatest act of fidelity to humanity and the "fundamental function in every age and particularly in ours is to direct man's gaze, to point the awareness and experience of the whole of humanity toward the mystery of God" (*Redemptor Hominis*, 10) — because of this you rightly alluded to the dimension of eternal life. It is indeed in this proclamation of eternal life that we hold up a great motive of hope for our people against the onslaughts of materialism, against rampant secularism and against moral permissiveness.

7. A sense of pastoral responsibility has also been genuinely expressed by individual bishops in their ministry as local pastors. To the great credit of their authors I would cite but two recent examples of pastoral letters issued in the United States. Both are examples of responsible pastoral initiatives. One of them deals with the issue of racism and vigorously denounces it. The other refers to homosexuality and deals with the issue, as should be done, with clarity and great pastoral charity, thus rendering a real service to truth and to those who are seeking this liberating truth.

Brothers in Christ: As we proclaim the truth in love, it is not possible for us to avoid all criticism nor is it possible to please everyone. But it is possible to work for the real benefit of everyone. And so we are humbly convinced that God is with us in our ministry of truth, and that he "did not give us a spirit of timidity but a spirit of power and love and self-control" (2 Tm. 1:7).

One of the greatest rights of the faithful is to receive the word of God in its purity and integrity as guaranteed by the magisterium of the universal church: the authentic magisterium of the bishops of the Catholic Church teaching in union with the pope. Dear brothers: We can be assured that the Holy Spirit is assisting us in our teaching if we remain absolutely faithful to the universal magisterium.

In this regard I wish to add an extremely important point which I recently emphasized in speaking to a group of bishops making their *ad limina visit:* "In the community of the faithful — which must always maintain Catholic unity with the bishops and the Apostolic See — there are great insights of faith. The Holy Spirit is active in enlightening the minds of the faithful with his truth and in inflaming their hearts with his love. But these insights of faith and this *sensus fidelium* are not independent of the magisterium of the church, which is an instrument of the same Holy Spirit and is assisted by him. It is only when the faithful have been nourished by the word of God, faithfully transmitted in its purity and integrity, that their own charisms are fully operative and fruitful. Once the word of God is faithfully proclaimed to the community and is accepted, it brings forth fruits of justice and holiness of life in abundance. But the dynamism of the community in understanding and living the word of God depends on its receiving intact the *depositum fidei;* and for this precise purpose a special apostolic and pastoral charism has been given to the church. It is one and the same Spirit of truth who directs the hearts of the faithful and who guarantees the magisterium of the pastors of the flock.''

8. One of the greatest truths of which we are the humble custodians is the doctrine of the church's unity — that unity which is tarnished on the human face of the church by every form of sin, but which subsists indestructibly in the Catholic Church (cf. *Lumen Gentium*, 8; *Unitatis Redintegratio*, 2, 3).

A consciousness of sin calls us incessantly to conversion. The will of Christ impels us to work earnestly and perseveringly for unity with all our Christian brethren, being mindful that the unity we seek is one of perfect faith, a unity in truth and love. We must pray and study together, knowing however that intercommunion between divided Christians is not the answer to Christ's appeal for perfect unity. And with God's help we will continue to work humbly and resolutely to remove the real divisions that still exist, and thus to restore that full unity in faith which is the condition for sharing in the eucharist (cf. Address of May 4, 1979).

The commitment of the ecumenical council belongs to each of us as does the testament of Paul VI, who writing on ecumenism stated: ''Let the work of drawing near to our separated brethren go on, with much understanding, with much patience, with great love; but without deviating from the true Catholic doctrine.''

9. As bishops who are servants of truth, we are also called to be servants of unity in the communion of the church.

In the communion of holiness we ourselves are called, as I mentioned above, to conversion, so that we may preach with convincing power the message of Jesus: ''Reform your lives and believe in the Gospel.'' We have a special role to play in safeguarding the sacrament of reconciliation, so that, in fidelity to a divine precept, we and our people may experience in our innermost being that ''grace has far surpassed sin'' (Rom. 5:20). I, too, ratify the prophetic call of Paul VI, who urged the bishops to help their priests to ''deeply understand how closely they collaborate through the sacrament of penance with the Savior in the work of conversion'' (Address of April 20, 1978). In this regard I confirm again the norms of *Sacramentum Paenitentiae* which so wisely emphasize the ecclesial dimension of the sacrament of penance and

indicate the precise limits of general absolution, just as Paul VI did in his *ad limina* address to the American bishops.

Conversion by its very nature is the condition for that union with God which reaches its greatest expression in the eucharist. Our union with Christ in the eucharist presupposes, in turn, that our hearts are set on conversion, that they are pure. This is indeed an important part of our preaching to the people.

In my encyclical I endeavored to express it in these words: ''The Christ who calls to the eucharistic banquet is always the same Christ who exhorts us to penance and repeats his 'repent.' Without this constant and ever-renewed endeavor for conversion, partaking of the eucharist would lack its full redeeming effectiveness...'' (*Redemptor Hominis*, 20).

In the face of a widespread phenomenon of our time, namely that many of our people who are among the great numbers who receive communion make little use of confession, we must emphasize Christ's basic call to conversion. We must also stress that the personal encounter with the forgiving Jesus in the sacrament of reconciliation is a divine means which keeps alive in our hearts and in our communities a consciousness of sin in its perennial and tragic reality, and which actually brings forth, by the action of Jesus and the power of his Spirit, fruits of conversion in justice and holiness of life. By this sacrament we are renewed in fervor, strengthened in our resolves and buoyed up by divine encouragement.

10. As chosen leaders in a community of praise and prayer, it is our special joy to offer the eucharist and to give our people a sense of their vocation as an Easter people, with the ''Alleluia'' as their song. And let us always recall that the validity of all liturgical development and the effectiveness of every liturgical sign presupposes the great principle that the Catholic liturgy is theocentric, and that it is above all ''the worship of divine majesty'' (cf. *Sacrosanctum Concilium*, 33), in union with Jesus Christ. Our people have a supernatural sense whereby they look for reverence in all liturgy, especially in what touches the mystery of the eucharist. With deep faith our people understand that the eucharist — in the Mass and outside the Mass — is the body and blood of Jesus Christ, and therefore deserves the worship that is given to the living God and to him alone.

As ministers of a community of service, it is our privilege to proclaim the truth of Christ's union with his members in his body, the church. Hence we commend all service rendered in his name and to his brethren (cf. Mt. 25:45).

In a community of witness and evangelization may our testimony be clear and without reproach. In this regard the Catholic press and the other means of social communication are called to fulfill a special role of great dignity at the service of truth and charity. The church's aim in employing and sponsoring these media is linked to her mission of evangelization and of service to humanity; through the media the church hopes to promote ever more effectively the uplifting message of the Gospel.

11. And each individual church over which you preside and which you serve is a community founded on

the word of God and acting in the truth of this word. It is in fidelity to the communion of the universal church that our local unity is authenticated and made stable. In the communion of the universal church local churches find their own identity and enrichment ever more clearly. But all of this requires that the individual churches should maintain complete openness toward the universal church.

And this is the mystery that we celebrate today in proclaiming the holiness and truth and unity of the episcopal ministry.

Brothers: This ministry of ours makes us accountable to Christ and to his church. Jesus Christ, the chief shepherd (1 Pt. 5:4), loves us and sustains us. It is he who transmits his Father's word and consecrates us in truth, so that each of us may say in turn of our people: "For them I consecrate myself for their sake now, that they may be consecrated in truth." (Jn. 17:19).

Let us pray for and devote special energy to promoting and maintaining vocations to the sacred priesthood, so that the pastoral care of the priestly ministry may be ensured for future generations. I ask you to call upon parents and families, upon priests, Religious and laity to unite in fulfilling this vital responsibility of the entire community. And to the young people themselves let us hold up the full challenge of following Christ and of embracing his invitation with full generosity.

As we ourselves pursue every day the justice and holiness born of truth, let us look to Mary, mother of Jesus, queen of apostles, and cause of our joy. May St. Frances Xavier Cabrini, St. Elizabeth Ann Seton and St. John Neumann pray for you, and for all the people whom you are called to serve in holiness and truth and in the unity of Christ and his church.

Dear brothers: "Grace be with all who love our Lord Jesus Christ with unfailing love" (Eph. 5:24).

Homily at Mass in Grant Park, Chicago, Oct. 5

My brothers and sisters in Jesus Christ,

The readings of today's celebration place us immediately before the deep mystery of our calling as Christians.

Before Jesus was taken up to heaven, he gathered his disciples around him, and he explained to them once more the meaning of his mission of salvation: "Thus it is written," he said, "that the Messiah must suffer and rise from the dead on the third day. In his name, penance for the remission of sins is to be preached to all nations" (Lk. 24:46-47). At the moment that he took leave of his apostles he commanded them, and through them the whole church, each one of us, to go out and bring the message of redemption to all nations. St. Paul expresses this forcefully in his second Letter to the Corinthians: "He has entrusted the message of reconciliation to us. This makes us ambassadors of Christ. God as it were appealing through us" (2 Cor. 5:19-20).

Once again, the Lord places us fully in the mystery of humanity, a humanity that is in need of salvation. And

God has willed that the salvation of humanity should take place through the humanity of Christ, who for our sake died and was raised up (cf. 2 Cor. 5:15), and who also entrusted his redeeming mission to us. Yes, we are truly "ambassadors for Christ," and workers for evangelization.

In the apostolic exhortation *Evangelii Nuntiandi*, which he wrote at the request of the third general assembly of the Synod of Bishops, my predecessor in the See of St. Peter, Paul VI, invited the whole people of God to meditate on their basic duty of evangelization. He invited each one of us to examine in what way we might be true witnesses to the message of redemption, in what way we might comunicate to others the good news that we have received from Jesus through his church.

There are certain conditions that are necessary if we are to share in the evangelizing mission of the church. This afternoon I wish to stress one of these conditions in particular. I am speaking about the unity of the church, our unity in Jesus Christ. Let me repeat what Paul VI said about this unity: "The Lord's spiritual testament tells us that unity among his followers is not only the proof that we are his, but also the proof that he is sent by the Father. It is the test of credibility of Christians and of Christ himself...Yes, the destiny of evangelization is certainly bound up with the witness of unity given by the church"(*Evangelii Nuntiandi*, 77).

I am prompted to choose this particular aspect of evangelization by looking at the thousands of people whom I see gathered around me today. When I lift up my eyes, I see in you the people of God, united to sing the praises of the Lord and to celebrate his eucharist. I see also the whole people of America, one nation formed of many people: *E pluribus unum*.

In the first two centuries of your history as a nation, you have traveled a long road, always in search of a better future, in search of stable employment, in search of a homestead. You have traveled "from sea to shining sea" to find your identity, to discover each other along the way, and to find your own place in this immense country.

Your ancestors came from many different countries across the oceans to meet here with the people of different communities that were already established here. In every generation, the process has been repeated: new groups arrive, each one with a different history, to settle here and become part of something new. The same process still goes on when families move from the south to the north, from the east to the west. Each time they come with their own past to a new town or a new city, to become part of a new community. The pattern repeats itself over and over: *E pluribus unum* — the many form a new unity.

Yes, something new was created every time. You brought with you a different culture and you contributed your own distinctive richness to the whole; you had different skills and you put them to work, complementing each other, to create industry, agriculture and business; each group carried with it different human values and shared them with the others for the enrichment of your nation. *E pluribus unum:* You became a new entity, a new people, the true nature of which cannot be adequately explained as a mere putting together of various communities.

And so, looking at you, I see people who have thrown their destinies together and now write a common history. Different as you are, you have come to accept each other, at times imperfectly and even to the point of subjecting each other to various forms of discrimination; at times only after a long period of misunderstanding and rejection; even now still growing in understanding and appreciation of each other's differences. In expressing gratitude for the many blessings you have received, you also become aware of the duty you have toward the less favored in your own midst and in the rest of the world — a duty of sharing, of loving, of serving. As a people, you recognize God as the source of your many blessings, and you are open to his love and his law.

This is America in her ideal and her resolution: "one nation, under God, indivisible, with liberty and justice for all." This is the way America was conceived; this is what she was called to be. And for all this, we offer thanks to the Lord.

But there is another reality that I see when I look at you. It is even deeper and more demanding than the common history and union which you built from the richness of your different cultural and ethnic heritages — those heritages that you now rightly want to know and to preserve. History does not exhaust itself in material progress, in technological conquest or in cultural achievement only. Coming together around the altar of sacrifice to break the bread of the holy eucharist with the successor of Peter, you testify to this even deeper reality: to your unity as members of the people of God.

"We, though many, are one body in Christ" (Rom. 12:5). The church too is composed of many members and enriched by the diversity of those who make up the one community of faith and baptism, the one body of Christ. What brings us together and makes us one is our faith — the one apostolic faith. We are all one, because we have accepted Jesus Christ as the Son of God, the redeemer of the human race, the sole mediator between God and man. By the sacrament of baptism we have been truly incorporated into the crucified and glorified Christ, and through the action of the Holy Spirit we have become living members of his one body. Christ gave us the wonderful sacrament of the eucharist, by which the unity of the church is both expressed and continually brought about and perfected.

"One Lord, one faith, one baptism" (Eph. 4:5). Thus we are all bound together, as the people of God, the body of Christ, in a unity that transcends the diversity of our origin, culture, education and personality — in a unity that does not exclude a rich diversity in ministries and services. With St. Paul we proclaim: "Just as each of us has one body with many members, and not all the members have the same function, so too we, though many, are one body in Christ, and individually members one of another" (Rom. 12:4-5).

If then the church, the one body of Christ, is to be a forcefully discernible sign of the gospel message, all her members must show forth, in the words of Paul VI, that "harmony and consistency of doctrine, life and worship which marked the first days of her existence" (Apostolic Exhortation on Reconciliation within the Church, 2),

when Christians "devoted themselves to the apostles' teachings and fellowship, to the breaking of bread and the prayers" (Acts 2:42).

Our unity in faith must be complete, lest we fail to give witness to the Gospel, lest we cease to be evangelizing. No local ecclesial community therefore can cut itself off from the treasure of the faith as proclaimed by the church's teaching office, for it is to this teaching office of the church, to this magisterium, that the deposit of faith has been especially entrusted by Christ. With Paul VI I attest to the great truth: "While being translated into all expressions, the content of the faith must be neither impaired nor mutilated. While being clothed with the outward forms proper to each people...it must remain the content of the Catholic faith just exactly as the ecclesial magisterium has received it and transmits it" (*Evangelii Nuntiandi*, 65).

Finally, and above all, the mission of evangelization that is mine and yours, must be carried out through a constant unselfish witnessing to the unity of love. Love is the force that opens hearts to the word of Jesus and to his redemption. Love is the only basis for human relationships that respect in one another the dignity of the children of God created in his image and saved by the death and resurrection of Jesus; love is the only driving force that impels us to share with our brothers and sisters all that we are and have.

Love is the power that gives rise to dialogue, in which we listen to each other and learn from each other. Love gives rise, above all, to the dialogue of prayer in which we listen to God's word, which is alive in the Holy Bible and alive in the life of the church. Let love then build the bridges across our differences and at times our contrasting positions. Let love for each other and love for the truth be the answer to polarization, when factions are formed because of differing views in matters that relate to faith or to the priorities for action.

No one in the ecclesial community should ever feel alienated or unloved, even when tensions arise in the course of the common efforts to bring the fruits of the Gospel to society around us. Our unity as Christians, as Catholics, must always be a unity of love in Jesus Christ our Lord.

In a few moments, we shall celebrate our unity by renewing the sacrifice of Christ. Each one will bring a different gift to be presented in union with the offering of Jesus: dedication to the betterment of society; efforts to console those who suffer; the desire to give witness for justice; the resolve to work for peace and brotherhood; the joy of a united family; of suffering in body or mind. Different gifts, yes, but all united in the one great gift of Christ's love for his Father and for us — everything united in the unity of Christ and his sacrifice.

And in the strength and power, in the joy and peace of this sacred unity, we pledge ourselves anew — as one people — to fulfill the command of our Lord Jesus Christ: Go and teach all people my Gospel. By word and example give witness to my name. And, behold, I am with you always, until the end of the world.

Address on Arrival at the White House, Oct. 6

Mr. President,

I wish to express my most sincere thanks for your kind words of welcome to the White House. It is indeed a great honor for me to meet with the president of the United States during a visit of which the aims are spiritual and religious in nature. May I convey at the same time to you, and through you to all your fellow Americans, my profound respect for all the federal and state authorities of this nation and for its beloved people. In the course of the last few days, I have had the opportunity to see some of your cities and rural areas. My only regret is that the time is too short to bring my greetings personally to all parts of this country, but I want to assure you that my esteem and affection go out to every man, woman and child without distinction.

Divine providence in its own designs has called me from my native Poland to be the successor of Peter in the See of Rome and the leader of the Catholic Church. It gives me great joy to be the first pope in history to come to the capital of this nation, and I thank Almighty God for this blessing.

In accepting your courteous invitation, Mr. President, I have also hoped that our meeting today would serve the cause of world peace, international understanding and the promotion of full respect for human rights everywhere.

Mr. Speaker and honorable members of Congress, distinguished members of the Cabinet and of the judiciary, ladies and gentlemen,

Your presence here honors me greatly and I deeply appreciate the expression of respect which you thus extend to me. My gratitude goes to each one of you personally for your kind welcome, and to all I wish to say how profoundly I esteem your mission as stewards of the common good of all the people of America.

I come from a nation with a long tradition of deep Christian faith and with a national history marked by many upheavals. For more than 100 years Poland was even erased from the political map of Europe. But it is also a country marked by a deep veneration for those values without which no society can prosper: love of freedom, cultural creativity and the conviction that common endeavors for the good of society must be guided by a true moral sense.

My own spiritual and religious mission impels me to be the messenger of peace and brotherhood and to witness to the true greatness of every human person. This greatness derives from the love of God, who created us in his own likeness and gave us an eternal destiny. It is in this dignity of the human person that I see the meaning of history and that I find the principle that gives sense to the role which every human being has to assume for his or her own advancement and for the well-being of the society to which he or she belongs. It is with these sentiments that I greet in you the whole American people, a people that bases its concept of life on spiritual and moral values, on a deep religious sense, on respect for duty and on generosity in the service of humanity — noble traits which are embodied in a particular way in the nation's capital, with its monuments dedicated to such outstanding national figures as George Washington, Abraham Lincoln and Thomas Jefferson.

I greet the American people in their elected representatives, all of you who serve in Congress to chart, through legislation, the path that will lead every citizen of this country toward the fullest development of his or her potential, and the nation as a whole toward assuming its share of the responsibility for building a world of true freedom and justice. I greet America in all who are vested with authority, which can only be seen as an opportunity for serving your fellow citizens in the overall development of their true humanity and in the full and unimpeded enjoyment of all their fundamental rights.

I salute the people of this land also in the members of the judiciary, who are servants of humanity in the application of justice, and who thus hold in their hands the awesome power of profoundly affecting, by their decisions, the lives of every individual.

For all of you I pray to Almighty God that he may grant you the gift of wisdom in your decisions, prudence in your words and actions, and compassion in the exercise of the authority that is yours, so that in your noble office you will always render true service to the people.

God bless America!

Mr. President,

I am honored to have had, at your kind invitation, the opportunity for a meeting with you; for by your office as president of the United States of America you represent before the world the whole American nation and you hold the immense responsibility of leading this nation in the path of justice and peace. I thank you publicly for this meeting and I thank all those who have contributed to its success. I wish also to reiterate here my deep gratitude for the warm welcome and the many kindnesses which I have received from the American people on my pastoral journey through your beautiful land.

Mr. President,

In responding to the kind words which you have addressed to me, I take the liberty of beginning with the passage from the prophet Micah that you quoted at your inauguration: "You have been told, Oh man, what is good, and what the Lord requires of you: only to do right and to love goodness, and to walk humbly with your God" (Mi. 6:8). In recalling these words, I wish to greet you and all the authorities in the individual states and in the nation who are committed to the good of the citizens. There is indeed no other way to put oneself at the service of the whole human person except by seeking the good of every man and woman in all their commitments and activities.

Authority in the political community is based on the objective ethical principle that the basic duty of power is the solicitude of the common good of society and that it serves the inviolable rights of the human person. The individuals, families and various groups which compose the civic community are aware that by themselves they are unable to realize their human potential to the full, and therefore they recognize in a wider community the necessary condition for the ever better attainment of the common good.

I wish to commend those in public authority and all the people of the United States for having given, from the very beginning of the existence of the nation, a special place to some of the most important concerns of the common good. Three years ago, during the bicentennial celebration, which I was fortunate to participate in as the archbishop of Cracow, it was obvious to everyone that concern for what is human and spiritual is one of the basic principles governing the life of this community. It is superfluous to add that respect for the freedom and the dignity of every individual, whatever his origin, race, sex or creed, has been a cherished tenet of the civil creed of America, and that it has been backed up by courageous decisions and actions.

Mr. President, ladies and gentlemen,

I know and appreciate this country's efforts for arms limitation, especially of nuclear weapons. Everyone is aware of the terrible risk that the stockpiling of such weapons brings upon humanity. Since it is one of the greatest nations on earth, the United States plays a particularly important part in the quest for greater security in the world and for closer international collaboration. With all my heart I hope that there will be no relaxing of its efforts both to reduce the risk of a fatal and disastrous worldwide conflagration and to secure a prudent and progressive reduction of the destructive capacity of military arsenals. At the same time, by reason of its special position, may the United States succeed in influencing the other nations to join in a continuing commitment for disarmament. Without wholeheartedly accepting such a commitment how can any nation effectively serve humanity, whose deepest desire is true peace?

Address after Meeting with President Carter, Oct. 6

Attachment to human values and to ethical concerns, which have been a hallmark of the American people, must be situated, especially in the present context of the growing interdependence of peoples across the globe, within the framework of the view that the common good of society embraces not just the individual nation to which one belongs but the citizens of the whole world. I would encourage every action for the reinforcement of peace in the world, a peace based on liberty and justice, on charity and truth.

The present-day relationships between peoples and between nations demand the establishment of greater international cooperation also in the economic field. The more powerful a nation is, the greater becomes its international responsibility; the greater also must be its commitment to the betterment of the lot of those whose very humanity is constantly being threatened by want and need. It is my fervent hope that all the powerful nations in the world will deepen their awareness of the principle of human solidarity within the one great human family.

America, which in the past decades has demonstrated goodness and generosity in providing food for the hungry of the world, will, I am sure, be able to match this generosity with an equally convincing contribution to the establishing of a world order that will create the necessary economic and trade conditions for a more just relationship between all the nations of the world, in respect for their dignity and their own personality. Since people are suffering under international inequality, there can be no question of giving up the pursuit of international solidarity, even if it involves a notable change in the attitudes and lifestyles of those blessed with a larger share of the world's goods.

Mr. President, ladies and gentlemen,

In touching upon the common good, which embodies the aspiration of all human beings to the full development of their capacities and the proper protection of their rights, I have dealt with areas where the church that I represent and the political community that is the state share a common concern: the safeguarding of the dignity of the human person and the search for justice and peace. In their own proper spheres, the political community and the church are mutually independent and self-governing. Yet, by a different title, each serves the personal and social vocation of the same human beings.

For her part, the Catholic Church will continue her efforts to cooperate in promoting justice, peace and dignity through the commitment of her leaders and the members of her communities, and through her incessant proclamation that all human beings are created to the image and likeness of God and that they are brothers and sisters, children of one heavenly Father.

May Almighty God bless and sustain America in her quest for the fullness of liberty, justice and peace.

Address to Organization of American States, Oct. 6

Mr. President, Mr. Secretary General, ladies and gentlemen,

1. It is indeed a pleasure for me to have this opportunity to greet all the distinguished representatives of the different member nations of the Organization of American States. My sincere gratitude goes to you, Mr. President, for the cordial words of welcome you have extended to me. I thank also the secretary general for his thoughtful invitation to come and visit the headquarters of the oldest of the regional international organizations. It is fitting that, after my visit to the United Nations organization, the Organization of American States should be the first one among the many intergovernmental organizations and agencies to which I am privileged to address a message of peace and friendship.

The Holy See follows with great interest, and may I say, with special attention, the events and developments that touch upon the well-being of the peoples of the Americas. It felt therefore greatly honored by the invitation to send its own permanent observer to this institution — an invitation extended last year by a unanimous decision of the General Assembly. The Holy See sees in regional organizations such as yours intermediary structures that promote a greater internal diversity and vitality in a given area within the global community of nations. The fact that the American continent is provided with an organization concerned with ensuring more continuity for the dialogue between governments, with promoting peace, with advancing full development in solidarity and with protecting man, his dignity and his rights is a factor contributing to the health of the whole human family. The Gospel and Christianity have entered deeply into your history and your cultures. I would like to call on this common tradition in order to present to you some reflections, in full respect for your personal convictions and your own competence, in order to bring to your endeavors an original contribution in a spirit of service.

2. Peace is a most precious blessing that you seek to preserve for your peoples. You are in agreement with me that it is not by accumulating arms that this peace can be ensured in a stable way. Apart from the fact that such accumulation increases in practice the danger of having recourse to arms to settle the disputes that may arise, it takes away considerable material and human resources from the great peaceful tasks of development that are so urgent. It can also tempt some to think that the order built on arms is sufficient to ensure internal peace in the single countries.

I solemnly call on you to do everything in your power to restrain the arms race on this continent. There are no differences between your countries that cannot be peacefully overcome. What a relief it would be to your peoples, what new opportunities it would provide for their economic, social and cultural progress, and how contagious an example it would give the world, if the difficult enterprise of disarmament were here to find a realistic solution!

3. The painful experience of the history of my own country, Poland, has shown me how important national sovereignty is when it is served by a state worthy of the name and free in its decisions; how important it is for the protection not only of a people's legitimate material interests, but also of its culture and its soul. Your organization is an organization of states, founded on respect for the full national sovereignty of each, on equal participation in common tasks and on solidarity between your peoples. The legitimate demand by the states to participate on a basis of equality in the organization's common decisions must be matched by the will to promote within each country an ever more effective participation by the citizens in the responsibility and decisions of the nation through ways that take into account particular traditions, difficulties and historical experiences.

4. However, while such difficulties and experiences can at times call for exceptional measures and a certain period of maturation in preparation for new advances in shared responsibility, they never, never justify any attack on the inviolable dignity of the human person and on the authentic rights that protect this dignity. If certain ideologies and certain ways of interpreting legitimate

concern for national security were to result in subjugating to the state man and his rights and dignity, they would to that extent cease to be human and would be unable to claim without gross deception any Christian reference. In the church's thinking it is a fundamental principle that social organization is at the service of man, not vice versa. That holds good also for the highest levels of society, where the power of coercion is wielded and where abuses, when they occur, are particularly serious. Besides, a security in which the peoples no longer feel involved, because it no longer protects them in their very humanity, is only a sham; as it grows more and more rigid, it will show symptoms of increasing weakness and rapidly approaching ruin.

Without undue interference, your organization can, by the spirit with which it tackles all the problems in its competence, do much throughout the continent to advance a concept of the state and its sovereignty that is truly human, and that is therefore the basis for the legitimacy of the states and of their acknowledged prerogatives for the service of man.

5. Man! Man is the decisive criterion that dictates and directs all your undertakings, the living value for whose service new initiatives are unceasingly demanded. The words that are most filled with meaning for man — words such as justice, peace, development, solidarity, human rights — are sometimes belittled as a result of systematic suspicion or party and sectarian ideological censure. They then lose their power to mobilize and attract. They will recover it only if respect for the human person and commitment to the human person are explicitly brought back to the center of all considerations.

When we speak of the right to life, to physical and moral integrity, to nourishment, to housing, to education, to health care, to employment, to shared responsibility in the life of the nation, we speak of the human person. It is this human person whom faith makes us recognize as created in the image of God and destined for an eternal goal. It is this human person that is often threatened and hungry, without decent housing and employment, without access to the cultural heritage of his or her people or of humanity, and without a voice to make his or her distress heard. The great cause of full development in solidarity must be given new life by those who in one degree or another enjoy these blessings, for the service of all those — and there are many of them still on your continent — who are deprived of them to a sometimes dramatic extent.

6. The challenge of development deserves your full attention. In this field too what you achieve can be an example for humanity. The problems of rural and urban areas, of industry and agriculture, and of the environment are to a large extent a common task. The energetic pursuit of these will help to spread throughout the continent a sentiment of universal fraternity that extends beyond borders and regimes. Without any disregard for the responsibilities of sovereign states, you discover that it is a logical requirement for you to deal with problems, such as unemployment, migration and trade, as common concerns whose continental dimension increasingly demands more organic solutions on a continental scale. All that you do for the human person will halt violence and the threats of

subversion and destabilization. For, by accepting courageous revisions demanded by "this single fundamental point of view, namely the welfare of man — or, let us say, of the person in the community — which must, as a fundamental factor in the common good, constitute the essential criterion for all programs, systems and regimes" (*Redemptor Hominis*, 17), you direct the energies of your peoples toward the peaceful satisfaction of their aspirations.

7. The Holy See will always be happy to make its own disinterested contribution to this work. The local churches in the Americas will do the same within the framework of their various responsibilities. By advancing the human person and his or her dignity and rights, they serve the earthly city, its cohesion and its lawful authorities. The full religious freedom that they ask for is in order to serve, not in order to oppose the legitimate autonomy of civil society and of its own means of action. The more all citizens are able to exercise habitually their freedoms in the life of the nation, the more readily will the Christian communities be able to dedicate themselves to the central task of evangelization, namely the preaching of the Gospel of Jesus Christ, the source of life, strength, justice and peace.

With fervent prayers for prosperity and concord, I invoke upon this important assembly, upon the representatives of all the member states and their families, upon all the beloved peoples of the Americas, the choicest favors and blessings of Almighty God.

My visit here, in the Hall of the Americas, before this noble assembly dedicated to inter-American collaboration, expresses at the same time a wish and a prayer. My wish is that, in all the nations of this continent, no man, woman or child may ever feel abandoned by the constituted authorities, to whom they are ready to accord their full confidence to the extent that those authorities seek the good of all. My prayer is that Almighty God may grant his light to the peoples and the governments, that they may always discover new means of collaboration for building up a fraternal and just society.

One last word before I leave you — with great regret — after this first brief visit to your esteemed organization. When I visited Mexico, at the beginning of the year, I was amazed at the enthusiasm, spontaneity and joy of living of its people. I am convinced that you will succeed in preserving the rich human and cultural heritage of all your peoples and thus maintain the indispensable basis for true progress, which is constituted, always and everywhere, by respect for the supreme dignity of man.

Address to Washington Diplomatic Corps, Oct. 6

Your excellencies, ladies and gentlemen,

It pleases me greatly that, in the midst of a program that is at the same time demanding and enjoyable, the opportunity has been offered to me to meet tonight with the distinguished members of the diplomatic corps in this city of Washington.

I thank you most cordially for the honor you bestow upon me by your presence, an honor given not only to my person but to the leader of the Catholic Church. I also see in your courteous gesture an encouragement for the activity of the Catholic Church and of the Holy See in the service of humanity.

In this cause of service to humanity the diplomatic corps and the Holy See stand together, each one in its own sphere, each one faithfully pursuing its own mission, but united in the great cause of understanding and solidarity among peoples and nations.

Yours is a noble task. Despite unavoidable difficulties, setbacks and failures, diplomacy retains its importance as one of the roads that must be traveled in the search for peace and progress for all mankind. "Diplomacy," in the words of my predecessor Paul VI, "is the art of making peace" (Address to the Diplomatic Corps, Rome, Jan. 12, 1974). The efforts of diplomats, whether in a bilateral or in a multilateral setting, do not always succeed in establishing or in maintaining peace, but they must always be encouraged, today as in the past, so that new initiatives will be born, new paths tried with the patience and tenacity that are the eminent qualities of the deserving diplomat. As one who speaks in the name of Christ, who called himself "the way, the truth, and the life" (Jn. 14:6), I would also like to make a plea for the fostering of other qualities that are indispensable if today's diplomacy is to justify the hopes that are placed in it: the ever deeper insertion of the supreme values of the moral and spiritual order into the aims of peoples and into the methods used in pursuit of these aims.

First among the ethical imperatives that must preside over the relations among nations and peoples is truth. As the theme for the 13th World Day of Peace (Jan. 1, 1980), I have chosen: "Truth, the Power of Peace." I am confident that the governments and the nations which you represent will, as they have so admirably done in the past, associate themselves once again with this lofty aim: to instill truth into all relationships, be they political or economic, bilateral or multinational.

All too often, falsehood is met in personal as well as in collective life, and thus suspicion arises where truth is called for, and the ensuing reluctance to enter into dialogue makes any collaboration or understanding almost impossible. Bringing truth into all relations is to work for peace, for it will make it possible to apply to the problems of the world the solutions that are in conformity with reason and with justice — in a word, with the truth about man.

And this brings me to the second point I would like to make. If it is to be true and lasting, peace must be truly human. The desire for peace is universal. It is embedded in the hearts of all human beings and it cannot be achieved unless the human person is placed at the center of every effort to bring about unity and brotherhood among nations.

Your mission as diplomats is based on the mandate you receive from those who hold responsibility for the well-being of your nations. The power you partake of cannot be separated from the objective demands of the moral order or from the destiny of every human being. May I repeat here what I stated in my first encyclical letter:

"The fundamental duty of power is solicitude for the common good of society; this is what gives power its fundamental rights. Precisely in the name of these premises of the objective ethical order, the rights of power can only be understood on the basis of respect for the objective and inviolable rights of man. The common good that authority in the state serves is brought to full realization only when all the citizens are sure of their rights. The lack of this leads to the dissolution of society, opposition by citizens to authority, or a situation of oppression, intimidation, violence and terrorism, of which many examples have been provided by the totalitarianisms of this century. Thus the principle of human rights is of profound concern to the area of social justice and is the measure by which it can be tested in the life of the political bodies" (*Redemptor Hominis*, 17).

These considerations assume their full relevance also in the area of your immediate concern, the quest for international peace, for justice among nations and for cooperation in solidarity by all peoples. The success of today's diplomacy will, in the final analysis, be the victory of the truth about man.

I invoke from Almighty God abundant blessings upon your mission, which requires you to foster the interests of your own nation, and to place it in the context of universal peace; upon you personally — who are in such a distinguished way artisans of peace; upon your spouses and families, who support and encourage you; and finally upon all who count on your dedicated service to see their own human dignity respected and enhanced. May God's peace be always in your hearts.

Address to Religious Sisters, Washington, Oct. 7

My first desire in this National Shrine of the Immaculate Conception is to direct my thoughts, to turn my heart, to the woman of salvation history.

In the eternal design of God, this woman, Mary, was chosen to enter into the work of the incarnation and redemption. And this design of God was to be actuated through her free decision given in obedience to the divine will.

Through her yes — a yes that pervades and is reflected in all history, she consented to be the Virgin Mother of our saving God, the handmaid of the Lord and at the same time, the mother of all the faithful who in the course of centuries would become the brothers and sisters of her son.

Through her, the Sun of Justice was to rise in the world. Through her, the great healer of humanity, the reconciler of hearts and consciences — her son, the God-man Jesus Christ — was to transform the human condition and, by his death and resurrection, uplift the entire human family.

As a great sign that appeared in the heavens in the fullness of time, the woman dominates all history as the Virgin Mother of the Son, and as the spouse of the Holy Spirit — as the handmaid of humanity.

And the woman becomes also — by association with her son — the sign of contradiction to the world and, at the same time, the sign of hope whom all generations shall call blessed: the woman who conceived spiritually before she conceived physically; the woman who accepted the word of God; the woman who was inserted intimately and irrevocably into the mystery of the church, exercising a spiritual motherhood with regard to all people; the woman who is honored as Queen of Apostles, without herself being inserted into the hierarchical constitution of the church. And yet this woman made all hierarchy possible, because she gave to the world the shepherd and bishop of our souls.

This woman, this Mary of the Gospels, who is not mentioned as being at the Last Supper, comes back again at the foot of the cross, in order to consummate her contribution to salvation history. By her courageous act, she prefigures and anticipates the courage of all women throughout the ages who concur in bringing forth Christ in every generation.

At Pentecost, the Virgin Mother once again comes forward to exercise her role in union with the apostles, with and in and over the church. Yet again she conceives of the Holy Spirit, to bring forth Jesus in the fullness of his body, the church — never to leave him, never to abandon him, but to continue to love and serve him through the ages.

This is the woman of history and destiny, who inspires us today: the woman who speaks to us of femininity, human dignity and love, and who is the greatest expression of total consecration to Jesus Christ, in whose name we are gathered today.

Dear Sisters,

May the grace, love and peace of God our Father and our Lord Jesus Christ be with you.

I welcome this opportunity to speak with you today. I am happy for this occasion because of my esteem for religious life, and my gratitude to women religious for their invaluable contribution to the mission and very life of the church.

I am especially pleased that we are gathered here in the National Shrine of the Immaculate Conception, for the Virgin Mary is the model of the church, the mother of the faithful and the perfect example of consecrated life.

1. On the day of our baptism, we received the greatest gift God can bestow on any man or woman. No other honor, no other distinction will equal its value. For we were freed from sin and incorporated into Christ Jesus and his body, the church. That day and every day after, we were chosen "to live through love in his presence" (Eph. 1:4).

In the years that followed our baptism, we grew in awareness — even wonder — of the mystery of Christ. By listening to the Beatitudes, by meditating on the cross, conversing with Christ in prayer and receiving him in the Eucharist, we progressed toward the day, that particular moment of our life, when we solemnly ratified with full awareness and freedom our baptismal consecration. We affirmed our determination to live always in union with Christ and to be, according to the gifts given us by the Holy Spirit, a generous and loving member of the people of God.

2. Your religious consecration builds on this common foundation which all Christians share in the body of Christ. Desiring to perfect and intensify what God had begun in your life by baptism, and discerning that God was indeed offering you the gift of the evangelical counsels, you willed to follow Christ more closely, to conform your life more completely to that of Jesus Christ, in and through a distinctive religious community.

This is the essence of religious consecration: to profess within and for the benefit of the church, poverty, chastity and obedience in response to God's special invitation, in order to praise and serve God in greater freedom of heart (cf. 1 Cor. 7:34-35) and to have one's life more closely conformed to Christ in the manner of life chosen by him and his blessed mother (cf. *Perfectae Caritatis*, 1; *Lumen Gentium*, 46).

3. Religious consecration not only deepens your personal commitment to Christ, but it also strengthens your relationship to his spouse, the church. Religious consecration is a distinctive manner of living in the church, a particular way of fulfilling the life of faith and service begun in baptism.

On her part, the church assists you in your discernment of God's will. Having accepted and authenticated the charisms of your various institutes, she then unites your religious profession to the celebration of Christ's paschal mystery.

You are called by Jesus himself to verify and manifest in your lives and in your activities your deepened relationship with his church. This bond of union with the church must also be shown in the spirit and apostolic endeavors of every religious institute. For faithfulness to Christ, especially in religious life, can never be separated from faithfulness to the church.

This ecclesial dimension of the vocation of religious consecration has many important practical consequences for institutes themselves and for each individual member. It implies, for example, a greater public witness to the Gospel, since you represent, in a special way as women Religious, the spousal relationship of the church to Christ. The ecclesial dimension also requires, on the part of individual members as well as entire institutes, a faithfulness to the original charisms which God has given to his church, through your founders and foundresses. It means that institutes are called to continue to foster, in dynamic faithfulness, those corporate commitments which were related to the original charism, which were authenticated by the church and which still fulfill important needs of the people of God.

A good example in this regard would be the Catholic school system which has been invaluable for the church in the United States, an excellent means not only for communicating the Gospel of Christ to the students, but also for permeating the entire community with Christ's truth and his love. It is one of the apostolates in which women Religious have made, and are still making, an incomparable contribution.

4. Dear Sisters in Christ: Jesus must always be first in your lives. His person must be at the center of your activities — the activities of every day. No other person and no activity can take precedence over him. For your whole life has been consecrated to him. With St. Paul you have to say: "All I want is to know Christ and the power of his resurrection and to share his sufferings by reproducing the pattern of his death" (Phil. 3:10).

Christ remains primary in your life only when he enjoys the first place in your mind and heart. Thus you must continuously unite yourself to him in prayer. Without prayer, religious life has no meaning. It has lost contact with its source, it has emptied itself of substance and it no longer can fulfill its goal. Without prayer there can be no joy, no hope, no peace. For prayer is what keeps us in touch with Christ. The incisive words written in *Evangelica Testificatio* cause us all to reflect: "Do not forget the witness of history: faithfulness to prayer or its abandonment is the test of the vitality or decadence of religious life" (*Evangelica Testificatio*, 42).

5. Two dynamic forces are operative in religious life: your love for Jesus — and, in Jesus, for all who belong to him — and his love for you.

We cannot live without love. If we do not encounter love, if we do not experience it and make it our own, and if we do not participate intimately in it, our life is meaningless. Without love we remain incomprehensible to ourselves (cf. *Redemptor Hominis*, 10).

Thus every one of you needs a vibrant relationship of love to the Lord, a profound loving union with Christ, your spouse, a love like that expressed in the psalm:

"God, you are my God whom I seek, for you my flesh pines and my soul thirsts like the earth, parched, lifeless and without water. Thus have I gazed toward you in the sanctuary to see your power and your glory" (Ps. 63:1-2).

Yet far more important than your love for Christ is God's love for you. You have been called by him, made a member of his body, consecrated in a life of the evangelical counsels and destined by him to have a share in the mission that Christ has entrusted to the church: his mission of salvation.

For this reason, you center your life on the Eucharist. In the Eucharist, you celebrate his death and resurrection and receive from him the bread of eternal life. And it is in the Eucharist especially that you are united to the one who is the object of all your love. Here, with him, you find ever greater reasons to love and serve his brothers and sisters. Here, with him — with Christ — you find greater understanding and compassion for God's people. And here you find the strength to persevere in your commitment to selfless service.

6. Your service in the church is then an extension of Christ to whom you have dedicated your life. For it is not yourself that you put forward, but Christ Jesus as Lord. Like John the Baptist, you know that for Christ to increase, you must decrease. And so your life must be characterized by a complete availability: a readiness to serve as the needs of the church require, a readiness to give public witness to the Christ whom we love.

The need for this public witness becomes a constant call to inner conversion, to justice and holiness of life on the part of each religious. It also becomes an invitation to each institute to reflect on the purity of its corporate ecclesial witness. And it is for this reason that in my address last November to the International Union of Superiors General I mentioned that it is not unimportant that your consecration to God should be manifested in the permanent exterior sign of a simple and suitable religious garb. This is not only my personal conviction, but also the desire of the church, often expressed by so many of the faithful.

As daughters of the church — a title cherished by so many of your great saints — you are called to a generous and loving adherence to the authentic magisterium of the church, which is a solid guarantee of the fruitfulness of all your apostolates and an indispensable condition for the proper interpretation of the "signs of the times."

7. The contemplative life occupies today and forever a place of great honor in the church. The prayer of contemplation was found in the life of Jesus himself and has been a part of religious life in every age. I take this opportunity therefore — as I did in Rome, in Mexico and in Poland — to encourage again all who are members of contemplative communities.

Know that you shall always fulfill an important place in the church, in her mission of salvation, in her service to the whole community of the people of God. Continue faithfully, confidently and prayerfully, in the rich tradition that has been handed down to you.

In closing, I remind you, with sentiments of admiration and love, that the aim of religious life is to render praise and glory to the most Holy Trinity and, through your consecration, to help humanity enter into fullness of life in the Father, and in the Son and in the Holy Spirit.

In all your planning and in all your activities, try also to keep this aim before you. There is no greater service you can give; there is no greater fulfillment you can receive.

Dear Sisters, today and forever: Praised be Jesus Christ!

Address to Catholic Educators, Washington, Oct. 7

Dear brothers and sisters in Christ,

1. Our meeting today gives me great pleasure, and I thank you sincerely for your cordial welcome. My own association with the university world, and more particularly with the Pontifical Theological Faculty of Cracow, makes our encounter all the more gratifying for me. I cannot but feel at home with you. The sincere expressions with which the chancellor and the president of the Catholic University of America have confirmed, in the name of all of you, the faithful adherence to Christ and the generous commitment to the service of truth and charity of your Catholic associations and institutions of higher learning are appreciated.

Ninety-one years ago Cardinal Gibbons and the American bishops requested the foundation of the Catholic University of America, as a university "destined to provide the church with worthy ministers for the salvation of souls and the propagation of religion and to give the republic most worthy citizens." It seems appropriate to me on this occasion to address myself not only to this great

institution, so irrevocably linked to the bishops of the United States, who have founded it and who generously support it, but also to all the Catholic universities, colleges and academies of post-secondary learning in your land, those with formal and sometimes juridical links with the Holy See, as well as all those who are "Catholic."

2. Before doing so, though, allow me first to mention the ecclesiastical faculties, three of which are established here at the Catholic University of America. I greet these faculties and all who dedicate their best talents in them. I offer my prayers for the prosperous development and the unfailing fidelity and success of these faculties. In the apostolic constitution *Sapientia Christiana*, I have dealt directly with these institutions in order to provide guidance and to ensure that they fulfill their role in meeting the needs of the Christian community in today's rapidly changing circumstances.

I also wish to address a word of praise and admiration for the men and women, especially priests and Religious, who dedicate themselves to all forms of campus ministry. Their sacrifices and efforts to bring the true message of Christ to the university world, whether secular or Catholic, cannot go unnoticed.

The church also greatly appreciates the work and witness of those of her sons and daughters whose vocation places them in non-Catholic universities in your country. I am sure that their Christian hope and Catholic patrimony, bring an enriching and irreplaceable dimension to the world of higher studies.

A special word of gratitude and appreciation also goes to the parents and students who, sometimes at the price of great personal and financial sacrifice, look toward the Catholic universities and colleges for the training that unites faith and science, culture and the gospel values.

To all engaged in administration, teaching or study in Catholic colleges and universities I would apply the words of Daniel: "They who are learned shall shine like the brightness of the firmament and those that instruct many in justice as stars for all eternity" (Dn. 12:3). Sacrifice and generosity have accomplished heroic results in the foundation and development of these institutions. Despite immense financial strain, enrollment problems and other obstacles, divine providence and the commitment of the whole people of God have allowed us to see these Catholic institutions flourish and advance.

3. I would repeat here before you what I told the professors and students of the Catholic universities in Mexico when I indicated three aims that are to be pursued. A Catholic university or college must make a specific contribution to the church and to society through high-quality scientific research, in-depth study of problems, and a just sense of history, together with the concern to show the full meaning of the human person regenerated in Christ, thus favoring the complete development of the person.

Furthermore, the Catholic university or college must train young men and women of outstanding knowledge who, having made a personal synthesis between faith and culture, will be both capable and willing to assume tasks in the service of the community and of society in general, and to bear witness to their faith before the world. And finally, to be what it ought to be, a

Catholic college or university must set up, among its faculty and students, a real community which bears witness to a living and operative Christianity, a community where sincere commitment to scientific research and study goes together with a deep commitment to authentic Christian living.

This is your identity. This is your vocation. Every university or college is qualified by a specific mode of being. Yours is the qualification of being Catholic, of affirming God, his revelation and the Catholic Church as the guardian and interpreter of that revelation. The term "Catholic" will never be a mere label, either added or dropped according to the pressures of varying factors.

4. As one who for long years has been a university professor, I will never tire of insisting on the eminent role of the university, which is to instruct but also to be a place of scientific research. In both these fields, its activity is closely related to the deepest and noblest aspiration of the human person: the desire to come to the knowledge of truth.

No university can deserve the rightful esteem of the world of learning unless it applies the highest standards of scientific research, constantly updating its methods and working instruments, and unless it excels in seriousness and therefore in freedom of investigation. Truth and science are not gratuitous conquests, but the result of a surrender to objectivity and of the exploration of all aspects of nature and man.

Whenever man himself becomes the object of investigation, no single method or combination of methods can fail to take into account, beyond any purely natural approach, the full nature of man. Because he is bound by the total truth on man, the Christian will, in his research and in his teaching, reject any partial vision of human reality, but he will let himself be enlightened by his faith in the creation of God and the redemption of Christ.

The relationship to truth explains therefore the historical bond between the university and the church. Because she herself finds her origin and her growth in the words of Christ, which are the liberating truth (cf. Jn. 8:32), the church has always tried to stand by the institutions that serve, and cannot but serve, the knowledge of truth.

The church can rightfully boast of being in a sense the mother of universities. The names of Bologna, Padua, Prague and Paris shine in the earliest history of intellectual endeavor and human progress. The continuity of the historic tradition in this field has come down to our day.

5. An undiminished dedication to intellectual honesty and academic excellence are seen, in a Catholic university, in the perspective of the church's mission of evangelization and service. This is why the church asks these institutions, your institutions, to set out without equivocation your Catholic nature. This is what I have desired to emphasize in my apostolic constitution *Sapientia Christiana*, where I stated:

"Indeed, the church's mission of spreading the Gospel not only demands that the good news be preached ever more widely and to ever greater numbers of men and women, but that the very power of the Gospel should permeate thought patterns, standards of judgment and the norms of behavior. In a word, it is necessary that the whole of human culture be steeped in the Gospel. The cultural atmosphere in which a human being lives has a great influence upon his or her way of thinking and, thus, of acting. Therefore, a division between faith and culture is more than a small impediment to evangelization, while a culture penetrated with the Christian spirit is an instrument that favors the spreading of the good news" (*Sapientia Christiana*, I).

The goals of Catholic higher education go beyond education for production, professional competence, technological and scientific competence. They aim at the ultimate destiny of the human person, at the full justice and holiness born of truth (cf. Eph. 4:24).

6. If then your universities and colleges are institutionally committed to the Christian message, and if they are part of the Catholic community of evangelization, it follows that they have an essential relationship to the hierarchy of the church. And here I want to say a special word of gratitude, encouragement and guidance for the theologians.

The church needs her theologians, particularly in this time and age so profoundly marked by deep changes in all areas of life and society. The bishops of the church, to whom the Lord has entrusted the keeping of the unity of the faith and the preaching of the message — individual bishops for their dioceses, and bishops collegially with the successor of Peter for the universal church — we all need your work, your dedication and the fruits of your reflection. We desire to listen to you and we are eager to receive the valued assistance of your responsible scholarship.

But true theological scholarship, and by the same token theological teaching, cannot exist and be fruitful without seeking its inspiration and its source in the word of God as contained in sacred scripture and in the sacred tradition of the church, as interpreted by the authentic magisterium throughout history. (cf. *Dei Verbum*, 10). True academic freedom must be seen in relation to the finality of the academic enterprise which looks to the total truth of the human person.

The theologian's contribution will be enriching for the church only if it takes into account the proper function of the bishops and the rights of the faithful. It devolves upon the bishops of the church to safeguard the Christian authenticity and unity of faith and moral teaching, in accordance with the injunction of the apostle Paul: "Proclaim the message and, welcome or unwelcome, insist on it. Refute falsehood, correct error, call to obedience" (2 Tim. 4:2).

It is the right of the faithful not to be troubled by theories and hypotheses that they are not expert in judging or that are easily simplified or manipulated by public opinion for ends that are alien to the truth. On the day of his death, John Paul I stated: "Among the rights of the faithful, one of the greatest is the right to receive God's word in all its entirety and purity." (Sept. 28, 1979).

It behooves the theologian to be free, but with the freedom that is openness to the truth and the light that comes from faith and from fidelity to the church.

In concluding I express to you once more my joy in

being with you today. I remain very close to your work and your concerns. May the Holy Spirit guide you. May the intercession of Mary, seat of wisdom, sustain you always in your irreplaceable service of humanity and the church. God bless you.

Address to non-Catholic Religious Leaders, Washington, Oct. 7

Dearly beloved in Christ,

1. I am grateful to the providence of God that permits me on my visit to the United States of America to have this meeting with other religious leaders, and to be able to join with you in prayer for the unity of all Christians.

It is indeed fitting that our meeting should occur just a short time before the observance of the 15th anniversary of the Second Vatican Council's Decree of Ecumenism, *Unitatis Redintegratio*. Since the inception of my pontificate, almost a year ago, I have endeavored to devote myself to the service of Christian unity. For, as I stated in my first encyclical, it is certain "that in the present historical situation of Christianity and of the world, the only possibility we see in fulfilling the church's universal mission, with regard to ecumenical questions, is that of seeking sincerely, perseveringly, humbly and also courageously the ways of drawing closer and of union" (*Redemptor Hominis*, 6).

On a previous occasion, I said that the problem of division within Christianity is "binding in a special way on the bishop of the ancient church of Rome, founded on the preaching and the testimonies of the martyrdom of Sts. Peter and Paul" (General Audience, Jan. 17, 1979). And today I wish to reiterate before you the same conviction.

2. With great satisfaction and joy I welcome the opportunity to embrace you, in the charity of Christ, as beloved Christian brethren and fellow disciples of the Lord Jesus. It is a privilege to be able, in your presence and together with you, to give expression to the testimony of John, that "Jesus Christ is the Son of God" (1 Jn. 4:15), and to proclaim that "there is one mediator between God and men, the man Christ Jesus" (1 Tm. 2:5).

In the united confession of faith in the divinity of Jesus Christ, we feel great love for each other and great hope for all humanity. We experience immense gratitude to the Father, who has sent his Son to be our Savior, "the expiation for our sins, and not for ours only but for the sins of the whole world" (1 Jn. 2:2).

By divine grace we are united in esteem and love for sacred scripture, which we recognize as the inspired word of God. And it is precisely in this word of God that we learn how much he wants us to be fully one in him and in his Father. Jesus prays that his followers may be one "so that the world may believe" (Jn 17:21). That the credibility of evangelization should, by God's plan, depend on the unity of his followers is a subject of inexhaustible meditation for all of us.

3. I wish to pay homage here to the many splendid ecumenical initiatives that have been realized in this country through the action of the Holy Spirit. In the last 15 years there has been a positive response to ecumenism by the bishops of the United States. Through their Committee for Ecumenical and Interreligious Affairs, they have established a fraternal relationship with other churches and ecclesial communities — a relationship which, I pray, will continue to deepen in the coming years.

Conversations are in progress with our brothers from the East, the Orthodox. Here I wish to note that this relationship has been strong in the United States and that soon a theological dialogue will begin on a worldwide basis in an attempt to resolve those difficulties which hinder full unity.

There are also American dialogues with the Anglicans, the Lutherans, the Reformed churches, the Methodists and the Disciples of Christ — all having a counterpart on the international level. A fraternal exchange exists likewise between the Southern Baptists and American theologians.

My gratitude goes to all who collaborate in the matter of joint theological investigation, the aim of which is always the full evangelical and Christian dimension of truth. It is to be hoped that through such investigation persons who are well-prepared by a solid grounding in their own traditions will contribute to a deepening of the full historical and doctrinal understanding of the issues.

The particular climate and traditions of the United States have been conducive to joint witness in the defense of the rights of the human person, in the pursuit of goals of social justice and peace, and in questions of public morality. These areas of concern must continue to benefit from creative ecumenical action, as must the fostering of esteem for the sacredness of marriage and the support of a healthy family life as a major contribution to the well-being of the nation. In this context, recognition must be given to the deep division which still exists over moral and ethical matters. The moral life and the life of faith are so deeply united that it is impossible to divide them.

4. Much has been accomplished, but there is still much to be done. We must go forward, however, with a spirit of hope. Even the very desire for the complete unity in faith — which is lacking between us, and which must be achieved before we can lovingly celebrate the eucharist together in truth — is itself a gift of the Holy Spirit, for which we offer humble praise to God. We are confident that through our common prayer the Lord Jesus will lead us, at the moment dependent on the sovereign action of his Holy Spirit, to the fullness of ecclesial unity.

Faithfulness to the Holy Spirit calls for interior conversion and fervent prayer. In the words of the Second Vatican Council: "This change of heart and holiness of life, along with public and private prayer for the unity of Christians, should be regarded as the soul of the whole ecumenical movement" (*Unitatis Redintegratio*, 8).

It is important that every individual Christian search his or her heart to see what may obstruct the attainment of full union among Christians. And let us all pray that the genuine need for the patience to await God's hour will never occasion complacency in the status quo of division in faith. By divine grace may the need for patience never become a substitute for the definitive and generous response which God asks that there be given to his invitation to perfect unity in Christ.

And so, as we are gathered here to celebrate the love of God that is poured out in our hearts by the Holy Spirit, let us be conscious of the call to show supreme fidelity to the will of Christ. Let us together perseveringly ask the Holy Spirit to remove all divisions from our faith, to give us that perfect unity in truth and love for which Christ prayed, for which Christ died — "to gather together in unity the scattered children of God" (Jn. 11:52).

I offer my respectful greeting of grace and peace to those whom you represent, to each of your respective congregations, to all who long for the coming of "our great God and savior Jesus Christ" (Ti. 2:14).

Address to Journalists, Washington, Oct. 7

My dear friends of the communications media,

Here we are together again at the end of another journey — a journey which this time has brought me to Ireland, to the United Nations and to the United States of America.

The purpose of this journey was to permit the pope to exercise his function as a herald of peace, in the name of Christ, who was referred to as the Prince of Peace. This message of peace was announced especially in those places and before those audiences where the problem of war and peace is perceived with particular sensitivity and where there exist the conditions of understanding, of good will and of the means necessary to building peace and cooperation among all nations and among all peoples.

The word "peace" is a synthesis. It has many components. I have touched on several of these during this journey, and you have diligently reported on these reflections. You have commented on them; you have interpreted them; you have performed the service of stimulating people to think about how they might contribute to a firmer foundation for peace, for cooperation and for justice among all persons.

Now we find ourselves at the moment of parting, in this capital city of one of the most powerful nations in the world. The power of this country, I believe, comes not only from material wealth but from a richness of spirit.

In fact, the name of this city and of the tall monument which dominates it recalls the spirit of George Washington, the first president of the nation, who — with Thomas Jefferson, for whom an imposing memorial also exists here, and with other enlightened individuals — established this country on a foundation which was not only human but also profoundly religious.

As a consequence, the Catholic Church has been able to flourish here. The millions of faithful who belong to the church testify to that fact as they exercise the rights and duties which flow from their faith with full freedom. The great National Shrine of the Immaculate Conception in this city testifies to that fact. The existence in this capital city of two Catholic universities — Georgetown and the Catholic University of America — testifies to that fact. I have observed that the people of the United States of America proudly and gratefully pledge allegiance to their republic as "one nation under God."

This one nation is made up of many members — members of all races, of all religions, of all conditions of life — so that it is a type of microcosm of the world community and accurately reflects the motto, *E Pluribus Unum.* As this country courageously abolished the plague of slavery under the presidency of Abraham Lincoln, may it never stop striving for the effective good of all the inhabitants of this one nation and for that unity which reflects its national motto. For this reason, the United States of America gives to all cause to reflect on a spirit which, if well applied, can bring beneficial results for peace in the world community.

I sincerely hope that all of you have profited from this journey, and that you have had the opportunity to reflect anew on the values which have come from Christianity to the civilization of this new continent. Most of all, however, we can draw hope for a peaceful world community from the example of persons of all races, of all nationalities and of all religions living together in peace and unity.

As we prepare to part, my dear friends, I am consoled by the fact that you will continue to inform and to form world public opinion with a profound consciousness of your responsibility and with the realization that so many persons depend on you.

Finally, I say goodbye to you and to America. I thank you again, and with all my heart I ask God to bless you and your families.

Homily at Mass on Washington Mall, Oct. 7

Dear brothers and sisters in Jesus Christ,

1. In his dialogue with his listeners, Jesus was faced one day with an attempt by some Pharisees to get him to endorse their current views regarding the nature of marriage.

Jesus answered by reaffirming the teaching of scripture: "At the beginning of creation God made them male and female; for this reason a man shall leave his father and mother and the two shall become one. They are no longer two but one in flesh. Therefore let no man separate what God has joined" (Mk. 10:6-9).

The Gospel according to Mark immediately adds the description of a scene with which we are all familiar. This scene shows Jesus becoming indignant when he noticed how his own disciples tried to prevent the people from bringing their children closer to him. And so he said: "Let the children come to me and do not hinder them. It is to just such as these that the kingdom of God belongs....Then he embraced them and blessed them, placing his hands on them" (Mk. 10:14-16).

In proposing these readings, today's liturgy invites all of us to reflect on the nature of marriage, on the family and on the value of life — three themes that are so closely interconnected.

2. I shall all the more gladly lead you in reflecting on the word of God as proposed by the church today, because all over the world the bishops are discussing marriage and family life as they are lived in all dioceses and nations. The bishops are doing this in preparation for the next world Synod of Bishops, which has as its theme: "The Role of the Christian Family in the Contemporary World."

Your own bishops have designated next year as a year of study, planning and pastoral renewal with regard to the family. For a variety of reasons there is a renewed interest throughout the world in marriage, in family life and in the value of all human life.

This very Sunday marks the beginning of the annual Respect Life program, through which the church in the United States intends to reiterate its conviction regarding the inviolability of human life in all stages. Let us then, all together, renew our esteem for the value of human life, remembering also that, through Christ, all human life has been redeemed.

3. I do not hesitate to proclaim before you and before the world that all human life — from the moment of conception and through all subsequent stages — is sacred, because human life is created in the image and likeness of God.

Nothing surpasses the greatness or dignity of a human person. Human life is not just an idea or an abstraction. Human life is the concrete reality of a being that lives, that acts, that grows and develops. Human life is the concrete reality of a being that is capable of love and of service to humanity.

Let me repeat what I told the people during my recent pilgrimage to my homeland: "If a person's right to life is violated at the moment in which he is first conceived in his mother's womb, an indirect blow is struck also at the whole of the moral order which serves to ensure the inviolable goods of man. Among those goods, life occupies the first place. The church defends the right to life, not only in regard to the majesty of the Creator, who is the first giver of this life, but also in respect of the essential good of the human person" (June 8, 1979).

4. Human life is precious because it is the gift of a God whose love is infinite; and when God gives life, it is forever. Life is also precious because it is the expression and the fruit of love. This is why life should spring up within the setting of marriage, and why marriage and the partners' love for one another should be marked by generosity in self-giving.

The great danger for family life in the midst of any society whose idols are pleasure, comfort and independence, lies in the fact that people close their hearts and become selfish. The fear of making permanent commitments can change the mutual love of husband and wife into two loves of self — two loves existing side by side, until they end in separation.

In the sacrament of marriage, a man and a woman — who at baptism became members of Christ and hence have the duty of manifesting Christ's attitudes in their lives — are assured of the help they need to develop their love in a faithful and indissoluble union and to respond with generosity to the gift of parenthood. As the Second Vatican Council declared: Through this sacrament, Christ himself becomes present in the life of the married couple and accompanies them, so that they may love each other and their children, just as Christ loved his church by giving himself up for her (cf. *Gaudium et Spes*, 48; cf. Eph. 5:25).

5. In order that Christian marriage may favor the total good and development of the married couple, it must be inspired by the Gospel, and thus be open to new life — new life to be given and accepted generously. The couple is also called to create a family atmosphere in which children can be happy and lead full and worthy human and Christian lives.

To maintain a joyful family requires much from both the parents and the children. Each member of the family has to become, in a special way, the servant of the others and share their burdens (cf. Gal. 6:2; Phil. 2:2). Each one must show concern, not only for his or her own life, but also for the lives of the other members of the family: their needs, their hopes, their ideals.

Decisions about the number of children and the sacrifices to be made for them must not be taken only with a view to adding to comfort and preserving a peaceful existence. Reflecting upon this matter before God, with the graces drawn from the sacrament and guided by the teaching of the church, parents will remind themselves that it is certainly less serious to deny their children certain comforts or material advantages than to deprive them of the presence of brothers and sisters who could help them to grow in humanity and to realize the beauty of life at all its stages and in all its variety.

If parents fully realized the demands and the opportunities that this great sacrament brings, they could not fail to join in Mary's hymn to the author of life — to God — who has made them his chosen fellow workers.

All human beings ought to value every person for his or her uniqueness as a creature of God, called to be a brother or sister of Christ by reason of the incarnation and the universal redemption. For us, the sacredness of human life is based on these premises. And it is on these same premises that there is based our celebration of life — all human life. This explains our efforts to defend human life against every influence or action that threatens or weakens it, as well as our endeavors to make every life more human in all its aspects.

And so, we will stand up every time that human life is threatened.

— When the sacredness of life before birth is attacked, we will stand up and proclaim that no one ever has the authority to destroy unborn life.

— When a child is described as a burden or looked upon only as a means to satisfy an emotional need, we will stand up and insist that every child is a unique and unrepeatable gift of God, with the right to a loving and united family.

— When the institution of marriage is abandoned to human selfishness or reduced to a temporary, conditional arrangement that can easily be terminated, we will stand up and affirm the indissolubility of the marriage bond.

— When the value of the family is threatened

because of social and economic pressures, we will stand up and reaffirm that the family is "necessary not only for the private good of every person, but also for the common good of every society, nation and state" (General Audience, Jan. 3, 1979).

— When freedom is used to dominate the weak, to squander natural resources and energy, and to deny basic necessities to people, we will stand up and reaffirm the demands of justice and social love.

— When the sick, the aged or the dying are abandoned in loneliness, we will stand up and proclaim that they are worthy of love, care and respect.

I make my own the words which Paul VI spoke last year to the American bishops:

"We are convinced, moreover, that all efforts made to safeguard human rights actually benefit life itself. Everything aimed at banishing discrimination — in law or in fact — which is based on race, origin, color, culture, sex or religion (cf. *Octogesima Adveniens*, 16) is a service to life. When the rights of minorities are fostered, when the mentally or physically handicapped are assisted, when those on the margin of society are given a voice — in all these instances the dignity of life, and the sacredness of human life are furthered....In particular, every contribution made to better the moral climate of society, to oppose permissiveness and hedonism, and all assistance to the family, which is the source of new life, effectively uphold the values of life" (May 26, 1978).

Much remains to be done to support those whose lives are wounded and to restore hope to those who are afraid of life. Courage is needed to resist pressures and false slogans, to proclaim the supreme dignity of all life, and to demand that society itself give it its protection.

A distinguished American, Thomas Jefferson, once stated: "The care of human life and happiness and not their destruction is the just and only legitimate object of good government" (March 31, 1809). I wish therefore to praise all the members of the Catholic Church and other Christian churches, all men and women of the Judeo-Christian heritage, as well as all people of good will who unite in common dedication for the defense of life in its fullness and for the promotion of all human rights.

Our celebration of life forms part of the celebration of the eucharist. Our Lord and Savior, through his death and resurrection, has become for us "the bread of life" and the pledge of eternal life. In him we find the courage, perseverance and inventiveness which we need to promote and defend life within our families and throughout the world.

Dear brothers and sisters: We are confident that Mary, the mother of God and the mother of life, will give us her help so that our way of living will always reflect our admiration and gratitude for God's gift of love that is life. We know that she will help us to use every day that is given to us as an opportunity to defend the life of the unborn and to render more human the lives of all our fellow human beings, wherever they may be.

And through the intercession of Our Lady of the Rosary, whose feast we celebrate today, may we come one day to the fullness of eternal life in Christ Jesus our Lord.

Address on Departure from Washington, Oct. 7

My dear friends in America, and my brothers and sisters in the faith of our Lord Jesus Christ,

As I leave the capital city of Washington, I wish to express my gratitude to the president of the United States and to all the religious and civil authorities of this country.

My thoughts turn likewise to all the American people: to all Catholics, Protestants and Jews, and to all men and women of good will; to people of every ethnic origin, and in particular to the descendants of the first inhabitants of this land, the American Indians; to all of you whom I have greeted personally; those who have been close to me through the providential media of press, radio and television; those who have opened their hearts to me in so many ways. Your hospitality has been warm and filled with love, and I am grateful for all your kindness.

I believe strongly in the message of hope that I have held up to you, in the justice and love and truth that I have extolled, and in the peace that I have asked the Lord to give to all of you.

And now I must leave the United States and return to Rome. But all of you will constantly be remembered in my prayers, which I look upon as the best expression of my loyalty and friendship.

Today, therefore, my final prayer is this: that God will bless America, so that she may increasingly become — and truly be — and long remain — "One nation, under God, indivisible. With liberty and justice for all."

God bless America.

God bless America.